*Intersections*

Published by ANU E Press
The Australian National University
Canberra ACT 0200, Australia
Email: anuepress@anu.edu.au
This title is also available online at http://epress.anu.edu.au

National Library of Australia Cataloguing-in-Publication entry

| | |
|---|---|
| Author: | Lal, Brij V |
| Title: | Intersections : history, memory, discipline / Brij V. Lal |
| ISBN: | 9781922144379 (pbk.) 9781922144386 (ebook) |
| Notes | Includes bibliographical references. |
| Subjects: | Lal, Brij V. |
| | East Indians - Fiji. |
| | Fiji - Politics and government - 20th century. |
| | Fiji - Politics and government - 21st century. |
| | Australian |
| Dewey Number: | 591.53 |

All rights reserved. No part of this publication may be reproduced, stored in a retrieval system or transmitted in any form or by any means, electronic, mechanical, photocopying or otherwise, without the prior permission of the publisher.

Design and layout by Noel Wendtman Design
Cover photgraph istockphoto.com/wsfurlan

Originally published by Fiji Institute of Applied Studies 2011
This edition © 2012 ANU E Press

# *Intersections*

HISTORY, MEMORY, DISCIPLINE

**BRIJ V LAL**

E PRESS

*For*
Jayan & His Daadi

# Contents

| | | |
|---|---|---|
| Foreword: Doug Munro | | vii |
| 1. | When It Is Over | 1 |
| 2. | Heartbreak Islands | 8 |
| 3. | Making History, Becoming History | 22 |
| 4. | While the Gun is Still Smoking | 39 |
| 5. | Where Has All The Music Gone? | 58 |
| 6. | Chance Hai: On the Hustings, 1999 and 2006 | 79 |
| 7. | The Ungiven Speech | 102 |
| 8. | Road from Laucala Bay | 110 |
| 9. | Coombs 4240: A Room of My Own | 127 |
| 10. | People In-Between | 139 |
| 11. | The Surinam Lecture | 156 |
| 12. | A Hundred Years in a Lifetime | 165 |
| 13. | One Life, Three Worlds | 186 |
| 14. | Primary Texts | 201 |
| 15. | Blurred Lines | 208 |
| 16. | Frequent Flyers | 220 |
| 17. | Waituri to Nelspruit and Places In Between | 231 |
| 18. | Sairusi, Tom, Mr Bechu Prasad, Sir Paul Reeves | 264 |
| 19. | Caught in the Web | 279 |
| 20. | From the Sidelines | 287 |
| 21. | Speaking to Power | 303 |
| Acknowledgments | | 307 |
| Notes | | 309 |
| About the Author | | 321 |

# Foreword

## What you see is what you get

Doug Munro

Brij Lal is what the English would call a 'scholarship boy,' one of those lads from the provinces who would not have received a tertiary education but for their fees and allowances being met through the award of a competitive scholarship—in Lal's case it started with a Canadian Third Country Scholarship, in 1971, to study at the recently-founded University of the South Pacific. Thus did the boy from the back blocks of Labasa, whose parents were unlettered, start on the journey that would lead to a stellar career as a historian of the Pacific Islands and especially of Fiji. He is not simply the most distinguished graduate of the University of the South Pacific but would grace the roll of graduates of any university in the world. For over thirty years Lal has moved purposefully through the major periods of Fiji's history. As well as having eight academic monographs to his name, he has been involved with some twenty-five edited collections. The starting point was the revision of his doctoral dissertation (*Girmitiyas: the origins of the Fiji Indians*, 1983; reissued 2004) but the emphasis thereafter has increasingly focused on the political history of twentieth century Fiji, including biographies of A.D. Patel (*A Vision for Change*, 1997) and Jai Ram Reddy (*In the Eye of the Storm*, 2010). I've lost count of the number of journal articles and book chapters that Lal has written. They began to appear in 1979, the centennial of *girmit*, and the output has not slackened.

The present book comprises a selection of these shorter pieces, but it is a selection of a selection. Many of Lal's journal articles on the indenture system in Fiji have already been republished within single covers (*Chalo Jahaji: On a journey through indenture in Fiji*, 2000; reissued 2006) and his more creative writings ('faction') have appeared in a number of volumes, beginning with *Mr Tulsi's Store* (2001). The present book completes the circle with a broad selection of his writings on more recent events in Fiji and beyond, and puts on parade Lal's versatility as an historian and writer. Although he has largely confined his research to Fiji, both the form and content of his writings are eclectic, ranging in style from academic non-fiction, popular 'faction' and serious journalism; and in geographic range (anywhere his travels take him), and this includes following the Indian diaspora to the Caribbean and recounting his impressions of London.

Lal has often used the metaphors of travel to denote both historical processes and individual experiences—'journey', 'odyssey', 'voyage', 'banishment', 'sojourn'. Journeys might involve changes of direction, hence one of Lal's 'faction' books being entitled *Turnings* (2008). Now there are 'intersections', those often happenstance criss-crossings between life and events—or as Lal puts more precisely, the 'series of haphazard intersections between the primitive and the modern, colonial and postcolonial, past and present, and scholarship and political activism'—and these are what drives the present volume. Lal is fond of quoting the Australian historian Ken Inglis to the effect that 'A lot of history is concealed autobiography,' precisely because it describes the extent to which his own writings are forged through a specific mind intersecting with particular experiences. For that reason, to give one small example, the scholarship boy who made his way on the basis of merit is hardly likely to barrack for chiefly privilege. A broader intersection between mind and matter is that History, for Lal, is not so many dispassionate words on paper but the recounting of real and lived experience. Lal, moreover, needs a sense of involvement and attachment before he can warm to a subject, and in his earlier work on the indenture system in Fiji he found a topic where the heart and the head came together: his choice of subject stemmed from relevance and a sense of engagement with his own roots. There is more to it. His writings on indenture always contained a strong argumentative line, often accompanied by a moral stance: the labourers *were* exploited and women labourers especially so; labourers soon learned *not* to engage in confrontational resistance to the plantation system; women were *not* the major cause of the high suicide rates on the plantations.

These same features apply to his work on the contemporary history of Fiji. Its personal salience lies in writing about the recent history of his country of birth, which, incidentally, he started doing well before the 1987 coups. What the coups did do was to impart a sense of urgency and fuel the moral dimension. Lal said to me in the late 1990s that 'there is something fundamentally wrong and immoral about deposing a duly elected democratic government through a military coup', and he has not deviated from that position from that day to this. Democracy has had a strange journey in Fiji: the winners at the ballot box claim it as the source of their legitimacy whereas the losers condemn democracy as a foreign flower, sublimely unaware on this line of reasoning that Christianity must fall into the same noxious-weed category. When *Broken Waves*, his history of twentieth century Fiji, appeared in 1992 as a volume in the Pacific Islands Monograph

## Foreword

Series, the series editor, Robert C Kiste, rightly pointed out that *Broken Waves* 'is a history with a point of view; it is neither impartial nor ambiguous and may well provoke controversy. Lal's own perspectives and value judgments are explicit, and he does not conceal his disappointment and even anguish over the failure to create a truly democratic multi-racial society.'

Never were truer words spoken—and in the same way, I openly acknowledge that I was completely biased when co-authoring a book on the collapse of the National Bank of Fiji: 'Yes, that's right. I am biased against imprudent banking practices, political cover-ups, the looting of the state and the bad governance that encourages such behaviour. Damned right I'm biased!' To assume the posture of the detached scholar, as Oskar Spate once put it, is none other than a feigned 'impartiality which evades responsibility by saying nothing, the partiality which masks its bias by presenting slanted facts with an air of cold objectivity—these are a thousand time more dangerous than an open declaration of where one stands; then at least those who disagree can take one's measure with confidence.' In like fashion, Lal's readers can be assured that what they see is what they get. There is no question of his flying in under false colours. In fact, Lal cannot abide people in any walk of life, and especially public figures, who say one thing and then do another, or who are models of unprincipled inconsistency and consistent only in adherence to their own self-interest.

Many of the pieces in the present book bear witness to Lal's role as a 'participant historian', which has a long pedigree in Pacific Islands historiography. He needs to engage with his subject matter—to get his hands dirty—and he mounts a spirited defence of his position in this book. Of course there are various levels of participation in the events that one writes about and Lal's deepest immersion was being appointed one of the three members of the Reeves Commission to review the 1990 Fiji Constitution. For the most part, however, Lal has been a close observer of the political scene in Fiji but at the edges of action. Although I suspect he would feel uneasy at being labelled a public intellectual, that is what he is: he has recognised expertise and an acknowledged reputation (or cultural authority), he is willing to express his views in a variety of media, and he has a constituency. But speaking truth to power can be a dangerous thing and Lal has been exiled from the country of his birth and where he hoped to retire—or at least he sets foot inside Fiji at his physical peril. There have been other setbacks, not least the abrogation of the 1997 Fiji Constitution which he helped to create, and further coups. He does not dwell on any sense of personal disappointment, real though it is, and instead is more concerned about the overall situation in Fiji and the absence of any light at the end of the tunnel. More than once he has said to me, regarding his research on Fiji, that it is 'so painful to visit the past, and a failed past at that.' At least he does not feel the sense of irretrievable waste that has beset Jai Ram Reddy, whose biography he has written: 'I gave up thirty years of my life for nothing,' [he said to Lal], with a palpable trace of disappointment and hurt in his voice. 'All that sacrifice: what for?' That is not to say that Lal is upbeat about Fiji's future. He is under no illusions that 'there will be future coups in Fiji long after I am gone. All I can do is to say my piece and state where I stand.'

Lal is also disappointed at the lack of a widespread reading culture in Fiji, as will be evident from the latter pages of this book. Life for him would be insupportable without books. He is also aghast at slovenliness of written expression, not least amongst fellow academics. The present book, in both matter and manner, is one person's attempt to lead by example and to show that serious writing can be read to be enjoyed—just as Oskar Spate often said in a slightly different context, 'You don't have to be solemn to be serious'. In an essay not published in this book, Lal presented his credo that both History and how it is written and practised really matters:

> I belong to a tradition and a generation which does not regard a few lines of mangled English as fine poetry. Grammatically incorrect English that passes for modish prose is, for me, an exercise in language abuse. Shakespeare, Matthew Arnold and John Steinbeck are not, for me, Dead White Males whose works have no relevance. I have read them with the same devotion and interest as I read Albert Wendt and MG Vassanji, Chinua Achebe and VS Naipaul. And great poetry often provides deeper insights into the human condition than post-modern theory… Let us not reject out of hand the humane, intellectually liberal and morally engaged discipline of our founding ancestors. Let us engage in the intelligent language of ordinary discourse. Let's continue to search for tangible, verifiable and knowable truths with passion and imagination. Let us once again proclaim the fundamental truth that History matters.[1]

As well as being an exemplar of the possibilities of written English, *Intersections* provides historical perspective on the 'Fiji situation.' Let us not reject out of hand the possibility that something can be retrieved from the repeated failures of Fiji's postcolonial past. There is still a remote hope that the clouds might clear. So neither should we reject out of hand, however faint the possibility, that post-independence Fiji may yet be able to forge a just multi-racial society, a viable

*Foreword*

economy and an equitable political system where the result of the ballot box is accepted and where people's civil rights are not abused. The spirit that pervades Brij Lal's *Intersections* offers indirect but instructive insight as to how these objectives might be achieved and for that reason repays careful attention.

Doug Munro
Wellington, New Zealand
April 2011

# One

## When It Is Over

*When it is over, I don't want to wonder*
*If I have made of my life something particular, and real.*
*I don't want to find myself sighing and frightened,*
*Or full of argument.*
*I don't want to end up simply having visited this world.*

Mary Oliver, 'When Death Comes'

Travelling is an occupational hazard of academic life, especially in Australia where the 'tyranny of distance' takes its toll more than in most other places. Long plane journeys are a particular problem especially if you travel the crowded cattle class, as most impecunious conference-attending academics invariably do. The drinks trolley should desirably be avoided for good health reasons, you are advised, and there are warnings to be heeded about deep vein thrombosis and the need periodically to wiggle your toes to get the blood flowing. There is so much time to kill on long flights, and flights to and from Australia are invariably long. A movie or two may be taken in, but mostly I read. Just as often I write. For that, all I need is a pad and a pen. I still do most of my creative and even lecture writing in longhand, a legacy no doubt of my prehistoric educational background and a Luddite's lurking trepidation about technology. People of my generation have become remnants in their own time (though we cheerfully live with the certainty that today's jaunty avan garde folk will in the fullness of time also become footnotes in other peoples' texts).

Many pieces collected here were conceived and written on long-distance flights to and from Australia to far-flung corners of the globe: Africa, the Caribbean, Europe, Southeast Asia, the Americas. Of varying length, written in different moods for different audiences (and sometimes for no audience at all), these essays emerged from the first rough drafts composed on these journeys. They are about people and places I have encountered actually or vicariously, about events which provoked a particular response in me, about topics and themes I had to have a word on, and about my unease with developments and digressions in my own area of academic specialisation. Sometimes writing things down is nothing more than an act of resistance against the ravages of failing memory. We all daily struggle with a range of emotions but seldom contemplate them in any serious way. The moment passes and the memory fades, replaced the next day by another thought, another emotion. More often now than before, I have a strong urge to commit the lived experience to paper, to shore up the fragments against the lengthening shadow, if nothing else. Nothing I have thought about or experienced or observed is 'really real' until it acquires concrete shape in the form of words. Words are the tools I use to structure thought and clarify emotion. Writing gives concreteness and form to reality, helps to 'clasp the net over the butterfly,' as EL Doctorow puts it.

Reading and writing has been an integral part of my life for the better part of three decades. Reading is second nature to me, writing much less so. Writing for me is a way of thinking more deeply about experience. It is a skill I have learned over time. It has not been easy, and many gaps remain. We came late to the English language. Its intricate structures and nuances were beyond easy comprehension, and the rules of grammar were elusive, as they still are. There were other hurdles as well. I do not come from a social or historical background grounded in intellectual pursuit. My grandparents were indentured labourers—*girmitiyas*—who had come to Fiji in early 20th century, and my parents were struggling cane growers in rural Vanua Levu, living on the outer edges of encroaching poverty. I vividly recall the acute pain—embarrassment—I felt when I was once asked to do an exercise from a New Zealand textbook requiring me to ask my parents which two books they had most enjoyed reading and why, and then to tell the class what I had learnt about these books. My parents were non-literate, both in English and in their own native language.

People of my generation growing up in rural Fiji in the post-war years often came from impoverished families scratching a meagre living from small cane or rice farms. There were no books in our homes, except some religious texts which were invariably more revered than actually read. There was no way of knowing about the world beyond the village horizon. School texts helped, but education had an instrumentalist intent to get us out of the predicament that had so blighted the life of our parents growing up in the shadow of indenture. Schooling in Fiji's late colonial period was not about enlarging the mind or encouraging exploration and discovery. The emphasis was squarely on learning, rote learning, the alphabets to acquire some elementary trade skills, to become better, more productive law-abiding citizens. The lucky ones might find a career in the lower rungs of the colonial bureaucracy, no more. The glass ceiling for those of the 'wrong colour' or class was real. The fact that some of us broke the invisible but very real boundaries did so despite, not because of, the education we received. We were often the first ones in our families to receive secondary schooling and to have a vocation other than farming. We were pioneers in the true sense of the word, with all the limitations that went with it.

It is fashionable these days to talk about relevance and empowerment in school curricula. I understand the intellectual and emotional impulse that prompts such talk. There was nothing relevant or empowering about what we learned at school. On the contrary, local experience—cultural, social, historical, economic—hardly ever featured in the school curriculum. Our past was simply far too fractured and far too contested to lend itself to a warm, uplifting nation-building narrative. It was safer to learn about other peoples' places and pasts than your own. This sort of education is now routinely condemned by our postcolonial critics as part of an insidious imperial strategy to control and dominate subject peoples. That may be so, but we did not have a written past of our own upon which to draw for intellectual and cultural sustenance (and which the evil colonial masters could subvert for their own selfish purposes). Reading stories from the Caribbean or Africa in our remote rural school, we felt connected to other parts of the world. The stories and pictures opened up new horizons for us, helped us momentarily escape the mindless routine of village life. That in its own way was also an empowering, enlarging experience. We understood that bad as things were around us and for us, we were not alone in our miseries and predicaments. The need to know, to connect with the world around us has remained with me. The passion to know more has only intensified with time

Reading was fun but writing was another matter. It was one thing to learn about split infinitives, and subordinate and co-ordinate clauses, quite another to recognize them in the texts we were required to read. Think of the agony of a child with the most elementary knowledge of the English alphabets being asked to distinguish between wrote and rote, wretch and retch, wrest and rest, to explain the meaning of onomatopoeia or malapropism. We simply reproduced on the page what we rote-learned in the books. We did set-pieces in composition and comprehension exercises about exotic people and places because there was no opportunity to write about our own surroundings. And there were no role models to follow either. We were lucky in high school and university to have teachers who cared about the English language and taught us, however unsuccessfully, to write fluent and agile prose, to pause and appreciate sentences of nuance and rhythm. They took care in teaching. In my own university career, I have been lucky to have friends and colleagues who wrote as if they owned the English language, and whose example was inspiring, although well neigh impossible to emulate. I think in this respect of Hank Nelson, Donald Denoon and Tessa Morris-Suzuki in my own department here in Canberra. Doug Munro in Wellington read virtually everything I wrote and corrected my prose with gentle admonition. Other friends introduced me to such great cultural artefacts of the modern world as *The Times Literary Supplement*, *New York Review of Books* and the incomparable *New Yorker*. It has been my great fortune to have a circle of friends who take reading and writing as seriously as I do, for whom style matters, and to whom I often turn for advice and inspiration.

Academic writing today has its own specific rules of engagement and its own specialized audience. Scholars these days often write about themselves, for themselves and for a like-minded, narrowly-focused fraternity of specialists. Some of this is understandable: citation indices have to be kept in mind and starred journals as well, for they matter hugely in promotion stakes; but taken to excess it loses its purpose, the converted talking to the converted about arcane bits and pieces of knowledge of no great consequence to the world at large. This sort of intellectually myopic incestuousness has no appeal for me. Truth to tell, I am repelled by it. I live at the interface of scholarship and practical engagement with society. I am what the French might call *spectateur engage*, a politically engaged but independent intellectual (although intellectual is not a label I am comfortable with). I take my rights, roles and responsibilities as a citizen seriously. I live in society, not above or outside it. I am part of the history about which I write. I write to communicate, not obfuscate, to be read rather than simply to get ahead. I would like to have my voice heard on matters of consequence, to make a difference, if I can. Writing as accessibly as I can is my private act of resistance and revenge against some of the dominant intellectual fashions of our time.

But this passion of mine is not shared by some of my younger colleagues, formed by different experiences and influences, who accuse me—us—not unfairly, I should say, of being part of the assimilationist tradition of scholarship. We learnt the rituals and protocols of higher learning sanctioned by metropolitan universities and reproduced them faithfully to specified standards for validation by our peers and superiors. We worked within an approved epistemological framework, not questioning its assumptions and understandings, its limits and limitations, the insidious ways in which it marginalised 'unauthorized' thought. In short, we played along. Some of the younger generation is aggressively non-conformist. They flout the rules of English grammar and openly subvert its narrative structures in the name of creativity and innovation. They want to be different and they want that difference to be acknowledged and accommodated. They want the world to understand their way of telling their stories, their unconventional and unorthodox approaches, and defiant stance against the conventions of the past. I understand their courage and ambition, and sometimes even support it, though I also share the view that the narcissism of the younger generation sometimes erases the historical subject itself. But my eclectic disposition notwithstanding, I have some difficulty accepting mangled English which passes for modish poetry. It is for me too late to change. Nor, if truth be told, would I want to.

I have come to the conclusion after a lifetime of reading and writing that accessible prose is valued by the lay reader. Stories draw people in. Story telling, as Hannah Arendt once wrote, 'reveals meaning without committing the error of defining it.' The sharing of experience creates the possibilities for individual acts of imagination. The reaction to my *Mr Tulsi's Store* from readers around the world has been overwhelming. That book, for readers unfamiliar with it, is my effort creatively, through the device of 'faction,' to recreate the village world of my childhood. It is by far the most widely read of my books. In my journey, my contemporaries heard echoes of their own footsteps, markers of their own special moments, and they responded generously. Imaginative works have that special power to connect. The book also raises larger questions about writing about societies where no written records exist and where public memory is not neatly archived. How do you write about unwritten pasts? Or is that world lost to historical reconstruction?

Scholarly work occupies a very large part of my time, but not all of it. The tumultuous events in Fiji over the last decade or so have pulled me back to the present, and a considerable part of my time and energy is spent on commentary and analysis of contemporary events in that country. This is time consuming and often repetitive, but it is a responsibility and an obligation that I cannot escape, nor would I want to. Silence in the face of oppression is not an option for me, nor is the defense of democratic values and the rule of law a crime. 'A society in which citizens cannot criticize the policy of the state,' the great American historian Arthur Schlesinger Jr. once wrote, 'is a society without the means of correcting its course.' The fundamental truth of that statement is unchallengeable. There is also much wisdom in Joseph Schumpeter's words: 'To realise the relative validity of one's conviction and yet stand for them unflinchingly is what distinguishes a civilised man from a barbarian.'

All this should suggest that I have a lived a fairly unconventional academic life. I constantly move between the present and the past. The link between the two engages my intellectual interests and energy, and 'Intersections' best captures the range and scope of what I do. I inhabit the borderlands between scholarly endeavour and practical political engagement, between writing about the past in the conventional scholarly fashion and writing imaginatively about the world of living memory. The world of in-betweenity, of flux, suits my temperament. I have lived my life in different junction zones of history at different times. I was born in the late colonial period in Fiji, came of age when it became independent and have borne witness to its various postcolonial traumas. I have vivid recollection of my ancient indentured grandparents and through them have established a vicarious connection to another past. I now live forcibly exiled from the land of my birth. The world that formed and deformed me is vanishing before my eyes as I struggle to cope with the technology-driven, new fangled ways of the present. Not only the physical, material world, but the world of ideas and values with which I grew up and which I cherish are being trampled upon, forced to the margins, by men drunk on power: ideas about the sanctity of the ballot box, for instance, and the importance of the rule of law. 'Change in all things is sweet,' Aristotle said. May be, but Matthew Arnold is also right that too much change 'doth unknit the tranquil strength of men.'

This volume admits the readers to my peripatetic world with the hope that they will write down their own experience of life and affairs. Preserving memory for future generations is a responsibility we cannot evade. But self indulgence is not the primary reason for putting this collection together. I have done so principally in response to requests from complete strangers from around the world seeking information and reading material about their parents' or grandparents' place of birth. The need to know, to trace one's roots, is deep and urgent and very moving in its own way. And there are frequent requests from nieces and nephews in Australia, New Zealand and North America who write regularly to introduce themselves, establish family connections long forgotten, and ask for more relevant things to read. The younger ones ask me to go onto the Facebook. I do not know how and I am not sure, from what I have been told, whether I would welcome the inevitable intrusion and exposure that would entail. Others have urged me to create my own Web Page. That is a possibility but when: I cannot say. A Luddite's lame response, I know, to avoid facing the excruciating truth about our mental anguish, our crippling incapabilities with modern technology. This collection of essays will have to do in the meantime. Some friends and colleagues in Fiji have complained, and justifiably so, that I have not reciprocated their generous acts of assistance over the years. I feel that burden more acutely now that I cannot return to that country for the foreseeable future. This volume, offered at an affordable price, is my gesture of gratitude. It is a paltry gesture, I know, but it is the best I can do in the circumstances. Please accept it with the sincerity with which it is offered.

I was once asked by a student after a talk in Fiji why I wrote, and how I found time to write. I was stumped. It was not a question I had considered in any systematic way before. Invoking VS Naipaul, I spoke of my 'fear of extinction,' and of the deep urge to transcend the 'familiar temporariness' of life. I also invoked the name of Elizabeth Hardwick who was fond of saying that there were principally two reasons for writing: desperation and revenge. But I was still unsatisfied. Years later, I read Mary Oliver's poem 'When Death Comes.' The concluding lines of that great piece of art, quoted at the beginning of this introduction, sum up my feelings much better. When the end comes, I do not want to wonder if 'I have made of my life something particular, and real.' That will do me for an epitaph.

# Two

# Heartbreak Islands (2003)

*Chamkte Chaand Ko Toota Hua Tara Bana Dala*
*They have reduced a shining moon to a shooting star*

Fiji is a paradox and a pity. A paradox because this island nation endowed with wonderful natural resources, a talented and multi-ethnic population with an enviable literacy rate, a sophisticated (but now crumbling) public infrastructure where drinkable piped water was once guaranteed, public roads had few potholes, poverty and crime and squatters were visible but contained, hospitals were uncrowded, children went cheerfully to schools, and respect for law and order was assured: this nation is tragically prone to self-inflicted wounds with crippling consequences. One coup is bad enough for any country, but three in thirteen years staggers the imagination. And a pity because there is no resolution in sight of the country's deep-seated political and economic problems as its leaders dither and the country drifts divided. The battle lines are clearly drawn in a deadly zero-sum game. The militant nationalists, happily nonchalant about the implications of their actions, threaten violent retribution if their agenda for political supremacy is marginalised in mainstream public discourse. Compounding the problem on top of all this is a manifest lack of political will to exorcise the country of the demons that terrorise its soul.

The tragedy of Fiji politics has been that rosy rhetoric has always won over the hard reality on the ground, blinding its people to the deep-seated problems that beset the country, or at least causing them a sense of slight unease in probing too deeply into the inner dynamics of national body politic lest they discover some discomforting truth about themselves that they would rather not know about. If the emperor had no clothes, it was better not to find out. Fiji portrayed itself to the world as a model of functioning democracy, largely free of ethnic tension and conflict that plagued many developing countries, the way the world should be, as Pope John Paul II intoned after a fleeting visit to the islands in 1985. There was little public acknowledgement, let alone public discussion, of inter- and intra-ethnic tensions, and the deep reservations the different communities had about the structure of power relations in the country, the deeply contested struggle for a definition and clarification of Fijian political identity that preceded independence. The illusion of harmony and amicable understanding in the post-independence era was just that, an illusion, and just as misleading and fraught and dangerous as the impression of balance and equilibrium conveyed by an earlier metaphor of Fiji as a three-legged stool.[1]

The truth is that Fiji never had a genuinely shared sense among its citizens about what kind of constitutional arrangement was appropriate for it. It was an issue that had bedevilled the country's politics since the late 1920s. Fijian and European leaders, with active official support, argued for separate racial representation. For them, primordial loyalties were paramount. The Indo-Fijians, on the other hand, championed a non-racial common roll, privileging sectarian ideology over ethnicity. The issue dominated political debate throughout the 1960s, leading to a boycott of the Legislative Council in 1967 and tense elections and by-elections a year later.[2] The communal voice won in the end, largely because of Fijian and European adamancy but partly also because of the Indo-Fijian leaders' lack of genuine commitment to the idea, following the death of AD Patel, the tireless advocate of common roll. Their compromise—in truth compromised—agreement was enshrined in the secretly negotiated independence constitution, which retained ethnicity as the principal vehicle of political participation while making half-hearted commitment to non-racial politics as a long term national objective.[3]

Unsurprisingly, race dominated post-independence politics. Political parties, the Alliance and the National Federation, were essentially race-based, the former among Fijians and Europeans and a sprinkling of Indo-Fijians, and the latter among Indo-Fijians. In time, virtually every issue of public policy came to be viewed through racial lenses: affirmative action, poverty alleviation, allocation of scholarships for tertiary education, opportunities for training and promotion in the public service. The intent to create a more level playing field, to assist the indigenous community to participate more effectively in the public sector was laudable, but race-based, rather than needs-based, policies inevitably corroded inter-ethnic harmony. Public memory was racially archived even though in daily life the salience of race was suspect. Citizens were asked for their 'race' when they opened a bank account, took out driver's licence, left or entered the country. 'Race is a fact of life,' Ratu Sir Kamisese Mara, Fiji's first and longest serving prime minister, kept reiterating. Under his administration, it almost became a way of life. Political leaders on both sides opportunistically championed moderate multiracialism, but actually played the race card on every occasion to secure power.

But with time, other realities intruded that questioned the legitimacy and value of a political edifice constructed on the foundations of ethnic compartmentalisation. Forces of change, rapid in their pace and bewildering in their implications, were fast eroding old assumptions of public discourse. The television and video brought new and strange images into people's homes. Urbanisation proceeded apace, spawning problems that transcended race and attenuated traditional links and attachments. Improved roads speeded up communication, and cash cropping inculcated more individualistic values. As RG Ward put it in 1986, 'the combined introduction of new skills, new technology and money have weakened the functional cement which binds native Fijian village society. This does not mean that the structure has collapsed, or will do so in the near future. It does mean that the risk of disintegration exists if other factors shake the edifice.'[4] Decades earlier, OHK Spate, RF Watters and CS Belshaw, among others, had made essentially similar points, but were dismissed by traditionalists afraid of change and by the colonial government too timid or tied down to orthodoxy to embrace potentially progressive ideas.[5] An opportunity was thus missed to enable and empower the Fijians to embrace the forces of modernity engulfing their lives, largely on their own terms and at their own pace. For this failure, they would pay a heavy price later.

Things came to a head in 1987, the year of the first two coups, when a democratically elected, nominally left-leaning Labour-led coalition was ousted after a month in office. Some commentators saw the crisis as a straight-out 'racial fight' between the Fijians and Indo-Fijians. Others saw the conflict as a class struggle between the haves and the have nots, Fijian commoners and Indo-Fijian working class joining hands against the dominance of chiefs and the Indo-Fijian business elite.[6] The importance of both race and class is acknowledged, but the coup can also be seen as an effort to turn the clock back, to fortify old structures and values which sustained them against forces of change, to shore up the importance of rural areas as well as the power of traditional leaders at a time when the new government was determined to democratise elements of the traditional order.[7] As Dr Timoci Bavadra, the deposed Labour prime minister, told his rallies, the individual's democratic right to vote did not mean a compulsion to vote for a chief. It was a free choice. 'By restricting the Fijian people to their communal way of lifestyle in the face of a rapidly developing cash economy, the average Fijian has become more and more backward. This is particularly invidious when the leaders themselves have amassed huge personal wealth by making use of their traditional and political powers.'[8] These were revolutionary words in the context of the time and the place, a call to action by an indigenous Fijian no less, against a system already under siege. They could not be ignored and had to be quelled quickly.

The traditionalists rallied to restore the status quo. The post-coup 1990 constitution, decreed by presidential edict, predictably privileged rural Fijians over their urban counterparts, allocating 30 of the 37 Fijian seats to them and only 7 to urban and peri-urban areas, even though nearly 40 per cent of Fijians were urban dwellers. Moreover, a candidate had to be registered in the *Vola Ni Kawa Bula* (the Register of Native Births) of the constituency in which he or she was standing, further entrenching provincialism in Fijian politics.[9] Provincial and regional affiliations, often opening up pre-colonial social cleavages, acquired a public and symbolic significance that tested the fragile, colonially-created notion of an overarching Fijian cultural and social identity. It also had the practical effect of weakening the operation of political parties among Fijians. Candidates were endorsed by the provincial councils, and their first loyalty therefore was to their provincial power base. Leaders of political parties had limited influence over their selection and little power to discipline them for insubordination or breach of party discipline. The result was an undisciplined proliferation of political parties among Fijians, formed by disgruntled or discarded candidates flying regional flags or camouflaging their private agendas under the umbrella of 'Fijian interest.'

To prevent political fragmentation, Fijian leaders had the Great Council of Chiefs sponsoring a party to unite disparate Fijian opinion and interests under one umbrella.[10] A new political party, the Soqosoqo ni Vakavulewa ni Taukei (SVT), was launched in 1990 but the hope for unity was still-born, as many Fijians questioned the wisdom of a chiefly body getting embroiled in party politics and the assumption that Fijians were of one mind on all things political. In an ironic twist, a commoner, albeit an uncommon one—Sitiveni Rabuka—was elected president of the party over one of the highest ranking chiefs, Adi Lady Lala Mara. Unsurprisingly, dissension built up, opposition emerged, rival factions developed, and alternative parties launched, such as the Fijian Association Party, privately supported by Mara, and All National Congress and later the Party of National Unity in western Viti Levu. The SVT was dislodged from power in 1999 by a combination of factors, but among the most important was the political fragmentation of the Fijians.[11] That trend will continue to hobble party politics among the Fijians, now that provincialism is back in business and flourishing and Fijian leaders are seeking to institutionalise provincial administration along the Melanesian model. 'We are still coming out of provincialism,' Sitiveni Rabuka says, 'and having that form of system will be counter to creating national cohesiveness.'[12] He is right.

The party presently in government, Soqosoqo Duavata ni Lewenivanua, launched in 2000 on a nationalist platform to woo the supporters of the coup, was able to win power by adopting a fiercely nationalist platform and by outbidding moderate Fijian parties. Its effort to consolidate its position included a promise to review the constitution to entrench Fijian political control, and pursue race-based, pro-Fijian affirmative action policies in commerce, education and the public service.[13] It also bought off potential significant opposition by diplomatic postings and through other employment opportunities: Ratu Inoke Kubuabola, a key nationalist and coup supporter, is now Fiji's High Commissioner to PNG. Isikia Savua, police commissioner at the time of the 2000 coup, and allegedly involved in it, is Fiji's Ambassador to the United Nations, and Adi Samanunu Talakuli, a known Speight supporter from the Kubuna Confederacy, is Fiji's High Commissioner to Malaysia. Berenado Vunibobo, a George Speight sympathiser, has recently handled several diplomatic assignments for the government. And several people publicly known to have been associated with the coup—Apisai Tora, Josefa Dimuri, Ratu Inoke Takikaievata, Reverend Tomasi Kanailagi, are in the Senate, and George Speight's choice for President, Ratu Jope Seniloli, is now the Vice President. Political patronage has yielded the government much needed short-term benefits, but what will happen when the well runs dry, when there are no more perks to be distributed? How will the disgruntled elements be pacified then?

The present government has made a review of the constitution a key plank in its political platform. Indeed, while heading the interim administration set up soon after the 2000 coup, Laisenia Qarase established a constitution review committee headed by Professor Asesela Ravuvu, a known nationalist-leaning former University of the South Pacific academic, to recommend changes.[14] But the committee, set up without public consultation, and filled with hand-picked men of dubious credibility (certainly in the Indo-Fijian community)[15] lacked legitimacy and was disbanded after a few months. A summary of its report—the full report, although taxpayer-funded, has not been released—suggested a hardline nationalist position requiring *vulagis*—guests, foreigners such as Indo-Fijians—to accept the primacy of the *taukei*—the indigenous people, the first settlers—in politics. The fundamental argument is that Fiji is a Fijian country, and its political leadership should therefore always rest in Fijian hands. Others can live in Fiji, make money, contribute to the development of the country, but not aspire to political leadership. That acceptance, in the nationalist view, is a precondition for political stability.

Although that position will be unpalatable to believers in liberal democracy, it will, I suspect, be broadly embraced by many indigenous Fijians as a symbolic recognition of the indigeneity of the country. There was political stability in Fiji from independence to 1987 because a Fijian, who had the confidence of his people, was at the helm, many Fijians say. When his hold on power was threatened, as in 1977 and again in 1982, retribution was threatened. And when he actually lost power in 1987, violence was used to reinstate him. In other words, democracy would be viable only with an indigenous Fijian at the helm. Perhaps. But Ratu Mara led the country under a constitution forged through consensus, flawed though it was in many respects. Astute and skilful manipulation of the electoral system put the Alliance Party in power, not a constitutional requirement for an indigenous Fijian as head of government. Any constitution that breaches human right conventions embraced by the international community will be rejected outright. That much is certain. A constitution that discriminates on the grounds of race is doomed from the start.

There are other issues to consider as well. Fijian society is much more diverse now than before. It is cris-crossed with a host of class, regional, provincial, and rural-urban interests.[16] There is no one leader who commands the respect and loyalty of all Fijians as Ratu Mara once did. The question is not really having a Fijian head of government but rather which Fijian leader would be acceptable to a particular group of Fijians at any given point in time. Sitiveni Rabuka was a Fijian, and he was defeated by Fijian votes, first in 1994 and again in 1999. Ratu Sir Kamisese Mara was a high chief, and he was forced to resign as president after the 2000 coups by Fijians. Frank Bainimarama is a Fijian, but his leadership of the armed forces was challenged by Fijian members of the military in a bloody mutiny in November 2000. George Speight claims he is Fijian (of sorts) and he is languishing in jail for a crime whose beneficiaries are ruling the country.

Fijians of all ranks and backgrounds talk wistfully about forging indigenous political unity, but as the Fiji Constitution Review Commission argued, that goal is simply unattainable. In the past, Fijians lived in villages, for the most part isolated from the other communities and dependent on subsistence agriculture. They had their own 'Native Regulations' and programs of work under the leadership of traditional leaders. But Fijian society has changed dramatically in the years since independence. Now, over 41 per cent live in urban or peri-urban areas,[17] participate in the cash economy, have the benefit of tertiary education, and are well represented in the professions and the public sector.[18] A sizeable, self-made Fijian middle class is an undeniable social fact in contemporary Fiji. It is therefore unrealistic to expect one political party to accommodate and represent a whole multiplicity of complex and competing interests. It also constrains the choices available to Fijian people who will not be able to vote a Fijian government from office if it does not deliver on its promises. Fijians, like other citizens, have the same regard for effectiveness and efficiency. 'The idea that a Fijian government must be maintained in office at all costs has grave consequences for political accountability,' the Commission argued. 'It requires setting aside the normal democratic control on a government's performance in office. This is bad for the Fijian community as well as for the country as a whole.'[19]

But perhaps, as Stewart Firth suggests, Fijian politics increasingly is not about delivering on promises but rather about taking turns at the helm balancing regional, provincial and social interests by virtue of traditional power calculations rather than competence or merit.[20] In this equation, non-Fijians matter little. Demographic reality dictates increasingly that the nature and direction of Fiji politics in future will be influenced by indigenous concerns and calculations. The projected population of Fiji in 2002 was 824,596 of which indigenous Fijians numbered 441, 363 (53.5 percent), while the Indo-Fijians, 328, 059, constituted 39.8 per cent.[21] This trend will continue with continuing Indo-Fijian migration and lower birth rates. Provincial and confederacy calculations will, as they already do, determine appointments and promotions and other opportunities. Frank Bainimarama, from the Kubuna confederacy, was appointed commander of the Fiji Military Forces in part because the two previous holders of the position, Sitiveni Rabuka and Ratu Epeli Ganilau, were from Tovata. Sitiveni Rabuka complained how, under the 1990 constitution, under which Fijian members were elected to parliament from the provinces, he had to ensure that all the provinces were represented in the cabinet, irrespective of ability and talent. Not to do so would have been interpreted as a slight on the province's name and incur their wrath. But as Fijian numbers increase, the Fijian people will realise that good governance and not the calculations of provincial representation will be in their best interests.

Leadership is a problem for both the Fijian as well as Indo-Fijian communities. Among Fijians, the era of the dominance of paramount chiefs with overarching influence across the whole spectrum of Fijian society, tutored for national leadership by the British in the post-war years, has ended.[22] The paramounts are gone: Ratu George Cakobau, Ratu Edward Cakobau, Ratu Penaia Ganilau and now Ratu Mara. These Fijian leaders brought with them practical experience of public service—Mara was a district officer in the predominantly Indo-Fijian sugar district of Ba—and a broad educational background in Fiji and overseas. Whatever else may be said of them and their politics, they believed in the principles of good, accountable governance, no doubt a legacy of their experience in the colonial civil service. For the most part, they also had a multiracial circle of friends, including Europeans and Indo-Fijians.

Their successors lack their broad experience and background. Many latter day Fijian leaders went from racially exclusive provincial schools to predominantly Fijian schools, such as the Queen Victoria School, their formative years uninformed and uninfluenced by any meaningful exposure to the cultures of other communities.[23] They were thus ill-equipped to meet the leadership challenges on the national stage, embroiled as they often were—and are—in provincial and regional politics to carve a national niche for themselves. In district administration, too, senior military leaders, facing dead-end careers but politically well connected, were plucked to become district commissioners, serving in areas and among people whose culture they did not understand, unlike their colonial counterparts who were expected to have some fluency in the dominant language of the area (Hindustani or Fijian as the case might have been). The government has no plans to develop the cross-cultural skills of its district-level administrators.

Leadership is a problem in the Indo-Fijian community too. Over the years, there has been a marked shift in the social and educational background of Indo-Fijian leaders. At the time of independence—and before—the majority of Indo-Fijian politicians were lawyers. Now, the base has diversified, with increasing numbers coming from the trade union movement and the academia and from the ranks of retired school teachers and civil servants looking for second careers. They, too, for the most part, are handicapped by limitations similar to those experienced by the Fijians. Few, for instance, are fluent in Fijian. And not many have a direct experience of Fijian culture. Those who do are not always appreciated. When a Labour member of parliament made his maiden speech in his Nadroga dialect, there were disapproving voices among his colleagues. The present minister of multi-ethnic affairs, George Shiu Raj, is a fluent Fijian speaker, at ease in both the cultures, but his cross-cultural skill is sometimes derided. The message seems to be that you cannot be an 'authentic' Fijian or Indo-Fijian if you are cross-culturally fluent or transgress ethnic and cultural boundaries.

The trade union culture, at least the way it has evolved in Fiji, is not conducive to negotiating the complex currents of Fiji politics. That was one of Mahendra Chaudhry's main handicaps. Few disagreed with his prognosis of the problems facing Fiji, but they demurred at the manner in which he articulated them: forthright, testy, even confrontational, little appreciating that the Fijian mode of both private and public discourse is allusive and tempered by protocol. In the trade union politics, often the ends justify the means, but in national politics, the means, articulated in the glare of intense public scrutiny, is probably just as important as the end. Chaudhry often chanted the mantra of electoral mandate to justify his uncompromising pursuit of his election promises. To be sure, he had the mandate of the voters, but that, he discovered to his cost, was only one mandate among many. The Great Council of Chiefs had its mandate for the indigenous Fijians; the Native Land Trust Board had its mandate, the Fijian dominated army its own. The art of political leadership in such a situation lay in negotiating one mandate among many competing and often incompatible mandates. Chaudhry's tragedy was that he ignored this crucial fact or at least showed an insufficient appreciation of it.

Multi-ethnic societies, with divergent traditions of discourse, are prone to mis-communication and misunderstanding. Fiji is no exception. Indo-Fijians are heirs to centuries old tradition of open, robust public debate often conducted without subtlety or irony. It can be direct, frontal and confrontational. The Fijian tradition of public discourse is the opposite, allusive, indirect, hedged in by cultural protocol and a sensitive sense of person and place. Sometimes, what is not said is probably just as important as what is. The problem is accentuated by the colonial legacy of racial compartmentalisation, the absence of shared cultural traditions and language (except English), attachment to different faiths and, more recently, the corrosive effects of the coups.

Misunderstandings are not only linguistic but cultural as well. Let me illustrate. Most Indo-Fijians routinely assert that Fijians have over 80 per cent of all the land in Fiji. That is true, but only a small percentage of it is economically useful. Moreover, land is not owned by one monolithic entity but by thousands of social units scattered throughout the islands. Some Fijians have ample land, while many are effectively landless. But these internal facts of uneven patterns of native landownership and land distribution escape Indo-Fijian comprehension. There is something more. Sir Vijay R Singh: 'To most non-Fijians, land is an item of economic utility, a basis for an income, to be acquired, used and disposed of, if the occasion arises, without much emotional wrench. To most Fijians, on the other hand, and almost every rural Fijian, it is part of his being, his soul; it was his forebears' and shall be his progeny's till time immemorial. And the Indian sees large stretches of land between Suva and Sigatoka and Nausori and Rakiraki lying idle and can't understand it. He even becomes angry and bitter when he sees where his former flourishing farm is now, after he was denied renewal of his lease, bush and scrub. The Fijian does not see it that way. Sufficient for him that it is there.'[24]

But just as Indo-Fijians do not grasp the Fijians' almost mystical attachment to their vanua,[25] Fijians have little understanding of the deeper impulses which inform the Indo-Fijian mind-set. The two most crucial concepts in Indo-Fijian thought are *izzat* (honour) and *insaf* (justice).²⁶ 'Do what is right, not what is opportunistic,' the *Bhagvad Gita* teaches. Islam sanctions jihad in the face of oppression. Death is preferable to dishonour. 'A no muttered from the deepest convictions is better and greater,' AD Patel told his rallies in the 1960s, quoting Mahatma Gandhi, 'than a yes muttered merely to please, or worse, to avoid trouble,' because in the end, truth will triumph (*Satyame Vijayte*). Indo-Fijians would accept an outcome, even if it is disadvantageous to them, provided it is transparently fair and does not affront their sense of dignity, honour and self-respect. Indo-Fijian leaders pushed for a common roll of voting—one person, one vote, one value—in the 1920s when they were a minority in the population. As HLS Polak told Colonial Office in 1929, 'everywhere they [Indians] stand by the principle of the common franchise as symbol of equal citizenship.'²⁷ In the 1960s, the overwhelming majority rallied to that cause because the cause was just, not because it was politically advantageous or indeed achievable. Privately, many Indo-Fijians will probably accept a Fijian head of government if that outcome was achieved through political negotiation, but never as a unilaterally declared constitutional right. In 1997, for example, Indo-Fijians put aside their longstanding demand for political parity with the Fijians and accepted proportionality in the reserved (twenty three Fijian and nineteen Indo-Fijian) because the allocation was based on demographic composition of the two groups. It is difficult to convey how deeply offensive the words 'second class citizenship' are to the Indo-Fijians' sense of honour and self-worth.

Many Fijians feel that the Great Council of Chiefs should play a more active role in national politics.²⁸ Since its formal establishment after Cession in 1874, it has been the principal advisor to colonial and post-colonial governments on matters relating to the indigenous community. In the 1970 independence constitution, it nominees in the Senate had the power of veto over all legislation touching indigenous Fijian interests and concerns. The 1997 constitution, for the first time, recognised the GCC as a constitutionally established institution (as opposed to one established by an Act of Parliament). Its 14 nominees in an upper house of 34 members enjoy veto powers similar to the provisions of the 1970 constitution. The GCC also nominates the President and the Vice President of Fiji. In short, its role and authority are an important political as well as constitutional fact and, perhaps more important, beyond dispute.

The supporters of a greater role for GCC see it as an important force for good in restraining ethnic chauvinism, in facilitating ethnic accommodation, and bridging ethnic.²⁹ Perhaps, though the evidence is contestable. In 1987, the GCC convened to legitimise the overthrow of the Labour Coalition government, its proceedings dominated by its more hardline elements. Rabuka was hailed as a hero and inducted as a life-member. In 2000, it similarly convened, at the behest of Speight supporters, to demand changes to the 1997 constitution—a constitution it had blessed without reservation—to accommodate the nationalist Fijian demand. Such inconsistency or opportunism undermines the Council's moral authority and legitimacy among non-Fijians. The current chair of the GCC, Ratu Epeli Ganilau, says he is a 'keen to involve Indian leaders in the chiefs' council to discuss sensitive issues such as land.'[30] That is a welcome gesture, but it would require a consistent effort to ensure that the Indo-Fijians are able to make genuine representation of their concerns, interests and aspirations. There are, however, some Fijian chiefs who have argued that the chiefly council should represent the concerns of the indigenous community only, and that anything else would detract from its central purpose and mission.[31]

There are few avenues available for inter-ethnic dialogue outside the political arena where talk is inevitably shrill and antennas tuned to political partisanship and advantage. Religious organisations have few opportunities for regular inter-faith conversation. The Methodist Church, to which the majority of Fijians belong, has been strongly nationalistic since the 1987 coups.[32] The Church is now trying to have the soldiers involved in the 2000 mutiny pardoned as a part of the reconciliation process.[33] In the mid-1990s, the various faiths were able to establish an Inter-Faith Search to seek common ground to pave the way for national healing and reconciliation, but corrosive effects of ethnic and religious politics have eroded its foundations.[34] Fijians have their traditional avenues for intra-Fijian dialogue and dispute resolution through district and provincial councils, and through the machinery of the Fijian administration. But these are unavailable to the Indo-Fijians. The Girmit Council, an organisation of various Indo-Fijian social and cultural organisations formed to mark the centenary of Indian arrival in Fiji, is virtually defunct, while the Indian Summit, convened in the aftermath of the 2000 coup, has achieved little. Indo-Fijians have their village committees and voluntary social and cultural associations, but these are ill-equipped to facilitate cross-cultural, inter-ethnic dialogue. What is urgently required is a proper and properly equipped forum for an exchange of views between the two communities outside the political arena.[35]

Perhaps in this context, a recommendation of the Reeves Commission is worth re-visiting. A number of Indo-Fijian organisations and community leaders asked the Commission to recommend the creation of a representative Indo-Fijian umbrella body similar to the Great Council of Chiefs. The Commission reported: 'We endorse the principle behind the suggestion, but think that, initially, it should be taken up informally by the Indo-Fijian community. If there is agreement about the basis for the selection of the members of such a body, and it is able to meet and work in a way that demonstrates broad support for its composition and role, consideration should then be given to providing it with a statutory constitutional base.'[36] But the Fiji Labour Party has already rejected the idea. An Indian Council, it says, would 'only serve to further divide the people [and] compartmentalise through the creation of racial institutions.'[37] In view of such opposition, the prospects look bleak.

The one bright light in an otherwise dim scene is the work of various Non-Government Organisations, most of which emerged after the coups of 1987. Fiji Women's Rights Movement and the Women's Crisis Centre have done much to educate the public about issues relating to gender and domestic violence, even though both are urban-based. Ecumenical Centre for Research, Education and Advocacy has sponsored important research on sensitive issues of social justice.[38] The Fiji branch of Moral Re-armament has its part in trying to build cross-cultural bridges. But perhaps the most important, and the most controversial, has been the Citizens Constitutional Forum. Formed in the mid-1990s, it has convened numerous meetings and sponsored conferences, workshops and publications to educate the public about their constitutional and human rights.[39] It fought court cases challenging the abrogation of the 1997 constitution, and most recently, sought Supreme Court ruling on the legality of the Qarase government's unwillingness to form a multi-party government with the Labour party as provided for in the constitution. The CCF has been a sharp critic of the government's race-based affirmative action policies. Stung by CCF's criticism, the government de-registered it, but its spirit remains undaunted. I believe that organisations like these, which seek non-violent resolution to the country's deep-seated problems through non-racial means, have a lot to contribute to the daunting task of nation building.

Recent crises have severely tested the fabric of race relations in Fiji. On the surface things look calm. People play and work together, mingle in the markets, and children attend schools together, but the underlying tone is apprehension and anxiety. The government's affirmative action for indigenous Fijians, approved in some form or other by many Fijians, is resented by most Indo-Fijians because they are not transparent and are based on assumptions that defy the experience of daily life: large sections of the Indo-Fijians live in desperate poverty. They look in dread at the glass ceiling in the public sector. Sugar cane growers, for the most part uneducated and unskilled, are forced to relocate and start all over again as leases expire and their formerly productive fields revert to bush, generations of effort vanishing at the stroke of the pen or an official edict. The talk of reviewing the constitution to further entrench Fijian control causes them deep anxiety. I asked a prominent Indo-Fijian lawyer married to an indigenous Fijian what the future held for the Indo-Fijians. Her response: 'There is little future for them here unless the present government changes its policies.' Unwanted and uprooted, Indo-Fijians leave. Since 1987, over 80,000 have left, and more will leave if they could, draining the country of skills and resources Fiji can ill-afford to lose.[40] But now, more and more indigenous Fijians are leaving as well, to give themselves and their children a better future. The Indo-Fijians are caught in a bind. They are leaving because they don't see a future for themselves and especially their children, and the government is reluctant to spend money on training and educating a group it knows will one day go.

To heal the wounds, the government has set up a Department of National Reconciliation and Unity to promote racial harmony and cohesion through social, cultural, educational and sporting activities. But inter-ethnic reconciliation is only one part of the government's effort. An important role for the department is to 'promote greater unity within the indigenous Fijian community through various programmes and activities at village, *tikina*, provincial and national levels.'[41] Political self-interest and survival instincts drive the reconciliation effort, for the government knows that its chances of success depend crucially on Fijian unity, however illusive that prospect might be. It is precisely for that reason that, however much it may wish it, and I know that members of the government at the highest level want justice done, the government cannot afford to be seen to be proactive in pursuing the course of justice. It is for that reason that the government has reportedly asked the military to be lenient on those convicted of mutiny. It is for that reason that coup supporters have been dealt with lightly, and why the government is loathe to reprimand ministers who utter racist remarks under the cover of parliamentary privilege.[42] It is for that reason that a man accused of aiding and abetting treason, the deputy speaker of the House Ratu Rakuita Vakalalabure, still occupies the chair. The government recognises that having aroused Fijian expectations with ambitious but costly promises, it cannot now retreat. To appear to be making compromises in the national interest, would be seen as a sign of defeat and retreat. The government is riding a tiger it cannot dismount at will.

True and enduring reconciliation, which all the people of Fiji want, will come only when the truth of the past is confronted honestly and dispassionately. In 1987, opportunistic leaders looked the other way when the coup took place. Sitiveni Rabuka was not only hailed as a cultural hero of the Fijian people— 'Steve: The Hand of God' the tee-shirts proclaimed. What interests and concerns supported the overthrow of the Labour Coalition government were never investigated. Again that reluctance to look too deeply into the heart of the nation's problems. Thirteen years later, Fiji experienced another, and more, violent over throw of a democratically elected government. And if the causes of the present crisis are not investigated, Fiji will, as surely as night follows day, encounter more violent turbulence on its ill-fated journey into the future. The politicisation of the military, the police force and the public service will have to cease. The culture of corruption and nepotism nourished after 1987 will have to be confronted, the political ambitions of the 'Children 1987' to take the front seat as a matter of ethnic right curtailed. Regard for law and order would have to be re-introduced to groups of people, often young, unskilled, marginalised in the march to modernisation and vulnerable to emotional exploitation by would-be politicians. Only then will a solid base for economic development and investment be built.

Beyond that, the people of Fiji would have to re-examine the foundations of a political culture they have inherited. It is my firm view that a very large part of Fiji's problems derives from having a political system based on race.[43] An obsession with race encourages ethnic chauvinism, poisons multi-ethnic discourse, and hinders the search for solutions to Fiji's deep seated social and economic problems which have little to do with race but everything to do with colour-blind forces of globalization. Marginalizing the Indo-Fijians and discriminating against them will not solve the problems facing the Fijian people. Using race as an escape goat will lead Fiji nowhere. Indo-Fijians do not threaten the foundations of Fijian culture and traditional society: modernity does. Asesela Ravuvu: 'The new political system emphasises equal opportunity and individual rights, which diminish the status and authority of chiefs. Equal opportunities in education and equal treatment under the law have further diminished the privileges which chiefs enjoyed under colonial rule and traditional life before…Although village chiefs are still the focus of many ceremonial functions and communal village activities, their roles and positions are increasingly of a ritualistic nature.'[44] Sitiveni Rabuka: 'I believe that the dominance of customary chiefs in government is coming to an end and that the role of merit chiefs will eventually overcome those of traditional chiefs: the replacement of traditional aristocracy with meritocracy.'[45] Ropate Qalo: '[Traditional authority] is a farce, because Fijians want the new God, not the old traditional Dakuwaqa or Degei. The new God is money, and the new chapel is the World Bank. Like all the rest of the world, traditional authority has to go or be marginalised.'[46] And it goes. As the late Oscar Spate used to say, you can turn the hands of the clock, but it won't do the clock any good. To reclaim the potential that is hers, Fiji will have to reject the old, exhausted orthodoxies of the past, old ways of thinking and doing things. A past unexorcised of its demons will continue to haunt the country's future.

# Three

## Making History, Becoming History

Early in March 1995, when the telephone call came from Mr Jai Ram Reddy, Fiji's Leader of the Opposition and the long-term leader of the Indo-Fijian community, asking me to be his nominee on the Constitution Review Commission, I was naturally overwhelmed. The appointment was not unexpected: I had been asked several months earlier about my willingness to serve but the enormity of the task ahead dawned on me at that moment. Many friends in Fiji had cautioned me. The review, they said, was a charade, a cynical exercise in public relations by a coup-tainted government eager to refurbish its image in the eyes of the international community. Rabuka was still Rabuka: leopards do not change their spots. The presence of Tomasi Vakatora, a member of the 1988 cabinet subcommittee whose recommendations had formed the basis of the contested 1990 constitution, proclaimed the government's real intention. But I was undeterred. At a celebratory dinner with friends that evening, my son Niraj, then just eleven, piped up proudly. 'Dad,' he said innocently, 'You have taught history and written history. Now you can make history and then become history.' Nervous laughter greeted his remark.

Niraj was more prophetic than anyone of us realized. Four tumultuous years after the commission completed its report, Fiji is back on the road to ruin. The 1997 constitution, based on our commission's report, unanimously approved by parliament, and blessed by the Great Council of Chiefs, lies in limbo. A democratically elected government, with an absolute majority, was ousted by a coup, the country subjected to a reign of terror and violence unprecedented in Fiji's history. The fabric of race relations, just beginning to be repaired after years of strain following the coups of a decade earlier, is in tatters. The economy is down, and the best and the brightest are looking for greener pastures. The May coup and the ensuing mayhem have taken Fiji back by a generation. As I write (in November 2000), the people of Fiji are intensely debating the future political direction of the country, including the formulation of a new constitution.

The Fiji saga has received more than its share of regional and international notice. Coups attract attention, for there is something deeply unsettling and immoral about using the bayonet to overturn the verdict of the ballot box, not once but thrice in thirteen years, the first two as tragedy, the third as farce. Fiji's situation highlights dilemmas faced by other multiethnic countries in the developing world. What framework of government is appropriate for multicultural, multiethnic nations like Fiji (or Guyana or Malaysia)? How and in what ways should the constitution of a country enlarge and enrich the common space of equal citizenship without infringing on the unique and rich cultural and spiritual traditions of the various components making up the larger society? Fiji's case also raises questions about the tension between the privileged claims of the first settlers—the indigenous people—and those of the later arrivals. Should the basis of political affiliation be blood rather than belief, primordiality rather than ideology? Our commission provided a set of recommendations to resolve these complex questions, but the latest coup-makers and their supporters did not approve of them. A vision has vanished beyond recall.

Between the beneficiaries of the coup in the interim administration and those deposed from power, a war of words is raging to win the hearts and minds of the local people and of the international community. The deposed government insists that any constitutional solution to the present crisis should be sought within the framework of the 1997 constitution; its rein-statement is for them a prerequisite for any future dialogue and reconciliation. But the coup supporters insist that the 1997 constitution is dead and buried and that a fresh start, favouring indigenous Fijian interests and needs, is necessary to resolve the crisis. What the outcome will be remains unclear. I am not convinced that the constitution has failed the people of Fiji. More to the point, the people of Fiji have failed the constitution. It will take many years of toil and tears to recover what Fiji has lost in its moment of madness, just as it did following the 1987 coups.

The destroyers of the 1997 constitution have advanced many arguments to support their cause. To begin with, George Speight and his supporters circulated a twenty-six-point document to the Great Council of Chiefs soon after hijacking parliament.[1] Their main points were that the 1997 constitution was not in the interests of the Fijian people, as seen in the rejection of it by a majority of the Fijian provinces; that it was not properly explained to the Fijian people; and that it was introduced by stealth. The democratic principles that the constitution enshrines were, in their view, foreign flowers unsuited to Fijian soil and antithetical to the central tenets of indigenous Fijian society. They further claimed that Chaudhry was 'Indianizing' the public sector by appointing more Indo-Fijians to senior positions. Chaudhry, they said, had 'a long history of arguing for racial equality under the umbrella of democracy whilst pursuing an underlying secret agenda of entrenching the interests of Indians in Fiji as supreme.' The prime minister

(Chaudhry) was confrontational in his style and insensitive to Fijian interests and concerns, particularly in relation to the ever-sensitive issue of land. His government, they complained, had 'contributed to the impoverishment and disaffection of indigenous Fijians and his rule was the culmination of thirty fraught years of modern indigenous Fijian leadership that have sacrificed the economic and cultural well being of Fijians for the advancement of a few.' In short, both the constitution and the government elected under it failed to serve the interests of the indigenous people and so had to be removed by force. Speight and his gunmen did what most Fijians had secretly desired. Speight should thus be treated as a hero and not as a treasonous criminal.

There are two sets of issues here, one constitutional and the other political; one involving the rules and regulations of government, and the other dealing with the way the party in government promulgated policies promised in their election manifesto and handled the business of administration. The two have often conveniently been conflated in Fiji, the shortcomings of the government of the day hitched to the supposed shortcomings of the constitution, and the constitution blamed for the outcome of the election. The coupling of the two is a politically expedient but unconvincing ploy; they must be separated and considered separately.

The 1997 constitution was not introduced by stealth, preceded as it was by the most comprehensive process of review and consultation ever carried out in Fiji, far more even than the 1970 constitution. This process began with the appointment of the Constitution Review Commission.[2] Its members were chosen by parliament, which also drew up the commission's terms of reference. These required the commission to review the 1990 constitution and produce a report recommending constitutional arrangements that would meet the present and future needs of the people of Fiji; promote racial harmony, national unity, and the economic and social advancement of all communities; take into account internationally recognized principles and standards of individual and group rights; guarantee full protection and promotion of the rights, interests, and concerns of the indigenous Fijian and Rotuman people; and have full regard for the rights, interests, and concerns of all ethnic groups in Fiji.

The commission itself consulted widely. It travelled to all the provinces and major settlements throughout the group and received well over eight hundred written and oral submissions from individuals, non-government organizations, church and community groups, and all the major political parties.[3] These submissions were printed in the media and broadcast over television and radio. The commission also requested research papers from local as well as overseas experts on the matters it was called to consider. These papers, too, were published.[4] In addition, the commission visited three countries with constitutional arrangements that had some bearing on the Fiji case, including Malaysia, a multiracial country with a significant indigenous population enjoying constitutionally guaranteed affirmative action policies; Mauritius, a small island state in the Indian Ocean whose constitutional structure had facilitated enviable economic growth that far outstripped Fiji's (although at the time of independence in 1968 it had lagged behind Fiji in virtually every sphere); and South Africa which, in the mid-1990s, was engaged in a massive effort to formulate an appropriate constitution to facilitate the change from apartheid to a multiparty democracy.

The commission's thoroughness and sensitivity received wide praise both locally and internationally. Introducing the report to parliament, President Ratu Sir Kamisese Mara commended the commissioners 'first for their willingness to undertake this important task, and second for the devotion and commitment they and their staff have shown in accomplishing it. We are all very much in their debt.' Prime Minister Sitiveni Rabuka extended his 'warmest gratitude and congratulations for a work well done,' and went on, 'The Commission had painstakingly canvassed views and consulted widely throughout Fiji. With meticulous care and with patience, they then compiled their report. The unanimity with which they have submitted their recommendations clearly demonstrates the seriousness with which they had approached their task, and their determination to speak as one is suggesting to us the best way forward for our country.' Opposition Leader Jai Ram Reddy was equally fulsome in his praise of a 'thorough and comprehensive document.'[5] Internationally, the commission's modus operandi was recommended by the Commonwealth Secretariat and the United Nations' Electoral Assistance Division as a model for other constitutional review exercises.

A multiparty, multiethnic Joint Parliamentary Select Committee considered the commission's report for a whole year, before producing a report that formed the basis of the constitution, was debated in parliament, and was approved unanimously. Subsequently, the Great Council of Chiefs blessed the document unreservedly. It is true that many provincial councils had rejected the commission's report at the instigation of leaders opposed to the review process. But the same people were also members of parliament, indeed members' of the Joint Parliamentary Select Committee that had approved the constitution, as well as members of the Great Council of Chiefs.

Nor is it valid to argue that the constitution could not be understood by ordinary people because it was not translated into the Fijian language (or Hindi, for that matter). Translating a complex document like a constitution is not an easy task, although the Citizens Constitutional Forum, a nongovernment organization, explained its basic features in all the three principal languages of Fiji. More important, the people who worked against the constitution were not ordinary, unlettered Fijians, but members of parliament who understood the document and had voted for it.

Is democracy a foreign flower unsuited to Fijian soil? It is of course true that democracy is foreign to Fiji, but so too are some of the most cherished institutions and practices of modern Fijian society.[6] The Fijian state itself is a creation of British colonialism, for before the middle of the nineteenth century, the islands of Fiji comprised a warring collection of *matanitu* (traditional confederacies), clamouring for political supremacy, a semblance of which was eventually achieved under Ratu Seru Cakobau, the self-styled king of Fiji. Christianity, too, is a foreign flower, having arrived in the islands via Tonga in 1835. The Great Council of Chiefs, the powerful umbrella organization of traditional Fijian leaders, and the established principles of Fijian land tenure are both, in different degrees, foreign flowers in Fiji.

The advocates of the foreign-flower argument ignore the fact that Fiji had practised kind of democracy since independence in 1970. The legitimacy of democracy was not questioned then because the Fijian establishment always won. Only when they lost power in 1987 and in 1999 was the issue raised. Even the interim administration does not question the validity of a democratic form of government for Fiji. They simply want a democracy that will always put Fijians—or more correctly, the most vocal sections of them—in power. The independence constitution, and those that followed it, did include provisions that became entrenched, effectively quarantining indigenous Fijian interests from general public debate, and giving the power of veto over them to the representatives of the Great Council of Chiefs in the Senate. That was as it should be, and those protective provisions were the product of national consensus. If Fiji jettisons democracy and all that it represents—the sovereignty of parliament as the repository of the peoples' will, an independent judiciary, an impartial civil service: what alternative will be put in its place? Monarchy? Ethnocracy? Theocracy?

Some coup supporters argued that the 1997 constitution did not protect the 'paramountcy of Fijian interests.' These words have a peculiar origin in Fijian history, their significance distorted by meanings invested in them by different groups over the years. Many have mistakenly traced them back to the Deed of Cession in 1874, by which Fiji became a Crown colony. Those words are not found there; instead, the document records the chiefs' desire to 'tender unconditionally' the sovereignty of the islands to Queen Victoria and her successors, 'relying upon the justice and generosity' of Her Majesty in dealing with her subject peoples. Cession, the chiefs hoped, would promote 'Civilization' and 'Christianity'—both foreign flowers—in the islands along with a secure and stable government—another foreign flower. In turn the Crown promised that 'the rights and interests of the said Tui Viti and other high chiefs the ceding parties hereto shall be recognised so far as is and shall be consistent with British Sovereignty and Colonial form government.' This is paramountcy within parameters. In early colonial usage, 'paramountcy of Fijian interests' meant the protection (and the insulation) of those institutions and social practices that had a particular significance to the Fijian people—their land tenure system, 'native policies' designed to preserve the neotraditional structure of their society, a separate system of administration, matters of chiefly titles and genealogies. On these matters, the view of the Fijian people, expressed through the Great Council of Chiefs, prevailed. The European planters invoked the principle of Fijian paramountcy in the 1920s, not to support Fijians, but to halt political equality demanded by Indo-Fijians. Nonetheless, until the middle of the twentieth century, the words were used in a protective sense.

That changed when independence became imminent in the 1960s. Then, Fijian leaders began to interpret the 'paramountcy of Fijian interests' to mean 'political paramountcy,' as was most forcefully articulated in 1963 in the now famous 'Wakaya Letter'[7] In it, Fijian leaders laid down preconditions for further political change toward greater internal self-government, including declaring Fiji a Christian state, seeking security of landownership, demanding Fijian parity in the public service, and recognizing a continuing constitutional link with Britain, a link 'forged in a spirit of mutual trust and goodwill that should never be severed,' and 'building on and strengthening the spirit and substance of the Deed of Cession.' The letter was a negotiating document, and a successful one. The 1965 constitution gave Fijians two additional seats over the Indo-Fijians, thus upsetting the principle of balance that had under-pinned the colonial pattern of political representation, and sowing seeds of further political instability for the remainder of the 1960s. The 1970 constitution camouflaged the issue through a complex system of political representation. Fijians and Indo-Fijians each had 22 seats in a 52-seat Lower house, 10 elected on national or cross-voting seats and 12 on straight communal seats. General voters had 8 seats. Because General Voters tended to side with Fijians and the Indo-Fijian community was prone to splitting, the dominance of the Fijian leadership was ensured. But beyond politics, paramount chiefs were at the helm of national leadership—Ratu Sir Kamisese Mara, Ratu Sir Penaia Ganilau, Ratu Sir George Cakobau, and Ratu Sir Edward Cakobau, assuring Fijians of continuity with the past.

The conventional wisdom of communal compartmentalization that under-pinned Fiji's political system was that ethnicity would drive the engine of party politics. That view as was threatened by social and economic developments in the post-independence era and the widespread changes they brought in their wake. Modern, multiracial education opened new doors. Urban drift introduced people to new and often unsettling challenges. The video and then the electronic revolution introduced ideas and values once alien or inaccessible. Improved communications and increased cash cropping in rural areas brought the subsistence sector more centrally into the modern, monetary economy. New horizons opened, more opportunities presented themselves, and old assumptions about politics changed. New ideas manifested themselves in the emergence in 1985 of a multiracial Fiji Labour Party whose non-racial social and economic philosophy challenged the old order. Seen this way, the coups of 1987 represented an effort to turn the clock back, by force.

Three years later, the post-coup administration decreed a new constitution weighted in favour of the indigenous Fijians to 'realise the aims of the coup.' Important offices of state, including that of the prime minister, were reserved for them. Special, racially exclusive affirmative action programs for Fijians and Rotumans were legislated. And in parliament, the indigenous Fijians enjoyed an outright majority of seats, with 37 of the 71 seats in the House of Representatives. For indigenous Fijians election to parliament took place from their traditional provinces; urban Fijians, more than a third of the Fijian population, were severely underrepresented. With rural weighting and an outright parliamentary majority, the architects of the 1990 constitution hoped that Fijians would always remain in power, that Fijian political paramountcy would prevail. That did not eventuate. Soon after its formation, a party backed by the Great Council of Chiefs (the Soqosoqo ni Vakavulewa ni Taukei SVT), splintered, with rival parties forming to contest its legitimacy, including the Mara-backed Fijian Association Party and the All National Congress launched by Apisai Tora in the west. Part of the fragmentation arose from dissatisfaction with Rabuka's erratic leadership, part from regional factionalism, and part from class tensions—Rabuka, a commoner, had beaten high chief Ro Lady Lala Mara for the presidency of the new party. Electing candidates from provinces encouraged provincial loyalties, paralysing the operation of effective party politics with a national agenda and vision. Rabuka's party won the 1992 election but not in sufficient numbers to form a government on its own. It could do so only with the support of the Fiji Labour Party, backed in the main by the Indo-Fijian community, the very people so recently deposed.

The clear lesson of 1990 was that Fijian numerical supremacy in parliament was no guarantee of Fijian political paramountcy. This fact was further clearly demonstrated in the 1999 elections, when Fijian fragmentation reached epidemic proportions with some twelve ethnic Fijian parties contesting the election.[8] Division among the Fijians, not political unity among Indo-Fijians, led to the fall of the Rabuka government. Since the coup of 19 May 2000, regionalism and confederacy-based politics have become rife, dividing the Fijian community as never before, and not likely to end anytime soon. Other factors must be noted: Precisely what constitutes 'the Fijian interest,' besides those items already given watertight protection in the 1997 constitution, remains unclear. Fijian interests are more diffuse now than ever before. Over 40 percent of the indigenous population now resides in urban and peri-urban areas, exposed to all the challenges of living in a complex monetary economy. Increasingly, their needs are not the needs of their rural counterparts. Weighting representation in parliament in favour of the rural dwellers—as election from the provinces will inevitably entail—will marginalize urban Fijians even more.

Given the diversity of Fijian society across class and region, the goal of permanent political unity also puts enormous strains on the Fijian community. It is difficult, if not impossible, the Constitution Review Commission argued, for one party to accommodate the multiplicity of interests that embrace Fijians. The quest for political unity also puts strains on traditional institutions. The Great Council of Chiefs' sponsorship of one political party divided the Fijians, who wanted the Council to provide leadership to all Fijians irrespective of political affiliation. The emphasis on Fijian unity also means that Fijians will not be free to vote out a Fijian government if it does not deliver what they expect. Those expectations go beyond fulfilment of the government's election promises to improve the conditions of life for Fijians, who, like other citizens, want the same standards of integrity, efficiency, and effectiveness from those they elect. The idea that a Fijian government must be maintained in office at all costs has grave consequences for political accountability. It requires setting aside the normal democratic controls on a government's performance in office, and this is bad for the Fijian community as well as for the country as a whole.

Supporters of the coups have invoked various international instruments on indigenous rights in support of their claim for political paramountcy. Their argument rests on a misreading of these instruments. The conventions most commonly cited in support are ILO Convention No 169 on Indigenous and Tribal Peoples and the draft 'Declaration on the Rights of Indigenous Peoples.'[5] The ILO Convention was adopted in June 1989 as a revision of ILO Convention No 107 on Indigenous and Tribal Populations. The Convention was based on the assumption that all relevant decisions on the living and working conditions of indigenous and tribal peoples would be taken into account by the government and that eventually the indigenous and tribal peoples would be assimilated into the broader community. But the goal and philosophy of assimilation has been discredited, and Convention 169 accepts that the indigenous and tribal peoples will continue to enjoy a separate cultural identity within the national society. The draft declaration provides for greater autonomy for these groups within states where they and their lands are now situated. These and other instruments apply, or are intended to apply, to indigenous and tribal communities whose lands, culture, and separate identity are at risk of marginalization as a result of colonization, such as the Hawaiians, the Maori, and Australian Aborigines, as well as tribal groups in North and South America. For that reason, they are not wholly relevant to indigenous Fijians, who have always enjoyed autonomy in the management of their administrative affairs and are secure in the possession of their lands and a vibrant cultural identity.

At the heart of these instruments lie two ideas: that indigenous peoples will remain a distinct community, and that they will enjoy equal rights with other members of society. The clear implication is that at the national level the political and other rights of the indigenous and tribal peoples are on exactly the same footing as those of other members of the national society. Both instruments see the special rights of indigenous peoples as distinct communities as supplementing the fundamental human rights and freedoms they already share with all other citizens. Nothing in either instrument gives an indigenous people superior or paramount rights in participating in the government of their society. Sometimes, indigenous activists raise the issue of 'self-determination.' The declaration (Article 3) states, 'Indigenous peoples have the right of self-determination. By virtue of that right they freely determine their political status and freely pursue their economic, social and cultural development.' But the phrase 'freely determine their political status' refers to their political status in taking control of their own affairs, not to their political status as it affects their participation in the national government. The article does not sanction secession. Nor does 'self-determination' authorize a particular 'people' within a country, whether or not indigenous, to exercise political domination over other 'peoples' as citizens. No political community, by reference to either 'self-determination' or 'sovereignty,' can legitimately claim it has political rights that entitle it to a position of dominance over other groups forming part of the same national society.

The word 'rights' is often used in conjunction with sovereignty and self-determination. What are Fijian rights? An important Fijian right is the right to own land. This is guaranteed through the recognition of customary title in the Native Land Act. The Native Land Trust Act provides that Fijians may not dispose of their lands except to the government through the Native Land Trust Board. Fijian traditional fishing rights are protected by the Fisheries Act. And the constitution gives all landowners, including indigenous Fijians, the right to a share of the royalties from the exploitation of minerals in the subsoil of their land or the seabed over which they have traditional fishing rights. Fijians also have rights to their traditional institutions, including the Great Council of Chiefs, and other separate administrative systems set up for their governance under the Fijian Affairs Act. The 1997 constitution for the first time recognized the council as a constitutional body and empowered it to nominate both the president and the vice president of the republic. The separate system of Fijian administration is also protected. But political paramountcy is not, and cannot be, a right. As mentioned, international standards, including the two instruments dealing with indigenous peoples, and the concepts of 'self-determination' and 'sovereignty' give no support to that proposition.

Some Fijians also argue that they have a 'right' to affirmative action programs. This is a complex area involving an interplay of many perceptions about the present circumstances of different communities; the philosophy of giving state assistance to individuals by reason of their membership in a particular community or group; the principles on which appointments should be made to public service; how programs for the benefit of a particular community or groups are reconciled with the right of equality before the law and freedom from discrimination on the constitutionally prohibited grounds; the desirable balance between the resources used for those purposes and other social justice programs for the needy members of all communities; and the question of whether the assistance given to enhance the position of particular communities and groups achieves the desired results.

Nonetheless, affirmative action for the indigenous Fijians was an accepted fact of public policy in post-independence Fiji. Since the 1970s, for example, following the report of the 1969 Education Commission, 50 percent of all government scholarships for tertiary education was reserved for them on a parallel-block basis, despite demonstrably inferior performance. The Fiji Development Bank initiated a number of commercial and business schemes to assist indigenous Fijians in the commercial sector[9], a function that the National Bank of Fiji assumed between 1987 and 1995. After 1987, the government set up special funds to purchase freehold lands and give them back to the indigenous landowners. And a special scholarship fund was set up by the Fijian Affairs Board to help indigenous Fijian students gain tertiary qualifications. The results of these efforts did not match expectations. The 1990 Constitution explicitly provided for affirmative action for indigenous Fijians and Rotumans. Section 21, entitled 'Protection and Enhancement of Fijian and Rotuman Interests,' authorized and directed parliament to put in place affirmative action programs for their benefit: 'Parliament shall, with the object of promoting and safeguarding the economic, social, educational, cultural, traditional and other interests of the Fijian and

Rotuman people, enact laws for those objects and shall direct the Government to adopt any programme or activity for the attainment of the said objectives.' The Cabinet could authorize government departments and statutory commissions to reserve scholarships and other training opportunities and business permits and licenses to attain the aims of the section. The constitution also contained specific provisions that sought to secure a minimum 50 percent representation of Fijians and Rotumans in government departments and among the holders of judicial and legal offices.

There is no quarrel with the principle of affirmative action, but the selective manner of its application, as well as the failure to reach expectations, has become a bone of contention. No matter of sensitive public policy such as affirmative action can succeed without public or national consensus. In the case of post-coup Fiji, no such consensus existed. Nor is any program of this kind likely to succeed unless the specific goals, and the means through which they are to be achieved, are clearly indicated. To succeed, there must be performance indicators for judging the efficacy of the program in achieving its goals, and criteria for selecting the individuals who will be entitled to the privileges and advantages. A blanket 'Fijian' or 'Rotuman' criterion is not good enough because, as mentioned, these communities are as diverse as others in the distribution of wealth among them. Prescribing ethnicity as the sole criterion for affirmative action is problematic for other reasons as well. For one, it ignores other criteria, such as gender; and women are grossly underrepresented in the public sector. For another, it assumes that other communities, in particular the Indo-Fijians, do not need affirmative action. This is not true, as the level of Indo-Fijian participation in the public sector has been declining markedly. In 1985, Fijians made up 46.4 percent of established public servants, Indo-Fijians 48 percent, and General Voters and expatriates 5.6 percent. The corresponding figures in 1995 were Fijians 57.3 percent, Indo-Fijians 38.6 percent, and General Voters and expatriates 4.1 percent. In 1995, of the 31 permanent secretaries, 22 were Fijians, 6 Indo-Fijians, and 3 were General Voters. Furthermore, virtually every study of income levels and poverty in Fiji in recent years has shown that, among Fijian and Indo-Fijian households, each group has a roughly comparable percentage living in poverty. Although incomes of Indo-Fijian households, on the whole, were higher than those of Fijian households, income disparity was significantly greater among Indo-Fijian households

The Fiji Constitution Review Commission therefore recommended that the government 'put in place not only affirmative action programmes for the benefit of the Fijian and Rotuman people, but similar programmes for other ethnic communities, and for women, and for all other disadvantaged citizens or groups in the Republic of the Fiji Islands.' The Compact of the 1997 constitution (Section k) agreed that 'affirmative action and social justice programmes to secure effective equality of access to opportunities, amenities or services for the Fijian and Rotuman people, as well as for other communities, for women as well as men, and for all disadvantaged citizens or groups, are based on an allocation of resources broadly accept-able to all communities.' The phrase 'broadly acceptable to all communities' is important: it implies consensus as well as the principle of proportionality. In effect it means that since the Fijian and Rotuman people now constitute more than 50 percent of the population they are legitimately entitled to 50 percent of affirmative action resources.

The current interim administration has proposed reimplementation of a race-based affirmative action program. It has promised to establish a Fijian and Rotuman Trust Fund to support indigenous development projects; to start a national saving scheme for Fijians and Rotumans to finance increased Fijian equity and other forms of participation in business as well as investment in education; to give tax exemptions to Fijian companies for an unspecified period; to set up a Fijian Development Trust Fund and a Fijian Education Fund to provide scholarships to students and grants to Fijian schools; and to reserve for indigenous Fijians 50 percent of government shares in commercial companies, 50 percent of all licenses and permits, and 50 percent of all government contracts. All this in addition to transferring all Crown Schedule A and B lands to the Native Land Trust Board and establishing a Land Claims Tribunal to deal with long-standing claims for native lands acquired for public purposes. These proposals are designed to appease the Fijian nationalist fringe: the interim administration wants to be seen to be implementing policies that favour Fijians. But such policies and initiatives have been in place for a long time and have failed to deliver the desired outcome. It must be asked whether more affirmative action is the answer, or are the problems, in the commercial field, for example, more deep-seated and culturally based than money alone can remedy. And what of the principles of efficiency, accountability, transparency, merit, and effective delivery of state services? Playing the 'race' card, blaming other ethnic groups for the poor performance of indigenous Fijians, as is often done, is no longer convincing. Deeper soul searching about the role of culture and tradition would yield more fruitful results.

In my opinion, then, the 1997 Constitution did not fail. The people of Fiji failed the Constitution. The next question is: Did the People's Coalition government fail, or in some way dilute Fijian interests? The People's Coalition government included disparate political parties with diverse interests and agendas. They came together not necessarily because of a shared vision for the nation but because of what might be termed 'negative' sentiments. The Fijian parties in the coalition joined with the Labour Party because they wanted Rabuka out of office as punishment for the sorry record of his government in the 1990s, tainted as it was by mismanagement, corruption, indecisive leadership, and the scandals in his private life. They also opposed the 1997 constitution, which Rabuka, working closely with Jai Ram Reddy, had been instrumental in shepherding through parliament. The Christian Democratic Alliance, a member of the People's Coalition, wanted Fiji to become a Christian state and wanted the constitution to be revised to address Fijian concerns, especially the issue of Fijian political paramountcy. Soon after forming a government, rifts emerged in the coalition. A faction of the Fijian Association Parry opposed the government in which its own leader, Adi Kuini Bavadra Speed, was the deputy prime minister. And Apisai Tora, the founding leader of another coalition partner, the Parry of National Unity, attacked the prime minister and opposed the government even though two of his own colleagues were members of the cabinet. So the coalition government was hobbled by internal friction and division, that threatened its unity and cohesiveness.

The Labour Party was the dominant partner in the coalition, with 37 out of the 71 seats giving it an outright majority in parliament. But because the constitution prescribed compulsory power sharing in cabinet—any political party with more than ten percent of seats in parliament was entitled to be invited to join the government—Chaudhry's hands were tied: he had to share power with parties not in his coalition. As leader of the largest party in parliament, Chaudhry became prime minister, although several of his own colleagues would have preferred an indigenous Fijian in that office. Perhaps the manner in which he attained that office might have been different, through more consultation and dialogue, but Chaudhry did the right thing. The fact that President Ratu Sir Kamisese Mara persuaded recalcitrant Fijian parties to rally behind Chaudhry (in whose government Mara's own family members were ministers), raised suspicions among Fijians long distrustful of Mara's rule about his dynastic ambitions for himself and his traditional power base in the eastern parts of Fiji. Chaudhry's ability to secure the president's support, along with that of factions of Fijian parties in his coalition (successfully practicing the kind of politics Fijian leaders had played with the Indo-Fijian community since independence), was seen, rightly or wrongly, as a strategy to divide the Fijians.

Chaudhry's own personal style compounded problems. An intelligent and battle-hardened trade union leader, he had been the single most painful thorn in the side of post-coup regimes, his uncompromising defense of the trade union movement and the principles of non-racial democracy earning him enemies among important, unforgiving sections of the Fijian community. Although more Fijians than Indo-Fijians were in the cabinet, there was no doubt in his opponents' minds that real power was wielded by Chaudhry, who himself controlled the portfolios of prime minister, minister of finance, sugar, public service, and information. Such centralization was consistent with his personal style of leadership as well as a tacit acknowledgement of dearth of ministerial talent in his coalition. Some of his decisions invited public censure, such as appointing his own son, not a civil servant, as his personal secretary on the public payroll. He was criticized for practising the very kind of nepotism he had condemned while in opposition, and the perception of a government that favoured its own grew among those already disapproving of it. The government's confrontational approach to the media did not help matters. To every criticism and every opposition, the government responded with the mantra: it had the people's mandate to implement policies promised in its manifesto. Of course, the government did have the mandate, but astute political leadership in Fiji would have understood that parliamentary mandate is one among several mandates in Fiji. Repeated invocation of the mantra of mandate irritated those already fearful of the government's huge majority in parliament. The government's hectic legislative program, institutional reforms, and the shedding of deadwood from the public sector heightened those fears.

The issue that raised the greatest emotion was land, not its ownership, but the imminent expiry of thirty-year leases granted under the Agricultural Land and Tenant Act, first passed in 1969. Some Fijian landowners wanted their land back, either to cultivate it themselves, to re-zone it for commercial or residential purposes, or to use the threat of nonrenewal to extract more rent from their tenants. They were led by Marika Qarikau, head of the Native Land Trust Board, an abrasive, hardline nationalist who used every means possible, from addressing the provincial councils to using the network of the Fijian Methodist Church, to rally the landowners behind him and against the government. The government did not contest the right of the landowners to reclaim their land, but neither could it ignore the plight of tenants, most unskilled, poor, uneducated, evicted from the land, thus causing a massive social problem for the country. The government offered the displaced tenants F$28,000 to get started in some other occupation, and the landlords F$8,000 to equip themselves as cultivators. It was a pragmatic interim solution to an intractable problem.

At the same time, the government attempted to establish a Land Use Commission to work with landowners to identify idle lands that could be put to productive use, including, if possible, resettling displaced tenants on them. With Qarikau on the warpath, the government went directly to the landowners, and sent a delegation of chiefs to Malaysia (Sarawak) to familiarize themselves with the work of a similar commission there and to dispel any fears they might have about the government's intentions. To everyone's surprise, the chiefs returned impressed, but by then Qarikau had already orchestrated an unqualified rejection of the proposal from many provincial councils. Qarikau feared that if the concept of a Land Use Commission were accepted, the power of his own political base, the Native Land Trust Board, might be irredeemably impaired. With provincial criticism swirling, the government did what it should have done in the first place: it took the proposal to the Great Council of Chiefs, which blessed it and asked the government and the Board to work cooperatively to finalize the details.

This hard-fought victory was short-lived, for just as the government felt it was gaining the upper hand over its critics, protest marches began around the country, led in virtually every instance by defeated politicians, Ratu Tevita Bolobolo and Apisai Tora among others. The protests gained momentum, energized by the government's dismissive stance toward the marches as the work of a few misguided miscreants. The cry 'Fijian Rights in Danger' rallied many behind the reinvigorated Taukei Movement, and roadblocks and threatening antigovernment banners went up. The climax came on 19 May when George Speight and six other armed gunmen hijacked parliament, tore up the constitution, and unleashed a reign of terror and violence on an unsuspecting population. Even if the Chaudhry government was not everyone's choice, even if it was drunk on the power of its numbers in parliament, to justify a coup on these grounds is plainly untenable. For, if style were the criterion, then coups would be the order of the day in many of the most advanced democracies of the world. Saying that just because Chaudhry was unacceptable to the nationalists, no other Indo-Fijian should ever aspire to lead the government of Fiji equally boggles the mind. Whether it realized it or not, the Chaudhry government was forced to share the political space with competing centres of power. No law affecting the indigenous Fijians could be changed without the support of the nominees of the Great Council of Chiefs in the Senate. The Fijian Affairs Act specified the rules and procedures for the governance of indigenous Fijians. The power of the Native Land and Fisheries Commission to adjudicate ownership disputes among indigenous Fijians was absolute. The Chaudhry government did not threaten to cancel programs put in place for indigenous Fijians by previous governments; it merely asked for more accountability and transparency in their administration.

In one respect, however, the People's Coalition government did threaten the established habits of thought and political behaviour in Fiji. In however small a way, its emphasis on non-racial solutions to the country's deep-seated social and economic problems threatened to undermine the way of thinking that has long seen the country's problems and remedies through the prism of race and ethnicity. Those who viewed race not only as a 'fact' of life but also as a 'way of life' saw the Chaudhry government as undermining a system that had kept them in positions of power for more than a generation. Over the years, many had been led to believe that only a Fijian prime minister, not an Indo-Fijian one, could be trusted to govern the country and maintain the security of Fijian interests. Chaudhry's success, as seen in soaring public opinion polls on the eve of the coup in May, would have undermined a fundamental tenet of their beliefs. Chaudhry had to go before he and his vision for Fiji became too deeply entrenched.

The interim administration has proposed a new constitution, which it says must enshrine Fijian political paramountcy. In his address to the United Nations in September woo, Interim Prime Minister Qarase hinted at the kinds of things that the constitution might include. Because over 50 percent of the population is Christian, Fiji might be declared a Christian state. Qarase also said that the amount and value of landownership should also be reflected in the composition of parliament. The Soqosoqo ni Vakavulewa ni Taukei is more specific. Indigenous Fijians, it says, must have 70 percent of all parliamentary seats; Fijian culture and language should be made the national language and culture; the first-past the-post system should be used in national voting rather than the alternative voting system prescribed in the 1997 constitution; open (non-racial) seats should be turned into national seats (that is, cross-voting seats where the ethnicity of the candidate is specified but all vote); and there should be greater decentralization of political, fiscal, and administrative structures. The salience of these points can be debated at length—can a small island state like Fiji, for example, afford the financial burden of more decentralization? Why have national seats when everyone knows them to be compromised and discredited? Why use the first-past-the-post system when it is universally regarded as obsolete? Why give the Fijian people the right to vote and then insist that they vote for only Fijian candidates? Decentralization is fine in theory, but Indo-Fijians are excluded from Fijian provincial and district councils.

The real issue underlying the demands of the Soqosoqo ni Vakavulewa ni Taukei is Fijian political paramountcy. A Fijian must be the head of state, and of government, and if possible of important statutory positions as well. Fiji has travelled that route before, under the 1990 constitution, with disastrous results. The question for the Fijian people is not whether a Fijian must be the head of government, but which or what kind of, Fijian. For some, Ratu Sir Kamisese Mara was the 'wrong' kind of Fijian leader. Others rejected Sitiveni Rabuka because he was a commoner, albeit an uncommon one. Dr Timoci Bavadra, too, could not be trusted by everyone. For yet others, George Speight (now calling himself

Ilikini Naitini) is an unacceptable face of Fijian nationalism. Increasingly, too, many Fijians are thinking in terms of their provinces and confederacies, all wanting to take turns at the helm of the ship of state. Taking turns: that is what the debate is about, not about social, economic, and national development in an era of unprecedented change and globalization.

Now, Fijians will take turns without the 'threat' of Indo-Fijian dominance. Thousands of Indo-Fijians left the country after the coups of 1987, and now many more will leave, depriving the country of much-needed talent and skills. The reduced number of Indo-Fijians will open up space for more debate among Fijians as provincial, regional, and confederacy tensions and rivalries come to the fore, as they have already begun to do since the 19 May coup. Their situation is aggravated by the absence on the national scene of experienced and trusted leaders with overarching national influence. The departure of Ratu Sir Kamisese Mara has brought to an end the rule of paramount chiefs tutored for national leadership by the colonial government in the years following the Second World War. The new generation of Fijian leaders is embroiled in local and regional politics, their wider influence limited or tainted by involvement in the events of the last decade or so. In the absence of any alternative, Fijian people may discover the 'foreign flower' of democracy as their political saviour.

In recent months, I have often revisited in my mind the work of the Fiji Constitution Review Commission. I continue to be inspired by its vision of Fiji as a vibrant, multiethnic, democratic state that celebrates the indigeneity of Fiji, recognizes the equal rights of all citizens, maintains the separation of church and state, provides a basis on which all citizens can describe themselves by a common name, and encourages every community to regard the major concerns of other communities as national, not sectional, concerns. A multiethnic state, I fervently believe, should strive for multiethnic government achieved through the voluntary cooperation of political parties, or increased support for a genuinely multiethnic party. It must recognize and celebrate the distinctive character of its diverse constituent parts while enlarging the common space and opportunities of equal citizenship. Consensus, not coercion, is the way forward to genuine reconciliation. The Fijian powers that be may wish to turn back the clock, but it would not do the clock any good. The Fijian tragedy once again underlines the fundamental truth that those who do not learn from history are condemned to repeat it.

*Four*

## While the Gun Is Still Smoking

'A lot of history is concealed autobiography,' the distinguished Australian historian KS Inglis once wrote.[1] That observation rings true to me. So, too, does EH Carr's contention that every historian is in some sense 'a social phenomenon, both the product and the conscious and unconscious spokesman of the society to which he belongs.'[2] And Jim Davidson seems right as well when he says that the 'initial impetus towards the study of modern history not infrequently derives from the students' own sense of involvement in his own society.'[3] The nature and quality of that engagement, I would argue, shape our understandings and assumptions about the world we live in, and frame the identity, orientation and style of our work. I do not wish to suggest a simple mechanistic correlation between class, ideology and intellectual work. History is a liberal, broad minded discipline of multiple, overlapping identities, which admits a variety of approaches, techniques and sources. Its boundaries are porous and flexible. What I do suggest is a dynamic and dialectical relationship between social and historical experience and intellectual endeavour, underlining the fundamental truth that we live in our own histories.

The subject of this paper is contemporary history, in particular, eyewitness and participant history. It is necessarily autobiographical, as these projects usually are,[4] but I use my experience to raise issues about the limitations, attractions and opportunities that present themselves to historians who live at the interface of history and practical action. What forces and impulses pull them in that direction of practical engagement? Does participation or engagement hinder or help one's understanding of the society's history? How does it affect the analysis and interpretation of the event in which one is a participant? Does engagement provide new insights into the dynamics of the practical affairs of state, or does it simply reinforce existing prejudices? There is, in my particular case, the added complication of being a historian participating in the affairs of my own country.[5]

Participant and eye witness history of the type I discuss here, without drawing a sharp distinction between them, are decidedly out of fashion even, or especially, among historians. The conventional, not to say unconvincing, objections are well known. Participant and eye witness accounts are partial and biased; they distort; they lack perspective; they are unable to separate matters of residual from matters of cardinal importance; they are, at best, the first primitive draft, a small building block, nothing more, in the larger edifice of later historiography produced in the course of time by detachment and objectivity. Attachment, it is argued, constricts accuracy, and advocacy, of whatever kind, is the stuff of propaganda. History should be objective, not reductionist or directly utilitarian in intent, and the historian should try to tell 'how it actually happened.' Disapproval also comes from cultural relativists and the new social historians who decry the narratives of 'total' history and the search for complete explanation, wary of creating structures and imposing interpretations which suffocate variety and deny diversity. Scepticism, doubt, ambiguity, tentativeness and partiality of knowledge, a firm belief in the impotence of human reason and the injustice of universal moral judgements, are markers of this discourse. These are words and concepts would seem incongruous to most participant historians. And *their* organising concepts—political power, the nation state, democracy, human rights, for example—and *their* efforts to search for patterns and meanings, to create structures which unite and enlarge the common space, are dismissed as hopelessly obsolete, relics of a past long gone and mercifully forgotten. I exaggerate slightly, but the suspicions and the tensions are real.

In the Pacific islands many scholars, including historians, have been active participants in the affairs of their societies. Nowhere in the region has this been more marked than in my own country of Fiji, where the list of academic departees is impressively long. The drift began with Rusiate Nayacakalou, trained in anthropology at the London School of Economics by Raymond Firth and tenured at Sydney, who gave up a promising academic career to return to Fiji to head the Native Land Trust Board, Isireli Lasaqa, with a doctorate in geography, left an academic position at the University of he South Pacific for a senior position in the Fiji public service, Ahmed Ali gave up academia for national politics, followed by Satendra Nandan, Tupeni Baba, Jo Nacola and Meli Waqa, Ganesh Chand, Isimeli Cokanisiga and, for a while, Wadan Narsey. I mention only the names of those who took the direct plunge from university teaching into parliamentary politics, but many Fiji staff, both Fijian and Indo-Fijian, have long been politically active in a variety of capacities. One hopes that in due course some of them will reflect on their transition and transformations and tell us how their training and experience as academics has tempered their practical work.

Participation came naturally to the generation of students attending the University of the South Pacific in its salad days of the 1970s. The regional university, which opened in 1968, was required by its founding mission to train manpower to meet the anticipated development needs of a rapidly decolonizing region. A Programme Planning Seminar at the Laucala Bay campus in May 1968 took its cue from the charter of the university which provided that the 'objects of the University shall be the maintenance, advancement and dissemination of knowledge by teaching, consultancy and research and otherwise and the provision at appropriate levels of equation and training responsive to the well-being and needs of the communities of the South Pacific. At the seminar, 'the decision was taken to adopt the general organisation of groups of discipline located within Schools of broad developmental rather than the more common departmental and faculty structure.' The initial schools, two of which have been re-named since, were Education, Natural Resources and Social and Economic Development. The developmental intellectual climate set the framework of learning in practical ways. Specialization was discouraged, a broad-based education deemed the best preparation for training future administrators and teachers. The political environment of decolonisation provided an affirming context for the intellectual course charted by the new university. My own evolution as a historian engaged in practical issues derives largely from that experience.

Like other Pacific island historians—Sione Latukefu, Malama Meleisea, John Waiko—I focussed on the history of my own people for my first piece of sustained graduate research, writing my dissertation on the social and cultural background of the Indian indentured migrants to Fiji. At the same time, I expanded my research to include the workings of contemporary politics, which began through a series of election studies and commentaries. Living in Fiji, and called upon to comment on the political campaigns, I could not, nor did I want to, escape the challenge and opportunity to participate, albeit as an interested bystander, in contemporary debates in my own country; and what could be more interesting than covering a heated political campaign? With time, an incidental interest evolved into a major professional preoccupation, resulting in a series of detailed political studies, and culminating in my appointment to the Fiji Constitution Review Commission in 1995. That appointment itself was preceded by several years of active opposition to the coups of 1987 and the divisive public culture of racialized governance they spawned. From the very beginning I was opposed to the overthrow of the Labour Coalition government. I felt then, as I feel now, that there was something profoundly wrong about overturning the verdict of the ballot box by the bayonet.

The coups presented, for me, a deep political as well as moral crisis. One either supported the coups or opposed them: there could be no middle ground. I lost patience with those who treated the coups as a 'on the one hand and on the other' kind of discourse. Perhaps I spoke too firmly, but at least there was no doubt in anyone's mind about where I stood. Taking a stand: those words have a familiar ring to those caught in the middle of a fray, both participants and historians. My opposition intensified with time. I intervened through radio and television interviews, mostly unsuccessfully, to correct what I construed to be misrepresentations and misconceptions. I learnt the rude lesson that in the public domain facts, when they come in the way of a dramatic story, are not welcome. Complex facts do not engage the public imagination, which wants simple, vivid, preferably provocative answers to quotable 'newsworthy' questions, delivered in attractive sound bites. By intervening the way I did, I may have compromised my objectivity, but I remained staunch in my support for liberal, representative democracy while emphasising the need to acknowledge and celebrate and constitutionally recognized sacred and important institutions of Fijian society. In this respect, I share Oscar Spate's wise advice to declare one's hand to the readers:

> The impartiality which evades responsibility by saying nothing, the partiality which masks its bias by presenting slanted facts with an air of cold objectivity—these are a thousand time more dangerous than an open declaration of where one stands; then at least those who disagree can take one's measure with confidence: 'that is why he said thus,'....The important points are that inference must be based on evidence, as carefully verified as possible; and that the choice shall be made from the evidence, and not from pre-conceived ideas.[6]

This is the approach I used in my *Power and Prejudice: The making of the Fiji crisis* (1988). I was a target of the coup perpetrators because of my ethnicity and political stance: the book was written while the gun was still smoking. Nonetheless, I brought to my analysis the training and approach of the historian. I gathered all the available evidence as assiduously as I could against which I tested a number of prevailing hypotheses, many of which failed to measure up. One such, which had reached melodramatic proportions soon after the coups, saw the American Central Intelligence Agency (CIA) as the principal instigator of the overthrow a left-leaning government supposedly hostile to American strategic interests in the Pacific. The presence in Fiji around the time of the coups of some senior American officials alleged to be veterans of coups in other parts of the world, added fuel to the fire. But all this was nothing more than the product of a hyperactive, conspiratorial imagination. Nothing that I saw convinced me that the hypothesis was tenable. Americans may have known, perhaps given a knowing wink or looked the other way when they knew that something was afoot, but they did not mastermind the coups. The search for the extent of foreign involvement, I argued, should not be allowed to distort the larger picture. Often those who pursue the theory of external causation pay insufficient attention to the role of local forces and local leaders in the making of their own history.[7]

A decade later, I have no reason to change my view, but at the time I was accused of being a puppet of the State Department for not holding American responsible for the Fiji crisis. Another hypothesis portrayed the coup as a simple racial conflict, between indigenous Fijians and Indo-Fijians, an assertion of indigenous power against an economically powerful and demographically preponderant immigrant-derived community. On the surface the hypothesis sounded convincing, but was superficial upon closer analysis. Ethnicity was both a cause as well as a scapegoat of the crisis. I saw the coups as flowing from a complex interplay of a range of factors, none of which by themselves could be sufficient. I argued:

> Fiji coups were more about frustrated politicians bent upon recapturing power lost at the polls then they were about ethnic prejudice; the importance of the latter cannot be—and here is not—lightly dismissed. I argue further that the basic reasons for the coups will be found not so much in the machinations of outside agencies—which no doubt played a role in aiding and abetting forces opposed to the Coalition government—as within the dynamics of local history and politics, and in the actions and machinations of specific individuals within Fiji without whose active participation nothing could have been accomplished. It is possible to discern the premonitions of the present crisis in the silent footsteps of modern Fijian history; but to argue that the coups were historically predetermined is to falsify a very complicated story and misjudge its essence. There was nothing really inevitable about the Fiji coups. In the ultimate analysis, the Fiji crisis was caused by a complex combination of incipient class conflicts, provincial tensions among the indigenous Fijians and deep-seated racial antagonisms long embedded in the very structure of Fiji's society and politics.[8]

Over a decade since this analysis was written, many books, some by participants, have been published and some new information has come to light, but my fundamental thesis stands. At least, I stand by it. Indeed, I am tempted to say that it grows stronger as new information comes to light. An important reason is that I wrote the account as a trained historian. We do not deal with certainties but with probabilities. We try to draw conclusions from the facts, as carefully and objectively assembled and verified as possible, rather than fit them into preconceived conclusions. No one explanation by itself 'will satisfactorily account for the complex character of the Fijian crisis,' I wrote in 1988, nor was 'it desirable to put the Fijian story into the straitjacket of political and social theories derived from other contexts and experiences.' This is no unique insight: it is simply sound historical practice of the type we employ in the course of our regular work.

While historians are good at predicting the past, they by and large make bad prophets, especially historians of the contemporary scene. Engrossed in the details and drama of events unfolding before their eyes, they miss the wood for the trees. I was no exception. When I wrote, I was deeply pessimistic about Fiji returning to normalcy in my own lifetime. In 1988, the architects of the coup were in power, implementing policies designed to entrench Fijian paramountcy. The economy was on the brink of collapse. Fiji was out of the Commonwealth. Capital drained out of the country and people queued outside foreign embassies seeking visas for permanent migration. The army was on the streets. The opposition was demoralised. The world did not seem to care. But Fiji did, within a decade, return to embrace a new constitution, without violence and bloodshed, to launch the country tentatively in a new direction of inclusive multiracial democracy, only to have it shattered by George Speight's intervention—another case of historians not seeing what was coming. With hindsight, I should have glimpsed the shape of future developments. I had argued that provincial tensions, class interests and individual ambitions for power had led to the coup, along with ethnic fears. It should have been apparent that once the fears which had sparked the crisis had gone, these interests and concerns would have, in the course of time, gone on their own divergent paths. I should have seen that the politically expedient unity of Fijian interests was a chimera, that politics among Fijians, like any other community, was driven by vested social interests and personal ambitions. And my knowledge of history should have taught me that authoritarian structures imposed on a populace through force do not enjoy a long and happy life.

As I read the accounts of the coups, including my own, long after the dust has settled and the army returned to the barracks, I am impressed by the depth and detail of the narratives produced while the gun was still smoking. They convey passion, urgency and immediacy that are difficult for me to conjure up now. The authors argue different theses. There were few points of agreement between them then, and they remain as far apart even now. Time has not erased the difference, and it never will. The idea that one day when all the facts are available, when the first primitive drafts of contemporary, or eye witness history, will be transformed by a master historian into a standard, universally uncontested account, about the full significance of what happened in the past, is mere fantasy.[9] Three of the earliest accounts of the coup were all written by professional historians.[10] The imprint of their training and approach is clear. The texts are well documented, but they also rely on types of evidence that go beyond the narrow range of sources typically deployed in conventional political histories.

My own analysis draws upon newspaper accounts and other published sources in the public domain. But it also draws upon other material, much of which is now probably lost to posterity: hand bills, draft copies of speeches, transcripts of radio broadcasts, television footage and interviews. In the future, those wanting to know the initial reaction of the people might turn to the handbills distributed on the streets of the major towns and centres. I reproduced two in my book to give the reader a sense of what was being said and heard as the crisis was unfolding. They capture some of the anxiety, frustration, suppressed anger, and trauma at the time in a way that a latter day historian working from conventional sources might be unable to construct. I also used personal observation: the shops clogged with frenzied people buying emergency food supplies; shop windows barricaded behind hurricane shutters; the commandeered vehicles speeding along deserted streets; anxious, armed, balaclava-clad soldiers atop strategic buildings; the long queues seeking to emigrate, the hushed conversations in cars. These are the kind of details a future novelist writing about this event might find to be of primary importance. A contemporary historian, especially one working in societies where the culture of preserving the historical record is undeveloped and unappreciated, carries the dual burden of being an archivist and an observer as well as an interpreter of events.

Eyewitness history also provides the historian the opportunity to corroborate evidence through interviews, which is unavailable to those working on more remote periods A case in point is the role of the judiciary in resolving the early stages of the first (May) coup. The matter was understandably shrouded in secrecy, encouraging rumours and false impressions about what was happening at the Government House. What advice had the judges given the Governor General? Had their advice been sought? What was the legal status of the suspended constitution and other authority flowing from it? Wanting to find out, I rang the Chief Justice at his residence, and, much to my surprise, he readily agreed to see me that very morning. When I met him, the Chief Justice not only gave me a detailed account of the difficulties he had encountered in contacting the Governor General—he gave me the names of individuals impeding that effort—he also gave me a copy of the high court judges' submission to the Governor General, which is reproduced in my book. The judges' advice that the 'purported suspension of the Constitution of Fiji by the military regime which has assumed de facto power is illegal and invalid,' and that the independence constitution 'remains in force and unchanged,' when it finally reached the Governor General, changed his mind. He proclaimed himself deeply disturbed by 'unlawful seizure of members of my government' 'which must not be allowed to continue.' The role of the judiciary was a crucial one, and one which I would not have understood properly without the assistance of the Chief Justice. I would be surprised if the Chief Justice would still be able to recall all the details and the emotion as vividly as he did a few hours after the event.

I would not today be able to write the book I wrote in 1988. Is that an indictment of contemporary history? I do not think so. My own response is well put by David Butler: 'If one is trying to summarize an event as it seemed at the time, trying to get the facts together, the less one is contaminated by posterior wisdom, by looking back at the events with a knowledge of the consequences, the greater the force and immediacy of one's narrative.'[11] Events and emotions which loomed large at a critical moment in time have a reality and identity of their own, irrespective of their place in the later assessment of history. Their meaning and importance, ethnographic historians will argue, should not be contingent upon the meaning placed upon them by posterity. To 're-present what actually happened in its specificity' is important in its own right. But having said that, I am also mindful of Doug Munro's contention that 'contemporary or participant history should not necessarily be regarded as intrinsically deficient or de facto primary source for future historians.' 'Every work of history, no matter the distance between the description and the event,' he argues, 'has this same quality of transience, some more than others of course.' Historians, as Greg Dening has reminded us, live with the certainty that they will one day become someone else's historiography.[12]

Writing about your own society as a participant historian requires great sensitivity and tact and a certain degree of self-censorship. The quest for truth and objective understanding has to be balanced against the demands of other, sometimes equally, demanding factors. In a small island state, everyone is known to virtually everyone else, and news travels fast on the coconut wireless. Criticism and adverse comment, no matter how justified, are often taken personally. And they can easily be misconstrued in a country like Fiji which has two contrasting traditions of discourse. One, practised by the Indo-Fijian community, is at home in open, robust, democratic debate. The other, rooted in traditional communal culture, is presented in subtle, indirect ways, conscious of the rank and status of both the speaker and the person spoken about. Commenting on electoral politics in Fiji in the early 1980s, I was acutely conscious of the need to be cautious in my comments and analysis for fear of being misunderstood or, worse still, labelled.

I practised a degree of self-censorship in my public comments though not in my writing, from the safety of a foreign university. In a divided society such as Fiji, everything is seen and assessed through the prism of ethnicity. Public memory is racially archived. Birth and death certificates register ethnicity; one is asked to indicate one's ethnic identity when opening a bank account or when taking out a driving licence. Upon leaving and entering Fiji, the citizens are required to declare their ethnic identity. In South Africa, the immigration forms distinguish five categories of ethnicity. In Fiji, the number is seven. Markers of ethnicity are everywhere. In the mid-1990s, when the National Bank of Fiji was on the verge of bankruptcy brought about by breathtakingly bad management, and the matter was raised in parliament by the Indo-Fijian Leader of the Opposition Jai Ram Reddy, the indigenous Fijian Foreign Minister (Filipe Bole) attributed the criticism to racism because many of the Bank's employees were Fijians and Rotumans.[13] When some Opposition Indo-Fijian members of parliament criticised French nuclear testing in French Polynesia, Rabuka denounced his critics as anti-Fijian, because his (Fijian) government had tried to cultivate relations with the French. When I dared to suggest that Ratu Sukuna's policies had, at least in part, disadvantaged many ordinary Fijians because he saw no value in academic education for his people—as distinct from chiefly Fijians, who, thus equipped, could then go on to perpetuate chiefly dominance while other ethnic groups were marching ahead in the professions, I was labelled an anti-Fijian for my audacity to criticise the work and legacy of a high chief.[14] Physical distance now diminishes the impact of these criticisms, but they can be oppressive and dangerous to those living with them on a daily basis.

Academics resolve the dilemma in several ways. Some present their views openly, without being overly concerned about the consequences. Isireli Lasaqa, analysing the development dilemmas facing the Fijian people, writes forthrightly about 'Fijian life and thought, Fijian needs and aspirations, how they see their neighbours, and the Fijian scene and beyond.'[15] If one is labelled a racist for representing a racial point of view, so be it. Some attempt a 'middle course between partiality on the one hand and impartiality on the other,' satisfying no one, while others take the grandiose view that 'there is a lot to be said on both sides.'[16] Some resort to anonymous but editorially sanctioned essays in the newspapers, getting their ideas into the public arena without revealing their identity. This approach, to me, seems cowardly. Others have used the path of fiction to circumvent the dilemma. The best exponent of this approach in the Pacific Islands is Epeli Hau'ofa. His justifiably well known satire, *Tales of the Tikongs*, deals with the problems of aid, development, corruption and mismanagement, conflict between traditional customs and modern attitudes, in the tiny island of Tiko. The issues are identified, and the message gets across without the messenger being persecuted. Sudesh Mishra's searing poems on the coups and subsequent developments also achieve the same goal, but whether his work is read by those who are its target is another matter.[17]

Participation enables one to see history in the making. It is a sobering experience to see how 'truth' emerges from a vast, chaotic mass of experience and activity, how small things get magnified, torn out of context and used in unexpected ways that change the course of history. One example will suffice. In 1982, Jai Ram Reddy, the leader of the National Federation Party, was fighting a tough election against the ruling Alliance Party which, for its part, wanted to wean away sufficient Indian voters from his party to destroy, once and for all, the NFP's claim to be the voice of the Indian community. The campaign was closely contested and very tense. In the course of one speech in Labasa, Reddy said that Mara was so desperate for Indian votes that he would even open a toilet block in order capture Indian votes![18] A harmless enough remark given the context, but printed in the papers next day, it aroused more emotion and acrimony than I had ever seen before. Reddy, many Fijians said, had committed a serious breach of protocol, which in ancient times would have seen him clubbed. He had insulted not only a great man, but also insulted the vanua of Lau, of which Mara was the paramount chief, and the Fijian people generally. How dare an Indian suggest that a high chief like Mara would ever stoop so low to get Indian votes. Seizing the moment, Mara said in a deeply injured tone that those who had attacked him will not be forgiven or forgotten. Protest marches were held throughout Fiji, demanding Reddy's resignation. Racial rhetoric reached dangerous levels. Up went the call for Fijian unity. Reddy lost the election, winning 24 seats to Alliance's 26, but his words remained firmly in people's minds for a long time. Indeed, a few months after the election, at a meeting of the Great Council of Chiefs, opened for the first time by a reigning monarch, the chiefs vented their anger at the remarks made by the *kaitani*, foreigners, and passed resolutions demanding Fijian dominance in parliament.[19] A stray comment, uttered in the middle of a heated campaign, inflamed racial passions and brought Fiji to the brink of potentially explosive political conflict. Such is the nature of politics in an ethnically divided society.

The participant historian also learns from personal experience that sometimes the public record does not reflect reality, and may in fact be contrary to it. When that happens, should the participant expose the facts and face the consequences, knowing that left uncorrected, the historical record would forever remain distorted? One example will suffice. During the course of public hearings organised by the Fiji Constitution Review Commission, I was attacked several times by a number of nationalist Fijians, who questioned my credentials and credibility and integrity to be on the Commission. The attacks were vicious and hurtful, accusing me of being an incompetent, anti-Fijian bigot. They were broadcast on the television and published in the newspapers, and several years later, people still remember the incident. The Commission expressed full confidence in me, but I was discomfited by such brutal and unfounded attack especially when I could not respond without damaging the standing of the Commission. Much later, when I met one accuser in an airport lounge, and another at a social gathering, I gently asked why they had been so hard on me. The first, wrapping his arms around my shoulders said that he was trying to 'soften me up,' a routine tactic politicians use against all new opponents, trying to get their measure. That came as a surprise to me. The other, equally frank, regretted attacking me, but revealed a personal agenda. He was contesting a by-election in Tailevu, one of several caused by the disqualification of Adi Samanunu, as a member of the Fijian nationalist organisation Vanua Tako Lavo Party, a nationalist Fijian political organisation. Attacking me, he said, would assure him automatic publicity and national news coverage as a champion of the Fijian people, standing up against this 'smart Indian.' Not that it did him any good, because he lost the by-election by a huge margin.

Serving on the Commission also made me realise how limited, and limiting, media coverage is or can be. Things are done on the run, deadlines have to be met, there is limited space in the news column, the story, important in its own right, does not have 'sale' value. Often, only the sensational bits and pieces get reported, and even then they are torn out of context. For instance, the future historian of the Fiji's constitutional evolution will read, from the newspapers, that the reason why the Commission was unable to submit its report on time was that Tomasi Vakatora and I were bitterly opposed to each other and were unable to agree on the most important points. I will not deny that we had our difficult days, but the reason had nothing to do with us: the delay was caused by the sheer amount of work we were asked to accomplish. For the record, the main details about the structure of the executive and legislative branches of the government were resolved by January 1996, several months before we submitted our report! This fact will be known only to those who care to comb the record of the Commission rather than relying on the newspapers. Sometimes, what is said never comes to light, again distorting the public record. Let me illustrate this with an example. One prominent advocate of separate representation for Muslims, then a civil servant, asked for a private audience with the Commission to plead his case. The request was granted. He repeated the usual arguments: Muslims were a separate group, apart from the larger Indian community into which they were lumped for the sake of administrative convenience. He also favoured making Fiji a Christian state, largely to win the support of the Fijians for his cause. How could he, a Muslim, agree to Fiji becoming a Christian state? Was there not a contradiction here? His response: his exact words were: 'No, because Islam is a heresy of Christianity anyway! Christians we don't mind, it's the Hindu gatekeepers we cannot abide.'

There were many others like him, saying one thing in public and another in private for reasons of pure political expediency that perplexed me. Take the Sunday Ban, for instance, a strict observance of the Sabbath, which came into force in 1988, proscribing all unauthorised commercial and recreational activity on Sunday. Many people, including, especially, indigenous Fijians, suffered from the ban on pubic transport, making it difficult for them to attend church or go to hospitals or access other essential services, and the closure of shops denied them the normal foodstuff such as bread, tea, sugar, all staples in the countryside. They wanted the ban removed, they said in private, but in public they remained steadfast in support of it. It was a similar situation on provincial representation. Many Fijians in private deplored its deleterious effects, sowing the seeds of provincial division and rivalry, impeding the development of an effective national political party not tethered to local provincial interests. They wanted us to recommend reversion to the constituency-based electoral system of the pre-coup era. Yet, these same individuals remained disconcertingly silent in public or actively joined the chorus to retain the status quo. In a meeting of the Joint Parliamentary Committee, one participant arguing for change pointed out the absurdity of Filipe Bole not being able to stand from Suva, where he lived, but standing from Lau, where he was born but where he had not lived for decades. Many members agreed with the absurdity of the situation, but voted against the proposal. The public heard that the Fijian members of parliament were unanimously in favour of retaining the provincial system of election. Some of the most eloquent defenders of the status quo were among the most passionate pleaders for change in private.

For a historian, it is interesting as well as instructive to see how history is understood and used at the popular level. I was both impressed and dismayed by what I saw and heard during the Commission's hearings. Historical facts and events were often invoked in support of various demands. Often, the seemingly incontrovertible truth being presented was either wrong or misleading, acquired through heresay, prejudice masquerading as principle, but the submitters did not know or care. The most troubling example of this was the SVT submission which used, unacknowledged, some thirty quotations from my book *Broken Waves*. Wrenched out of context, the words were used to support themes that directly contradicted my own position. So, Governor Sir Murchison Fletcher is quoted saying that Indians who had gone to Fiji had come from 'the most ignorant and backward part of India,' and he saw danger in 'placing power in the hands of untutored people.' But Fletcher wrote this to argue the more limited position that Indians were not worthy of equal franchise. Sir Maynard Hedstrom, an implacable foe of Indo-Fijian demands for political equality, is quoted approvingly. The 'British race,' Hedstrom was quoted as saying, must continue to govern Fiji to safeguard the paramountcy of Fijian interests, because 'the Indian race has not yet in modern times completely proved its capacity for self-government.' And yet the same person wanted more native land to be converted to freehold title! The Great Council of Chiefs resolution of 1933 is quoted: 'The immigrant Indian population should neither directly nor indirectly have any part in the control or direction of matters affecting the Fijian race.' The chiefs were asserting the right to complete, unfettered internal self-administration, but now those words were stretched to mean denying the Indo-Fijians equal political rights. Ratu Epeli Ganilau is quoted as objecting 'to being ruled by Indians, as we always have regarded British to be sole foundation of honour, justice and fairness.' But Indians were not demanding the right to rule Fijians; they wanted equality with other British subjects. The context of these quotations is missing, the political and ideological logic behind them ignored.

Elementary errors of composition and argument are accompanied by more serious and deliberate misreading and manipulation of history. I will cite two examples mentioned most frequently to the Commission to illustrate the point. One concerns Lord Salisbury's Despatch of 1875, in which the Secretary of State for India asked the Government of India whether it would, after consultation with the various provincial governments, intervene to facilitate the recruitment and emigration of Indian indentured labourers to the British colonies.[20] In return, the India Office promised to ask the colonies to grant the Indian settlers 'rights and privileges no whit inferior to those of any other class of Her Majesty's subjects resident in the colonies.' The provinces declined the request, the Government of India advised London accordingly, and the matter was dropped. The SVT argued that the promise made in the Despatch also lapsed, forfeiting any claim to legal authority. But this interested reading ignores the crucial fact that the intention of equality was never abandoned by India. In fact, it underpinned India's policy on indentured emigration throughout. It was explicitly reiterated in 1910 in these words:

> The present administration itself fully recognises the value of Indians as permanent settlers and is willing to concede them

the enjoyment of equal civil rights. The whole tenor of the correspondence between India and the colony shows that it was on this condition that indentured immigration in Fiji has been allowed in the past, and any measures leading towards lowering the political status of the immigrants or reducing their economic freedom would, in our opinion, involve a breach of faith with those affected.

The vagueness of the promises in Salisbury's Despatch is contrasted with the firm assurances given in the Deed of Cession by which the leading chiefs of Fiji ceded the islands in 1874. That important document has been invested with a range of meanings, beyond the weight the document itself can reasonably be made to carry. It has come to be seen as a document of trust between the Fijian people and the British Crown, a compact, a solemn pledge, a charter that not only promised to protect Fijian rights, but also guaranteed the paramountcy of Fijian rights over all. What many Fijians wanted, they told the Commission, was a unequivocal restatement of that right, fulfilling a solemn pledge made by Queen Victoria. To those unfamiliar with the document, the supposed promise of paramountcy and the British failure to fulfil it would seem a grave breach of trust. But in fact, the words 'paramountcy of Fijian interests,' are not mentioned even once in the Deed of Cession. The Deed acknowledges the unconditional surrender of the islands to the United Kingdom, promises to promote 'civilization and trade' in the islands, while Fijian rights 'shall be recognised so far as is and shall be consistent with British Sovereignty and Colonial form of government.' All claims to financial liabilities made by the chiefs would be carefully scrutinized according to principles of justice and sound public policy.

Throughout the 20th century, the colonial government and especially the local members of the 'British race' continually invoked the concept to forestall Indo-Fijian claims for elected political representation on the basis of universal franchise and a common roll. To acquiesce in that project would be to relinquish a solemn pledge to the Fijians—and safeguard their own vested interests, allowing political change to proceed at a pace acceptable to the colonial establishment. Nonetheless, the concept of paramountcy was used in a broadly protective sense. That is, in matters pertaining to the internal structure and administration of Fijian society—determination of land and chiefly titles, the drawing of traditional land boundaries, the allocation of the roles and responsibilities within society, sanctions for breaches of traditional, customary practices—the Fijian people themselves, through their customary elders and the Great Council of Chiefs, would exercise the paramount power. In this protective sense, it was intended to shield the Fijian people from the demands and corrosive pressures of the modern world. As independence approached, paramountcy was transformed from a protective sense to an assertive one. The Fijian leaders began to argue that the paramountcy of Fijian interests could only be guaranteed if Fijians had political paramountcy. Legislative and constitutional safeguards were deemed to be insufficient. A concept, not found in a document to which its origin was attributed, was transformed from a protective instrument into an assertive tool for political dominance, and invested with historically unsustainable meanings and symbolism.

My second example is the now famous Wakaya Letter which was also invoked before the Commission on numerous occasions. This was a letter signed by the members of the Fijian Affairs Board, the administrative and policy-advisory arm of the Great Council of Chiefs, and which had as its members all the highest ranking chiefs of Fiji, including Ratu Mara, and presented to Nigel Fisher, the parliamentary Under Secretary of State for the Colonies in 1963. The signatories demanded certain preconditions before Fijians would discuss even the possibility of independence. Fiji, they said, had a special relationship with the British Crown, which had to be clarified and codified. Fijian ownership of native land should be guaranteed, in consultation with the Great Council of Chiefs. The Fijian Affairs Board should have the veto power over all legislation affecting Fijian rights and interests. Fijian wishes for Fiji to be declared a Christian state should be recognized, and the Public Service should ensure racial parity in the public sector. 'Subject to a satisfactory resolution of the issues we have raised in the foregoing memorial,' the signatories concluded, 'we would be prepared to initiate, in co-operation with the other principal races, further moves towards internal self government.' The fact that Fijian leaders cooperated actively in the movement towards greater self government from the mid-1960s onwards suggests that their preconditions had been met, if not in full. The Wakaya Letter was only a negotiating document. But many people kept reminding the Commission of the document in support of their claim for political paramountcy, and especially in support of making Fiji a Christian state. It was difficult to convince the people that the Wakaya letter was designed for a specific purpose for a particular moment, and that its import was now purely historical, superseded by another compact, the constitution which gave Fiji its independence. Assertions get transformed into unassailable facts before your eyes, one learns quickly, historical truth a matter of perception.

A participant is privy to information given in a variety of ways: a heavy hint, a slanted joke, a throwaway remark masking a serious point or indicating a point of view to be noted, malicious gossip of no permanent value but clearly intended to harm an opponent (though it is of permanent value to the perpetrator!). It is often assumed, although seldom explicitly articulated, that things are being said in confidence. Much of this kind of evidence can be discarded or forgotten. But some information, from recounted conversations, and eye witness accounts about important players or critical events and episodes, raise troublesome questions. Uttered in confidence, or the expectation of confidence, how does one use it, especially if it relates to something of great public importance? An example. During the 1999 election campaign, Sitiveni Rabuka claimed that he had not acted alone in carrying out the coups, that in fact he was the 'fall guy' who had refused to fall. He named some of the co-conspirators and left others unnamed. A year later, through his authorised biography, he implicated Ratu Sir Kamisese Mara in the pre-coup machinations, recounting a conversation he had with Mara on a golf course where Mara had tried to sooth the nerves of a clearly worried colonel about the possible intervention of foreign countries, especially the United States and the United Kingdom in the event of a military coup in Fiji, by saying, 'Leave these to me.'[21] For the record, Mara has denied the conversation. The accusation caused an uproar in Fiji, but Rabuka's account was a public secret in Fiji long before it appeared in print. Some years ago, he had told me—and several other people as well—what his recent biographer has since revealed: that his biography, if ever one was written, should be titled 'The Fall Guy' or 'The Kleenex Man,' the allusion to being used and then discarded like paper tissue. As a historian, I noted his remark, because in my own account of the Fijian coups, I had written generally that Rabuka could not have acted alone, and that circumstantial evidence pointed to the involvement, or at the very least the acquiescence, of others. But important as Rabuka's information was, I could not use it. First, I could not document or verify it. Second, since the information was given privately, and thus off the record, Rabuka could, if he so chose, deny it, leaving me to face the very likely prospect of a libel action. So both personal interest as well as ethical concerns about broadcasting the contents of a private conversation, led me to commit the information to my files.

I was chastened from an earlier experience, when a speaker flatly denied saying what he had, in fact, said. In the early 1980s, a former Fijian colleague from the University of the South Pacific, visited the East West Centre in Honolulu. During the course of an informal presentation, he was asked about the increasing rate of Indo-Fijian emigration, and its effects on the Fijian economy. The sooner more of them leave the better, he said, to uneasy laughter from the audience. I thought the remark inappropriate. I cannot now recall when or how I recounted this conversation to an acquaintance. The next day, to my horror, an Indian candidate at the Civic Auditorium in Suva recounted the substance of my conversation, alleging that the Fijian candidate was anti-Indian. The accused candidate, of course, denied the allegation the next day, and threatened a libel action. Fortunately, the allegation was never repeated, and soon swamped by other issues and forgotten, but the pragmatic need for discretion has remained with me ever since.

The possession of privately acquired potentially explosive information creates its own problems. The obligations of scholarship, the disinterested pursuit of knowledge and truth should require full disclosure. This obligation, however, has to be assessed in the context of other competing obligations. Will the release of the information do more harm than good? Might it, for example, lead to civil strife, loss of life, poison race relations, affect the welfare of innocent people caught in the cross fire, or bring down a government? The question is: who is to act as the arbiter? What right does the possessor of important information have to withhold information from the public? The answer can never be clear cut. In my own case as a constitutional commissioner, there are certain things that my oath of secrecy requires me never to make public, however important they are. Some discussions, treating sensitive issues were never recorded. Such was the case with the proceedings of the Joint Parliamentary Committee which deliberated on the Reeves Commission report and produced the draft constitution. Recording the proceedings, it was felt, would impede free flow of discussion, make people wary of the fact that their words were recorded, which might harden positions. In the Commission's own deliberations, discussion was recorded without attribution for the very same reason. But having said that, I should state that the substance of what I saw or was told and believed, I have reproduced in an indirect, allusive way, without specifying details. This is unsatisfactory, to be sure, but there does not seem to be any way around it.

There is an unmatchable excitement about doing contemporary history. One sees events in the raw, unprocessed, unfolding haphazardly, with little sense of where they might lead. One thrills to the particularities of events, to their uniqueness and integrity. Human beings can never be reduced to abstract categories no matter how subtle or intricate they appear. One sees how history is created, and how messy and unpredictable the process is. Often what one reads in the media or in the official reports is not how one saw it at the time. One becomes acutely aware of how only a tiny fragment of what happens finds it way into the historical record. One learns painfully how complex seemingly simple things can be. One becomes aware of the role of contingency, fortuity, ignorance, chance and stupidity in human affairs. Participation humanises history, and reinforces belief in human agency. It is humbling to realise the limits and limitations within which instantaneous choices are made. One begins to develop a more sympathetic understanding of human frailties and human ambitions.

Fijians who want political power to control their destiny are not necessarily racist chauvinists, but people who feel besieged, threatened, caught in the grips of forces beyond their control. They are saddened by the sight of their cherished world of childhood vanishing before their eyes, hurt to see things they believed to be beyond comment—the institution of chieftainship, for example—dragged into the cauldron of ordinary debate, thus debasing their culture. They want political power, enabling them to adjust to the world at their own pace. That is the romance of the idea. The Indo-Fijians do not necessarily want power to dominate others. They want equal rights, as human beings, to live with dignity and freedom. They invoke universal principles and their enormous contribution to the country in support of their claims, while Fijians support theirs by invoking the arguments of cultural uniqueness.

Can I be objective about what I write as a participant historian? Partial or biased scholarship is not the peculiarity of any one period or of a particular type of scholarship. As Walter Laqueur puts it, 'Violent prejudices are nursed and maintained more easily in sheltered academic surroundings than on the political stage, which provided on many occasions welcome corrections and may even teach patience and tolerance.'[22] 'The only completely unbiased historian,' says David Thomson, quoting Mark Twain, 'is the Recording Angel, whose works are unpublished: and even he, said Mark Twain, doubtless has convictions which, to Satan, might look like prejudices.' Thomson goes on:

> If prejudice is inevitable, and it comes from the 'spirit of the age' as well as from more individual inclinations, it should perhaps be welcomed and made use of. It may be argued that it is, indeed, as indispensable to the historian as is resistance to the autocrat who knows that, without resistance to his rule, he has no leverage to rely on. The battle against his own prejudices can be invigorating for the historian and an aid to him in his battle to find the truth. But only a few bold spirits among professionals accept the subjective element in historiography as not regrettable and not merely unavoidable, but as positively vitalizing and perhaps indispensable to it as an intellectual endeavour.[23]

Meaningful participation requires attachment and commitment and an informed and long term engagement with the subject of one's research. And it can never be undertaken from intellectual inertia.[24] But these qualities are coming under threat from the changing culture within the academy. Financial cutbacks to universities have demanded increasing rationalisation of resources.

Classes become bigger and teaching loads increase, reducing the already limited time for research. In an age of out-sourcing, research funding is increasingly becoming outcome-oriented. Relevant research related in some way to Australia's (or the United Kingdom's of the United States') national and strategic interests gets priority. And when the currently fashionable research agenda—governance, poverty reduction, capacity building, structural reform– passes, emphasis moves on to some equally fashionable and equally transient topic.

Some of this policy-related work is important, but counterproductive when it is allowed at the expense of more fundamental, long-term, culturally informed research. The culture which nurtures participant history is also challenged by the current intellectual fashion in fields such as Cultural Studies which 'unsettles, destabilizes, and complicates the discourses of the humanities,' where the 'line between words and things, subject and object, inside and outside, humanity and nature, idea and matter becomes blurred and indistinct, and new configuration of the relation of action and language is set in place.'[25] This kind of exercise maybe stimulating in a graduate seminar, but unhelpful when dealing with the practicalities of the real world.[26] Generally, people, I have come to believe, want to entertain the possibility of hope, of change and progress, rather than dwell in the quagmire of self-pity and despair, disabled by doubt. They want clarity, not complication, stability, not uncertainty, rules, not anarchy. But they also want the simplicity that evades truth, that denies the complexities, contradictions and dynamics. That is what makes our task demanding—to get clarity and subtlety, clarity which includes discomforting exceptions and gaps in the evidence. We want to be able to write so that those who were there say, yes, that is the way it was—and learn something. Participant historians learn to live with the inescapable truth that we all live in our histories. 'The world is what it is,' VS Naipaul has written. 'Men who are nothing, who allow themselves to become nothing, have no place in it.' These words provide participant historians with both their challenge as well as their opportunity.

*Five*

# Where Has All The Music Gone?

*On the whole it is better to explore history rather than to repress or deny it* [1]

Edward Said

*It is not enough to stand at a tangent of other peoples' conventions; we should be the most unforgiving critics of our own* [2]

Tony Judt

*'[There is a] difference between the silence after the music, and the silence when there is no more music.* [3]

Vincent O'Sullivan

On 10 October 2010, Fiji will mark the fortieth anniversary of its independence from the United Kingdom after ninety six years of colonial rule. What a tumultuous forty years it has been in the ill-fated history of that otherwise richly endowed country: coups and constitutional crises, state-sponsored constitutional engineering, more coups and endless cul-de-sacs. The prospect of stability, peace and prosperity at the time of independence, the sense that Fiji, as a multi-ethnic society, might have a lesson to teach similarly situated countries in the developing world at the end of colonial rule seems like a bad dream now. What was once thought to be the fate of newly independent countries in Africa and Latin America whose fledgling democratic values were regularly subverted by the military in the name of good governance has now become an integral part of Fiji's postcolonial journey. And there is no end in sight to its unpredictable future.

I was in my final year of high school when Fiji became independent. I remember the occasion vividly. Lollies were distributed at the morning assembly along with miniature plastic navy blue Fiji flag, the Union Jack came down for the last time as we dutifully recited 'God Save the Queen' for the last time, speeches were made by Mr Sukru Rehman, chairman of the school's Board of Governors, and by the District Commissioner (Mr Dodds?), and words were spoken about achieving independence with tolerance, harmony and justice and about the legacy the British were leaving us: a sense of fair play, the rule of law and the fundamentals of parliamentary democracy. It was a proud moment in our youthful lives and we were told never to forget it. I did not know it then that I would spend a lifetime variously engaged with Fiji's history and politics. I am a part of the history I now seek to understand. I cannot and do not claim detachment and objectivity. But I will say that what I express is not entirely idiosyncratic, that in some ample measure, it reflects the opinion and experience of a section of the community from which I come, and those of the generation of which I am a part. In the sounds of my footsteps many would recognize the echoes of their own.

The late 1960s were one of the most dynamic decades in Fijian history, comparable in some senses to the 1990s, full of animated debate and discussion about what kind of political culture was appropriate for a multi-ethnic society such as Fiji. Opinion was genuinely divided. The National Federation Party, with its base in the Indo-Fijian community, advocated a non-racial common roll of voting with one person, one vote, one value. The Alliance, nominally multiracial but solidly backed by the Fijian and European communities, wanted nothing less than the retention of full communal, that is, race-based rolls. The NFP wanted Fiji to become independent with an elected Fijian head of state, while the Alliance was lukewarm about independence and wanted ties to the British monarchy maintained. Questions were asked about such sensitive subjects as the role and place of traditional social and cultural institutions in the fabric of the wider society, and about the social, cultural and institutional impediments to change and growth in Fijian society.[4]

These were questions which I came upon much later at university. Living in rural Labasa on the island of Vanua Levu, in a village without running water, paved roads or electricity, where the radio was still a novelty in many households and newspapers an expensive luxury which only a few could afford, we lived largely in blissful ignorance. We had few means of finding out what was going on in the world. We had no contact with Fijians who lived on the outer edges of our settlement, no comprehension of their concerns, aspirations and needs just as they were innocent about ours. We were preoccupied with making do with whatever little we had, which was very little indeed. More than national politics, the affairs of the sugar industry, then under the mighty Colonial Sugar

Refining Company, were of much greater concern to us. The sugar industry sustained us. It was our lifeblood. It was the reason why we were in Fiji. The news of national politics came to us via the occasional Hindi newspapers such as *Jagriti*, *Shanti Dut* and the *Fiji Samachar*. More immediately, it came through occasional visiting politicians, important men, impressively dressed, who talked about independence, about pride and sacrifice, about a new future, things which few of us actually understood. Our cane-growing village was solid Federation country. It was 'our party.' It had fought the CSR on our behalf. It carried our hopes and aspirations. There were a few Alliance supporters in the village, such as my eldest brother, for which I was sometimes taunted at school as a traitor to our community; but since such people were few and far-between, they were generally tolerated as misguided men with misplaced loyalties, harmless.

At high school, politics was taboo, even in the higher grades. The colonial protocol of separating politics from education was strictly observed. It was as if nothing was happening in the country that truly mattered to us. In our high school debates, we chose (or, rather our teachers chosen them for us) topics such as 'Alcoholics should have no place in society' and 'Why students should be allowed to wear thongs to school,' but nothing more serious.[5] Politics was dangerous, destabilizing territory, best left unexplored. The colonial educational bureaucracy kept a close, watchful eye on what went on in the classroom, and we were all focused on preparing for the final exam which would determine our fate and our school's ranking in the colonial prestige system. In our history classes, we learned about the unification of Germany and Italy, about the causes and consequences of the First World War and the Russian Revolution, but nothing about Fiji itself, or the broader Pacific region for that matter. Colonial rule was no longer fashionable and its defense problematic. The irony is glaringly obvious now. Here we were, people who would inherit the challenges and opportunities of independence, its next generation of leaders, completely unaware of important developments taking place all around us. And as products of largely mono-racial schools, we would be called upon to play national leadership roles on a multiracial stage for which we were spectacularly ill-prepared. No wonder, Fiji foundered on its postcolonial journey.

Fiji embarked on this postcolonial journey as we entered university. The opening of the University of the South Pacific in Suva must count as one of the turning points in modern South Pacific history, availing higher education to masses of students from poor homes who would have, before then, been deprived of the opportunities of tertiary education altogether; higher education in colonial Fiji was the privilege of a selected elite: usually a dozen or so scholars sent to Australia and New Zealand to study 'useful' subjects in preparation for careers in the teaching profession and in low level administration. The university was for us an enlarging and enriching experience but no more informative about what was going on in political circles in Fiji. Once again, we had our sports, hiking, social and cultural clubs; we staged plays, read poetry, went bushwalking, but serious discussion of politics was absent, or confined to a few individuals. The Indo-Fijians generally assumed that their Fijian counterparts were supporters of the Alliance Party while they, in turn, suspected us of being Federation sympathisers. Given that the political parties were essentially race-based, we were conscious of the ever-present danger that any criticism of a political party could easily be interpreted as a provocative attack on an ethnic group; and so the boundaries remained intact, and we kept our thoughts largely to ourselves.

Other Pacific island students, from Samoa, Tonga, the Cook Islands and the Solomons, talked proudly of their 'history' as beneficial and nourishing influences in their lives. They had a history to celebrate, which had a coherence borne of ancient heritage or forged in response to colonial rule (the Mau movement in Samoa, Maasina Rule in the Solomon Islands, the monarchy in Tonga). Their obvious pride in their 'national identity' was a source of envy for us. We had no overarching sense a common identity; we were 'Indians' and 'Fijians,' separate in our conceptions of the past and divergent in our understanding of the present. We hardly spoke each others' language. Our memory was racially compartmentalised. While one group lauded the policies of colonial rule, the other rejected it. In our vision of what Fiji as a multi-ethnic society should be like, we were poles apart, symbolised most immediately in the different attachments to communal and common roll system of voting. Our traditions of political discourse were different: one was open and robust, the other hedged in by a careful observance of rituals and protocols of hierarchy. The space of common concerns was small although in the lived experience of daily life, social boundaries were freely breached. For us, history could not serve a serviceable ideology of nation-building as it could and did for many of our Pacific neighbours.

This was the unspoken reality on the ground, but our national myth evoked a different image. The early years of independence were warm and fuzzy. We had become independent without strife. Our links with the British monarchy remained intact. The old colonial pattern of political representation, with paramountcy for Fijians and privilege for Europeans was maintained, with Indo-Fijians having to content themselves with the illusion of parity in the overall scheme of things. We were paraded before the world as a model of multiracial democracy. 'The Way the World Should Be,' Pope John Paul II had intoned on a fleeting visit to the country in 1985. That became our national mantra, shamelessly self promotional. But deep inside us, I am not sure if we really believed this myth. Independence had arrived peacefully, but none of the deep underlying problems about power sharing, land leases, the underpinnings of affirmative action, had been resolved. We were reluctant to look too closely into the abyss which faced us in the eye.

In truth, we had merely papered over the cracks and fractures that lay just beneath the surface. There were certain assumptions and understandings which underpinned the independence order which lay unexplored lest we discovered the hollowness that lay beneath the centre of our public life. Race, we were repeatedly told, was a fact of life; in truth, it was on its way to becoming a way of life. Every issue of public policy came to be viewed through the prism of race. You were asked for your race when you opened a back account, took out a driving licence, left or entered the country. In the award of scholarships, in promotions in the public service, race became a consequential factor in the national equation of affirmative action. 'Blood will flow,' Ratu Mara said, if Fijian sensitivities about land and leadership were ever breached. Race serviced a convenient political ideology but it was also deeply flawed. Neither the Fijians nor the Indo-Fijians were homogenous communities. There were interests and concerns which transgressed communal boundaries in many parts of Fiji. Nonetheless, the overall architecture of national life was race-based.

Expatriate academic analysts scratched the surface and developed the theory of 'Three Fijis.'[6] There was some truth to this characterization although fundamental structural changes in the economy were surreptitiously unsettling established orthodoxies. The Fijians were behind in some sectors but considerably ahead in others (ownership of land. timber and marine resources, for example). The Fijian government of the day adopted affirmative action policy in favour of indigenous Fijians in the field of education which affected us most directly. An education commission in 1969 had recommended that fifty percent of all government scholarship should be reserved for indigenous Fijians, the unexpended funds designated specifically for Fijian educational projects. Fijian disadvantage in education and in the professions generally, was a direct result of the policies and visions of an earlier generation of Fijian leaders, principally Ratu Sir Lala Sukuna, who thought the place for his people was in the subsistence sector in the villages under the guidance of chiefly leadership, and that higher education was to remain the preserve of the chiefly elite. In the abstract, the policy of racial balance made sense, but it was quite another matter at the personal level to see Fijian students getting scholarships on far lower marks to Indo-Fijian students. That policy of discrimination inevitably bred resentment. We felt as if we were the stepchildren of the state. In the civil service, senior Indo-Fijians stared blankly at the glass ceiling.[7] The feeling of disappointment was muted, but it was real.

A few years after independence, the warm mantra of multiracialism espoused by the leaders, seemed strangely cold.

Things went from bad to worse after the mid-1970s. In 1974, former Alliance assistant minister, Sakeasi Butadroka, founded the Fijian Nationalist Party with its motto, 'Fiji for Fijians.' The following year, he moved a provocative motion in parliament on the fifth anniversary of Fiji's independence, to have the Indians deported from Fiji, with the expense of relocation to be paid by the British government. In hindsight, the motion seems ludicrous, a rhetorical flourish of the Fijian nationalist fringe, nothing more. But at the time, it had a powerful, unsettling effect on us. In 1974, Idi Amin had expelled long-settled Indians from Uganda for no other reason than their industry and hard earned prosperity. If it could happen in Uganda (and expulsion of Indians had taken place in Burma earlier), there was no obvious reason why it could not happen in Fiji. The Alliance government's political point scoring response to the motion, condemning Butadroka but affirming support of the rights of all citizens, not only Indians, who were its specific targets, deepened our sense of alienation, especially when it became clear that the motion's sentiment, in varying degrees, was shared fairly widely in the Fijian community according to Ratu David Toganivalu, himself a man of widespread cross-cultural friendships. For the first time, many Indo-Fijians began to feel that Fiji might not, after all, be their permanent home. The Canadian prime minister Pierre Trudeau's more liberal, skills-based migration policy opened doors that began to attract many. A gradual drift began.

Two years later, the tremors of the earthquake started by Butadroka was felt when the Alliance lost the general election in April 1977 with 25 per cent of the Fijian votes going to the Nationalists. Five months later, the Alliance recaptured its natural constituency by effectively jettisoning its multiracial philosophy and embracing an openly ethnic one. The Alliance learnt anew the truth of a central assumption that underpinned the independence settlement: that Fijians would remain in power provided they remained united. Henceforth, the main preoccupation of the Alliance would be the preservation of Fijian ethnic solidarity. A similar consolidation was taking place on the Indo-Fijian side. Having won the April elections by the narrowest of margins (two seats), the NFP tried for four days to have a coalition government with the Alliance, an offer which the party flatly refused, the dithering allowing the Governor General, Ratu Sir George Cakobau, to appoint a minority government headed by Ratu Sir Kamisese Mara. NFP's delay in forming government and its internal but well publicized leadership skirmishes were blamed for the appointment of the minority government but everyone knew privately that an 'Indian' prime minister would not be acceptable to Fijians, proclamations of democratic principles and multiracial values notwithstanding. One by one, all the founding Indo-Fijian members of the Alliance party left, or were forced to leave on one pretext or another, finding a welcoming home in the National Federation Party headed by its new leader Jai Ram Reddy. Reddy had not been part of the bitter ideological fights of the pre-independence era. He wanted all Indians united under one umbrella, precisely the goal that Ratu Mara had in mind for the Fijians. Racial polarization was almost complete. We could feel it in our bones.

In 1982, things nearly boiled over. Indo-Fijians had joined hands with some western Fijians leaders disgruntled with the Alliance government's development policies, especially about the lucrative pine industry, and succeeded in nearly toppling the Fijian government. Racism raised its ugly head again. Calls were made to deport Indo-Fijian leaders, refuse renewal of leases to Indo-Fijian tenants unless they agreed to Fijian political control, amend the constitution to enshrine Fijian paramountcy. Crises were manufactured and events staged to arouse peoples' emotions. Old timers will remember the 'Four Corners' program and the Carroll Report.[8] Once again, the reluctance of the Fijian establishment to concede power or to share it except on its own terms was on full display. The tensions generated by the political debates percolated down to the grassroots, subtly influencing (and infecting) cross-cultural attitudes and perceptions. There was cordiality in public but a great deal of circumspection in private. Not everything, however, was as the Alliance narrative portrayed it to be. Villages and settlements were changing in significant ways as the tentacles of the modern cash economy reached the hitherto isolated sections of the community.[9] Travel and technology were transforming urban attitudes and relationships. More and more children were attending multiracial schools, and people of all ethnicities were feeling the effects of a stalled economy and lengthened unemployment lines caused, in part, by World Bank inspired policies. A multiracial working class was haphazardly in the making. Old polarities and binary oppositions were making less and less sense.

One result of the dissatisfaction with the existing orthodoxies and power arrangements in the country was the formation of a (nominally) multiracial Fiji Labour Party in 1985. Rhetorically left-leaning, it was in fact cautiously pragmatic, or pragmatically cautious, but its emergence posed a potential threat to the established order of things Fijian where the conventional wisdom held that the business of leadership was the prerogative of chiefs. Its criticism of the eastern chiefs who had dominated Fijian political discourse for much of the twentieth century caused further alarm in minds used to deference and acquiescence to duly constituted authority. It came as little surprise that the Fiji Labour Party-National Federation Party Coalition which won the 1987 general elections was swiftly deposed by the Fijian military in the name of the 'Fijian race.' I argued at the time that the coup was more than a simple racial contest that it was made out to be by the supporters of the coup and by the international media, that it was more about defeated politicians taking back power by any means possible. This narrative lacked traction in those emotionally charged days when 'race' was the privileged explanatory factor of the coup.[10]

The story of the 1987 coups is too well known to be re-told here. The wounds it inflicted on the body politic, social fabric and inter-ethnic relations were profound and enduring. The daily harassment of people, mostly Indo-Fijian supporters of the Coalition, including members of my own extended family, perpetuated religious bigotry and fanaticism that found its culmination in the infamous 'Sunday Ban,' the threatened non-renewal of leases, the rampant discrimination in the public service, left a deep wound on the Indo-Fijian psyche. The sense of rejection and humiliation was deep: just how deep would become clear a few years later. I think I misjudged the depth of the hurt. The 1999 general elections were the first time that Rabuka had to seek Indo-Fijian support to govern. Under the 1990 Constitution, which was completely race-based, he only had to court the Fijian electorate, but there were twenty five 'Open,' that is, non-racial seats under the 1997 Constitution. The Indo-Fijians rejected his overtures for partnership in opening a new chapter in Fiji's political evolution. All his achievements in helping give Fiji the most liberal constitution it ever had, counted for little. To be sure, there were good reasons why the Rabuka government was unpopular: his administration was riddled with corruption and mismanagement and scandals that nearly drove the country to the brink of bankruptcy. Politics of patronage was the order of the day. Beyond all this, though, was a feeling of revenge and retribution. The man had done something terribly wrong and he could not go unpunished. Mahendra Chaudhry, the Labour leader, understood the Indian psychology well and exploited it adeptly for his own purposes even though it was his support that had enabled Sitiveni Rabuka to become prime minister in 1992 in the first place. But sadly it turned out to be a pyrrhic victory for him.

The 1987 coup sent an important message to the Indo-Fijian community. As Rabuka said at the time, they could live in Fiji and make as much money as they wanted, but they should never aspire to political power which should always remain in Fijian hands. The Indo-Fijian community was caught in a cul-de-sac. With very little to fall back on—the land leases were expiring at a rapid rate, there was rampant discrimination in the public sector—many Indo-Fijians began to contemplate migration, which had started in earnest soon after the May military takeover. A trickle turned into a torrent. Precise figures are understandably uncertain but a conservative estimate would put the numbers of those who left after the first coup at over one hundred and twenty thousand. The size of the Indo-Fijian population as a result has declined from around forty nine percent in 1987 to around thirty three per cent now. And the decline will continue well into the future through a continuously falling birth rate and unceasing migration

This huge demographic transformation is full of important implications. To start with, the fear of 'Indian domination' which so plagued the dynamics of Fiji politics since the end of the Second World War, when the Indo-Fijians for the first time exceeded the indigenous Fijians, has gone forever. You can feel this in the texture and tenor of ordinary conversation with Fijians who know it in their hearts that Fiji is once again 'their country.' This transformation has demonstrated the potential for the reconfiguration of Fiji politics. It has, for instance, opened up more space for democratic debate among Fijians about such sensitive topics as chiefly titles and inheritance, for example, in ways that would have been unimaginable during the reign of paramount chiefs in the early years of independence. In the 1990s, there was a proliferation of Fijian political parties, each with their own specific agendas that opened up and re-energized the discussion of intra-Fijian issues. The carefully nurtured artefact of 'Fijian unity' was visibly fractured, aided by the departure from the political stage of paramount chiefs who had once wielded overarching, unifying influence over their people, and the disappearance of traditional gatekeepers of knowledge and information by the advent of modern technology: radio, television, the internet, and the visual and print media. This is going to be the future order of the day. 'Race' has lost its edge in ordinary conversation and behaviour.

The bulk of those who left were people of talent and education whose skills were in great demand overseas, especially in Australia and New Zealand: doctors, nurses, accountants, science teachers, mechanics, businessmen. The best and the brightest have left, are leaving, and will leave. On that there is general consensus. Among the migrants are members of my own family: three brothers in Brisbane, a sister in Darwin and nieces and nephews and cousins scattered across the globe. Those who remain in Fiji do so for reasons of business, lifestyle, or enduring commitment, but have their families and their investments safely 'parked' elsewhere: the word is theirs, not mine. Some who are overseas talk of retiring 'back home,' but few so far have taken the opportunity of becoming permanent residents or citizens now on offer. They are keeping their options open: once bitten, twice shy. Among those leaving are people who in the normal course of events might have been expected to take a more moderate, longer term view of the future. Their departure affected the power base of the National Federation Party, playing an important part in its downfall in the 1999 elections. Those who remained behind and who could not leave —unskilled workers, farmers, the elderly—who had nothing to lose by demanding the sky, fell prey to the demagoguery and vaguely emancipating, empowering rhetoric of the Fiji Labour Party. Among those left in Fiji are the desperately poor with few hopes and little opportunity. They will continue to be vulnerable to the entreaties of opportunistic politicians preying on the needs and aspirations of the truly desperate. And the young will continue to migrate through family sponsorships, arranged marriages or other means. Many are taking courses at tertiary institutions in the hope of improving their chances in the migration stakes.

The creation of the Fijian diaspora in Australia and New Zealand, in particular, is an important recent social phenomenon. We are not talking about 'migrant communities' in the old sense of a rupture of a more or less a permanent kind. They might more accurately be described as 'transmigrant' communities whose links with their former homelands are never severed but nurtured in a variety of ways of novel ways. People maintain contact with friends and family back home through the internet (emails, Facebook), through regular telephone conversations (via Skype) and through periodic visits. Air travel is not as prohibitively expensive as it once was, and physical proximity helps: Australia and New Zealand are just a few hours away by plane. People help with scholarships, refurbishment of temples and schools, medical supplies and relief efforts during the natural calamities which visit Fiji with mundane regularity every year. Clusters form around places of origin in Fiji (Ba, Labasa) or around religious or cultural affiliation (Sangam, Muslim League, Sanatan Dharam and Arya Samaj) to provide more targeted assistance in times of need. This sort of contribution is difficult to measure but it is real, and it is increasing. The principle of gift-giving is no longer the preserve of 'traditional' societies much studied by anthropologists.

Many migrants left Fiji in emotionally difficult circumstances, giving up secure jobs which once held the prospect of promotion and permanency, selling homes and other property for a fraction of their normal price, rupturing relations built over generations, taking a journey into the unknown from which, they know, there will be no return. The pain of dislocation is real if never fully expressed. Understandably, their attitude towards those whose policies led to their displacement in the first place is suffused with a mixture of bitterness and deep anger. Many became strong supporters of the Fiji Labour Party and vocal critics of the more moderate and consensus building strategies of its opponent, the National Federation Party. Jai Ram Reddy's plea to make a fresh start, to let bygones be bygones, fell on deaf ears. Labour's red-hot, punitive rhetoric was more to their liking. It came as little surprise that many Indo-Fijian residents in Australia and New Zealand also became vocal supporters of Frank Bainimarama's latest coups for a variety of motives, not the least of which was revenge. Fijians had caused a lot of misery to Indo-Fijians in the past, enthusiastically endorsing the nationalist rhetoric of previous coups. Now it was time for them to 'taste their own medicine,' as the phrase goes in Fiji. There is a reluctance amongst many to believe anything but a positive narrative of the ongoing Fijian saga. That is, whatever the present state of affairs, Bainimarama will come good in the end. He, therefore, needs support, not opposition.

While migration was proceeding apace, there were other developments in the 1980s and 1990s which were aiding the alienation of the Indo-Fijian community in Fiji. Among them were the Rabuka government's avowedly pro-Fijian policies, especially during its first term, when he seemed overtly indifferent to the concerns of the Indo-Fijians. He allocated government funds to enable Fijian landowning units to purchase freehold land on the market but appeared to do little to address the anxieties of Indo-Fijian tenants evicted from expiring leases. Scandals rocked the government. The economic rationalist policies of Finance Minister Jim Ah Koy affected all workers, Fijian and Indo-Fijian alike, especially at the lower levels. Jobs were lost and unemployment lines lengthened. The man who had committed the coup was now embarking on a course that was compounding Indo-Fijian misery.

The expiry of the thirty-year agricultural leases under the Agricultural Landlord and Tenant Act in the 1990s caused havoc in the Indo-Fijian farming community.[11] Leases were not renewed partly because Fijian landowners themselves wanted to enter the industry in which until then they were bystanders. But land was power, too, Fijian power: around eighty three per cent of the land was owned in inalienable right by Fijians. People like Marika Qarikau, the Fijian nationalist manager of the Native Land Trust Board, realised this early and used land as a blunt instrument to extract maximum political concessions from the Indo-Fijians. Tenancies would be renewed, the message went out, if Indo-Fijians accepted the principle of Fijian political control. The threat of non-renewal of leases came at a particularly inopportune time for struggling farmers: the ancient milling structures were collapsing, husbandry practices had deteriorated, tonnage per acre produced was low, and the preferential access to the European Union under the Lome Agreement was about to expire. It was always in the nature of the leases that they would end one day, and the theoretical possibility was held constantly at the back of the mind of the growers. But the reality when it finally eventuated, was different. The experience of uprooting after generations of living in a place and then seeing your formerly productive farm revert to bush, of having to start afresh in a new occupation in a new place, often amongst complete strangers, was wrenching. It left many deeply traumatised and unforgiving of those whose policies had brought about their demise as cane growers, including members of my own extended family.

Ironically, many positive things were happening in the country concurrently, the most important of them being the review of the racially-lopsided 1990 Constitution in which Rabuka, along with Jai Ram Reddy, played a genuinely important role in establishing. It was a courageous move, going against the grain of nationalist Fijian opinion completely averse to any concession in the direction of political partnership with the Indo-Fijian community. The 1997 Constitution was a genuine improvement over its previous counterparts. There was limited but important movement in the direction of non-racialism. Race had been removed as factor in the allocation of affirmative action programs. The constitution had significant human rights provisions. Most importantly, the power sharing arrangements of the constitution ensured that Indo-Fijians, if they won a sufficient number of seats in the House of Representatives would, as a matter of right, not grace, be entitled to an invitation into cabinet. This is what the community had been struggling towards for nearly a century, and the opportunity was now within its grasp. But in the countryside, emptying from the non-renewal of leases, and in the mushrooming squatter settlements fringing the main urban centres of Fiji, where memories of deprivation and displacement were fresh and deep and the struggle for sustainable living getting more difficult by the day, constitutional reform counted for little. The constitution won't put food on the table, opportunistic politicians told the people, who believed them. Among them was a former university academic.

Mahendra Chaudhry's Fiji Labour Party was the clear beneficiary of the gradually growing reservoir of Indo-Fijian hurt and grievance.[12] He won the 1999 general elections by annihilating his old enemy, the National Federation Party, which failed to win a single seat. Apart from anything else, the Indo-Fijian electorate was unforgiving of NFP's embracing of Sitiveni Rabuka. Grudges run deep in the Indo-Fijian psyche. But the Chaudhry government lasted only a year in office when it was toppled from office in a quasi-military coup by insurgents led by the improbably self-styled Fijian nationalist George Speight. It was a dark moment for Fiji, but darker still for the Indo-Fijian community which saw, yet again, a government elected by them overturned by force. It did not matter that the causes of the Speight insurrection were complex and had more to do with intra-Fijian rivalries and struggles for power. The overthrow simply reinforced the feeling of rejection and marginalisation already well entrenched in the broader narrative of the Indo-Fijian experience in the postcolonial period. The fact that Chaudhry's rather abrasive style, developed in the cauldron of Fiji's combative trade union movement, his ill-advised confrontation with the media, his untimely an reportedly unilateral pursuit of policies of land reform which could have been postponed to more propitious times, might have contributed to his fate were ignored. The fact that a prime minister of Indo-Fijian descent had been overthrown was enough for many. Chaudhry, it should be emphasised, was not the cause of George Speight's insurrection though he might have contributed to it unwittingly.

What followed made matters even worse, deepening Indo-Fijian disenchantment with the unfolding events. An interim administration set up by the military and led by the merchant banker and former head of the Fiji Development Bank, Laisenia Qarase, which morphed into a new political party, the Soqosoqo Duavata ni Lewenivanua (SDL) won the general elections in 2001 and remained in power until 2006. The tragedy was that Qarase in his first term had not learned the lessons of Fiji's recent history. Everything he did repudiated the spirit of consensus building of the 1990s. He openly courted Fijian nationalist fringe to remain in power.[13] He gave the Fiji Labour Party miniscule portfolios of no significance, which Labour rightly refused, seeking Supreme Court ruling on the numerical composition of the multi-party cabinet. The fundamental thrust of his government's policy was to address the concerns and needs of the indigenous Fijian community to the exclusion of virtually everything else. His reading of the Fijian scene was as dated as it was blinkered, premised upon the notion that the Fijians were the disadvantaged community needing special assistance while Indo-Fijians were the well-to-do ones: this when every piece of objective, verifiable evidence showed that poverty and disadvantage paid no respect to ethnic boundaries but freely transgressed them, that, indeed, rural Indo-Fijians comprised some of the most disadvantaged groups in Fiji society (as shown in various studies done by Wadan Narsey).[14] His 'Fijian Blueprint' promised massive assistance for specifically Fijian projects. His education policies directed special assistance to Fijian-run schools when many urban Indian-run schools had more Fijian students than Indian but which missed out because they were not Fijian. The overall narrative of the first Qarase government was Fijian empowerment and Indo-Fijian disempowerment.

After the 2006 elections, looking ahead at his last term in parliament and with an eye on his place in history, Qarase tried to make amends for his errant, explicitly race-based politics of the past. He now honoured the spirit of the power-sharing provisions of the 1997 Constitution by giving Labour nine senior ministries in his cabinet. Labour ministers in cabinet felt there was a genuine effort to make power-sharing work. Qarase himself was, as he told me, full of praise for his Labour colleagues in cabinet. The mood among Indo-Fijians, and in the country at large, was buoyant, filled with optimism that at long last Fiji might be turning the corner of racially-divisive confrontational politics. But by then, Mahendra Chaudhry, the Labour leader, was completely disaffected. He thought, unlike most other people in Fiji, that the elections had been rigged. There may have been inconsistencies here and there but nothing that would have changed the outcome of the election. As party leader, he wanted to allocate portfolios to his minsters, and he wanted them to be accountable to him rather than to the prime minister as the Westminster convention requires. This was crude politics designed to destabilise the multi-party government. When his ministers balked, punishing them in the name of party solidarity became Chaudhry's prime concern, pursued relentlessly. At that point, the multi-party government was doomed.

Qarase did not help his cause by attempting to fulfil some of his controversial campaign promises which could, and should, have been left for consideration later in the life of his government, if implemented at all. These included returning the ownership of the foreshore to the indigenous owners (the Qoliqoli Bill) which deeply angered developers, hoteliers and non-Fijians generally, investigating the basis of land purchases in the 19th century with a view to returning illegally or fraudulently acquired lands to the traditional owners, and, most controversially, bypassing established judicial procedures to release from jail people convicted of coup related crimes. The story is more complex than it is possible to discuss here, suffused with a variety of motives. None of the bills actually came before parliament, but the damage to the government's reputation for probity and fairness was significant, providing powerful ammunition to its critics. Among these critics was Commodore Frank Bainimarama, the head of the Fiji military. His wrath focused particularly on the use of the Compulsory Supervision Order to effect early release of prisoners convicted for their role in the mutiny in November 2000 in which several loyal soldiers lost their lives and which nearly claimed the life of Bainimarama himself. He was angry, too, at the prospect of facing a reduction in the size of the top-heavy military force recommended in a White Paper commissioned by the government. There were issues also surrounding the length and duration of Bainimarama's contract. Deep personal animosity between military commander and prime minister did not help. For these and other reasons, Bainimarama's unleashed his coup on 5 December 2006.

Fijian anger at the overthrow of a Fijian government, elected with overwhelming indigenous Fijian support, was understandable. No one had ever contemplated the possibility of a Fijian military confronting a Fijian government, or the unceremonious humbling and humiliation of the central institutions of Fijian society, the Great Council of Chiefs and the Methodist Church. The reaction of the Indo-Fijian community was revealing. In 1987 and in 2000, there was immediate outrage: strikes were threatened or mounted, trade unions mobilized, international sanctions sought. But there was none of that in 2006. There were many reasons. To begin with, there was the nature of the coup itself. The 2006 Fiji coup would have to be one of the most advertised coups in the history of the world, announced several years before it actually materialised: a coup by haemorrhage. When the dénouement finally came, it was received not so much with surprise as with relief that the deed was finally done. It was not a coup, Bainimarama said; it was a 'clean up campaign.' The catchphrase caught on; it resonated in the experience of many who had witnessed or been victims of bourgeoning bribery and corruption in Fiji. Baksheesh was fast becoming a way of life in the country. Reports of government largesse being channelled to constituents for political, vote-buying purposes were well known. Many genuinely believed that Bainimarama meant business when he promised to halt the looting of the public purse for political purposes.

A new dimension to Indo-Fijian thinking was added in January 2007 when Labour leader Mahendra Chaudhry joined the military administration as its Finance Minister. There are many in Fiji who believe that Chaudhry was in on the game from the very beginning, a charge he denies vehemently, and for which he must be taken at his word. Nonetheless, throughout the steadily building crisis, Chaudhry was quietly seeking audience with Bainimarama after-hours, keeping his powder dry, keeping abreast of the latest developments and taking every opportunity to criticise the Qarase government and his own ministers in it. Perhaps like Bainimarama, Chaudhry too was haunted by a past which had denied him his just dues and why he was determined not to forgive his enemies. Chaudhry was the leader of the Indo-Fijian community and many, for that reason alone, followed his lead. There were other Indo-Fijian leaders, of the National Federation Party, for instance, who opposed the coup, but theirs was a minority voice. Perhaps Chaudhry thought he might be able to use his vast political experience to steer the novices in military regime into a desirable direction, the tail that might wag the dog, but in this view he was seriously mistaken. A year later, he was unceremoniously dumped from the military cabinet, but by then the damage brought about by his involvement had been done. Chaudhry's participation had given the military regime a certain cloak of much-needed legitimacy at a time when it mattered most. Bainimarama had been able to buy off valuable time to consolidate himself in power and fend off criticism at home and from abroad. Chaudhry now finds himself hobbled on the margins, taking occasional pot shots at various government policies from his website. His once strongly organised community is similarly disabled.

The Indo-Fijian business community switched sides in quick time, which comes as no surprise to anyone familiar with its past record. When the coup took place, many were heard to say that the country would bounce back to normalcy within six months. It did not, which forced them to take a longer term view of things, including courting elements of the military. There were some who supported the new regime because of their experience with corruption in the previous administrations, but for many, money making was their main priority, the end which any means could justify. The authoritarian environment suited their purpose. Some are known to have direct access to the members of the shadowy Military Council. The commitment of the business community to Fiji is suspect. It has been so for a while. Many have moved their nesteggs safely elsewhere, to Australia and New Zealand in particular, where many have permanent residence. Businessmen with conscience and commitment have been rare in Fiji.

More surprising has been the reaction of the Indo-Fijian moral community. After the obligatory disapproving tones, many Indo-Fijian religious leaders quickly fell in line. The head of the largest Hindu organisation in Fiji, the Sanatan Dharam Pratinidhi Sabha of Fiji, declared quiet support for the stated goals of the coup. The acting president of the Arya Samaj, the wife of a high court judge, joined the military administration's National Council for Building a Better Fiji and urged an understanding of the military regime's plans for Fiji. From western Viti Levu, the perennially changeable politician, Swani Maharaj, a member of several political parties in the past, gave similar assurances of support. The South Indian cultural organisation, Sangam, expressed opposition while the Fiji Muslim League, whose leaders were close to the Qarase administration, maintained strategic silence. But the overall narrative was of compliance.

A part of the reason for the support was pragmatic. There were personal business interests to consider. The regime in power had to be courted to receive special grants and other favours for schools and community projects because it looked likely that the regime would remain in power for longer than originally thought. But an important part of the reason for supporting the regime was grievance and grudge. People remembered the excesses of the Sunday Ban of the late 1980s, the mindless acts of religious vandalism, the burning of mosques and temples and other places of worship, with the support of the leaders of the Methodist Church—Reverend Tomasi Raikivi, Reverend Manasa Lasaro and Reverend Viliame Gonelevu, to mention just three. For this reason, many welcomed Bainimarama's punitive approach to the Methodist Church leaders. It was the same with the humbling and humiliation of the Great Council of Chiefs, which had supported coups in the past and which many thought was anachronistic in the modern era. Why should this body alone decide who should be the President and Vice President of Fiji?

In the past, academics and tertiary students played a prominent role in rallying public opinion against the coups. But now, with one or two notable exceptions, they took a back seat. In the early days, many of them were seduced by the 'Clean Up Campaign' message, their strategic silence quietly encouraged by the leadership of these institutions of higher learning fearing reprisals. And anonymous late-night phone calls. Many believed in the possibility of the Bainimarama coup being a good coup, a means to an end, the end being the creation of a better governed, race-neutral society. They were therefore prepared to give the new regime the benefit of the doubt over Laisenia Qarase and Mahendra Chaudhry, two old practitioners of race-based politics. A focus on personalities detracted from the fundamental principles at stake: a military coup had deposed a democratically elected government. Qarase and Chaudhry may fall under the proverbial bus tomorrow, but the sanctity of the ballot box must be guarded at all times. Others offered old, tired extra-constitutional justifications such as the need sometimes to go outside the law to protect it. Students took their cue from their teachers. Their seeming indifference and apathy was dismaying, their involvement in the great moral issues of governance almost non-existent. Perhaps many were simply focused on acquiring the right qualifications to emigrate. Others saw opportunities for themselves and thought it undesirable to 'rock the boat.' Edward Said's words are apposite: 'You do not want to appear too political; you are afraid of seeming controversial; you need the approval of a boss or an authority figure; you want to have a reputation for being balanced, objective, moderate; your hope is to be asked back, to consult, to be on a board or prestigious committee, and so remain within the responsible mainstream; someday you hope to get an honorary degree, a big prize, perhaps even an ambassadorship.' [15] Said goes on to say that 'If anything can denature, neutralize, and finally kill a passionate intellectual life it is the internalization of such habits.'

From Fiji's émigré community came unexpected support for the coup, particularly retired Indo-Fijian expatriates. Many had left Fiji, or forced to leave it, in singularly unfortunate circumstances in the late 1980s, some summarily dismissed for suspected harbouring of pro-Coalition sympathies. Now in their retirement, they wanted to return to help set things right, to make Fiji a true, non-racial democracy, albeit on exorbitant consultants' salaries, almost obscene by local standards. Some were clearly opportunistic, yearning for a brief moment in the sun before the inevitable twilight. But there were also among them technocratic ideologues with little confidence in the institutions and practices of electoral politics to deliver desired outcomes. They had no time for wicked politicians who played the race card to win elections. Voters could not be trusted to know what was in their own best interests. Elections were problematic, low voter turnout endemic in developing countries, corruption and scandals rampant, alienation of people from the processes of governance growing, leading to the conclusion that democracy may not be the most appropriate form of government for all societies. They, therefore, threw their weight behind the so-called 'Peoples Charter,' a document full of motherhood statements lifted straight from Good Governance 101 course, to put the country onto autopilot, leaving elected politicians only to dot the i's and cross the t's. The Charter has now become the military regime's roadmap, its foundational document, but it is observed more in the breach as the regime tramples upon principles of natural justice and basic human rights in order to entrench itself. The Charter supporters are caught in a bind: they can neither condone the excesses of the regime which their participation helped to legitimise, nor can they condemn it outright. Like most Indo-Fijians, they too are caught in a cul-de-sac.

Some responses are easily categorized, but others are not. There are many Indo-Fijians, perhaps the majority, who have no view either way, whose standard of life has not changed much at all since 2006, quite the contrary, who live precariously on the charity and sufferance of others. People who have endured enough upheaval for the last two decades hope that this too will pass soon so that they can get on with the rest of their lives. It is resignation born not of indifference or fatalism, but of experience, an endless cycle of promises made and broken. I should at this point declare my own hand. I have been a strong opponent of military coups in Fiji. I was as opposed to them in 1987 as I was in 2006. For me, there is something deeply immoral (as well as illegal) about overturning the verdict of the ballot box by the bayonet. The history of the world shows that coups don't solve problems, they merely compound them. Violence as an instrument of policy is always counterproductive. And I believe deeply that the intellectual classes (but not only they alone), have the sacred responsibility to speak truth to power. If we don't, who will? I did that in my own small way, speaking and writing against coups and their consequences for Fiji and for which I paid the price. I was interrogated by the military in November 2009 and expelled from the country, the land of my birth. There is no rancour or bitterness: if that is the price that had to be paid for standing up for the values of democracy and the rule of law, than I am glad I paid it.

Four years after the 2006 coup, the Indo-Fijian community, diminished and demoralized, is caught between a rock and a hard place. The rhetoric providing the initial justification for the coup rings hollow now. The 'Clean Up Campaign' has yielded few results except more embarrassment for the military regime and its bungling Fiji Independent Commission Against Corruption(headed by a serving military officer). Like the Qarase administration, the military regime too has used the Compulsory Supervision Order to effect early release from prison of people convicted for various coup-related crimes, including manslaughter of civilians, thus denting its moral claims over the regime it deposed. It is now clear that the military will only countenance a new political order in which it will have a visible and permanent presence. A militarised democracy is in the offing. Burma as a comparison comes to mind. There are many Indo-Fijians who, having supported the coup thus far, feel that there can be no turning back. They have burned their bridges with the Fijian community. They know that they are seen by others, fairly or unfairly, as aiding and abetting the coup through various acts of omission or commission. If the coup fails, they know they are done for, and so out of desperate necessity they back Bainimarama because they know that he is the only one who stands between them and anarchy. Indeed, some are beginning to embrace him as their real leader, not Mahendra Chaudhry or anyone else.

The impulses underlying this kind of thinking are understandable but wrong-headed and in truth counterproductive. Rhetoric of non-racialism aside, the Bainimarama coup is morphing into a 'Fijian' coup as many Fijians take up opportunities left by the departing Indo-Fijians and as province after province lines up to 'apologize' to Bainimarama for opposing his regime. The presence in the interim administration of such notable former coup supporters and members of the hardline Taukei Movement as Inoke Kubuabola and Filipe Bole is reassuring to them. Bainimarama has vowed not to allow 1987 era politicians to stand for elections in the future and yet has rewarded two of them with senior positions in his administrations. There is talk of non-racial equality but not a word has been said about opening up the almost racially exclusive military to non-Fijians. The ethnic imbalance in the public sector is glaring. Military personnel increasingly take up senior civilian positions. Commodore Bainimarama promises to address the perennial land lease problem by making available unused Fijian land on ninety nine year leases for agricultural purposes. It sounds an attractive proposition on paper, but it is like locking the gate after the horse has already bolted. The sugar industry is dying and no amount of artificial resuscitation will revive it. Places in northern Vanua Levu—Wainikoro, Lagalaga, Naqiqi, Coqeloa—are emptying at a depressingly rapid rate as people move into the congested squatter settlements principally in the Suva-Nausori corridor where an estimated one third of the total population now lives, often in wretched conditions. Yet, those displaced from the farming country say they will never return to the perpetual uncertainties of the past. The umbilical cord is severed for good. Many are contemplating an overseas future for their children.

For the Indo-Fijians, as indeed for Fiji as a whole, the last forty years have been a time of frustration and bewilderment, the promise of independence gone awry. A large part of the problem lay with the architecture of the independence political order itself. It was constructed on the pillars of ethnic compartmentalisation while with time and with the advent of new forces of change, 'race' largely lost its relevance in daily life to all but the leaders who continued to embrace it a 'as a fact of life.' When power was finally wrested from the ruling elite at the ballot box, the military was unleashed to win it back. In a strange twist of irony, the military which was nurtured as the ultimate bastion of power for the Fijian establishment returned in 2006 to destroy its very foundations. It now looks unlikely that it will ever completely disappear from the political scene. Power concedes nothing without a struggle, and once out, soldiers do not voluntarily return to the barracks. The intense and deeply-felt debates over the last forty years about strengthening the institutions of parliamentary democracy –electoral systems, political parties, constitutional protection of rights, institutional mechanisms for strengthening the participation of citizens in the governance of the country –seem in the end to have been a wasted effort. There is poignant irony in the fact that a community committed broadly to non-violent Gandhian approach to politics, and which itself had been a victim of coups in the past, now endorses, however indirectly or tangentially, violence as an instrument of public policy in the desperate hope of a better outcome for itself. But one of the lessons learnt from history is that coups do not solve problems, they only compound them.

The Indo-Fijian community itself has changed almost beyond recognition in the last forty years. The self-contained, self-sustaining rural community built around the sugar industry is uprooted and adrift. The settlements in the cane areas which once hummed with life—local sports competitions, festivals and festivities—now look empty and forlorn. The land has ceased to be the sole source of livelihood for most families, including my own, that it once was. Villages are now essentially residential sites. There is a deep yearning among most young people still stranded in rural areas to leave for some place else. The rapid transformation of the rural scene is eroding a culture and a way of life which once formed the bedrock of Indo-Fijian society and provided a direct link to its foundational past. Cut from its cultural moorings, with declining support and sustenance from its roots, the community is vulnerable, much more at the mercy of forces of change beyond its control. It is, in truth, living on the sufferance of others. In the early 1970s, migration would have appeared a very distant prospect for most Indo-Fijians. It was something that only the wealthy and the well-connected might contemplate. It is a daily occurrence now, uppermost in the minds of most people, if not for themselves then certainly for their children. The community is emotionally uprooted. It is often said with some truth that there is hardly a single Indo-Fijian family in Fiji which does not have at least one member abroad. The emotional centre of gravity has shifted. Perhaps in time, 'From Immigration to Emigration' may become the dominant narrative in the overall experience of the Indo-Fijian community, its Fiji sojourn a momentary stopover in the life of a people condemned by fate to wander the world. By then, people of my generation would have moved on. In the words of John Dryden,

> *Not Heav'n itself upon the past*
> *Has pow'r*
> *But what has been has been, and I*
> *Have had my hour*

# Six

## Chance Hai
## On the hustings, 1999 and 2006

It has been a hard day on the campaign trail. We began early to reach the remote, rural sugarcane village of Daku in north Vanua Levu at around ten. The meandering road is a monstrosity, full of boulders and huge potholes as we bump along in a crowded jeep. Nothing much has changed in these parts since I left Labasa thirty years ago: the same sprawling cane fields now slowly creeping up the mountain slopes in the distance, rusting iron roof tops barely visible above the cane top, cows and goats grazing among overgrown grass by the roadside, men on cycles or horseback going about their business.

We arrive an hour later to find about a hundred men sitting on wooden benches in the school verandah, smoking, drinking yaqona, talking. These are simple rural folk, prematurely aged sons of the soil with furrowed sunburnt faces and skin cracked by excessive kava drinking. I grew up among them; I recognize some people in the crowd as my distant relatives whom I haven't seen for decades. They approach me, introduce themselves, and shake my hand with both of theirs as a gesture of respect. We move inside. People stub their cigarettes, have one last bowl of yaqona, clear their throats and follow us, sitting at their children's or grandchildren's desks.

The meeting starts with the party prayer about unity and peace. Then the speeches begin. The points have been well rehearsed and presented with practised ease. The party's strength and achievements are contrasted with the alleged weaknesses of the opponents.' Subtlety and truth, I quickly realize, are among the first casualties of an election campaign. The crowd is attentive and respectful and in awe of some of the candidates with big degrees from the land of the sahibs in subjects they have never heard of. Such as economics. Supporters of the opposing camp are at the back of the room listening intently, noting points they will refute and rubbish in their own meetings. Some of the older men watch the speakers with a wry smile; they have heard many such speeches full of fire and promise before.

Things have gone well, the candidates say over grog later. The planted questions—such are the tricks of the campaign trade—are fielded with flair. We leave the school for lunch around 3 at the home of the party's local branch president. Key supporters have also been invited. We sit on a *paal* (mat of stitched rough sack covers) on the cold cement verandah of the shop. The candidates seek advice, plant ideas, and promise to return. Families of opponents are identified and will be flooded with propaganda in the weeks ahead, cajoled and coerced into coming on board. Lunch, which we eat in a dimly lit kitchen, is delicious piping hot fish and free-ranging chicken curry. Women who have prepared the meal are behind the curtain in the adjacent room. Cultural protocol in rural areas even now demands that women maintain a discreet distance from strangers. A boy keeps piling our plates with food until we can eat no more. Such touching generosity, such loyalty to the party (or whatever).

We leave for another meeting in town on full stomach and fuller bladder. The thought of sitting through another set of thoroughly rehearsed speeches drains the spirit. The local candidate, recently retired from civil service and novice at politics, assures us of a good turn out. Only a dozen or so old men turn up. The speakers go through the tired routine. A local doctor, defeated in one of the previous elections, approaches me: he was my father's physician. Why wasn't he standing, I ask him. The voters are treacherous bastards, he says loudly. They will drink your yaqona, eat your pulau and vote for someone else. The doctor is drunk, embittered. Stand for elections? I can't even get this to stand, he says grabbing his crotch with both his hands, a cigarette dangling from his lips. I move on to mingle with others.

The meeting finishes around ten as we head for dinner at a candidate's place in a small rented and still incomplete ground flat in a nearby suburb. Yaqona is served, but I have had enough. Miraculously, a bottle of local gin appears. It is rough but effective—and much needed. People review the day and prepare for the next. There is much banter and relaxed idle talk. One candidate with poor English looks worried. When pressed, he turns to me and asks, 'Doc, tell us how to penetrate the women folk.' He was anxious about the absence of women from the rallies; hardly any had turned up at meetings that day. I gulp my drink and burst out laughing. Others join in, even the speaker after he realizes his *faux pas*. But he had intended a serious point. Women in rural are house-bound, often unlettered and unversed in matters beyond the family and the village, and completely dominated by men. Yet they will all vote—voting is compulsory—and each vote counts. But politics here is a man's game.

More meetings, more speeches, more irregular hours, more greasy food and bladder bursting marathon yaqona sessions, and endless cups of sweet syrupy tea in the days and weeks ahead. Each new audience will demand to see the candidates in person. No matter how exhausted, the candidates will dig deep, fake seriousness and make points they have made a thousand times before as if they were saying it for the first time. It is a gruelling experience like none other. I marvel at the madness as well as the majesty of democracy in action as I travel around the country. I feel strangely enthralled to see a new political culture emerging under a constitution based in large part on the report of the Fiji Constitution Review Commission, of which I was a member. Fiji is back in the Commonwealth and once more receptive to the principles of representative democracy and international human rights conventions. It is good to see the country moving in the right direction once again.

From coup to constitutionalism within a decade is not a journey many coup-scared nations have managed to undertake successfully. Fiji's political transformation is remarkable. So, too, is the transformation of its political leaders. Sitiveni Rabuka, the coup maker of 1987, is fighting the election alongside Jai Ram Reddy, the Indo-Fijian leader most hated by the supporters of the coup, seen as the evil genius behind Dr Bavadra's victory. Labour leader Mahendra Chaudhry's coalition partners include the Fijian Association Party whose candidate he had refused to support for Prime Minister in 1992, lending his numbers instead to Rabuka, whom Reddy had opposed. Fate, history and circumstance have combined to produce this strange permutation unimaginable only a few years ago.

Preparations for the elections begin soon after the promulgation of the constitution in July 1997. Twenty one parties and nearly three hundred candidates are vying for the 71 seats in parliament. But the main contest is between two coalitions, one led by the Labour Party under Mahendra Chaudhry and the other led by Sitiveni Rabuka and Jai Ram Reddy. The others are minor parties, ephemeral, some with such improbable, entertaining names as Multiracial Dynamic Party, Coin Party, the Party of Truth. Their presence frustrates the main players, but it is the way of the future. Democracy—once dubbed demon-crazy by nationalist Fijians—is alive and well in Fiji.

The campaign has a carnival atmosphere, free of the racial tensions and hostilities of the past. One candidate's approach captures the mood. He has written his campaign slogan in bold letters on a white cloth wrapped around a dozen cows grazing in scorching sun along the Queen's Highway. 'It's Time for a Change,' the slogan says. 'No Bull.' Poor cows! All major leaders are committed multiracialists, which has dampened extremist rhetoric. They have gone through a lot together in the constitution review, and the cross-cultural friendships are evident on the hustings. But inter-coalition rhetoric heats up as the campaign progresses.

Rabuka's record is ridiculed by his opponents who recite a long and dreary list of failed enterprises, scandals, abuse of office and arrogance of power. Labour has rehearsed its lines well: its message is sharp, focused, simple. Rabuka has to go, and with him his partner Reddy. Fijians regard the SVT leader as a man who has overreached his culturally-sanctioned authority and station: he is not duly deferential to his chiefs. Adding insult to chiefly injury, Rabuka, a commoner, claims achieved chiefly status for himself for his accomplishments, as his forebears did in pre-colonial Melanesian Fiji. Moralizing opponents point to the prime minister's rampant Bill Clinton-style philandering. A local newspaper headlines: 'I am not Kama Sutra, says Rabuka,' reporting an escapade that allegedly took place at the local golf course. The publication is timed for maximum embarrassment-- on Easter Friday. But Rabuka escapes serious electoral damage; bed-hopping is a common enough past time in Suva these days. A cabinet minister says to me only partly in jest, 'How come he gets all the luck!'

Criticism of Rabuka is relentless, unforgiving, hurtful. It is as if he is fair game. No other public figure in living memory has been so ridiculed. But some of the criticism is hypocritical. Christian Democratic Alliance leader, Poseci Bune, until recently a public servant and Fiji's Permanent Representative to the United Nations, accuses Rabuka of corruption, but he himself is the only Permanent Secretary so far to have been investigated for misuse of office. Other opponents, now self-styled champions of multiracialism—Viliame Gonelevu, Apisai Tora—are singled out by Rabuka as his coup-making associates, pricking their politically expedient balloons. Some cannot forgive Rabuka for his past sins, for staging the coup which he insists he did not carry out alone, and for which he asks forgiveness. He was the fall guy who refused to fall, he tells a meeting at the Girmit Centre in Lautoka. Others condemn him for embracing the creed of multiculturalism and betraying the aims of Fijian nationalism.

But if not Rabuka for prime minister then who, ask his supporters and the National Federation Party, which presents him to sceptical Indian audiences as the leader best equipped to take the country into the next millennium. By contrast, Fijian Association's Adi Kuini Bavadra, the re-married widow of the founding Labour leader Timoci Bavadra is unwell, untested and erratic. Apisai Tora is a serial, record-holding party swapper, having belonged to virtually every party in Fiji in a career spanning four decades; and Labour's intellectualising Tupeni Baba is new to politics and considered a lightweight. Rabuka stands above them all, his supporters argue: a transformed man, a true messiah of multiracialism.

Each party has prepared a manifesto, carried over the air and in the local dailies. But they are not taken seriously. These are things parties have to have, formalities of a campaign. Manifestos are forgotten the moment voting begins, a veteran politician says to me. Most voters, cynical through experience, agree. The real issue in rural areas are not about high principles but about roads, bridges, water supply, better hospitals, the price of bread, about how many times a politician has visited the area, attended funerals and marriages and donated to local charities. 'You cannot eat a constitution', a man says to me. 'Anyway, what has the constitution done for me,' he asks a candidate preaching its virtues. I know how he will vote.

The campaigns have changed in character over the last three decades. In the 1960s, major speeches were given at a few strategic places—in theatres, public parks and school compounds. They were grand affairs. Hired musicians sang specially composed songs extolling the party and its leaders. People travelled miles and waited for hours to listen to candidates. A rally was a major event in the village social calendar. But things have changed. Now, village pocket meetings and intense small group discussions with key individuals are the norm. What is said in these small gatherings, what propaganda and distortion go on, no one knows. Sometimes, major speeches are taped and distributed across the country, which is a godsend to novices who repeat them parrot-fashion without fully comprehending their content. Advertisements on air and on television have started, but the pocket meetings remain the major innovation and the prime focus.

Voters have become demanding. They are cynical about big promises, and no longer impressed by big names. They want to see people like themselves in parliament, not high-fee lawyers and smooth-talking political salesmen. 'Campaigning is a demeaning experience,' one candidate says to me. Voters have short memory, they are ignorant about larger issues, selfish and ungrateful. They seek the path of least resistance. In Labasa, people at a rally demand food and drink. One of the dailies reported them as saying 'If they cannot provide refreshment now like other parties are doing, then what will they give us when we vote them into parliament.' Voters can be deceptive as well. A Labour strategist tells his supporters to pluck coconuts (Labour symbol) by climbing the branches of the mango tree (Federation symbol). Translation: drink your opponents' yaqona, eat their food, go through their sheds but vote for Labour. It is effective advice, as many candidates later discover to their cost. Demeaning it might be for candidates, but voters are smarter than most people think.

Campaigns are serious business, but they are also about theatre. People want information as well as entertainment. Politicians know this, and the good ones are good actors. In the Yasawas, a predominantly Fijian constituency, Ratu Eteuate Tavai describes the mercurial character of his opponent Apisai Tora by invoking the image of cooking roti—Indian leavened bread. First you flip the bread on one side, then the other. Flip flop, flip flop: that was Tora. The audience roars with laughter; there is no need after that to say more about Tora's party. In Nadi, a candidate talks animatedly about all the things his party would do for the people if he got elected. He would get schools and hospitals built, scholarships for school children arranged, roads repaired, bridges built. All this is too much for a man who has heard big promises before. 'Bhaiya [brother], what's the use of a bridge when we have no river here?' he asks. The candidate says without blinking, 'Well, in that case, I will have a river dug up as well.'

At a meeting in Ba, a candidate is grilled about his credentials to stand in the constituency. 'You are from Labasa, your family lives in Australia, you work in Suva, and you are standing from Ba?' a man asks. A fair point. The candidate, quick thinking, points to a prayer pole flying a red pennant. He asks the questioner if he believed in God. 'Yes' came the reply. 'Have you ever seen Him?' 'No.' 'But you believe that God hears your prayers and answers your needs?' 'Certainly.' The candidate closes the trap. 'That is exactly right,' he says. 'I am like that. You may not see me here but like God the Invisible, I will be looking after you where it really counts, in the corridors of parliament.' Ripples of laughter sweep the crowd, drowning the larger point about representation and constituency accountability. In Lautoka, a candidate is attacking the leader of the opposing party for being too consistent and inflexible. Consistency, the man says, is not always a virtue. 'Politics is like fishing. If you fail to catch anything here, you pull up your anchor and move to some place else. You keep shifting your anchor until you get what you want.' The audience is rapt until an old man at the back pipes up, 'How would you know, *beta* [son]. You don't have any anchor at all.' Such repartee.

Humour is a great campaign weapon, but it has to be used judiciously. It should not be used to debase debate or detract from the credibility of the candidate. Voters expect their candidates to be serious, to use sharp language when the occasion demands it. Name calling, character assassination, taunts, jibes all provide spicy grist for the rhetorical mill on the hustings. Usually, religion and culture and ethnicity are left alone; some things are still taboo in public. But people have found ways around them, especially in small pocket meetings with like-minded people. 'Why another when you have your own' is a code word to vote for a candidate who belongs to your sub-cultural or religious or ethnic group. It is a repeat of the campaign strategies of the 1950s which the Fiji-born used to keep people like AD Patel out of the Legislative Council.

Fijian and Indo-Fijian campaign styles differ, which sometimes causes friction and confusion in the open seats. Fijian campaigns are a formal affair. Meetings are usually planned for late mid-morning. By then many a bowl of yaqona has been drunk. Chiefs and other prominent people sit apart, at the head of the gathering. The conversation is subdued, punctured by occasional thigh-slapping laughter. When the speakers arrive, there is a hush, a slight shuffle of feet. Formal ceremonies invoking ancestral spirits and establishing clan genealogies, welcome them to the occasion. Yaqona flows, hands are clapped and speeches begin. The points are made in broad terms, the attacks on the Fijian opponents indirect so as not to offend their vanua. Voice is not raised: to speak loudly is un-chiefly behaviour. So while not much may be said, much is conveyed and discussed over numerous tanoa of yaqona late into the evening.

Indo-Fijian campaigns are influenced by the individualistic lifestyle of the community, and a long tradition of robust democratic debate. Meetings are full of personal attacks and aggressive verbal jousting. People expect—and get— rousing, fiery rhetoric. Couplets from the scriptures and snippets of folk wisdom are used to underline points or close an argument. Much yaqona is drunk, but without ceremony or solemnity. Mixed Fijian—Indian meetings are restrained, good diplomacy triumphing over good argument. Sensitive issues are avoided or raised indirectly. Indians are concerned about the imminent expiry of leases on which generations of their families have grown. Fijian speakers assure them that everything will be resolved through dialogue and discussion. Precisely how and when is left alone. Indo-Fijians oppose plans to convert state land to native land. Fijians welcome the move for it was after all their land before the Europeans came. For Indo-Fijians state land is state property, to be used for the benefit of all, especially to re-settle displaced tenants. The divisions are smoothed by talk of racial tolerance, mutual understanding and national unity.

Fijians have long used regional, provincial and confederacy ties for political purposes to mobilize support or raise funds during elections. Indeed, the constitution provides for the election of twenty three Fijians from the provinces. Provincial sentiments, attachments, loyalties and connections are all effective campaign assets. Ties of blood and kinship matter. People of Lau say openly that they will vote only for the candidates loyal to the Tui Nayau household. That is why the otherwise liked and effective parliamentarian Viliame Cavuibati lost to novice Adi Koila Mara Nailatikau. Parties seek the blessings of leading chiefs in their provinces even though their actual influence has been diminishing in recent years.

Among Ind0-Fijians, cultural and social divisions are not institutionalized. The indenture experience destroyed caste as the principle of social relationships. Caste was replaced by other categories of differentiation, such as religion (Hindu, Muslim, Arya Samaj, Sanatan, Shia and Sunni), and regional origins of the migrants in India (Gujarati, Panjabi, North Indian, South Indian). It was not good form to manipulate these divisions for political purposes openly, but the selection of candidates often reflected the composition of Indo-Fijian society. In this election, however, culture and religion are exploited as never before. The NFP is a party of the South Indians, Labour rallies are told. It is time to have a North Indian as leader of the community, which it is said, has always been led by outsiders: AD Patel, a Gujarati, Siddiq Koya, a Muslim, Reddy a Madrasi. It was time for a North Indian leader now. And that leader is Mahendra Chaudhry. I have no doubt that other groups use similar tactics to bolster support for candidates belonging to their communities. The tactic may have won a few votes, but at the expense of divisions which will take a generation to heal.

Parties pitch candidates from the same cultural community against each other wherever there is a large presence of a particular group. You cut steel with steel, a party strategist tells me. It is as simple as that. Some have it both ways, like a North Indian candidate in Nadi who is married to a South Indian woman: a *bhaiya* among North Indians and a, *Anna* among the Southerners. In Tavua, a Muslim Labour candidate is popular in the electorate. A sitting parliamentarian, a good community worker, he would be hard to dislodge. He goes to funerals and attends *Ramayana* recitals, where he makes small donations, as is appropriate to do. Ten dollar bills are common. He is winning friends. Some Hindus in the rival camp attempt to neutralize his appeal by concocting a totally false, malicious story. They told me this themselves. This Muslim candidate, they tell people, is laughing behind their backs, telling Muslims how cheap the Sanatanis were, their votes bought for just ten dollars. But justice prevailed; the Muslim candidate won by a landslide.

Rumour, innuendo, outright fabrications, unfounded assertions transformed into unassailable facts right before your eyes, deliberate deception, cutting corners and shading the truth, are all a feature of this campaign. Politics without principles is the sixth sin, Jai Ram Reddy says over and over again, quoting Mahatma Gandhi, frustrated that his message is neutralized by the opposition. But many even in his own party do not share this view. For them, politics is not about morality and principles, it is about winning. One candidate who studied the history of the Third Reich at university tells me of Goebbels's advice about a lie repeated a thousand times acquiring an aura of truth. He is practising it in this campaign. It's all politics, he tells me nonchalantly.

Voting is compulsory in Fiji, which annoys some and confuses others. There is a $50 fine for not voting. A man turns up at a meeting brandishing a fresh $50 note from the bank, saying that he would rather pay the fine than vote for the party in government. 'Why,' the candidate asks, perplexed. 'Because this government has not done anything for the people: the roads are bad, there is no piped water, no electricity,' the man replies. The candidate says 'Why waste money, why not vote for another party?' 'Can I do that?' he asks. Another man asked his wife which party she would vote for. The one whose symbol is the tree, she says. The man thinks she would vote for the coconut tree, Labour symbol. But he wanted to be sure, so he returned after a few minutes and asked her which tree. 'The mango tree, of course,' she replied, for the NFP. The man said he would rather pay the fine than 'allow' his wife to vote for the 'wrong party.'

Candidates have their own ears and eyes in the electorate, friends, confidants, hangers-on. Their influence varies depending on their proximity to the candidate. They make contacts, devise strategy, raise funds, act as sounding board. Some are prominent people in the community, either retired or of independent means, who accompany the candidates and party leaders to meetings. These advisers are a curious breed. Some are of course genuine but many desire public recognition and social prestige. They have their own interests. If their party wins, they will make their move, asking to be nominated to statutory bodies, endorsed for municipal council elections, appointed to rural advisory committees, selected as justices of peace and, in a few more ambitious cases, appointed to the Senate. There are agendas within agendas, personal ambitions carefully camouflaged behind party interests and platforms.

At long last, the campaign is coming to an end. The candidates are exhausted, hoarse. The early enthusiasm has given way to cynicism about people and politics, about the frustration of reducing everything to the lowest common denominator, about having to counteract mischievous lies spread about by their opponents. It is always the other side, never one's own, which is trimming the truth, spreading malicious rumours. Campaigning together under intense pressure, and with so much at stake, has produced friction, criticism and disenchantment among candidates. The newcomers have been sizing each other up, forging alliances, assessing their future prospects and mapping out a route to rise to the top. But in a few rare instances, the campaign has also enhanced respect created friendships which will endure after the dust has settled.

The initial enthusiasm for the coalition arrangement has waned; campaign styles clash, tempers are frayed and disappointment aired to anyone who will listen. In Nadi, an Indo-Fijian open seat candidate complains bitterly about not being able to have direct access to the Fijian voters. She does not know how her Fijian voters view her. Her only contact is indirect, through a chiefly intermediary, a yaqona crazed man who assures her that all the votes are in the bag. He was wrong. 'I wish we were not in coalition with these fellows,' she says with resigned anger, but it is too late. Throughout Viti Levu, Indo-Fijian candidates and parties are complaining about how Fijians have approached the campaign. The NFP feels that the SVT is not pulling its weight behind the coalition, and Labour is bitter about Apisai Tora. 'Everything is set,' a Fijian campaigner tells a clearly anxious Indian candidate, which makes him panic even more. There is urgency, anxiety and the desire to make the last minute effort on the one side, and a relaxed, she- will- be- alright, we- will- get- there attitude on the other. There are reports of landlords threatening their tenants. In Sabeto, one threatens her Indo-Fijian tenants with eviction if they do not go through her shed and vote for her party. The tenants go through her shed alright, but vote Labour whose candidate defeats the party leader Tora. It is treachery, you might say, but it is sweet treachery: the revenge of the weak and helpless against the threats of the rich and powerful.

The last few days of the campaign are like the last leg of writing a thesis. All the ideas have been canvassed, research completed, points made. It is now about getting the niggly details right, the footnotes checked, the glossary prepared. It is the same with campaigns. In the last week, thought shifts from speeches to practicalities of getting voters to the booth. Sheds have to be erected, trusted people hired to man the polling booths, scan the rolls and issue registration numbers to voters. Food has to be prepared for the campaign workers. Usually it is vegetable pulau and tomato chutney, neutral fare for both Hindus and Muslims. Vehicles have to be hired and reliable drivers secured to get the voters. When voting was made compulsory, party leaders hoped that they would not have to get people to the polling booth, but in reality, things do not work that way. Voters are used to being transported to the booths, and they will have it no other way. Nothing can be done about this: the voter owns the vote. Names of people who have already voted are crossed out, vehicles sent to new locations. Party workers look anxiously at each others' sheds to estimate the size of the crowd to see how well they are doing. Rough and ready estimates float around. 'It is fifty-fifty around here,' people say, it is touch and go. That means it is desperation time.

Voting is spread over a long and exhausting week full of confusion, anxiety, doubt, fluctuating fortunes. Candidates watch and wait—and await the peoples' verdict. It is a sight to see: a politician, helpless, lost for words, waiting. Some glow with optimism, some know they are gone, most are on auto-pilot. Long queues form outside the polling booths, people waiting for hours in the scorching sun as counting officials deal with administrative cock-ups. In a few hours the candidates will know whether they will go to parliament or rue their loss and await another turn five years away, or leave politics altogether.

I carry with me a collage of images, a cacophony of speeches and a blur of faces as I leave the campaign trail. As I write this in my wintry Canberra office, I recall the sight and smell of simple food cooked in huge aluminium pots on open fires. I remember a candidate offering me sumptuous pulau and apologizing for lack of chairs and tables, saying 'Doc, please don't mind. Eat like a scavenger. After all we live like scavengers.' His own prosperity was protruding prominently. I remember a jovial rolly-polly chief in Nadroga welcoming me in Hindi, asking one of the men to serve me yaqona. *Chalao sale ke,* serve the bugger (the drink, not me!), *talo mada. Ham hiyan ke raja baitho,* he says to much laughter and applause. I am the king of this place. I remember a toothless almost blind Fijian man in Nabila welcoming Jai Ram Reddy with old farcical songs in Hindi and Tamil, accompanied by an Indian man making *dhamak, dhamak* drumming music with his mouth. I have never seen Jai Ram laugh so heartily as he did that day. I remember a man in Tau approaching him crouching in respect, saying *Prabhu ke Jai,*' 'Hail to the Lord! I remember a young Fijian man with Rastafarian gait and matted hair wearing a tee-shirt proclaiming a hand written slogan: '1999 General Erection.' I remember a candidate praising Sitiveni Rabuka as a well trained draught bull who did not need to be broken, unlike his opponents. I remember...

I rejoice at the triumph of democracy in Fiji, despite all the tensions and frustrations and misunderstandings and mis-communications. I celebrate the majesty and the madness, the mayhem and the method, of democracy at work. I leave Fiji elated and grateful to be present at a decisive moments in its history.

**Campaign 2006**
Balata, Dabota, Tagi Tagi, Garampani: these are distant, even vaguely exotic, names to this Labasa-born lad. They are, in fact, names of hauntingly beautiful places, evoking the sight, sound and smell of growing up in a rural settlement more than half a century ago. The same sprawling, rippling sea of cane fields, people going about their business on horseback or bicycle, weather-beaten faces of sons of the soil, their leathery skin cracked by excessive kava drinking. People show hospitality and humanity rural folk everywhere will recognize instantly. A hot cup of tea materializes quickly even in the poorest of homes, along with the invitation to stay over for a meal. These touching gestures remain with you long after you are gone.

I am travelling through western Viti Levu, trying to get some sense of what rural folk think about the election, the stories they might have to tell of what they have seen or heard. Everywhere I am greeted with respect and affection, even, or especially, by those who think mistakenly I am with the enemy, meaning the National Federation Party. At least you haven't become independent, one man says with a chuckle, a not too subtle reference to those, unable to secure a party ticket, who are standing as independents for one excuse or another. Astoundingly, in this election, the number of independents is over sixty. What impact they will have on the final outcome is causing concern to party strategists. (None, as it turned out in the end).

In rural areas, the normal rhythm of life continues largely undisturbed by what is happening in the country at large. A few pocket meetings here and there, the occasional talk by a visiting politician or the local candidate, but little more than that. In urban areas, it is a different story. There, the campaign in its early stages is full of talk of betrayal and treacherous preferencing, about intimidation and fear and vote rigging. Both the SDL and Labour accuse NFP of reneging on preference deals, which the NFP vehemently denies but not to any great effect. The party recognizes its minority status, a far cry from its glorious days when it was the major party of the Indo-Fijian community. It gives its first preferences to Labour in predominantly Indo-Fijian areas and to the SDL in several winnable open seats in south-eastern Viti Levu. Labour accuses NFP sarcastically of not knowing whether it was 'Arthur or Martha,' that is, whether it was a party of and for the Indo-Fijians first and foremost or whether it had a multi-ethnic identity and aspirations, while the SDL uses NFP's preference distribution to rally the Fijians behind it, telling them that both NFP and FLP were secretly consolidating Indo-Fijian support between them and that Fijians should do the same under its broad umbrella. Divide and rule is the name of the game, and all the parties know it: unite your own ethnic constituency and divide enough of your opponents to win. I find the charge of betrayal hollow.

I listen to the radio, religiously watch the evening news on television, buy and read all the newspapers. There are so many issues lurking in the background that desperately need to be discussed, but they aren't. It is as if everyone is avoiding hard, controversial topics in the campaign. The Reconciliation Truth and Unity Bill is one of them. The government says it wants to use the Bill to bring closure to the painful events of 2000, but its opponents see it as a barely veiled attempt to grant amnesty to the coup plotters whose support SDL needs especially among the nationalist sections of the Fijian community. The fact that some (notably former vice President Ratu Jope Seniloli) are released from prison on Compulsory Supervision Order raises doubts and nurtures suspicion about the government's true motives. There is massive objection to the Bill from community and non-government organizations. Petitions are sent in the hundreds and protest marches are organized, reminding me of the 'Back to May' movement against the May coup in 1987. The Fiji Military Forces commander, Fran Bainimarama, thunders ominously that the Bill will simply 'not happen.'

To emphasize his point and to remind the country of his authority, he joins five hundred of his fully armed men on a march through Suva the day parliament is dissolved. Bainimarama is angry, he says privately, because the government is not really in charge and the country is being run by two unelected men: Jioji Kotabalavu, the chief executive officer of the prime minister's office, and Senator Qoriniasi Bale, the Attorney General.

The country is deeply divided over the rift between the military and the government. There are some who applaud Bainimarama's tough, no-nonsense approach. Labour Party president, Jokapeci Koroi, asked on television about her views on the army's confrontational attitude to the government, says that she would have no qualms about the army overthrowing the Qarase government and putting Labour back in power to continue its 'unfinished business.' I am astounded by the utter brazenness of the statement from the head of a party which itself had been victim of the army's intervention in 1987. Later, seeking to deflect the issue, she says she was quoted out of context, but I have seen the interview with my own eyes, and she was not mis-quoted. The government calls for her resignation, but the matter is not followed through. As the campaign progress, the issue quietly slips away. In many places, I hear Indo-Fijians actually supporting the army's stance. As one person tells me, in Hindi, 'We will take aim at them [meaning the SDL] by placing the gun on the shoulders of the soldiers.' 'You need steel to cut steel,' another says to me in a tone that I find somewhat disturbing. 'The army is with us,' Labour tells the electorate. There will be no coup. Don't be afraid. Vote for us without fear.' The message is repeated in pocket meeting after pocket meeting. It is effective in rallying wavering supporters to the party in the dying days of the campaign.

On the Fijian side, there is genuine discomfort about the army's increasingly confronting statements. Many feel the army is overstepping its constitutionally defined role. In newspaper advertisements and on radio and television, Laisenia Qarase makes this point repeatedly. He wants the Supreme Court to rule on the proper constitutional position of the army in a Westminster type democracy. There are some who are calling for the government to discipline the commander and cannot fathom the government's reluctance to move. But there is confusion about the proper procedure for this to happen. On the eve of the elections, the widely-admired Vice President, Ratu Joni Madraiwiwi, a high chief in his own right, convenes a meeting between Qarase and Bainimarama to cool the temperature of the public spat between them. A vaguely worded accord is negotiated, and there is a palpable sigh of relief in the country, hedged in by a foreboding sense that things could go wrong at any time. As the campaign concludes, the army's strident intervention in the public arena has pushed many

Fijians to the SDL's side. Ironically, the army has achieved a result it wanted to prevent in the first place: SDL's increased popularity among Fijians.

In a radio interview, I am asked about the army's antics. My view is clear, and directly opposite to the military's which sees an increased role for itself in the public life of Fiji. 'It is better to prevent the mess at the outset,' one officer tells me, 'than to be called in to clean it up after the event.' Pakistan is cited as a model. I don't think it is the army's role to interpret the public's will, I say. Its role should be to enforce the public will, not to interpret or pre-empt it. My words are published in the papers and for a brief moment, I wonder whether I should be so incautious in my public statements. 'Watch out, doc,' a Fijian nationalist candidate says to me at the Dolphins in Suva, slapping me playfully on the shoulder. But for a brief moment only: I have to be truthful to my convictions.

Another issue burning in the background is the expiry of agricultural leases under the Agricultural Landlord and Tenant Act. The leases began expiring in the late 1990s. Now there are thousands of farmers whose leases have not been renewed, who are uprooted and beginning new careers as casual labourers, small vegetable growers and domestic hands, crowding the already clotted Suva-Nausori corridor. I am told that in the Nasinu constituency contested by Labour's Labasa-born Krishna Datt, fully 40 per cent of the voters are displaced Labasans. There is quiet resentment against them, resentment about their industry and enterprising spirit, their preparedness to work for any wage. 'This place stinks of Vanua Levu,' a taxi driver tells me, as we drive from Kinoya to Tacirua via the Khalsa road, not knowing that I, too, am from the Friendly North. There is intense competition for the squatter vote. But about a major cause of that problem, the expiry of leases, nothing much is said. SDL wants to renew the leases under the Native Land and Tenant Act which gives the landowner more say and greater flexibility on the renewal of leases, while Labour prefers the Agricultural Landlord and Tenant Act whose tenant-favouring 'hardship clause' places greater onus on the landowner to prove that his need to reoccupy his land is greater than the tenant's.

The National Federation Party proposes the concept of a 'Master Lease' under which the government would lease land from the landlords under the provisions of NLTA and then lease them to the tenants under the terms of ALTA. The idea was first proposed by Jai Ram Reddy and Wadan Narsey in the late 1990s, but it goes nowhere in this campaign. People are reluctant to engage with ideas and alternatives seriously, I begin to realize, preferring instead the comfort of the simple slogans. As I travel through the countryside, I see displaced tenants by the roadside selling root crops, vegetables and fish. The look on their sun-bathed, anguished, furrowed faces, touches the heart. Through no fault of their own, they have become refugees in their own homeland. I see formerly productive

*Chance Hai: On the hustings, 1999 and 2006*

cane fields slowly reverting to bush. A Fijian farmer, deep in the heartland of Viti Levu, tells me about the situation in his area. Many leases were not renewed and tenants had to move to the town. 'NLTA or Calcutta,' some village wit had remarked. But after a few years, the land owners realized their error and the absence of income that lease rents brought, and pleaded with the former tenants to return. Most refused.

The land issue is closely tied to the uncertain fortunes of the country's ailing sugar industry. The preferential access to the European Union markets will soon expire, forcing Fiji to sell sugar on an internationally competitive market. The sugar mills function on ancient machines habitually prone to repeated breakdowns. The increasing cost of transporting cane to the mills and of hiring labourers is being felt by the growers. The uncertainty of renewal of leases creates its own problems. The government has talked about re-structuring the sugar industry, following advice of an Indian team of experts, but its precise details are not spelled out. Strangely, it is not an issue in this campaign. Just as certain as night will follow day, Labour will oppose any solution proposed by the SDL. The reason: Politics. Keep politics out of the industry, people say, but that is naïve. Politics drives the sugar industry, always has. Mahendra Chaudhry's power base is in the cane belt; and he is the general secretary of the National Farmers Union. Farmers are slowly, visibly, descending into poverty, while their leaders play politics and manoeuvre for political advantage, like vultures hovering eagerly over a mortally wounded animal.

Every major party has prepared a manifesto, a grab-bag of ideas and proposals about how they will address the social and economic problems facing Fiji. These are attractive documents, professionally produced, accessibly written and widely distributed. Though there are vernacular versions as well the main one is in English. But these are for show really. Many candidates, with poor English, wave it furiously before their audiences, with all the pretended passion they can muster, urging them to read it when they themselves are innocent of its contents! Prepared speeches, rehearsed several times over, is the standard campaign fare. Politicians glibly tell people what they want to, not what they ought, to hear. But manifestoes have to be launched, a politician tells me, because without it, people would not take the party seriously. The ones loudest in their demands for manifestoes are those who don't read, a candidate says to me slightly cynically. Complex ideas are reduced to laughter-inducing slogans. Voters want entertainment as well as (some), enlightenment.

The method of campaigning in Fiji has changed dramatically over the years. When I first began writing about elections in the early 1980s, large rallies were the order of the day. People travelled miles to listen to speeches. There was no television in Fiji then, and the video revolution was just beginning. So people turned up for rallies because these were a major item in their limited social calendar. By the late 1980s, cassettes began to be mass produced, carrying the party's ideas into distant rural areas where people could listen to their leaders, while sitting around the tanoa. Sakiasi Butadroka, the fiery Fijian nationalist, was among the first to use this medium. By the 1990s, 'pocket' meetings came to prominence, used very effectively by the FLP. And with good reason too. Labour's organizational machinery, well-oiled and functioning efficiently, reached out to the grassroots. A handful of diehard supporters in each constituency were briefed –brainwashed may be a better word—to carry on the party propaganda while the candidate moved elsewhere. In the late 1990s, video cassettes were used, especially by the NFP to carry party leader Jai Ram Reddy's message on the constitution, but that trend did not catch on.

More recently, radio and television debates, phone-in programs, live interviews, and especially advertising on television, have come to dominate election campaign. SDL led the way in 2006, with slick advertisements—the white dove, the party's symbol, flying majestically against a navy blue background—reminding the people of all it had achieved in the last five years and asking them not to jeopardize their future by voting for other parties. Labour focused on the real and alleged failures of the SDL government, highlighting the problems of poor water supply, unemployment and increased cost of living. Its advertisements, featuring despairing down-and-out people needing food, shelter and clean water, were pointed and hard-hitting in the characteristically Labour style. The NFP, strapped for funds, dusted up its 2001 campaign video for the 2006 election, screening exactly the same images but with a changed voice over. No one noticed, which caused some bemused puzzlement among party leaders! The National Alliance launched a surprisingly well-funded media campaign, highlighting its connection to the legendary lights of the Fijian establishment: Ratu Sukuna, Ratu Edward Cakobau, Ratu George Cakobau, and Ratu Mara, with a gently smiling party leader Ratu Epeli Ganilau, holding up a lighted torch, marching towards a rising dawn. Slickly packaged television campaigns will be the order of the day in the future.

Campaign styles vary. Among Fijians, especially in rural areas, there is an acute awareness of cultural protocols governing public discourse. Voice is not raised and insulting language avoided. Un-chiefly conduct is frowned upon. I vividly recall a National Alliance meeting at Syria Park in Nausori. I was invited to the meeting. Ratu Epeli arrived in a new, rented four while drive. Making a good impression is important. About two dozen people, mostly Fijian women from the neighbouring hinterland, are seated in a temporary corrugated iron shelter. At the appointed time, Ratu Epeli enters the speaker's shelter with his chiefly wife. They are seated on two elegant chairs in the shed facing the audience. Ratu Epeli is introduced. He reads a prepared speech, some of it in English. He is a dignified man, chiefly, well spoken but wooden. He is critical about the SDL's policies, but never once does he directly attack the party or its leader. He is talking about the need for the various ethnic groups to work together. He eschews racial politics. He talks about Fiji as a multiracial family. He is against racial discrimination in any form, including reserved affirmative action for Fijians. People clap politely when he finishes. Yaqona is served in the traditional Fijian way. He mingles with the crowd rather awkwardly. Style and status count as much as the substance of the speech. Snippets appear on the evening news and in the following day's papers.

After Ratu Epeli finishes, he asks me whether I might like to say a word or two. This catches me by complete surprise; I am unprepared. I realize quickly that Ratu Epeli is not inviting me, he is actually asking me to speak in the traditional chiefly way. What to say? I begin with something I had read in the papers recently with some politician saying that racially-polarised politics were inevitable, necessary even, because Fijians and Indo-Fijians could not, could never, work together. History was proof enough of that. I said in response that our history showed the contrary to be the case. Fiji had encountered seemingly intractable problems in its recent history, but our leaders had been able to resolve deep-seated problems through discussion and dialogue. Independence was a contested issue, but it was eventually achieved amicably. Our leaders were able to work together to devise ALTA which had brought decades of prosperity to the country. Again, after the coups of 1987, they were able to retrieve the country from the brink of precipice and conflagration. In the 1990s, Jai Ram Reddy and Sitiveni Rabuka, once bitter foes—Reddy was, after all, the chief target of the Taukei Movement in 1987: 'Reddy the Gun, Bavadra the Bullet', the placards had proclaimed—had been able to join hands to give the country the best constitution it ever had. We can work together, I said.

The Prime Minister was telling his campaign audiences that Fijians were not ready for a non-indigenous prime minister. And some were suggesting that the constitution should be changed to reflect the Fijian wish for the country to be led by Fijians. I said that I myself did not have a problem with a Fijian leader of government, provided that arrangement was the outcome of a political negotiation rather than a constitutional requirement. If race were further entrenched in the constitution, specifically the requirement that the prime minister should be a Fijian, we will once again court international sanctions. We will be expelled from the Commonwealth and strain our relations with our neighbours. With the population trend favouring Fijians—they would be about two thirds of the population in a decade or so—it was likely that a Fijian would always head government. Repeating my oft-spoken words, I said that this preoccupation with race was a prescription for political paralysis.

My words, echoing the sentiment Ratu Epeli had aired a few minutes earlier, received a warm response. He shook my hands in appreciation, and the women sitting in the shed clapped gently. I was moved, but wondered how much of what I had said was understood by the audience, for I had spoken in English. How I wished then that I could speak fluent Fijian, rather than communicating with my fellow countrymen in a language that none of us owned or was truly comfortable with.

A week or so after the Nausori meeting, I attended a NFP rally in Suva. I had gone there to observe the proceedings and to catch up with old friends. I was a bit late and sat at the back of the room. Much to my surprise, the chairman announced my arrival to the audience and said, without my permission, that I would be speaking towards the end of the meeting! The speakers were full of fire and with a bagful of ideas about how to resolve the problems facing the country. Labour's strategies of 'boycott and high court' (someone mischievously added paraquat) was derided to quiet applause. In other meetings, as the campaign heated up, the rhetoric got hotter and more personal. Indo-Fijian audiences love chest-thumping, *masala,* talk.

After the last speaker had finished, I was invited to the front, still unclear in my mind about what to say. Then, all of a sudden, I remembered something I had read—or was told. In one of the meetings a year or two back, Mahendra Chaudhry had said that NFP stood for 'Not Fit for Parliament.' I began by reminding the audience that NFP had, in fact, played a very large role in Fiji's recent history. I asked the audience to name four of the most important achievements of Fiji in the last half a century. People look blankly. They are not used to this kind of interactive meeting. Achievement of independence, I said was one. People nod in agreement. The Denning Award of 1969 which led to the departure of the colonial Sugar Refining Company and brought prosperity to the sugar industry was another. People are listening intently now. The successful negotiation of the Agricultural Landlord and Tenant Bill after independence was also a milestone achievement. And finally, I asked people not to forget the promulgation of the 1997 constitution, a momentous achievement considering the circumstances prevailing in the 1990s. I then make two concluding points. In all these four achievements of national importance, the NFP had played a key role: that was a matter of historical record and no trimming of the truth could alter that fact. And second, I say that these achievements came about as a result of dialogue and discussion, patient negotiation and sensitive appreciation of the fears and aspirations of Fiji's different communities. People clap warmly as I sit down. I hadn't said anything terribly profound, but I realize as I ponder the event later that our people, even political leaders, have a poor understanding of history, even the recent history of their own party.

The NFP puts on a brave face, but even the most optimistic assessment by party insiders gives them just a handful of seats, anywhere between three and eight. They can't be kings, its leaders realize, but they could be king makers by distributing their preferences wisely and perhaps, as a bonus, get a senate seat or two. Its most critical handicap in this election is that there is no clear, and in the public's mind clearly identifiable, leader, the face of the party. Attar Singh, Pramod Rae and Raman Singh take turns to represent the party in various forums, but that only serves to compounds the problem. On this front, Labour has a considerable advantage. Mahendra Chaudhry is the public face of the party, its brand name. For many, Chaudhry is the Labour Party.

In the Fijian electorate, Laisenia Qarase enjoys a similar advantage. He is no longer the shy, awkward campaigner of 2001, unsure of himself and dependent on others for advice. In 2006, he is relaxed, confident, skilled at public speaking, engaging. He is the undisputed leader of the SDL which he had over the course of five years built into a cohesive, well-oiled fighting machine. His most prominent Fijian challenger, Ratu Epeli Ganilau, is also a well known name from a distinguished family, but his base is limited and his platform of multiracialism drowned out by the politics of racial polarization. Qarase's advocacy of race-based affirmative action policy and his frequently-aired view that Fijians must continue to lead the country fall on receptive ears. The fear of Chaudhry returning to lead pushes many Fijians into the SDL camp. 'Do you want Mr Chaudhry to lead this country?' Qarase asks his audiences repeatedly, and the response always is a thunderous 'No.' A Fijian taxi driver tells me that he admires Chaudhry for his courage, but he does not trust him. To him, the Labour leader is politically too smart for his opponents, he always has something up his sleeve. He was not alone in thinking that.

Personalities certainly matter, but both SDL and Labour have done their homework. Qarase has made sure that in his policies and programs, no province is left out. The provincial link is assiduously cultivated, and the party's network reaches deep into the Fijian hinterland. The SDL is not officially endorsed by the Great Council of Chiefs as the SVT was in the 1990s, but people know that its blessing is with it. Any opportunity to 'explain' the government's policies—the Reconciliation Bill, for example—to the provinces is seized to strengthen the party's connection with the grassroots, reminding them of what the government had accomplished. With the disestablishment of the Christian Alliance Matanitu Vanua Party, SDL became the umbrella party of the Fijian community. The SVT in 2001 is a ghost of its former self, fielding only one candidate, that too an Indo-Fijian! Like the SDL, Labour's machinery is strong. The National Farmers Union, the Fiji Public Service Association, the Fiji Teachers Union, are all identified with Labour. Parliamentarians are regularly required to keep in close touch with their constituents. Chaudhry himself sets the example which others can ignore only at their peril.

Voters have become more sophisticated over the years. Now, they are keenly aware of the power they have in their hands. They know that they own the vote. They expect the candidates to come to them, to sit down with them, serve them kava and cigarettes, attend their marriage and funeral functions. They expect to be picked up from their homes and transported to the polling booth—at a time convenient to themselves. Candidates from all political parties complain about the expense incurred in entertaining voters. Many say that they have spent more than $10,000 of their own money during the campaign, most of it on providing kava. I am amazed at how much kava is drunk these days. Any excuse to mix a bowl. A party worker tells me that in his constituency, meetings go well into the night. That's good, I say, thinking that people really engaged with the campaign. 'No, Doc, nothing like that. They want long meetings so that can drink more free grog.' In Fijian meetings I observe, yaqona is drunk, but protocol and rank are recognized. The spirit of the vanua is honoured and outsiders are formally welcomed. But among Indo-Fijians, it is consumed in copious amounts, without decorum or dignity. Excessive yaqona drinking among Indo-Fijian men is a major cause of domestic problems and extramarital affairs, which sometimes end in tragedy. The sad thing is that yaqona drinking is becoming increasingly popular among younger people.

Politicians try hard to meet their public obligations, but sometimes things go wrong. A man tells me that when his wife died in a tragic fire accident, the politician representing his constituency felt obliged to make an appearance. He walks up to the bereaved husband, and asks him if he knew who the dead woman was! The man decided there and then not to vote for that parliamentarian ever again. Another candidate told me that when she visited one particular household, an elderly lady told her that she would vote for her provided she increased her monthly allowance. She was honest enough to say that she would try but could not promise. The old woman abruptly shut the door on her. The changing voter behaviour, at least in the Indo-Fijian community, is producing a new kind politician, one who is attentive to the needs of his constituency almost to the exclusion of any other consideration, who spends most of his time and energy mixing with members of his constituency, ministering to their personal needs. Whether he would make a good parliamentarian and legislator capable of handling complex national policy issues is sadly a secondary matter.

I encounter a range of opinion as I travel the countryside. Most talks are depressing: non-renewal of leases, unemployment, discrimination in the public sector, people waiting hopefully for their children to emigrate so that they too could go. But there are light moments as well. Without humour, it would be difficult to cope, I realize. A middle-aged man in Tavua town assures me over a bowl of grog that there has been real progress in Fiji since 1987. Progress? How? 'Look, Doc,' the man says, 'in 1987, our government lasted one month, in 2000 it lasted one year. Next time, it will last two years, no?' A thigh-slapping laugh follows. 'Let's hope it lasts much longer,' I reply, joining in the laughter. A man in Rakiraki tells me he will vote Labour. Before I am able to say anything, he says, 'If Labour wins, there will be trouble. We will then have better chance to migrate.' This reminded me of an incident in Sydney when some protestors hoisted a banner saying 'Speight ke Maro Goli.' This could read as 'To Hell with Speight' or 'Shoot Speight.' The protestors had the latter in mind. A man tells me 'We will get ourselves photographed in front of parliament house and will use the photograph to claim political asylum in Australia!'

Other stories. A man says he will never vote for NFP because it is rich man's party. Another replies: 'Arre, you should vote for a rich man's party: what can a poor party's man do for you!' At another place, a man relates a story which has been around for a while. Someone says he will never vote for NFP because NFP was not known outside Fiji. There was a Labour party in the UK, and in Australia and New Zealand as well, but there was no NFP there. 'How can you expect help for a party no one knows about overseas?' A candidate in Tavua says they should vote for Mahendra Chaudhry because he is a man of courage. 'I was a hostage for nearly two months. I saw with my own eyes the terrible beating the soldiers gave to my leader. I saw blood on his face. His ribs were broken. But he did not flinch.' People are impressed. But a week later the local headmaster visits the area and is told the story. He is puzzled. How could the candidate have seen Chaudhry being beaten 'with his own eyes' when he was not in parliament and never incarcerated? Trimming the truth: everyone seems to be doing it.

People devise ingenious ways of getting their message across to the people. At one meeting, a candidate asks people to vote for the *vara*, the germinating coconut tree which is the Labour Party symbol. Why? Because coconut is offered to the gods in Hindu religious ceremonies. 'Coconut water is the purest form of water, untouched by human hands,' he says. What that has to do with politics is beyond me. But at another meeting, a NFP candidate responds to this by saying that, yes, coconut water is the purest form of water, but we offer it to the gods using the mango leaf. Mango tree is the symbol of the NFP!

There is much talk about the poor calibre of candidates standing in this election. How can candidates from limited educational backgrounds be entrusted with making decisions about the country's future, people ask. Many are barely able to put two sentences in English together: how will they be able digest complex bills in parliament? The point is taken though it is easy saying this while sitting on the sidelines. The calibre of Fijian candidates is better than the calibre of Indo-Fijian candidates. Fijians see a future in politics for themselves. Indo-Fijians don't. Some of them are standing because they are retired, have nothing useful to do, and are looking for a bit of fame and fortune before the flame is finally extinguished. Some are standing because they believe passionately in some cause or because their party has asked them to. Their sense of loyalty and perseverance commands respect.

At the beginning of the campaign, every candidate I speak with is hopeful about his or her prospect. *Chance hai.* We have a chance. But hope begins to vanish as the campaign proceeds. It is a sad spectacle. The saddest though is the fate of those who, having done their arithmetic, know from the very beginning that they have no hope of winning at all. But they put on a brave face, go through the motion and campaign house-to-house. How they can muster the energy and enthusiasm to go on the campaign trail in humid heat and dust day in, day out, over several weeks defies easy comprehension. I suppose hope springs eternal in the heart of every prospective politician. Some hope to make enough acquaintances which might help their business. For others, this is a trial run, an apprenticeship for the next time around. At least one candidate told me that the exposure he has gained in this campaign will help his chances for selection in the municipal elections.

As I travel around the countryside, usually by myself, I often think how things have changed over the years. I published my first Fiji election analysis in 1983 and my latest two decades later. There was no internet, then, no websites, no email, no googling, just the radio and the newspapers. Gathering data—about the demographic and ethnic composition of a constituency, for example, or getting hold of party manifestos, or profile of candidates—was tedious and time consuming. Luck played a large part in acquiring election marginalia so essential to understanding the mood of the campaign. But all that has changed. All the data you need are posted on the official election website. Both SDL and Labour have their own websites, displaying their manifestos and speeches by their leaders. All the major newspapers have their own websites, carrying both analysis as well as information. Expert commentary is copied and carried far and wide. It is possible now to 'know' what is happening on the hustings without leaving your computer desk. The kind of detailed analyses I wrote earlier seems inappropriate now because everyone who wants can have access to the same data set. I have become a remnant in my own lifetime!

As the day of reckoning draws near and all the campaign propaganda has been distributed, attention turns to the logistics of manning the polling booth: sheds will have to be erected, transport arranged, food and grog organized, trusted party workers found to look after the booth. And the waiting, the endless waiting for the D-Day. As I leave the campaign trail, I hope and pray that whatever the final outcome, the verdict of the ballot box will be respected and that citizens of this most beautiful of lands on earth will be given an opportunity to fashion a future of unity and prosperity that they so richly deserve and which is within their reach.

# Seven

## Ungiven Speech (2009)

*All this passed into silence:*
*unremembered and unacknowledged,*
*that's why I am telling you now*

Cate Kennedy

When Mr. Murray McKenzie invited me to address your convention, I told him in all my naiveté that I didn't know anything about Accountancy. 'Not many accountants do either,' he replied. That put my mind at rest. When he said that I should focus my address on the present and the future, I had to tell him that I made my living by predicting the past. He said reassuringly, 'You will do just fine.' So here I am, and I thank you for the privilege of being with you today.

The invitation to speak at this gathering was extended to me at a time that is no more. The constitution was still in place, even though it was observed more in the breach; a political dialogue process, although fraught and flawed in many ways, was under way; the international community was expressing a cautious and conditional willingness to get engaged to rescue Fiji from the cul-de-sac it was in; and there was a glimmer of hope—just a glimmer—that Fiji might finally find its feet on the ground again.

But all that is now gone. There is now no pretence about finding a solution to Fiji's political problems in a timely fashion, in consultation with its friends in the regional and the international community. Fiji is now telling the world: we will find solutions to Fiji's problems on our own terms, in our own time. The international community must not dictate terms. Fiji is a sovereign nation. Leave us alone. There is a palpable sense of exasperation in the voice of the interim administration: we are the guys who are on the right side of history; we are doing the right thing; why doesn't the world understand us? Why indeed.

This question goes to the heart of the topic given to me: 'Fiji and the International Community: Acceptance or Isolation: Are these the only choices?' My response is: No. I don't think Acceptance and Isolation are the only two choices available to the international community when dealing with Fiji. There is another alternative: Accommodation. And there is an alternative to Monologue: Dialogue. I shall return to this theme later.

This coup is in marked contrast to the first coup of 1987. The world then was a simpler place. The fax machine was the latest invention, and it was possible to deprive society of the oxygen of information and commentary. But the world since then has changed beyond recognition. Now censorship is enforced in Fiji and self-censorship encouraged, but technology cannot be so easily intimidated. Blogsites abound, spreading information as well as misinformation to all those who want them across the world. The boundaries are simply too porous to be easily policed. They are transgressed at the click of a button. The whole exercise of controlling speech is futile and self-defeating.

There is another difference with 1987. Then the message was clear, even though it was based on spurious assumptions. The message was the defense of indigenous rights against the interests and aspirations of an immigrant community. The international community, unable or unwilling to decipher the more unseemly motives of the principal actors, was willing to believe the message. But the message this time around is not clear, which is one reason for the present confusion. Initially the coup was justified as a 'Clean Up Campaign.' A few months later, another rationale crept in: electoral reform and the implementation of a so-called Peoples' Charter, the latter a kind of sophomoric development plan, presented to the people as the military's exist strategy and as a panacea for all the ills afflicting the nation. More recently, another rationale has crept in: to create a perfect, corruption free, politics-free society. As the interim prime minister puts it, 'I want to rid politics from decision making that has an impact on our economy, our future. We cannot be beholden to petty politics, communal politics, provincial politics and religious politics.' He did not use the word, but he could have been talking about creating a utopia. And when you are engaged in that mammoth task, timeliness and accountability are irrelevant.

In 1987, the military coup was always intended as a means to an end, and not an end in itself. The end was the entrenchment of Fijian control of the political process After a few chaotic months, Sitiveni Rabuka eventually handed power back to civilian rulers who then chalked the path back to parliamentary democracy. Now the situation is different. You do not have on the national stage chiefs of mana and overarching influence, such as Ratu Sir Kamisese Mara or Ratu Sir Penaia Ganilau, who can exercise a moderating, stabilizing influence on developments. Now, the military having hobbled indigenous institutions of power, is much more intent on being centrally involved in reshaping the future of the country in its own image. They are here to stay: that message comes out loud and clear from a whole raft of things the interim administration has done since abrogating the constitution on April 10th. Whether it is civil society organizations, the media or the Fiji Law Society, the message from the military is the same: we are in control, and we intend to remain in control for a very long time.

The military and the interim administration have tried very hard to convince the international community that their main aim is to create a truly democratic society in Fiji that is just and fair to everyone. They want an allegedly very undemocratic constitution to be re-written so that every citizen has equal rights. One would have to admit that there are some—perhaps many—people both in Fiji and abroad who are willing to believe this, and give the interim administration the benefit of the doubt. That is, they believe that the military is dead earnest about creating a perfect democracy, after which it would voluntarily leave the stage for politics to operate as normal.

I am prepared to accept this assertion for the sake of argument, just as those who embrace the military's vision must, by the same token, accept the position of those who express grave reservation, as many in the international community do. There is the argument that by simply having a non-racial system of voting will not remove race as a factor in politics. Just look at Guyana or Malaysia, to take just two examples, and the evidence is clear. There are those who argue that an electoral system, however perfect, is a means to an end, and not an end in itself. So a prior question has to be asked: what kind of political culture do you want to create in Fiji? I do not believe that this debate has taken place here. A view has been asserted, but it has not been properly argued.

But let us, again for the sake of argument, assume that the interim administration's proposed electoral system is adopted. Two questions then arise. What is the quid pro quo? Will the military then retreat to the barracks? And what happens if the results thrown up by the new system, whatever they are, are deemed unacceptable to the military? There is another point to consider. Now that we have no constitution in place, the interim administration can simply decree its preferred electoral model into existence and then proceed to hold elections under it, as happened under the 1990 constitution. At the back of my mind is another thought that I want to express in the hope of having it debated. And it is this. Increasingly, it seems to me, the powers-that-be are engaged in a project that goes beyond tinkering with the electoral system. They are intent on fundamentally re-structuring of society. To put it another way, they are engaged in creating utopia in Fiji, as I suggested earlier. This plants seeds of doubt in my mind about elections being held in 2014. 2024 perhaps, but certainly not 2014. I hope I am wrong.

A central plank in the interim administration's defense of defiant stance is the notion of sovereignty. Sovereignty, simply defined, is the line that distinguishes one nation state from another. Historically, there have been two philosophical positions on sovereignty: one by Thomas Hobbes and another by John Locke. The difference between the two lies in the extent of the obligation the state has to its citizens: in one minimal, in the other considerable. There is now another dimension to consider: globalization, which renders national boundaries porous through the impact of travel and technology. Sovereignty is now not an absolute concept, but a contingent one, intersected at various points by provisions of international law. From the Nuremburg trials onwards, the world has understood international law as not only adjudicating disputes between states but also holding states accountable for the fundamental violations of the human rights of its citizens. Look at international intervention in Afghanistan, Iraq, Rwanda, Somalia, East Timor and Kosovo, and you will see what I mean. So Fiji cannot and should not expect immunity or exception from international disapproval for what has happened here. The consciousness of civil, political and human rights is now too deeply entrenched in many international instruments and conventions to be ignored or violated with impunity.

Indeed, Fiji is a signatory to many of these instruments. Let us take the Biketawa Declaration. Its seven or so principles include 'Upholding democratic processes and institutions which reflect national and local circumstances, including the peaceful transfer of power, the rule of law and the independence of the judiciary, and just and honest government,' and 'Recognizing the importance of respecting and protecting indigenous rights and cultural values, traditions and customs.' And the Declaration stipulates the precise steps to be taken in the event of strife in a member country: the convening of Forum Foreign Ministers meeting, creating a Ministerial Action Group, appointing a fact-finding mission, and so on. And this is precisely what happened in the case of Fiji. So I am puzzled at Fiji's umbrage. A few days ago, Forum Secretary General Slade expressed a view that is worth pondering: 'The welfare of the region is inextricably tied up with the welfare of Fiji. But the present situation in Fiji involves clear disregard of the core values of democracy, good governance and the rule of law recognized by all Forum members, as well as the vast majority of the international community, as crucial to the future peace and prosperity of the Pacific Forum region.' That sentiment is unexceptionable.

Let me take another declaration, the Cotonou Agreement, about which many of you probably know a great deal. There are four fundamental principles which underpin the Agreement: Equality of Partners and Ownership of Development Strategies; Partnership; Dialogue and Mutual Obligation, and finally Differentiation and Regionalization. I would be happy to elaborate on these principles during discussion. But what is important in the context of Fiji is an additional provision in the Cotonou Agreement. Article 8, titled 'The Political Dimension,' provides that all parties to the Agreement 'shall contribute to peace, security and stability and promote a stable and democratic environment.' The dialogue 'shall also encompass a regular assessment of the developments concerning the respect for human rights, democratic principles, the rule of law,' and 'shall take full account of the objective of peace and democratic stability in the definition of priority areas of cooperation.' It is all there in black and white, and I am again at a loss to understand Fiji's puzzlement at being told that what it is doing is wrong and unacceptable. The EU will not relax its stance. That much is certain. This is not necessarily what I or many of us want. This is, quite simply, the way things are. And the sooner the people of Fiji are told the truth, the better it will be for everyone.

It is no secret that the interim administration is unhappy with the reaction of the international community, and it has singled out Australia and New Zealand for particular criticism in relation to their alleged interference in Forum decision making about Fiji. There are several points to consider. The Forum position has hardened over time in direct response to Fiji's intransigence. Tonga's Fred Sevele was sympathetic to Fiji in the beginning, as was PNG's Michael Somare. Both were disappointed at Fiji's snub of Pacific leaders' meeting in Niue and then in Port Moresby. Fiji needs to recognize that Pacific leaders are not pawns in the hands of Australia and New Zealand, and it is deeply offensive to Pacific Island leaders for Fiji to think so. And there is a further point to consider. Why should anyone express surprise that Australia and New Zealand are using their diplomatic leverage in the region to effect an outcome they want? You would surely expect democratic countries to champion values that underpin their own political culture and not condone practices which seek to subvert them. But having said that, I know that the international community does want to help, provided there is genuine willingness on the part of the interim administration to engage in inclusive dialogue. Fiji's siege mentality in the circumstances is understandable, but it is also a hindrance to progress.

It is perhaps this closed mindset that obscures a clear perception of the international reaction to Fiji. I recall what then Minister Mahendra Chaudhry said when the Rudd Labour government was elected into office. He welcomed the new government and said that he was hopeful that Canberra would show a more sympathetic appreciation of the situation in Fiji. I was asked to respond to this on a Hindi radio talk show. The whole world came crashing down on my head. I said that the change of government would not alter Australia's position on Fiji, and gave three reasons. One was that no Australian political party would ever condone a military coup against a democratically elected government. Two, that after thirteen years in the wilderness, the ALP having won power at the ballot box could hardly be expected to condone its violation in its own neighbourhood. And three, Australia would not take a position on Fiji without consulting its closest partner New Zealand, which had already condemned the coup in the strongest terms possible. All this was, or should have been, commonsense.

Today, some in the interim administration are making a similar noise about China. Let me say at the outset that I hope the interim administration is right and that Chinese aid, trade and investment will flow into Fiji in ample measure in the years to come. But I am not optimistic. Why? We have been on this route before, soon after the 1987 coups, when Fiji embarked on a 'Look North Policy' with great enthusiasm, not the least to teach Australia and New Zealand the lesson that they were not indispensable to Fiji's development. Nothing tangible came from that initiative. Nothing. And I am not sure that much will come out of the current China drive either. China's strategic interest in Fiji is limited. Its regional policy is driven by the Taiwan factor. At this time of global financial crisis, no country, including China, will invest in an environment characterized by systemic instability and periodic eruptions. And for China, Australia and New Zealand are far more important than Fiji. For that reason alone, China is unlikely to do anything in direct defiance of Canberra and Wellington.

The interim administration has repeatedly told the international community and anyone else who would listen, that merely having elections will not solve Fiji's problems. I agree. Elections by themselves don't solve anything. That is common sense. What they do is to provide the basis of legitimacy for governance. This fundamental point has escaped many who place trust and confidence in the military and the interim administration. Fiji tells the international community that Fiji's constitution is 'undemocratic' and that it has to go if Fiji is to develop into a fair and just society. I have alluded to this before, but let me make some additional points. I do not know what criterion is used to define democracy. What I do know is that international laws allow for a certain margin of appreciation to accommodate a country's unique culture and history and traditions and for these to be incorporated into its constitutional structure. There is no one-size-fits all.

Second, I know that the 1997 constitution attempted to deal with the most fundamental problem that has beset Fiji since the inception of party politics in

1966. That problem was not a flawed electoral system (although the first-past-the-post most certainly was), but the systematic exclusion of one community, the Indo-Fijians, from sharing power. They were the perennial 'Other' of Fijian politics. The compulsory power-sharing provision in the 1997 constitution was designed to address that problem. And in 2006, for the first time in Fiji's political history ever, there was a genuinely multi-ethnic, multi-party government in place. A new beginning was being made, however tentatively. Consider the sweet irony: Fijians and Indo-Fijians were in government, while the opposition was led by a General Voter!

Third, I know that there are other forms of democracy other than the Westminster variety, respected and practiced in many stable democracies. One such, upon which the 1997 constitution was partly founded, was what Arend Lijphart has called 'Consociationalism' whose principal characteristics are: a grand coalition of elites representing different segments of society; guaranteed group representation so that no major community is excluded from power; mutual veto over matters of particular concern to the different communities; proportionality in political representation; and segmental autonomy that allows for the maintenance of different cultural identities. This, too, a model of democracy, and Fiji's 1997 constitution meets its test fully. In this version, reserving seats for distinct communities is not the evil that the advocates of the Westminster model make it out to be.

Fourth, I know that no country will ever enjoy political stability so necessary for economic development unless there is basic respect for the rule of law. You may have the most perfect constitution in the world, the most perfect model of democracy on paper, but as long as you have a large standing military in an environment characterized by violence and disorder, there will always be a threat to peace.

The time for apportioning blame about what happened is over. The question now is: where do we go from here? First, we need to confront the inescapable truth that Fiji cannot go it alone, that sooner rather than later, it will have to engage with the international community Fiji will have to adopt a more open and inclusive approach. Many initiatives contemplated by the interim administration are praiseworthy, and I have no doubt that there would be a meeting of minds on many of them. That is why there is an urgent need of tact and diplomacy. Fiji is an island, I have said so many times before, but it is an island in the physical sense alone. The words of John Donne come to mind: 'No man is an Island, entire of itself; every man is a piece of the Continent, a part of the main; if a clod be washed away by the sea, Europe is the less, as well as if a promontory were, as well as if a manor of the thy friends or thine own were; any man's death diminishes me, because I am involved with Mankind.'

As a practical matter, the interim administration, if it is serious about returning Fiji to parliamentary democracy in a timely fashion—and I have already expressed my doubts before—it should deign backwards from 2014 and draw up a timetable for taking the country to elections. Without that demonstrable commitment, the international community will not engage. That much is clear. No one wants to be taken for a cheap ride.

It would also be helpful if the interim administration set out in specific detail what aspect of the abrogated 1997 constitution it finds problematic so that areas of agreement and disagreement among the different stakeholders can be clearly identified. The problems Fiji faces are huge, but they are surmountable. The international community will come to the party but it will have to be convinced of Fiji's genuine desire to engage in an inclusive dialogue. In the end, though, solutions to Fiji's problems will have to be found here, devised by the people of this country. And no solution will be sustainable and enduring unless it is based on tolerance and a sensitive understanding of this country's diverse inheritance. It must be based on the understanding that dissent does not mean disloyalty. President Obama said it well in Cairo earlier this month. He said that 'in order to move forward, we must say openly to each other the things we hold in our hearts and that too often are said only behind closed doors. There must be a sustained effort to listen to each other; to learn from each other; to respect one another; and to seek common ground.' Fiji can realize its potential that is so within its reach. That is its challenge and its opportunity.

I want to end by quoting again words from President Obama's Cairo address which are apt for my purposes. He said: 'I do have an unyielding belief that all people yearn for certain things: the ability to speak your own mind and have a say in how you are governed, confidence in the rule of law and equal administration of justice; government that is transparent and doesn't steal from people; the freedom to live as you choose. These are not just American ideas; they are human rights, and that is why we will support them everywhere.'

# Eight

## The Road from Laucala Bay

*You who will emerge from the*
*Flood*
*In which we have gone under*
*Remember*
*When you speak of our failings*
*The dark time too*
*Which you have escaped*

Berthold Brecht 'To Those Born Later.'

It is a singular honour to be allowed to pay tribute to the late Professor Ron Crocombe. Ron—as he wished, indeed, insisted on being called—walked tall, literally as well as metaphorically, among scholars facilitating and promoting Pacific Studies in the latter half of the 20th century. He was a man of many parts, quite unlike any other, unmatchable in his energy and enthusiasm for things Pacific, the likes of whom I know I shall not see in my own lifetime. Ron went to the University of the South Pacific in 1969 as its Foundation Professor of Pacific Studies, after several years leading social science research projects in the then Territory of Papua and New Guinea as the Field Director of the New Guinea Research Unit. At USP, he came into his own. He taught and researched, but his lasting legacy to the region was his indefatigable promotion of research and writing by Pacific Islanders themselves. For many of us at the university in its salad days, Ron was an example and a source of inspiration. Others more qualified than I will reflect on his legacy and contribution. I honour my teacher and sometime colleague. In this essay, however, I focus on my own experience of the university guided by the vision of its foundation professors such as Ron Crocombe, what it meant to us and what it taught, how it formed and deformed us, and the ways in which it influenced the journey I embarked upon at Laucala Bay, a journey which has taken me far away from the land of my birth and the place of my upbringing and early education. It is an improbable journey, I know, but not a unique one. I am confident that in the footsteps of my endless wanderings, many of my generation will recognize the echoes of their own.

It is now exactly forty years since I went to the University of the South Pacific to undertake an undergraduate degree in History and English.[1] I was on a government scholarship to prepare for a career as a high school teacher. The humanities were for the no-hopers, some people in the village said; bright students did law and medicine and other status-enhancing subjects that secured good marriages and prosperous careers. But just getting into university was for me at that time an achievement of singular importance. I was the first one in my entire extended family throughout Vanua Levu ever to complete high school and the first to head for tertiary education. A career as a high school teacher was nothing to scoff at: it paid well, teachers had a good reputation in the community as exemplars of proper moral behaviour, and the prospect of promotion up the ladder of the educational bureaucracy looked bright. For the generation before us, a lowly career in the colonial bureaucracy was all that could be hoped for at best. Otherwise it was back-breaking work in the cane fields. The timing was right for us. Fiji had just become independent (in 1970) and there was need for skilled manpower to propel the engine of postcolonial development. We would be the torch bearers of the independence generation.

The opening of the University of the South Pacific was a monumental achievement in the modern history of the Pacific Islands, a genuine turning point, much like the impact of the Second World War, or the beginnings of decolonisation in the 1960s. It placed higher education within the reach of all school children who passed the appropriate exams with requisite marks, not only those who (or whose parents) could afford it, or the select few who went overseas on a small number of government scholarships. It was in its own way a great leveller of hierarchy based on wealth and status. Unsurprisingly, university education on offer was unequivocally utilitarian, explicitly advertised in the names of the three foundational clusters of academic activity: School of Social and Economic Development, School of Natural Resources and the School of Education. All this did not matter to those of us lucky enough to get admission to the university in the first place; getting to the Laucala Campus was quite an achievement in itself. What a time it was. 'I sing of our youth,' New Zealand historian Keith Sinclair once wrote, 'And the fierce gladness of being in at the beginning.'[2]

Towards the end of my second year, after I had demonstrated a capacity for academic achievement, at least as measured in the final grades, the thought began to enter my head that an academic career might be worth contemplating and might not be beyond the realms of possibility. Reading in the library for endless hours was enthralling. What could be better than a life devoted to it? In this thought, I was anything but discouraged by some of the faculty, especially by my history lecturer June Cook, the chain-smoking Cambridge graduate who had come to the university after a stint in the United Nations (and who, I was to learn much later, had gone on to bat for me with people like Ron Crocombe whom she was tutoring in French). The occasional nod of acknowledgement from some of the academics in the corridors, the chance encounter in the Dining Room, occasionally being called by your first name (after high school where we remained anonymous, seldom recognised individually), suggested that perhaps one was being noticed, or at least was making a small impression.

The university was a liberating experience in many ways: escaping the confining ways of village life in Labasa, encountering new people from other Pacific islands, the new freedoms and opportunities. Intellectually it widened our horizons in previously unimaginable ways. In high school, we had no local history. For our higher exams, we had studied the great themes of European history: the Unification of Germany and Italy, the Causes of World War One, the Russian Revolution, the Rise of Fascism in Italy and Germany. In earlier grades we had studied aspects of New Zealand history: the economic policies of Sir Julius Vogel, the rise of the Liberal Party, the life of Sir Apirana Ngata. At university, Tony Chappell's year-long course introduced us to Pacific history, broadly including the cultural anthropology of Pacific island societies comprising Melanesia, Polynesia and Micronesia. Ron Crocombe, the lean, lanky Professor of Pacific Studies, deepened that knowledge through an extensive reading and anecdotally rich course in 'Advanced Pacific History.' As I have said elsewhere, Ron was not a disciplined teacher, but he was an electrifying one who spoke with deep personal knowledge of the people he had met and the places he had visited. He seemed to know virtually every scholar who mattered in Pacific studies. And as a teacher, he took us seriously, perhaps more seriously than we deserved. I recall vividly Ron giving me a brand new copy of *Pacific Islands Portrait*, edited by Jim Davidson and Deryck Scarr and asking me to write a review of it.[3] Such confidence in one's ability to say something meaningful when one was merely leaning the alphabets was daunting at the time, but it was also thrilling. Ron was already publishing third year research papers as small monographs under the auspices of the South Pacific Social Sciences Association, which he founded. Some essays found an outlet in *Pacific Perspective*, a new journal he started, typically with the collaboration of senior undergraduates and edited by a junior islander academic.[4] It's now gone. I tried to follow Ron's example in my own teaching career.[5]

Suddenly, history did not appear remote or unrelated. I remember distinctly the faces of our Solomon Island colleagues lighting up when the topic of the Pacific islands labour trade was discussed and names of such places as Koolambangra and Choiseul were mentioned. These were not just names on paper, but names of places intimately familiar to the students. The mention of Efate or Tanna evoked a similar response among the ni-Vanuatu crowd when the history of the sandalwood trade was discussed. Ahmed Ali's course on 'Colonialism in the Pacific' introduced us briefly to aspects of Fijian colonial history, complete with names of familiar people and places, such as Sir Henry Marks after which the Marks Street in Suva was named and familiar to us as the place for affordable Chinese food. John Harre's lectures on the social anthropology of family and kinship led us to Adrian Mayer's incomparable *Peasants in the Pacific*, whose description of rural Fiji Indian society was as authentic as it was real.[6] The rituals and ceremonies he described were a part of our life in rural Labasa. Ken Gillion's *Fiji's Indian Migrants* introduced us to the history of our people, their origins and early settlement.[7] Ahmed Ali once lent me his thesis to read.[8] More than the subject matter, a history of race and electoral representation in Fiji, was the artefact itself: to see in a perfectly bound volume of several hundred crisp pages neatly typed words about our own history. All of a sudden, everything became real. The thesis and the books we read whetted my appetite for history and planted the seeds of ambition that I too might try my hand at it one day. But it remained a private ambition, riddled with doubt about its actual realization. I wasn't very good at transformational grammar, which was a compulsory. Discussion of alpha clause and beta clause left me cold. And I was, after all, on a scholarship to become a high school teacher.

We were undergraduates at the university at a time of great political optimism in the region. Our islands were in the process of gaining independence, and some amongst us were already marked for great things in the future, such as Barak Sope, who would go on to a mixed political fortune in his native Vanuatu, and the frequently shirtless, tennis-playing Teberero Tito, who would become the president of Kiribati. Others would become diplomats, senior administrators and educators, a veritable 'USP Mafia' in the region. The atmosphere at university was suffused with the sense that, with the right kind of leadership, ordinary people could make a difference to nation building that was under way after nearly a century of colonial rule. This was nowhere more evident than at the conference on 'Social Issues in National Development,' which Ron Crocombe organised at the university in 1974.[9] The occasion was genuinely participatory, featuring international luminaries such as the anthropologist Sir Raymond Firth, local academics (Ahmed Ali), political practitioners (Fiji's Karam Ramrakha), and students (Vijay Naidu, Jone Dakuvula and Amelia Rokotuivuna). This emphasis on inclusiveness and islander participation, on dissolving differences of hierarchy and status, was pure Ron, and it was stirring. The problem of development was considered from a variety of perspectives: anthropological, sociological, economic, historical, political. There was no contrived coherence of themes, no scripted choreography. This, too, was Ron, assertively multidisciplinary. 'What kind of life do we want for ourselves?' Amelia asked. One that promoted human dignity and equitable development, she answered. 'We people of the Pacific islands are in the enviable position of being able to make a choice since most of our nations are just beginning the journey of nationhood.' Dakuvula pleaded for 'freedom to examine and criticise,' as the 'unorthodox and the ruled are worth trusting and listening to.' Such innocence of those salad days seems so touching in the light of subsequent developments in Fiji and the region generally. After the 2006 military coup in Fiji, Jone, the youthful anarchist, was working for the military regime. Disillusioned, he is now at Fiji's new national university as its Registrar.

The same spirit of innocence was evident in scholarship as well. In 1973, three senior students at the university, Sr Mary Stella, Asesela Ravuvu and Raymond Pillay, all Ron's students, published a joint paper, 'Pacific History and National Integrity,' which provided a distillation of thought current at the time.[10] 'An objective study of Pacific history,' they wrote, 'will contribute greatly towards overcoming the myth of white superiority which has so discouraged the Pacific peoples from asserting themselves.' An important function of history, and scholarship generally was to instil confidence in people 'eager to make their own contribution.' History thus had a constructive role to play 'in promoting the rehabilitation of the Pacific peoples because it restores their confidence and self-respect, and enables them to take their place in a new and changing world.' They went on:

> If the Pacific peoples are to avoid the pitfalls that have plagued the progress of more complex civilizations, they must glean the pages of history and profit from the experiences of those who have gone before. Leaders in the Pacific need such knowledge in order to make soundly based decisions in their dealings with their own people and with other nations. History will not provide ready made solutions, but the process of analysing the past can be fruitfully applied to the present.

Such optimism about the relevance of the past to the present were not confined to the University of the South Pacific students and faculty. It was part of the general currency at the time. Delivering the presidential address to the Australia and New Zealand Association for the Advancement of Science in 1970, Harry Maude, of the Australian National University, too, had proclaimed that history 'has a very practical and therapeutic role to enact in assisting the rehabilitation of the Pacific peoples at the end of a traumatic era of European political, economic and technological ascendancy by renewing their self-respect and providing them with a secure historical base to play their part as responsible citizens of independent or self-governing communities in a new world.'[11] Subsequent history would prove that noble sentiment to be sadly misplaced. Once entrenched in power, political leaders disdained discussion and suppressed dissent. As Thomas Jefferson once said, 'Whenever a man has cast a longing eye on offices, a rottenness begins in his conduct.' Pacific leaders were no exception. University graduates were expected to be pliant cogs in the wheels of government bureaucracy, agents of state-sponsored development programmes, not independent critics of its policies. Former students, who later became political leaders themselves, breached the principles of freedom of expression they had so stoutly championed in their youth. And not everywhere in the Pacific was there a single unitary tradition that could be utilized in nation-building effort. The Papuans were seeking separation from the New Guineans, there was a breakaway movement in the Western Solomon Islands, the ni-Vanuatu were grappling with the divided legacy of colonial rule bequeathed by the British and the French. In Fiji, Fijians and Indo-Fijians had sharply divergent views about the colonial past that seemed only to harden with time.

The age of innocence of the earlier years about the role and importance of history is now gone. History, as a discipline, is taught in schools as part of an amorphous, mind-numbing social science unit rather than as a separate subject in its own right. It is a devalued currency in modern education in the islands. In universities, the sanctity of disciplinary boundaries is rejected as archaic. We now speak of 'histories' in the plural, contested, 'problematized,' intersected along a myriad lines by a variety of concerns, interests, understandings and authorial subjectivities. We now live with the certainty that scholarship is partial in both senses of the term.[12] I accept these new developments intellectually though I am also troubled by them. Doubt in small dozes is salutary, but it can be disabling when taken to excess. Pluralism, diversity and fragmentation can be liberating, but so, too, can an exercise in synthesis, an overarching connected narrative to understand the larger shape of the human experience. I also tire quickly of the endless language games scholars play, usually for the edification and amusement of each other. The habits of thought I acquired in my undergraduate years about the place of the humanities in the broad cultural life of a civilized society have persisted. I am comfortable with that.

There were several other things about my USP background that I observed quietly at the time but whose full importance I did not grasp then. Among them was the literary renaissance that was taking place at the university in the 1970s and 1980s. Students and creative writers were beginning to write imaginatively about their own societies. Their works appeared first in the student journal *Unispac* and later in *Mana*, the publication of the South Pacific Creative Arts Society started, among others, by Marjorie and Ron Crocombe and Albert Wendt. I was particularly fascinated by stories about the Indo-Fijian community about which so little had been written, almost as if the world we came from was not worthy of literary exploration and critical engagement. We read pieces by Raymond Pillay, Anirudh Singh, Dhurup Chand, Sashi Kant Nair, Sulochana Chand and others. Raymond was everyone's favourite.[13] He wrote with unerring clarity and authenticity about the world of rural Indo-Fijians. We understood perfectly what he meant about the stillness of village life being a 'cloak, like the veil a woman wears before strangers, hiding private life full of tragedy and violence.' When he wrote about Bangaru being black as a baigan (eggplant), we knew exactly what he meant. There was a Bangaru in every village. Vanessa Griffin introduced us to the world of Fijians and Part-Europeans. Her word pictures were so true: 'This Fijian woman, any Fijian woman, was a common sight on the sea wall, sitting couched, with faded cotton skirt billowing in the wind, or standing against the sky,' with a 'basket plaited out of green coconut leaf' containing her bait.[14]

The voices that Raymond, Vanessa and others captured were not found in archival documents so beloved of historians. It seemed to me then, and the conviction has deepened with time, that these writers were better able to capture the lived experience, its mystery, its rich daily texture, far better than conventional scholars. These creative pieces and the idea that our people had such wonderful stories to tell lodged deep at the back of my mind, and I have the lingering suspicion that they had something to do with my own efforts at creative writing later in my career. Sadly, though, the promise of a literary renaissance at the Laucala campus was short lived, ruptured by the coups of 1987 when the leading artists left for other shores or stopped writing altogether. It was revived in the mid-1990s by the 'Niu Waves' group only to be disrupted by George Speight's insurrection in 2000. After the latest coup in 2006, a culture of silence and self-censorship has descended on Fiji's creative community, sadly with the silent support of its pliant academic hierarchy.

The idea of literature providing a window into the truth of the lived human experience was expressed most powerfully by Albert Wendt.[15] Two things he said stayed with me. The first was the notion that there was no one perfect way to write history, that it could be written from a variety of perspectives. 'A novel is a history,' he wrote, 'an analogue of the real world, written by someone for whom life is a perpetual question and for whom there are no sacred truths.' The world the novelist sought to create 'attempts to explore all his possibilities, tries to be total, to include even the dreams/fantasies/smells/prophesies/and diseases of a particular place which exists outside time.' The difference between the two was that 'a historian tries to recreate a world that, according to historical evidence, was, and save it for all time.' But it was still fiction 'because it is selective recreation, and Art being selection ain't life.' Both were custodians and creators of memories as mythographers and mythmakers who 'explore our possibilities: the novelist through supposedly 'imaginary' people and situations, the historian through people who supposedly existed. And in a world where the gods are dead, they both create their own meanings in the hope that those meanings will sustain them.'

At the time, Wendt's contentions seemed heretical, unsettling to those of us just beginning to learn the alphabets of academic disciplines. We were taught to believe that the past had a reality of its own which could be revealed through the use of proper methods of enquiry. We had our own codes and distinctive protocols of research, just as other disciplines had theirs. We were not in the business of 'creating our own meanings,' but telling objective truths ascertained through verifiable evidence, this being one of the central tents of historical scholarship.[16] The idea that historians were mythmakers seemed strange to us, disturbing: on the contrary, we fancied ourselves as myth busters, setting the record straight. But over time, I have come to accept the essential truth of Wendt's contention, though not perhaps all of it. And I have also become more mindful of historian Ken Inglis' observation that 'a lot of history is concealed autobiography.'[17] We live within, not outside, the histories we write. We end up creating texts which are partial. We reject the notion of value-free research in its entirety and of linear, one dimensional truth. We accept the role of imagination in the construction of human knowledge. And we readily acknowledge the distinct possibility of becoming a footnote in someone else's text in our own lifetime rather than penning transcending, timeless texts.

The other disturbing question Albert Wendt asked touched on issues of representing the past. It was not so much a question of who should or should not be allowed to write history. 'The crucial question,' Wendt argued, was 'Can a historian ever get into the brain and blood of someone whose culture is so different from his own, and write from inside that person? And should he pretend he can?' These are important questions and I am not sure I have a clear or adequate response to them. Meanwhile, I do have questions to raise. Is it ever possible for anyone to get into the blood and bones of people long dead and gone?

Isn't the past a foreign country to us all? Is it ever possible to know the 'really real?' Insider cultural knowledge certainly confers some advantages, but cultural traits are learned, not innate, and there are ample examples in Pacific studies of scholars writing sensitively about indigenous cultural matters and accepted as such by the people themselves. Think, for example, of Roger Keesing, David Hanlon and Marshall Sahlins, to take just three examples.

Over time, I have come to question some of the assumptions and parameters of positivist scholarship characteristic of an earlier generation. I do not deny the enormous value of archival research, but I have also become aware of its many limitations. Documents about the past are not neutral pieces of paper. They were written by people in particular contexts for particular purposes. They are instruments of and for power and authority. They have an agenda of their own. Those who questioned the foundations of the duly constituted architecture of power were dismissed as madmen, misfits and mavericks. Students of Fijian history would know the fate of the Fijian rebel Apolosi Nawai. In the 1960s, the Indo-Fijian leader AD Patel was subjected to sustained attacks for demanding independence. So it is important to read the historical records for what they say but perhaps equally importantly, for what they leave out. Sometimes, the silence can be deafening.

Archival research privileges a particular kind of historical narrative. The written word provides the foundation of the project, enlivened wherever possible with oral and anecdotal evidence, although until recent decades, non-written sources that could not be properly authenticated or verified, were not accorded much weight. But what about histories of pasts where memory is not properly archived and written evidence does not exist? What, in other words, about the histories of unwritten pasts and peoples. Let me give a concrete example of what I have in mind. I grew up in a rural settlement in Fiji in the 1950s and 1960s. People had begun to settle on haphazardly leased pieces of land in the settlement soon after the end of indenture in 1920. Of little interest to the government except for purposes of rudimentary administration, the Indo-Fijians had to rely on their own cultural resources to establish families and farmsteads, create institutions which regulated social life in the villages, adjudicated disputes, celebrated life and mourned its passing. It was in these settlements that the main features of Indo-Fijian culture were fashioned from bits and pieces of the remembered past and the accumulated experience of the new environment. I came from this world which formed me and the people of my generation, but there was hardly anything written about it. It was almost as if that world did not exist, or did not matter. How to write truthfully about this past began to preoccupy me more and more. Albert Wendt's advice about capturing the spirit of the place, not only its dry facts, kept returning to me.

To make some sense of my lived reality, I began to write what I have termed 'faction,' where I try to capture the actual lived experience in fictional or quasi-fictional terms.[18] I write about things I have observed or experienced, about stories I have been told: a family quarrel, the politics of running local schools, religious and cultural tensions—and I write about them creatively but with disciplined imagination. Unlike a novelist, I cannot conjure something out of thin air. I work with material given to me by direct experience or observation, and from that I create a connected narrative. Perhaps this is what novelists do as well, I do not know. My concern is to capture the inner truth rather than the factual accuracy of an experience. The experiment has worked for me over the years. I have received dozens of appreciative messages from readers across the world who have found my factional pieces authentic, reflecting their own experiences.[19] Understandably, there will be many who will question the scholarly 'value' of this kind work. The truth of what I write in factions cannot be verified as a piece of archival evidence might be, but that is the best way I know how to get to the truth of an unwritten experience, to the blood and bones of the people I write about. And the truth, as they say, lies in the taste of the pudding.

Albert Wendt's point about the possibility of writing the history of another culture also raises pertinent questions with which I have grappled in my own work. I recall Ron Crocombe once telling me that he vowed not to conduct research on Fiji when he took up his appointment at the university. He wanted complete freedom to research and write about things that mattered to him, without having to worry about the renewal of his work permit. If he could not write the truth as he saw it, he wouldn't even try. He kept his word. For a very different reason, I made a conscious decision from very early on to write about my own people and my own country. I do not want to be an intruder on someone else's past. There have been occasions when I have written about other places, but the primary site of my scholarly investigation has been Fiji. I am moved by a strong sense of belonging and attachment. It is where my head and my heart come together. I am a part of the history I write about. I may get things wrong, but at least it is my place and my history. I will bear the burden of my errors. I have a deep sense of responsibility and obligation to it. I care about the region of which I am a part, but not with the same passionate intensity that I feel about Fiji. My choice is political, not intellectual. I see no reason why an outsider cannot feel passionately involved about the place of his or her research endeavour. Nor do I feel particularly possessive about my site of research. The more research we have the better. It is the quality of engagement, not the colour of skin, that will matter in the end.

For a while, the 'ownership' of scholarship was a deeply contested and politically contentious issue in Pacific Studies.[20] Did outsiders have the right to 'appropriate' someone else's history? Some saw scholarship as a deeply political act, and the involvement of outsiders as complicit in the process of academic imperialism. I encountered this most directly at the University of Hawaii while teaching there in the 1980s where issues of dispossession, marginalization and indigenous sovereignty were acute and dominated public discourse as well. Unless history was taught from a particular ideological standpoint, deployed in the cause of indigenous empowerment, however defined, it was unacceptable and therefore to be rejected outright. Emotions were aroused and brought into sharp focus in an exchange between the anthropologist Roger Keesing and the Hawaiian scholar and activist Haunani-Kay Trask.[21] Trask accused Keesing of being an academic 'colonialist,' a part of a 'colonizing horde' who sought to 'take away from us [natives] the power to define who and what we are, and how we should behave politically and culturally.' Arguing that 'anthropologists without Natives are like entomologists without insects,' she accused Keesing and other expatriate anthropologists of 'profiting' from native cultures by studying and writing about them in academic institutions. Keesing accused Trask and others like her of 'romanticizing' the past of Pacific cultures and drawing too rigid a line between outsiders and insiders. 'The time is long past,' he argued, 'where those who are friends of Pacific Islanders and islands and those who are enemies can be sorted out on the basis of their genes or skin colours: there are plenty of 'insiders' many with Swiss bank accounts, busily selling their forests, their minerals, their fish –the lives and environments of the village cousins and their own children and grandchildren –to foreign interests.' Similar issues about representation and legitimacy were raised elsewhere in the Pacific, again producing rather more light than heat.

But these debates which were once so animated and controversial, have lost their relevance and potency. The boundaries of knowledge and power are more porous now, as are dated essentialised notions of cultural identity. The traditional gatekeepers of knowledge have had their function usurped by modern technology. Many practitioners of Pacific Studies today are Pacific islanders themselves, some in positions of power and influence.[22] Given the paucity of serious scholars engaged in serious study of the islands, people are grateful for knowledge and insight irrespective of their origin. In the scholarship produced in recent years, there has been a great degree of emphasis on local context and agency, on indigenous epistemology, with the result that some of the older criticism of imperialism and insensitivity has lost its effectiveness. It is also important that the geographical boundaries of the Pacific islands have greatly expanded thereby necessitating a re-thinking about what constitutes the 'real' Pacific.[23] There are many more Pacific islanders—Samoans, Tongans, Cook

Islanders, Niueans, Tokelauans—who now make their homes in Australia and New Zealand, thus complicating the outsider/insider paradigm. On the present evidence, these diasporic communities will gain in strength and influence in the future. The centre of gravity of island writing and scholarship is shifting to metropolitan locations. Further, some of the romance associated with the study of the Pacific islands that suffused the earlier generation of Pacific scholarship has now vanished in the face of the trouble and turbulence that is an enduring part of the contemporary Pacific. Pope John Paul's 1985 declaration of Fiji as 'The Way the World Should Be,' would now be seen by most people as a cruel joke.

The journey I began at the University of the South Pacific all those years ago was influenced by people who taught us, by their example and inspiration. It should be clear by now how much this has been a factor in my own intellectual development. We were trained to be generalists, and there was no provision for academic specialisation in the university curriculum. Karl Popper, Karl Marx and Max Weber made brief appearances in some courses, but there was no sustained engagement with their ideas. There were thus big gaps which had to be filled through private study. Scholarship in the western academy, or at least where I have worked, is organised along disciplinary lines with the result that a lot of time had to be spent simply learning the discipline's history, philosophy and development, the sort of thing that better undergraduate students in history in western universities would have encountered much earlier in their education (Lord Acton, RG Collingwood, EH Carr, GR Elton, EP Thompson). And the field's literature too had to be mastered. Pacific history could not be learned or taught in isolation from the histories of other regions or cognate areas about which we knew very little. We had no anthropology at the university and yet it was a discipline with special relevance for the study of Pacific history . The practice of reading for the sake of general knowledge and for sheer pleasure had to be cultivated, which was never easy for people coming from non-literate, oral cultures. Now reading is an integral part of my being, indispensible to sanity. For me, most knowledge still comes through the written text, not the latest technology.

People of my generation lacked a sense of entitlement that some now seem to have. Education in Australia is big business, and universities regularly compete for foreign students. Special help is assigned to them to improve their literacy and research skills. Everyone naturally wants to preserve the goose that lays the golden egg. But there was none of this for people of my vintage. We were expected to pick up the skills on our own as we went along by reading journals and books. And when it came to writing the dissertation, we were again very much on our own. I recall my designated advisor, Ken Gillion, telling me—my formal supervisor was Anthony Low who was then the Vice Chancellor—that if after six months of reading in the library, I was not on top of my subject, the most knowledgeable person in the world, I should not be doing graduate work. That kind of confidence could be debilitating, but it was fairly standard fair then. Students who had arrived on scholarship to pursue graduate work had gone through a rigorous process of selection, and the best thing that could be done for them, it was thought, was to leave them alone to get on with their work. And it worked.

After three years of labour, we were expected to submit three hard bound copies of our dissertation for examination by three scholars who were leaders in the field who had had no contact with the candidate. We were expected to make a distinctive and significant contribution to knowledge by the 'highest standards of contemporary scholarship.' The dissertation had to be as perfect as we could make it. Too many spelling errors and we could expect the examiners to reject it outright. Nothing could be worse for a young postgraduate student contemplating an academic career than to have his or dissertation rejected. There was a certain stigma attached to a dissertation which required re-submission. Word was quick to get out, and chances of securing a decent job at a decent university could be at risk. I was horrified some years ago when a candidate whose dissertation I had examined, pointing out numerous spelling and stylistic errors, telling me the advice his supervisor gave him. The examiners, he had said, would point out the errors which the student could then incorporate in his revision before the final submission. Such an advice would have been unthinkable in our day. Now, it seems, many (but by no means all) students expect to make corrections after examination as a matter of course.

Graduate research is now fairly commonplace, at least in Australia, and doctorate is not in as short a supply as it once used to be. But thirty years ago, the criterion for admission to graduate work was fairly strict. Scholarship, by convention, was given to students not much over thirty; anything beyond that age required special pleading. At least in the humanities and the social sciences, it was expected that students would go on to an academic career, not an unreasonable expectation at a time when universities were expanding rapidly. At any rate, graduate training was a prelude to a career. That is not universally the case now. There are now more mature age students in universities who pursue graduate work more out of interest rather than with any expectation of an academic career in prospect. Indeed, an academic career may not be the most lucrative either. In Australia at least, opportunities in the public sector can be financially and professionally more rewarding. Even those who pursue an academic career are now routinely resigned to the possibility of moving on to several jobs in a lifetime.

The research culture has also changed. 'Curiosity driven research' was the order of the day when I entered the academy, and for me it has remained that way ever since. We were expected to work on topics that interested us and on which we were expected to make significant original contribution. Historical research was essentially an individualized enterprise. That was the strength of the discipline. Articles were useful in alerting the world to our work, but ideally, historians were expected to write books at respectable intervals which would make a decisive intervention in the field and would have a longer shelf life. We might be expected to make the occasional foray into the public domain on some important event or controversy, but too much media exposure was not 'a good career move.' It detracted from detachment and objectivity. Now, media monitoring is a regular part of a university's public relations exercise. We are expected, indeed obliged, to go beyond the lecture hall to make our expertise available to the wider public. In appropriate doses, this is a healthy and welcome development as part of general public education and engagement, but the demands increase daily for briefing and commentary. Salesmanship and showmanship are increasingly becoming an integral part of a scholar's life. I suppose it could be argued that reaching the general public is an important obligation of taxpayer-funded universities. There are other new developments to which we have to respond. Now scholars are routinely expected to apply for research grants. Indeed, In some cases, the ability to attract grants becomes a criterion in appointments and promotions. Grants not only support individual research, they also sustain the overall infrastructure of an academic department.

On paper, the pursuit of grants seems eminently reasonable, but upon closer inspection much more problematic. To start with, grants are advertised with particular agendas in mind, focus on strategic areas with some relevance to the broader concerns of the Australian community: border protection, national security, asylum seekers, and so on. Areas which fall outside the prescribed parameters find it harder to get up. 'Cutting edge research' is often an important factor in assessment. Although it is not stated, the truth is that research that does not somehow fit in with the reigning theoretical paradigm or conceptual category would not ordinarily count as cutting edge research. Sometimes, what is cutting edge research today is yesterday's news tomorrow. It would seem to me that this requirement is more appropriate to policy-oriented, outcome-driven projects. We were brought up in the tradition of humanities requiring a deep immersion in the culture, language and traditions of the people about whom we wrote, our research informed by a lifetime's work. That tradition is now in jeopardy, which is a pity because the finest research on the Pacific islands came from those scholars who pursued individual research projects.[24] I am not convinced, on present evidence, that large grant-supported research necessarily produces more insightful or enduring scholarship, especially when the outcomes have to be produced in a hurry. I see some serious problems in historians and other practitioners of the humanities in being forced to march at the pace and tune set by economists and other social scientists whose intellectual agendas and approaches are significantly different. Reviewing a recent biography of historian Sir Keith Hancock, Geoffrey Bolton, himself an Australian historian of note, remarked how long it took the author to publish the book. 'How fortunate,' he wrote, that '[Jim] Davidson's university did not insist that he should instead churn out numerous articles in refereed journals as index of research productivity.'[25] How fortunate indeed. The question remains: Is the day of the big book, the fruit of a lifetime's learning and scholarship, over? Are we publishing more and more about less and less?

The pressures to conform are not likely to cease anytime soon. In a globalizing world, higher education is increasingly inter-connected. International ranking systems matter. Universities high in ranking and prestige attract more funding and better faculty as well as graduate students. Universities run on paper, and the more peer-reviewed paper is produced the better. In Australia, academic journals are ranked and research published there rewarded. The precise criterion of ranking is not clear, but their influence is beyond doubt. Emphasis on excellence in writing and research is vital and should receive priority in every academic institution worth its name. There is, moreover, a certain professional satisfaction in being published in peer-reviewed places. But sometimes, this becomes an end in itself, which leads to the question: what and for whom is the research being done. For fellow researchers, to be sure, but for those of us working on non-western regions such as the Pacific islands, the question is more complicated, touching on the issue of ethical responsibility we have towards people about whom we write.[26] Books published by prestige publishers are invariably beyond the reach of most of the reading public and most high ranking journals unaffordable.

So we end up being caught between two sets of loyalties: loyalty to the institutions where we work and its demands and expectations, and the needs and expectations of the people and places where we conduct our research. Sometimes the issue is complicated by the absence of any scholarly outlet in the islands themselves where our research could be published. There were once many, now there are few. There is, for instance, not a single scholarly journal in the humanities coming out of the University of the South Pacific, a curious regression considering that there were several two decades ago. Fortunately, the timely intervention of technology has helped, that is, the phenomenon of the internet and 'e' publishing. Works published by the ANU E Press, for instance, are available free of charge to everyone. Readers can download particular items in a book or the entire book itself. Electronic publishing may be the way of the future. It has not acquired the prestige of conventional publishing, but it is a matter of time. I understand and accept the reality of the changed circumstances of scholarly publishing, but it still takes some getting used to for people of my vintage for whom printed books are cherished cultural artefacts that occupy a privileged niche in the intellectual life of society, telescopes, compasses and sextants, as someone once said, which 'help us navigate the dangerous seas of human life.'

I have sometimes being accused by friends and foes alike of being an unrepentant elitist, once an insider but now looking austerely and judgmentally at the local scene from the comfort of a privileged chair from the outside. There may be a grain of truth in this perception, but it does genuinely dismay me to see opportunities not grasped and potential not realized among people who have much to contribute. It is particularly disheartening to see students being short changed by their mentors when what they most need is role models of scholarly excellence. Exalted polemic is no substitute for solid scholarship. I accept that a university is a not a social security institution. It is, as it has to be, an inherently elitist institution that rewards merit and meritocracy above all else. I believe that scholars have a vital role to play in society, none being more important than a willingness to speak truth to power. We should guard against the temptations of power, maintain a certain distance and detachment from it that keeps us alert to the ways in which public memory is hijacked in the service of those who govern our lives. Am I being unduly optimistic, hopelessly idealistic? 'Still bent to make some port he knows not where/ Still standing for some false impossible shore?'[27] But what, in this levelling world, is the alternative when, as New Zealand literary polymath CK Stead writes, 'universities which once set stiff requirements for entry now advertise for students and compete for 'market share.'[28]

Over time, I have become much more attuned to the political interests and concerns which underpin a lot of academic activity. Nothing is ever so simple or neutral as it seems. The day of the 'God Professors' who once ran academic departments with unfettered power, influencing individual destinies and broad directions of research, is over. So, too, is the once common practice of 'tapping someone the shoulder' for a job. The academic practice is much more open and transparent, at least on paper. But ideas of what is valid and proper vary from place to place. At the University of the South Pacific, the question most often asked at appointment times was: how many Pacific islanders are there on the staff, as opposed to expatriates or 'Indians.' Few raised questions about gender equity. Ethnicity of regional origin was the primary marker of identity. In Australia, certainly at my own university, gender equity is a very serious consideration in any appointment process. Women are often alerted to new employment opportunities and encouraged to apply. I am not sure if we seriously ask how many Pacific Islanders or Asians there are in centres of Asian and Pacific learning in Australia. These are important issues, and they speak to different political and cultural concerns and contexts. I just hope that in our quite legitimate concerns for social equity, we do not lose sight of what in the end the true purpose of a university is.

There is no shortcut to success. The journey was much harder for my generation, moving from the world of pre-literacy to literacy within the span of a single lifetime. Being an academic is not only an occupation, it is a sacred responsibility, a distinctive way of life with its own overarching cultural codes, protocols and rituals. To succeed, it requires discipline, a cultivation of solitude, cultural re-invention and a deep humility. As Longfellow said a long time ago, 'The talent for success is nothing more than doing what you can do well, and doing well whatever you do without a thought for fame.'[29] Our tasks ahead are clearly defined. We must continue to produce and publish research that adds a vital sentence to the larger global conversation of scholarship. There is no substitute for excellence. We owe that to those who laid the foundations for us in those distant and difficult days and to those who will inherit the torch from us in uncertain and demanding times. We must engage critically and sensitively with the outside world, breaking the mould of self-referential, 'ghettoising,' inward looking, academia. Our natural home should be the interface between the world of scholarship and the world of the lay public. And finally, in this era of galloping globalization, we should do everything in our power to revive the centrality of the humanities in the cultural life of humankind and in deepening our understanding of the human condition, past and present. As Stephen Garton and Elizabeth Webby argue, 'If our innovation culture is to prosper, it needs to be embedded in a deep understanding of humanity and cultural difference. This is why humanities are fundamental to human progress.'[30]

# Nine

## Coombs 4240: A Room of My Own

> *As between clear blue and cloud*
> *Between haystack and sunset sky*
> *Between oak tree and slate roof*
> *I had my existence. I was there.*
> *Me in place and the place in me.*
>
> Seamus Heaney, 'Human Chain.'

Coombs 4240 has been my 'place' for more than two decades. I am talking about Room 4240 in the Coombs Building at The Australian National University.[1] It is my second home. It is where I spend most of my waking hours. It is where all my writing is done. I feel possessive about it. It has long been a silent witness to a large part of my life and work, my thoughts, ambitions, indignations and illusions, my strengths and my frailties. It has seen me laugh and cry, hit the table in frustration when the words have not come, or punch the air with joy when they have. I pace its floor as I compose a paragraph in my head or read it aloud for clarity and flow. It has frequently heard me talk absentmindedly to no one in particular about something that is on my mind, recalling a conversation and rehearsing a reply. Coombs 4240 is more than just a physical space for me. It is my past and present, and my sanctuary from the alienations and asperities of the outside world.

We all shape spaces around us to suit our needs and reflect our temperament. There can be no mistaking that Coombs 4240 is a historian's office. There are books everywhere: on the wall-to-wall bookshelves, on the stand-alone shelves and on the floor for the overflow, monuments of the spirit and thoughts of times past. My writing desk is controlled chaos, papers and jottings in every which direction, piled one on top of the other, books and journals with pages marked for quotation. Controlled is the operative word, for despite all the apparent chaos, I can put my finger on anything I want with an ease that sometimes bemuses visitors unused to seeing such professorial clutter. 'Entombed in Catacombs,' as one of them wrote in an email. On the window wall, there are full page newspaper reviews of my work and stories of my various adventures over the years, photographs of our children: Niraj in primary school smiling innocently with one front tooth missing, Yogi receiving her diploma from some gowned university hierarch. There are framed diplomas and certificates haphazardly parked on the shelves that attest to this achievement or that. They are not for show or to impress visitors, but as daily reminders of my various journeys over the years, connections to different times and places now slowly receding from memory. There are two easy chairs for visitors and colleagues and students. There is an annex to Coombs 4240 which has my lifetime's research notes and papers piled high up on the floor. There is a table there for the occasional visitor, and I use it for light reading.

Above all, Coombs 4240 is my working library, home to books collected over a lifetime about several places from which I have been removed by history: an ancestral village in India, a home in Fiji, books about many passing worlds: a culture of scholarship, an empire, an aborted postcolonial Fiji. These books are my permanent, irreplaceable companions, always uncomplainingly there when I need them, markers of special moments in my peripatetic life. On the shelf next to me are the very first books I ever read in primary school all those years ago in Tabia: Pandit Amichand's Hindi *Pothis*, the *Caribbean Reader Introductory Book One* and *The Oxford English Readers for Africa* which we read in higher primary grades. We were a part of the British colonial empire after all, immensely proud of all the red patches on our well-thumbed Clarion Atlas. Beside them are books from my high school days as well as rare Hindi books and pamphlets and songs published in Fiji in the 1950s and earlier, such as *Jhankar* and *Fiji Digdarshan*, now lost to us forever. Next to them are books I have written myself. I have a fairly decent collection of books on the Pacific islands, a reminder of a time when I lectured on the subject to undergraduates. I don't lecture anymore. These will in due course go to some library somewhere, but I doubt if I will ever be able to part with my Fiji books. They are an integral part of me, indispensible; I can't imagine my life without them; they made me what I am. What will happen to them when I go, I sometimes wonder idly. Will they find as loving a home as they have found with me? But for the moment, they are safe and secure in Coombs 4240.

I clearly remember the first time I entered Coombs 4240. It was in 1981 for my viva, now known colloquially in Australia as the 'oral.' Unlike now, viva was a common practice then no matter how good a thesis. The great Oskar Spate was the chair of my examining committee, and 4240 was his office at that point. The other examiner was the South Asia historian Sinappah Arasaratnam, from the University of New England. (The third examiner, Ian Catanach of Canterbury, had sent his questions in writing). The feeling of trepidation is still vivid in my mind. Will I pass? Was I good enough to pass? Were there some hidden gremlins in the thesis that I might have overlooked? I had stayed up late the previous night fielding imaginary questions, reading over the text looking for typos, and feeling depressed at the few that I did find, hoping desperately that these would go unnoticed by the examiners (they were). Oskar opened with a few questions about why I had undertaken this study, about methodology and then went on—and on—about something else while I sat and nodded in deferential silence. Oskar, the geographer of the Indian subcontinent, knew the region I had written about in my thesis very well.[2] The longer he talked, I guessed, the less curly the questions I would have to answer! Arasa gently quizzed me on indenture historiography.[3] This was the easy bit, I thought; I was being softened up for really tough grilling that was surely bound to come. Mercifully, it did not. After about half an hour, I was asked to leave the room for a few minutes. When I was called back in, Oskar told me that I had passed, but nothing would be formal until I heard from the Registrar. Oh, and I could go to the University House and relax with a drink. That I certainly did, to my body and heart's content (and to my head's throbbing displeasure the next morning)!

I have vivid recollection of Spate's Coombs 4240. It was a spartan room, with hardly any books on the shelves. That seemed very odd to me: an academic office without books. On one wall there were specially built little cubby-holes filled with odd bits and pieces of paper and what I later came to know as off-prints. Oskar kept in his office only things he needed for his current project. His extensive private library was at his Black Mountain home. Oskar would now find his old office unrecognizable, alien to his geographer's neat temperament. I later found out that Coombs 4240 was once occupied by Ken Gillion, one of my mentors, while Oskar was on a study leave to research his magnificent trilogy, 'The Pacific Since Magellan.'[4] Ken had a very utilitarian approach to books. His office, too, was bare, and he sold his library to a second hand book seller when he retired and left Canberra.

Both Ken Gillion and Oskar Spate were scholars of the older generation. Ken was, of course, the author of the pioneering study of Indian indentured immigration and settlement in Fiji.[5] After teaching Indian history at the universities of Western Australia and Adelaide, he returned to the ANU to research the sequel to his first book.[6] When his five year research fellowship expired, and was not renewed, he retired from the academy at just forty nine.

Oskar had come to the ANU in 1951 as the Foundation Professor Geography, with his monumental general and regional geography of India in press. He was the author of the classic 1959 report on the social and economic problems of the Fijian people,[7] and was a member of the Fiji Education Commission in 1969. While Ken was shy and reserved, Oskar was formidably erudite and eccentric: he had the disconcerting habit of passing you in the corridors and seemingly failing to recognize you at all. In seminars he would doodle on a piece of paper, drawing the contour map of an imaginary 'tight little, right little island,' or perhaps jotting down a ditty, apparently absorbed, and then asking the most penetrating question that went straight to the heart of the talk.

Both these one-time inhabitants of Coombs 4240 taught me things that have stayed with me. Oskar was famous for saying 'One doesn't have to be solemn to be serious,' and he lived up to his credo. And Ken believed in 'Wearing your learning lightly.' Oskar was very witty, highly intelligent, extremely well read, and delightful company in his good moods: he was fully aware that he had a 'propensity to cantankerousness,' but a marvellous man: a true polymath. Both were craftsmen of a high order, especially Oskar, and from them I learnt the importance of clarity and economy of expression. I can never match them, of course, but I try to emulate their example. It grieves me that so few people in my College, of Asia and the Pacific no less, have no idea who Oskar was, what his accomplishments were: this man who was truly one of the intellectual giants of the ANU and whose work will be remembered and read long after many of us are gone. When I suggested to a colleague that our 'School of Culture History and Language' might be named after Oskar Spate, he thought that I was mischievously putting forward the name of George Speight, the Fiji coupster!

I returned to the ANU and to Coombs permanently in 1990. Oskar was still the occupant of Room 4240, to the chagrin of some senior faculty who did not approve of the idea of a long-retired academic occupying a professorial office, even if it was someone of Oskar's eminence and a former director of the Research School of Pacific Studies to boot. Oskar had by then completed his magnum opus and was in frail health, barely able to walk up the stairs even with the help of walking stick (but with a pipe seemingly permanently clenched between his teeth). As a visitor to the department (from the University of Hawaii on a year's sabbatical to work on my history of twentieth century Fiji[8]), I was asked to share Oskar's office. This arrangement worked well. Oskar came in infrequently, mostly around mid-afternoon to check his mail and to attend seminars and then, after a few months, stopped coming in altogether, having moved into a nursing home where he unhappily lingered for another ten years (saying more than once 'How I wish I could go to sleep and don't wake up the next morning'). I now became the sole occupant of 4240. This did not go down well at all with some of the hierarchs: a visitor occupying a professorial office. Word was heard of someone asking for my removal so that he could occupy an office befitting his status. Spare rooms were in short supply. By the time I had filled the room with my books and research notes, the matter of occupancy was settled firmly in my favour.

As I imbibed the folklore of the place, I became acutely aware of the arcane protocols of status, at least in the Research School of Pacific and Asian Studies. There was a marked hierarchy of status. The distinction between sahibs and subalterns was still alive and well though not publicly talked about and even disavowed. At the departmental pinnacle were the professors, God-professors, who automatically acted as heads and exercised great influence on the careers of their colleagues. Their authority was unchallenged; they were the acknowledged leaders and intermediaries to the outside world. Below them were Professorial Fellows, senior academics with still a few rungs to climb to the top. Below them were Senior Fellows and Fellows, roughly equivalent now to Associate Professors and Lecturers. All these were tenurable positions. At the top of the untenured ladder were Senior Research Fellows (Ken Gillion being an example) and Research Fellows. These untenured members of staff were often academics from other universities on sabbatical or extended research leave to write their books and then return to their home universities. Each department had a certain number of rotating, short-term fellowships for this purpose, reflecting ANU's Institute of Advanced Studies' unique role in Australian higher education, performing a role other teaching universities could not. Now the ANU is simply one among several universities, *primus inter pares*. This perhaps is the most depressing change I have witnessed in my time at the ANU over the last two decades: the steady diminution of a great institution, still leading the way but just barely. I can hear the detractor say, 'If at all.'

Hierarchy and difference were expressed in subtle ways. Professorial offices were of a certain size. Usually, they had two windows, not one. They had carpets whereas non-professorial offices did not. Their desks had a certain number of drawers, one or two more than those issued to scholars on the rungs below them. Professors were entitled to research assistants as well as secretaries who typed their work and borrowed books from the libraries, organised their travel and did the acquittals. Not all professors were of a type. Some were eccentric and deliberately unorthodox in their mannerisms. Jim Davidson, the Pacific history professor, I was told, delighted in flouting convention. He wore very short shorts to work which outraged his sartorially more conservative colleagues. On the other hand, Sir Keith Hancock was a pucca sahib who dressed accordingly and treated his junior staff in a suitably donnish manner: he would introduce himself as 'Professor Sir Keith Hancock.'[9] He was the pope of the historical profession in Australia.[10] The distinctions and hierarchies of yesteryear have now vanished almost beyond recall. Some of the old nomenclature survives in the Coombs Building though: we still have Fellows and Senior Fellows, but ranking and the protocols which went with it have become obsolete. The surprise colleagues expressed at my occupying a 'professorial' office in 1990 would hardly raise an eyebrow today.

All the old colleagues who were in the Coombs Building in 1990 when I returned are now gone or in retirement. Among the former are Dorothy Shineberg, the historian of sandalwood and Melanesian labour trade, and the indefatigably independent-minded Robert Langdon who ran the Pacific Manuscripts Bureau from its inception in 1968 until his retirement in the 1980s. Donald Denoon, Hank Nelson, Niel Gunson and Deryck Scarr have retired. I miss Hank Nelson the most, the boy from Boort in the Mallee country, humane and generous and dependable, who always read my work with care and who would be happy to know that I have not used 'however' in much of what I have written in recent years on account of his advice that it was a lazy writer's word, superfluous. Deryck's office, Coombs 4239, was directly opposite mine. We maintained civil relations and drank polite cups of tea in the Coombs Tea Room, but as students of Fijian history would know, we were, and are, chalk and cheese in our views about Fijian history and politics, and the gulf sadly has widened over time. Everyone knew that Deryck, the heir apparent to Jim Davidson, felt cheated of what he thought was his just due: the chair of Pacific history, which instead went to Gavan Daws and later to Donald Denoon. But personal differences aside, our corridor had a collective sense that the centre of the discipline of Pacific history was right here. There were other Pacific historians elsewhere, but they were our offshoots, people who lived in the provinces. That sense of confidence, not to say arrogance, is now a thing of the distant past.

With the gradual fading of the older generation has gone a world of academic life, the world of unhurried scholarship and of the virtue of curiosity-driven research and wide ranging erudition. It would be difficult to say now of a colleague what Hancock said of Oskar Spate: that he would be as much at home in a chair of English as he was in the chair of Geography. In my own time, Mark Elvin, an eminent professor of Chinese history, could publish three volumes of science fiction under a pseudonym (John Mark Dutton). I cannot think of many younger colleagues who will be able to match the literary accomplishments of my colleague Tessa Morris Suzuki who, in addition to writing path-breaking books in her field of Japanese and Korean history, has published fine poetry and children's stories.[11] Times have changed. By today's standards, the older generation might appear less productive (though, as I endlessly point out, they did not have the advantage of word processors and the internet). That was certainly true of some of them, but they produced scholarship which has stood the test of time and which will not be surpassed. More by any stretch of the imagination does not necessarily mean better. There is a difference, as the English historian David Cannadine has said somewhere, between the 'culture of productivity' and the 'culture of creativity.'[12]

Life in Coombs 4240 begins early, around eight, and ends about six. This has always been the pattern of work for me. Some colleagues use their offices to check emails, or attend to administrative duties but do all their writing at home. I now draw a sharp distinction between home and work, not the least in deference to my family who have suffered enough from my periodic bouts of absentmindedness. There are inevitable distractions and diversion from phone calls and casual visits. Discipline is crucial to manage time. Intrusions of the external world have to be dealt with promptly and archived. Like most people, the first thing I do, almost as a ritual, after a cup of tea, is to read my email. Routine matters, such as notices of meetings or edicts from the hierarchs about this change or that new policy, are noted and deleted. Personal queries are answered, but it is emails from complete strangers seeking information that tests the patience. Hardly a week goes by without a request from someone in the Indo Fijian diaspora wondering how they might be able to trace their roots back to India. Often the request is hopeless because they have nothing beyond the name of the person who went to Fiji, and even that is unreliable. I always provide pointers for more specific information. The profound yearning of the heart to know about one's roots is genuine and it is deeply felt.

Then there are elementary requests from students, mostly from North America, about research papers and dissertations they are writing on Fiji, requests for relevant sources and to read and comment on drafts. It is all so anonymous and distant; I am almost expected to put aside everything and attend to their requests. From academic journals from around the world come requests to review submissions made to them. Less frequent but very time-consuming are requests from academic presses for review of book manuscripts. The good publishable ones are not a problem; it is the bad ones that require detailed comment. Such obligations come with the territory. It is a part of one's professional obligation but none of it is taken into account by the bean counters of the educational bureaucracy or in the promotion stakes by Promotion and Selection Committees. The university is an enterprise that runs on paper, I was once told, and the more refereed paper you have under your name, the better. That is the brutal truth of academic life, rhetoric about service and outreach and teaching notwithstanding.

Such 'teaching' as I do is confined to Coombs 4240. That is where I interact with my 'students' most intensely. I am uncomfortable with the word 'student.' I arrived at the ANU more than thirty years ago not as a 'Student,' but as a 'Research Scholar.' That was our official designation. We were being trained for a lifetime of scholarship and expected to participate fully in the scholarly life of the department to learn the protocols and rituals of academic culture. We belonged to a community of scholars, and it helped that the formal conventions and protocols of relations between the senior staff and younger scholars were very relaxed, at least in Pacific History. We addressed each other by our first names, though behind the appearance of relaxed informality and cheerful banter at morning tea was an unstated expectation that at the end of our term of three years (extensions were rare), we would, as a matter of course, produce a world-class thesis. I recall Ken Gillion's words to me vividly when I arrived at the ANU: 'If you are not on top of the literature on your subject in six months, you should not be here.' I was despatched to the library to read everything there was to read on my subject and to prepare a thesis proposal for public defence before heading off to the field. It was daunting thought at the time, but I now appreciate the confidence my mentors had in me and the freedom they allowed for me to pursue my thoughts.

Nearly every Research Scholar in the Coombs Building was on a scholarship; private and fee-paying students were not around then as they are now. Getting one of these through open international competition was a mark of some distinction. Doctoral students had no course work, no special reading groups. Scholars were expected to master their fields on their own, in consultation with their supervisor and get on with research as soon as possible. Dorothy Shineberg, for example, agreed with her own PhD supervisor that 'if one couldn't work independently at this level, then one had no business seeking a doctorate.'[13] It was taken for granted that we had been taught the basics of our discipline at the undergraduate level, that we were acquainted with the philosophies of RH Collingwood, EH Carr and Geoffrey Elton, and if we were not, we would familiarise ourselves with them on our own. The main focus was on the researching and writing of the thesis; everything we did was geared to that end.

The committee system of supervision was slowly coming into vogue, but the model followed in practice was still the Oxbridge one of working with a single scholar and writing your dissertation under his or her supervision. Other senior scholars in the department might enquire politely about your work but refrained from 'interfering.' You were known as so-and-so's student, or working under the supervision of so-and-so. The process of mentoring was personalized. Friends might be prevailed upon to read your drafts, but there was no editorial support available in the department, even to people for whom English was not the first language. It was expected that as an ANU scholar, you would naturally write a competent thesis, meeting the highest standards of contemporary scholarly practice, in acceptable, error-free prose on your own. Anything less could not be countenanced. And it was let known that some examiners did not take kindly at all to typos in the thesis. Being asked to re-submit for whatever reason was an ineradicable blot on your name and could seriously jeopardise your prospects of employment at a decent university.

Some of the old practice survives. Even with the committee system now formally in place, students end up working closely with one scholar. But there is far more support available to students. Virtually every department has someone who provides editorial assistance. No one now submits hard bound copies for examination; it is soft, spiral-bound copies with the expectation that changes would be required and made to the final version. It may also be the case that the convenience of word processing makes examiners more ready to demand revisions, whereas in the days of typewriting and carbon copies there was an understandable reluctance to take such a step. Perhaps that is why such a premium was placed on fluent, typo-free prose. A certain managerial culture has crept into academic practice. Workshops are held, usually by people who have never supervised any students in their lives, to tell potential supervisors what their roles and responsibilities are, and what legally enforceable obligations the university has towards students. I was once told that we, the university, are 'service providers,' and students are our 'customers.' We were all told of a student who sued the university for not providing adequate supervision which, he said, had impeded his progress: he had put his regular work on hold to do a doctorate, and he was suing for income foregone. In my own time, I knew of cases of difficult supervisor-student relationships, some deteriorating to the point of no contact, but am not aware of anyone being sued. The idea was simply unthinkable. More generally, people of my generation had no sense of entitlement; we were grateful for what we had and the opportunities that came our way.

I have had my share of graduate students. Each is unique in his or her own way. Some have a good sense of what they would like to do and want simply to be allowed to simply get on with research. Others need guidance to help formulate a doable topic. Some brim with confidence, others lack it. Some call me by my first name while to some, usually from Asian and Pacific cultures, I am 'Prof.' or 'Dr Brij.' For them, addressing teachers by their first names is seen to be culturally inappropriate. I am not fussed but I respect their sensitivities. It took me ages to call Oskar Spate by his first name: he was always 'Prof.' to me. Ken Gillion, on the other hand, insisted on being called 'Ken.' Whatever the academic bureaucrats say, and all the legalese notwithstanding, the supervisor-student relationship must be based on trust and confidence and a large doze of mutual respect. It is an unequal, dependent relationship and it can be fraught. And it is always useful to remind students it is their own thesis they are writing, not their supervisor's. They are spending three years of their life writing their dissertation, and they must make the most of an opportunity that will not come their way again. Most of them do.

From my perch in Coombs 4240, I have noticed profound changes in the culture and practice of the academy. Technology has been a main driver of change. The latest invention when I completed my dissertation was the 'selectric' typewriter that dispensed with the messy whitener, and how grateful we were for it. (The senior academics who had their work typed by the departmental secretaries were less conscious of the change). Publishing regularly at decent intervals was expected and mostly done, but there was no annual accounting for brownie points distributed by the government's educational bureaucracy (although publications were listed in Annual Reports where they went unread). It was understood that decent scholarship would take time to produce; it was like making yoghurt, as one old-timer said to me: it could not be hurried. His own magnum opus came long after he had retired. Historians, as a rule, were expected to write books. Journal articles were small morsels better suited to the various disciplines in the social sciences; it was in the books that the big ideas were presented and upon which reputations were made. I am no longer sure that is the case today. Writing a big book takes time, but accounting of publications is done on an annual basis. Wittingly or unwittingly, we are forced to tread the path of the social sciences. In more recent years, with the advent of ERA [Excellence in Research in Australia] the emphasis is placed on publishing in A and A+ journals. How the journals have been ranked, who ranked them, remains a frustrating mystery, at least to me, but the bureaucrats brook no criticism: rules are rules and they have to be followed. It puts inordinate pressure on the younger faculty for whom such validation truly matters.

The troubling thing is how meekly academics have capitulated to such pressure. By our acquiescence we have been complicit in the making of the mess that confronts us today. We have an obligation to perform at the highest standards of scholarship, but publishing in places not as highly ranked does not diminish the quality of our scholarship. And there is an ethical dimension to our work as well, which may not be the case in the natural and physical sciences and perhaps not even in some of the social sciences. Some of us feel a moral duty to disseminate the fruits of our research among communities where we work. Not many there would be able to access the highly rated learned journals. Perhaps electronic publishing is the way of the future, but e-books presently do not score well in the prestige stakes.[14]

Coombs 4240 is an historian's office. It is also unmistakably a Fijian's office. On the front door is a print of a Fijian exhibition from the Turnbull Library with the words 'The Heart of Fiji' written on it. On top of it is an old print of the Fijian coat-of-arms: 'Rere vaka na kalou ka doka na Tui,' obey God and respect chiefs. Inside, there is a tapa cloth on the wall, and large blown up photographs of the Suva vegetable and fish markets and a clogged Waimanu road, of a village handicraft centre and a lone, loaded cane train with its Indo-Fijian driver standing beside it looking straight at the camera. On one wall is a framed painting of 'Mr Tulsi's Store,' and on another a print of the cover of my 'Bitter Sweet,' a young Indo-Fijian girl looking anxiously, nervously at the camera. These are constant reminders of the spirit, sound, sight and smell of a place that was once home to me, and intellectually and emotionally still is, even though I have been barred by the military regime from returning to it. In the front of a stand-alone bookshelf is a framed photograph of Fiji's first deposed Prime Minister Dr Timoci Bavadra, given to me in May 1987 by an Indo-Fijian clerk in the Ministry of Information's archival section in the basement of the old Government Buildings as a memento to keep of a time, he said, that would never come again. On the wall is a portrait of the multi party Laisenia Qarase government thrown out of office in a military coup in 2006. On the wall next to my table is a portrait of the Fiji Constitution Commission of which I was a member, and next to it is a small framed photograph of a smiling Sitiveni Rabuka sitting next to me in the Suva Town Hall in 2006. Directly on top is a *Canberra Times* cartoon of the 1987 coup titled 'Paradise Lost' with Rabuka in a tank, driving innocent, unclothed civilians into the bush. All these are constant reminders of the troubled past of my homeland and of the various efforts to fashion a different, more inclusive future for it.

It is in Coombs 4240 that I have done all my writing for the last twenty years. It is here that I have sought to understand the troubled history of my country. It is here, more than a decade ago, that I wrote the life of AD Patel, the Indo-Fijian leader who struggled for forty years for a non-racial democratic future for Fiji.[15] It is here that I wrote the life of Patel's successor Jai Ram Reddy. From the lives of these two men I became aware of the ceaseless, uphill struggle for a different future for Fiji.[16] Had their vision for social justice, equality and human dignity succeeded, Fiji might well have been spared its present fate. What is past is past. A large part of my life has been devoted to ensuring that the voices of the vanquished are not extinguished from public memory or the written record. 'Words,' Winston Churchill once said, 'are the only things that last forever.'[17]

And it is from Coombs 4240 that I have spoken out, and continue to speak out, against the coups in Fiji. I accept fully the fundamental truth of Arthur Schlesinger Jr's view that 'a society in which the citizens cannot criticise the policy of the state is a society without the means of correcting its course.'[18] Dissent in a democracy should never be construed as disloyalty. It should be the responsibility of every citizen, every civilized human being, to speak out against tyranny and oppression, against the subversion of democratic values and the rule of law. Scholarship should, as a matter of moral duty, speak truth to power; silence can never be an option. Violence as a tool of public policy is always counterproductive. There are certain values humanity has embraced as its own which transcend national and political boundaries, and which are worth defending. This much I have said from Coombs 4240, and more. And I have paid the price, the price of banishment from the country of my birth, cheated of my birthright. What is it about Fiji that I miss the most, I have often been asked. Not being able to say the final farewell to friends and family is the simple answer. But there is no regret: I could not have done anything else. I am at peace with myself.

Coombs 4240 is my private retreat and my site of resistance. Within its walls I have laughed and cried, talked and listened, taught and learned. It has enabled me to engage with the world on my own terms, not on someone else's. It is here that I have met people who have inspired me and enriched my life. It is here that I have glimpsed possibilities I never imagined. It is here that I have become what I am. It is here that I daily struggle to rescue memory from the shallow graveyards of forgetfulness and defend it against those who seek its extinction in the interests of the privileged and the powerful. To whatever quirk of fate that brought me to Coombs 4240, I am immeasurably grateful. The words of William Shakespeare are apposite: 'Within this wall of flesh/ There is soul that counts thee her creditor.'

# Ten

## People In-Between

There is a small Indian community in Canberra where I live. It is a replica of Indian communities found in many western countries. It has its temples, mosques, churches; its spice and grocery shops and video outlets, restaurants and takeaway joints. It has its voluntary organisations pursuing a variety of social and cultural objectives. Occasional classes are held to re-acquaint children with the culture of their parents or grandparents. Festivals, such as Diwali and Dasherra, Eid and Prophet Mohammed's birthday are celebrated with appropriate aplomb. Cultural evenings, of songs and music, form a regular part of the community's social calendar. Ancient prejudices and modern greed are alive and well, causing fissures and frictions which enliven the social life of its members.

No migrant community is complete without a newsletter, and the Canberra Indians have several, both the electronic as well as the conventional variety, disseminating news about cultural events, soliciting contributions for this cause or that, announcing news of death, birth and marriages. Some offer longer reflections. Here is an excerpt, which provides the text for may paper. 'Like an overflowing container, Indians have spilled all over the world,' says the writer. 'This spilling,' he continues with becoming modesty, 'has been by and large to the benefit of the world.' He goes on:

> We Indians are found in every corner of the world. One in every five human beings on this planet is an Indian. From Australia to Alaska and Britain to Bahrain, we are proudly carrying the flag of Indian culture and civilisation along with idlis, dosas and chicken curry. They say that when Hillary and Tenzing reached the peak of Mt Everest, they were served hot parathas and cold lassi at *Bhappe da Dhaba*. Hillary was so enthralled by these that he climbed Mt Everest twice. It is rumoured that the pathfinder on Mars found the thousand year relics of *Patel the Motel* among the rocks. You can find a Fiji Indian running an Indian grocery

shop on the North Pole selling spices, rice, atta and dhal, along with copies of Hindi movies boldly labelled 'Pirated.'[1]

It is true that Indians are found nearly everywhere in the world. In 1980, ancient history now, the Calcutta newspaper, *The Statesman*, claimed that there were, in fact, only five countries where Indians had 'not yet chosen to stay.'[2] These were Cape Verde Island, Guinea Bissau, Mauritania, North Korea, and Romania! This is impressive statistics about a people long regarded as landlubbers, bound to home and hearth by caste strictures forbidding the crossing of the dreaded *kala pani*, dark, pollution-producing sea. But despite its wide spread, the Indian diaspora is not nearly as large as other diasporas. In 1990, 8.6 million Indians were living outside the subcontinent, roughly one percent of the population living at home. By contrast, 11 million Jews lived outside Israel, compared to 3.5 million within it, while 22 million Chinese lived outside China compared to one billion at home.[3]

The claim about the popularity of Indian cuisine is also (partly) true. Even where Indian people themselves might not be welcomed, their food is. In Suva, Fiji, you will not find many mainstreams indigenous Fijian restaurant, even though Fijians now constitute more than half the population. You will, however, find Indian and Chinese restaurants in all the major urban centres. In Trinidad and Guyana, Indian 'busup-shut' and 'dhall-puris' are the standard fare in urban areas. In Paramaribo, Surinam, the most popular eating place in town is 'Roopram's Rotishop.' So Indian food, especially of the non-vegetarian variety, is well on its way to becoming a regular fare in most countries with Indian populations. In this respect, in the friendly competition of the culinary stakes, the Indian and Chinese communities are rivals. May this rivalry long continue.

But other assertions in the passage quoted above are more problematic and would bear closer scrutiny. I want to preface what follows by noting some of the conceptual difficulties involved in using such an encompassing term as 'Indian' to describe a literal and symbolic community of people who share a common ancestral culture. A Patel or a Punjabi or a peasant from Fiji, are not all peas in the same pod. I want to suggest a more complex, socially, occupationally and genealogically differentiated category. I conceive of social and cultural identity as 'multiply inflected and continuously reproduced,' to use the words of Aisha Khan, who goes on to argue that diaspora studies generally 'reflect the recognition that stability in points of origin, finality of destinations, and coherence of identities are notions that have all been questioned and reassessed in recent scholarship.'[4] This leads me to the second point about the nature and meaning of the relationship that diasporic Indians have with India, that is, whether all overseas Indians 'are proudly carrying the flag of Indian culture and civilisation,' or whether the relationship admits to a more complex reading.

The Indian diaspora, like most other movements and displacement of people, is the product of many causes and many crossings over an extended period of time. Historians differ over the precise timing and nature of the different phases of Indian migration, but for my purposes, three will do. The first phase occurs in the pre-European age, involving long distance trading voyages across the Indian Ocean to the east coast of Africa and, closer to home, Southeast Asia. Impelled by missionary zeal or the imperatives of commerce and trade, voluntary and individualistic in nature, the impact of the early excursions survive now in cultural and historical relics and in the archives of deep time.

The second phase of systematic organized labour migration was the result of European commercial and colonial expansion in the 18th and 19th centuries. The third phase, a product of imperial relationships and the opportunities for migration, education and settlement which it offered, is by and large a phenomenon of the 20th century. The British Commonwealth, particularly the United Kingdom, was the main destination of the Indian elite. The United States and Canada and to a lesser extent Australia and New Zealand followed later, and then in much smaller (but now increasing) numbers. The emigrants were well-to-do or well connected, and migrated freely and voluntarily. The contact with the motherland was maintained and nourished through arranged marriages and regular visits. These, especially the more recent migrants, are the true 'non-resident Indians.'

Another kind of Indian 'diaspora' has begun to emerge recently whose precise character and orientation is difficult to ascertain but which is likely to become an important part of the larger diasporic mosaic this century. This is the diaspora of the 'twice banished,' descendants of Indian settlers in the plantation colonies in the West Indies, Fiji, Mauritius, Africa, and parts of Southeast Asia. Although ancestrally Indian, they are products of many influences, western and others peculiar to the region of residence. (In the case of Fiji, for instance, Indian, Oceanic and Western, in the Caribbean, Indian, Black and Western). Forced by political turbulence and repression at home—Idi Amin in Uganda, Sitiveni Rabuka in Fiji, Forbes Burnham in Guyana—or because of a search of better prospects, the descendants of the pioneer Indian settlers in the tropical colonies now make home in Canada, the United States, Australasia and Europe. They acknowledge their Indian roots and can identify with the broad contours of Indian culture, but they are also acutely aware of their separate non-Indianness as well. Questions of 'culture,' 'homeland,' 'territoriality,' 'nation' so intimately tied to the a diasporic identity, always problematic even at the best of times, acquire a particular niche in their psyche.

I do not want to dwell on the trials and tribulations of this group, of which I myself am a part, but of their founding ancestors who left India during the second phase of migration from the subcontinent, a direct product of European colonial and commercial expansion in the 19th century. It began with the large scale migration of Indian indentured labour to the 'King Sugar' colonies of Natal, Mauritius, Guyana, Trinidad, Surinam, Fiji and, under slightly different system, to countries in Southeast Asia. Begun in 1834 to meet the shortage of labour following the abolition of slavery in the British Empire, indentured emigration transported nearly 1.3 million Indian people to the distant colonies until all emigration ceased in 1916.[5]

Indenture was a grand but ultimately flawed labour experiment. But it was a unique system, different from the various patterns of Chinese labour migration to Southeast Asia. The system was government regulated and supervised, for the emigrants were British subjects departing for employment under a five year contract.[6] That contract stipulated the terms and conditions of employment in the colonies, remuneration for the labour of the emigrants, state responsibility for provision of medical and housing facilities, rations for a specified period of time. The immigrants would work for five and half days a week on plantation and manufacturing work, for which adult males would be receive 12 pennies and women nine, and they would receive rations for six months on a scale prescribed by the government. Not surprisingly, these promises were seldom fulfilled, leading to grave abuses in the system, but at least on paper—and in fact more than on paper—the colonial governments were held accountable by the government of India for the performance or non-performance of the contracts.

One important feature of Indian indentured migration was the provision of a free return passage to all emigrants who had completed ten years of industrial residence in the colonies; they could return at their own expense after five. Colonial governments and planters everywhere protested and pleaded with India to revoke the provision. After having incurred huge expenses, they wanted the Indians to remain to provide a settled pool of cheap labour for the labour-intensive sugar economy. The Government of India refused to oblige, for to have done so would have been an act of deception. Many emigrants returned. Up to 1870, 21 per cent had returned. From Fiji nearly 24, 000 of the 60,000 migrants went back. But the majority stayed on, encouraged by the availability of new opportunities, and inertia. In the course of time, sojourners became settlers.

The rights and interests of these settlers were protected in legislation, at least on paper. First, the government of India insisted that its indentured subjects be allowed to enjoy the same rights and privileges as other subjects resident in the colonies. It was a requirement repeated over time. All the colonies were required to submit annual reports to both the Government of India and to the India Office in London. When exceptional abuses came to light, India intervened with the threat of cancelling emigration. The threat was effective. Official enquires were instituted, which brought some amelioration. By the beginning of the 20th century, Indian public opinion began to take interest in the affairs of the indentured Indians.[7] Their reports and comments, coinciding with a resurgence of Indian nationalism, galvanized Indian public opinion which eventually ended the indenture system. In the colonies, an extensive machinery supervised indentured labour, consisting of resident inspectors of immigrants, medical officers and others. At the apex of the system was the Agent General of Immigration, a colonial official who represented the concern of the immigrants in the Legislative Council. Not all officials were effective or sympathetic, but neither were they all invariably callous and colluding with the planters.

Another feature unique to indenture was the fixed ratio of men to women in the emigrating population. The ratio evolved gradually. Before the 1860s, the situation varied, but after the 1870s, the Government of India insisted that 40 women accompany every 100 men on each shipment. The colonies complained about the extra cost of paying for (women) labourers who might more likely become a burden than an asset, and recruiters complained of difficulties in recruiting them. Once again, though, India was adamant, and in most cases, the ratio was met, and not necessarily through coercion or kidnapping either. In the late 19th century, women from depressed rural areas of eastern Uttar Pradesh were on the move in search of employment, and it was from this uprooted mass that the migrants came.[8] The government's stipulation ameliorated what would have been a major social problem, but disparity in the sex ratio, while it lasted, caused uncertainty and instability in Indian social and married life. Nonetheless, the presence of women on the plantations helped the community retain a semblance of its cultural and social identity.

There is another feature of indentured emigration worth noting. The people who migrated were essentially non-literate labourers and petty cultivators, essentially representing a fair cross-section of rural India. The Patels and the Punjabis, the traders and the artisans, came much later or, in the case of East Africa, went either as temporary workers or as fortune-seeking free migrants. The impression that the quotation gives, and which many visitors have, of Indians as wealthy traders and entrepreneurs is misleading. In fact, long after indenture ended, the bulk of the descendants of the *girmitiyas* remained on the farm, as cultivators of rice, sugar, cotton, bananas and other commercial crops, as employees of plantation companies and as general casual labourers. Their visibility in the commercial and professional sector came much later, accompanied unsurprisingly by envy and suspicion of those whose dominance their efforts challenged.

Like the Indians, the Chinese have a long, almost unbroken, record of migration to neighbouring countries as sojourners in search of better opportunities. This migration, like its Indian counterpart, is divided into several phases. The first, from the seventh to the sixteenth centuries, the intra-Asian phase, commercial in nature and often officially sponsored, was confined to the neighbouring region in Southeast Asia B Formosa, the Malay Peninsula, the Philippines and the Dutch East Indies. The second phase, from the sixteenth to the nineteenth centuries, was also intra-Asian in scope, but stimulated by the entry of European powers in the intra-Asian trade sphere, with increased numbers of merchants, artisans, miners and agricultural workers going to the Philippines, Java, West Borneo, Sumatra, Thailand and the Malay Peninsula.[9]

In the third phase, during the nineteenth century, the Chinese, while expanding within Asia, branched out voluntarily as individuals to other areas, to such far away places as Fiji in the late 19th century, where they set up as retailers and rural shop keepers, often marrying into the indigenous communities. Some left for the Caribbean from the 1890s to the 1940s, and many of the present day Caribbean Chinese are descended from this group. However, the Chinese were vastly outnumbered by Indian indentured migrants.

Both the experience as well as the structure of Chinese and Indian indentured migration differed in significant respects. As already noted, the Indian indenture system was state sponsored and regulated. The Chinese indenture had its own unique characteristics which distinguished it from its Indian counterpart. Lai has identified six differences between Chinese and Indian patterns of indentured migration.[10] There was no provision for a return passage back to China after the end of the five year term, as there was in the case of the Indians. The contracts the Chinese had were less standardized than the contracts of Indian indenture, leading to confusion and misinterpretation. The Chinese contracts provided for a seven and half hour workday, while for Indians in Trinidad it was nine hours and seven hours in Guyana. The Chinese could have repayable loan advances as well as country payments for accompanying family members, whereas the Indians did not. The Indian indentured labourers were given rations for a limited period upon arrival in the colonies, after which they were expected to pay their own expenses, whereas Chinese indentured workers were sometimes allowed rations as well as wages and other benefits, including small garden grounds. Perhaps the most important difference was that Chinese women were not allowed to enter into contracts of indenture. Instead, they entered into contracts of residence which bound them to designated plantations for five years where they lived but where they were not obliged to work. Indian indentured women, on the other hand, were brought to the colonies as indentured workers in their own right and employed on the plantations as such. This complicated family life, imposed additional hardships on women and contributed to the neglect of young children, producing high, heart-rending mortality rates in the late 19th century.

Both the Chinese as well as the indentured Indian communities bore the brunt of the brutalizing routine of the plantation regime. Indeed, the plantation was the site of massive social and cultural transformation for both the communities. Smaller in number and strong in the early phase of indentured emigration to the West Indies, the Chinese were, on the whole, well received by the planters, and commended in official reports for their industry, thrift and law-abiding nature. The British Guinea Commission noted in 1871:

> The Chinese labourer possesses greater intelligence than either the Indian or the Negro, and is much quicker at learning to manage machinery than either of them. He is also very careful and neat in his work in the field or buildings; is much more independent than the Coolie, and is not easily led away by discontented persons, rarely making a frivolous complaint...Possessing a keen sense of justice where his own rights are concerned, he is very capable of strong resentment that appears to him unjust.[11]

This is from the perspective of officials and says little about the inner personal costs of work. In fact, physical abuse of the labourers was common, and the high level of stress and anxiety starkly indexed in high suicide rates, drug addiction, unlawful desertion and unauthorized absence from work, deliberate acts of vandalism against plantation property and in occasional strikes.

The fundamental difference between Chinese and Indian experiences was that in the West Indies by the 1870s, the heyday of the Chinese was over, replaced by indentured Indians who became the backbone of the sugar plantation economy. For this reason, they were more deeply affected by the rigours of the plantation economy. Indeed, in some places, such as Guyana, the Indians continued to depend on the nexus of the plantation economy for their survival well into the middle decades of the 20th century. Even when the Indians were freed from indenture, they continued to do agricultural work, remaining in rural areas as cane and rice growers, field labourers and mill hands. The drift towards the urban areas and into the skilled professions came later, and much more slowly.

In contrast, many Chinese left the confines of the plantations as soon as they were eligible and went into other professions, quicker in some colonies than in others.[12] In Trinidad, many entered the retail trade, while others became domestic servants, hawkers, cocoa and coconut growers, jewellers, saw millers, landlords, rum distillers and smugglers and owners of the hardware business. They did well, some exceptionally so, such as Wong Yan-Sau in British Guiana and John Ho-a-Shoo whose three sons attended the University of Edinburgh in the early 1990s and whose daughter, Asin, became a Fellow of the Royal College of Surgeons before settling in Hong Kong in 1915.

But any hope that this success might encourage the development of a larger Chinese community in the West Indies failed to materialise. On the contrary, the Chinese population continued to decline throughout the latter half of the 19th century. Despite some (half-hearted) attempts, there was no fresh injection of migrants from China once the system of Indian indentured emigration took root. Its success spelt the end of the Chinese experiment. Many Chinese did not marry, or had no children even when they entered into common law unions. Another reason for the decline was the mobility of the Chinese who dispersed to other parts of the Caribbean which seemed more commercially lucrative. Some returned to China, perhaps the most notable of them being Eugene Chen, a lawyer, who became Sun Yet Sen's foreign affairs advisor and personal secretary from 1912-1925, and a member of the Kuomintang Central Executive Committee. The Indians, on the other hand, were less occupationally mobile and certainly less prone to migration than the Chinese. About a quarter of the indentured Indians and their families and even descendants returned to India.

The Chinese and the Indians also differed in their approach to, and enthusiasm for, integration, into their host societies. The former responded to opportunities for integration more readily than the latter for a number of reasons, including the small size of the community, the great distance from China, the absence of regular cultural contact with the ancestral homeland and the realities in their new homeland. One of these realities was the paucity of Chinese women, and the willingness of Chinese men to form liaisons with local women, thereby lessening the potential for antipathy towards them. So intermarriage was a function of both necessity as well as choice. Overtime, a sizeable and important mixed race Chinese community developed, speaking the local language and often adopting anglicized names for the sake of convenience. Another facilitator of assimilation was the Chinese non-reluctance to convert to Christianity. The 1891 Trinidad census showed that 914 of the 1,006 Chinese had converted to the new faith, with the majority belonging to the Church of England, followed, in that order, by Roman Catholicism, Presbyterianism, and the Wesleyan Church. Still, despite these developments, there was no wholesale rejection of things Chinese. As Lai points out:

> Local-born Chinese ties to the homeland diminished progressively with the generational factor, even though Chinese ethnicity as a binding within the Chinese community was retained, but varying a great deal with individual families and diluted over time by the process of creolization/Americanization, cultural and racial. However, the China link remained, and indeed never died, side by side with the assimilation and creolization process.[13]

With the indentured Indians in the West Indies and elsewhere, the process of assimilation was much slower and much more measured. Indenture involved both fragmentation as well as reconstitution. Perhaps the great casualty of indentured migration was the caste system whose strict rules of social relationships, pollution and purity and other ritual strictures fell by the wayside on the long voyage to the colonies and, even more forcefully, on the plantations whose daily routine of labour and systems of reward acknowledged individual enterprise and initiative and not divinely sanctioned status. Another factor of importance was the background of the workers, who came from the middle to lower social and economic strata, people of the 'Little Tradition,' in Milton Singer's words, unversed in the higher, sacred texts of Hinduism. The absence of cultural leadership created confusion and hardship. The indifference of the colonial regime and the determination of the planters to keep the Indians in the labour force helped matters little.

For all this, though, there never was a complete breakdown of Indian social and cultural institutions on the plantations. The Indians developed a new culture, drawn from surviving fragments of the past and interweaving them with what they encountered in the colonies. As Leo Despres has written, there was continuity 'not only because the indentures had certain rights, but also because the immigration and labour laws which defined those rights served to confine the new immigrants to ethnic ghettos. As new indentures arrived in one wave after another for almost three-quarters of a century, they were mixed with those who came earlier. This served to reinforce traditional habits and customs and contributed to a continuity of cultural patterning.'[14] The contrast with the Chinese experience was marked.

Women played a critical role in the reconstitution and maintenance of Indian culture. As Jeremy Poynting writes, women were 'the main preservers of Indian domestic culture,' which, he argues, was 'initially the principal means whereby Indians maintained their identity.'[15] We should be careful not to blame the Indian women for the cultural and racial exclusiveness of the Indian society. The women were not instigators of this, but a part of a larger process of reconstitution. An important point to bear in mind is that unlike the Chinese, Indian men were never able to develop a collegial relationship with the local communities they encountered in the colonies. Part of this was due to the large size of their community which did not require interaction with outsiders. Partly also, they sometimes competed for similar jobs, which created friction. Cultural prejudice also played a part. The Indian immigrants in Fiji called the indigenous Fijians 'junglis,' bushmen lacking culture and sophistication while for their part, the Fijians saw little to admire in the 'Kai Idia' beasts of burden. In Guyana, the Blacks saw the Indians as unfortunate victims while they themselves were convinced that they 'enjoyed a superior position to the East Indian.' In Trinidad, Indians 'strenuously objected' to intermarriage with Blacks, and in Jamaica the Indians called them 'kafari' which means an infidel.

Religion also helped to maintain and reinforce Indian cultural identity among overseas Indians. From very early on, the migrants seemed determined to preserve their religion to provide support and solidarity among themselves. In the words of Roy Glasgow, 'the Indian's emphasis upon the values and worthwhileness of his culture was really a mode of expression of his desire to be treated on terms of equality within the Guyanese universe.'[16] In Fiji by the 1890s, the indentured labourers on the plantations were reading all the texts of popular Hinduism circulating in the Indo-Gangetic plains, the most important of all being the *Ramayana*, whose epic story of Lord Rama's banishment stuck a particular chord with the migrants. Rama was exiled for fourteen years for no fault of his own, but he did return: good eventually triumphed over evil. His story gave the indentured labourers hope that they, too, one day would triumph over their ordeals. Besides reading the religious texts, Indians in all the colonies celebrated Hindu and Muslim festivals such as Diwali, Holi, Eid and Mohurram.

Unlike the Chinese, the Indians did not embrace Christianity in large numbers. This was not for lack of trying on the part of the Christian missionaries, such as the Methodists in Fiji and the Presbyterians in the Caribbean. Christianity failed to impress the Indians for a number of reasons. The Indian immigrants, even though themselves illiterate, showed pride, often exaggerated pride, in their own culture and traditions, and the community was large enough to support institutions and practices which contributed to the retention of their culture. Within a few decades of settlement, Indian communities everywhere had their own temples and places of prayer and worship. They also established social and cultural institutions—the Arya Samaj, the Sanatan Dharam Sabhas, the Mandalis—which sustained their culture. There was also the added fact of Christianity being identified in the indentured labourers' mind with the religion of their oppressors, the colonial officials and the planters. And so, for a variety of factors, Christianity remained a minor religion among the Indians.

There was one other difference between the Indian and the Chinese communities. It has already been pointed out that the Chinese were more mobile occupationally as well as geographically. Their pragmatic decision to embrace assimilation improved their chances of success. But the mobility of the Indians was curtailed. In the case of Fiji, this was by law. Governor Sir Arthur Gordon's policies effectively kept the two main races separate and apart. The Fijians lived in the subsistence sector for most of the 20th century, while the Indians lived in scattered settlements in the sugar cane belts of the country. Legislation restricted Fijian mobility and prevented Indians from settling in the vicinity of Fijian villages. Separate schools were established for Fijian, Indian and European children. In politics, too, communal rolls provided for racially segregated representation in the colonial legislature. So the gulf between the different communities that resulted from culture, language and religion, was exacerbated by government policy and practice, with each community leaning on its own cultural and spiritual resources for success.

In time, the Indian communities in the 'King Sugar' colonies increased in size. In Mauritius, Fiji, Guyana and Trinidad, they became the dominant community in the decades following the end of indenture in 1920. Numerical increase and permanent settlement led to the demand for political representation which, in turn, led to the creation of political structures providing for various degrees and forms of political representation—limited franchise, communal representation, nomination—with the colonial government retaining the ultimate authority. Nonetheless, for all its imperfections, even the limited political representation enabled the representation of Indian concerns at the highest levels of government.[17]

In addition to political representation, the Indian community was able to mobilize its own cultural and economic resources for the purposes of education and social progress, tasks neglected by colonial governments keen to keep the Indians tied to land. Voluntary organisations were formed and cultural institutions established: the Arya Samaj, the Sanatan Dharam, Sangam, the Muslim League. Temples were built, schools established through the keenness of parents eager to escape the vicious cycle of poverty and the degradation of menial labour. These initiatives halted cultural deracination and laid the foundation of social and cultural development, the indifference and importunity of the colonial governments notwithstanding.

The indenture system regulated one kind of Indian labour migration. The other, which dominated in Southeast Asia was, was the Kangani system.[18] Most of the recruits under this system came from South India, and the numbers were large: between 1852 and 1937, 2, 595,000 Indian immigrants went to Burma, 1,529,000 to Ceylon and 1,189,000 to Malaya. The kanganis (or maistries in the case of Burma) were often experienced and trusted employees of the plantation or the estate who were dispatched to recruit labourers in their villages. The kanganis not only recruited the labourers, but at work also acted as intermediaries between the employees and the employers, with concomitant opportunities that this position brought to them. The absence of comprehensive protective legislation and written and legally enforceable contracts enhanced their position. Nalini Ranjan Chakravarti argues that in this respect, the kangani system was worse than its indentured counterpart.[19]

Among the Southeast countries, Malaya was the largest employer of South Indian indentured labour, importing, between 1844 and 1910, some 250,000 labourers. But this indenture differed in form, if not in spirit, from the indenture system discussed above. In the case of Malaya, the recruitment was carried out by speculators and private agents of employers, while licensed agents appointed by government officials carried out recruitment for the sugar colonies. The contract of service for Malaya was for three years, for the sugar colonies five; and it was not always a written, legally enforceable document. Another difference was that while the emigration agents for the sugar colonies bore the cost of transporting the recruits, the cost for Malaya was borne by the workers themselves, paid over time from their wages. And finally, because indentured emigration to the sugar colonies was state regulated, the government of India was in a position to demand the fulfilment of the terms and conditions specified in the Emigration Act, but the informal, non-written nature of the arrangements in Malaya did not permit close scrutiny. India could not, for example, enforce the sex-ratio of men to women that it could for the sugar colonies.

The indentured diaspora has spawned a diaspora of its own, with large numbers of Indo-Caribbeans and Indo-Fijians and other Indian communities now living in the United States, Canada, Australia and New Zealand and the United Kingdom. The people are twice removed form India. Most have never been to India. Many, especially in the West Indies, have lost the language, and have adopted western values and adapted to the demands and necessities of living in multicultural societies. A great deal of the imaginative literature produced particularly in the Caribbean deals with the troubled and often tumultuous relationship the people of Indian descent have had with the countries of their birth where they faced years of exclusion from power and discrimination in the public sector. Yet, while seeking to understand their relationship with their current homeland, they also attempt to come to terms with their own ancestral culture. The task is not easy.

This leads directly to the claim in the quotation about overseas Indians 'proudly carrying the flag of Indian culture and civilisation.' This assertion raises further questions. Which Indian culture, which civilization? Which overseas Indians? The indentured labourers took with them Singer's 'Little tradition' of Hinduism, that is, essentially folk culture of northern and southern India. The *girmitiyas* themselves were largely illiterate, from cultivating and labouring classes, young. The culture they resuscitated after the ravages of the long sea voyage and the rigours of the plantations was cobbled together from many fragments, a culture in which the recognised social institutions of Indian society, most especially the caste system, had no place. The plantation regime was a great leveller of hierarchy and status, rewarding workers for the quality and quantity of their effort and not for their traditional status. The more recent Indian migrants to western countries, the literate professional classes, come generally from the 'Great tradition' of Indian society. The *Bhagvada Gita* rather than the *Ramayana* is likely to be their text. The two do not mix easily.

The process of cultural reconstitution took place everywhere, but its exact nature depended on a number of conditions.[20] One was the timing of the migration. The earlier migrants, particularly those who left India before the 1870s, faced greater difficulties in retaining their ancestral culture. Another important variable was the distance between India and the colonies where the indentured labourers went. As a general rule, the further away the colony, the less the contact with India and consequently lesser knowledge of the ancestral country. The policy of the colonial power and the role and influence of agents of western influence—Christianity, for example—also played an important role in determining the nature of the 'Indian' society that eventually emerged in the colonies. What was retained and what was jettisoned depended on these factors. The exact nature of the reconstituted society depended on the conditions in each colony. Each indentured Indian community developed its own unique relationship with and view of India.

Let me illustrate this by comparing the Fijian experience with that of Trinidad. What most strikes the casual visitor to these two island nations both with substantial Indian communities is the difference in the degree to which one has retained its Indian culture, and the other lost it. In Fiji, a significant proportion of the population reads and understands Hindi. There are 24 hour Hindi radio stations and there are Hindi newspapers. Hindi is one of the three official languages recognized by the constitution. Hinduism and Islam are the major religions of the Indian community, with only a small fraction professing Christianity. There is regular contact with India through periodic visit to the island by Indian religious missionaries and artists. In Trinidad few people speak Hindi, although many regret its loss and are now trying to learn the language. English is the primary language of most Indians. The Presbyterian mission was able to convert more Indians to its faith than the Methodist church was able to do in Fiji. Trinidadian Indians follow Hindi music and Bollywood cinema, but without understanding the language.

There are many reasons for the differences between Trinidad and Fiji. Indentured emigration to Fiji began much later, in 1879, by when there was an already well established Indian community in Trinidad. India showed far greater interest in Fiji than it did in other colonies, partly because of reports of greater abuses of Indian labourers on the Colonial Sugar Refining Company plantations. The Christian missions were not able to penetrate the Fijian Indian community to the extent they did the Trinidadian Indian partly because they concentrated their efforts on the indigenous Fijians and partly because of the stiff resistance of the Indians to the overtures of the new faith. The colonial policy towards the Indian community in Fiji forced the Fiji Indians to rely on their own efforts, which encouraged the retention of Indian culture. The emergence of voluntary social and cultural organisations from very early on also contributed towards that end. In Trinidad, the absence of an indigenous community, with its own demands and needs which the colonial government was obligated to respect—as it had to in Fiji—produced its own effects.

There is, thus, diversity, even among the indentured populations coming from a similar ancestral stock in India and with a shared history of servitude. But the diversity between the descendants of indentured migrants and the 'indigenous' Indians living in the West is greater, producing friction and misunderstanding. The sub-continental Indians, with little experience of the 'Little Tradition', remark patronizingly on the folkloric and rustic nature of many overseas Indian customs and rituals. The put-down is offensive and deeply hurtful to the overseas Indians who value these rituals as their cherished badges of cultural identity as 'Indians.' For many sub-continental Indians, the cultural rituals and ceremonies of the descendants of indentured Indians smack of archaic relics of a past which has vanished beyond recall in modern India. Modern India, they say, has moved on, while the overseas Indians are trapped in a vanishing past.

For their part, the overseas Indians decry what they see as retrograde aspects of Indian culture. For example, most see the caste system as a deeply oppressive and degrading social system with no redeeming features for those at the lower rungs of society and thankful that caste has disappeared in overseas

Indian communities. Other things cause bemusement as well, among them the Indian practice of arranged marriages, and the elaborate rituals of negotiation that accompany them. The Indian attachment to status, hierarchy, protocol, tradition, superstition—addiction to horoscope and astrology, for instance—sits uneasily with the overseas Indian preference for individualism, egalitarianism, a zest for living here and now, impatience with protocol. The intensity and violence of religious conflict on the Indian subcontinent confounds overseas Indians who have learnt to practice the virtues of religious pluralism.

India's relationship with overseas Indians has gone through several phases over the last century. In the 19th century, there was little public awareness of, or agitation about, the emigration of Indian indentured labourers, beyond the occasional comment about abuses in the recruitment system. It was an age of ignorance and darkness. That changed in the early years of this century, partly because Mahatma Gandhi's struggles in South Africa brought the overseas Indian question on to a broader public stage. From this flowed a number of enquiries, official and non-official, on the conditions on the Fijian plantations. Reports by sympathetic missionaries such as JW Burton and harrowing accounts by indentured labourer Totaram Sanadhya contributed to the end of the indenture system. The Indian interest was partly fuelled by the sense that treatment meted out to the indentured labourers was a reflection of India's lowly position in the international community.

The second phase, of more sustained Indian interest in the life of the overseas Indians, followed the end of indenture in 1920. Once the Indians had decided to settle in the colonies to which their forbears had migrated, the question of the political status of the Indians came to the fore. That is, what kind of arrangements would be appropriate which would retain political power in the hands of the colonial government while providing a semblance of representation to the Indians. India's intervention proved decisive at critical points. In the case of Fiji, for example, it was India's intervention which secured the Indian community political representation which the colonial government was reluctant to grant. India's support for common roll, however, was not successful. Similarly, Indian pressure on the land question helped, in part, to resolve the perennially thorny land question, forcing the colonial government to enact legislation regularising land leases to Indian tenants. India felt a degree of moral and political obligation to keep a sympathetic eye on Indians overseas.

When India gained its independence, the situation changed from one of active concern about the welfare of overseas Indians to one of passive interest. India understandably became preoccupied with the problems and challenges that independence brought. In foreign policy, India championed the cause of non-alignment and the interests of the Third World, and concerns of overseas Indians were seen and assessed in that light. Overseas Indians: that is how India began to see the people it had previously viewed as Indians overseas. Nehru explicitly asked the overseas Indians to identify closely with the interests and aspirations of the countries of their residence, and cease looking at India as their 'motherland.' This pragmatic and sensible advice underlined a reality the overseas Indians had come to accept themselves. So beyond private advice or legal assistance in constitutional negotiations at the time of independence, India became a silent player.

The third stage came with the independence of the former sugar colonies, a process which began in the late 1950s and the early 1960s. During this phase, the overseas Indian communities began consciously to think about their place, their roles and responsibilities as citizens of new countries. In many cases, they were in the vanguard of the movement for independence though in many places—Guyana, Fiji—they were fated to spend considerable periods of time in the political wilderness. India was represented in these newly emerging nations through high commissions, but otherwise the contact was limited to a few visiting cultural performers. Gradually, the 'overseas' Indians became Indo-Fijians, Indo-Guyanese and Indo-Trinidadians, the shift encapsulating a new, hyphenated identity. Retention or accentuation of Indian culture was interpreted as an index of unassimilability of the people, beyond the recognition of a few festivals as national holidays. Increasing influence of western culture, ideas and institutions also produced its effects.

Nonetheless, the link with India, however tenuous, still persists. The overseas Indians cannot comprehend the intensity of caste or religious conflict on the Indian subcontinent. They lament the absence of Indian civic pride, the degradation of the Indian environment, but they find it difficult to be indifferent to India. VS Naipaul's troubled and tumultuous relationship with India reflects, I think, a fairly common pattern of response.[21] Brinsley Samaroo's observation is equally apt that overseas Indians, no matter where they are or how long they have been away from India, cannot escape the legacy of their Indian heritage. They will have to come to terms with it. The hyphenated nature of their cultural identity will not be easily erased.[22]

I would like to end this discussion with some personal reflections which, I think, reflect wider and widely held concerns. The overseas Indians should acknowledge that they carry in their minds images of India, derived from mythological dramas and fantasy films, or from fragments of culture that survived the crossing, and that these do not necessarily reflect the reality of India. That India has moved on. It is no longer simply the land of Mahatma Gandhi or Jawaharlal Nehru.

The classical heritage of music, art, literature and philosophical thought co-exist with the froth of popular, westernized culture. That the land of their ancestors is scarred with the remains of religious and social conflict and violence beyond their imaginative understanding. Nor should they expect India to waive the magic wand on their behalf in international diplomacy, and expect its intervention to produce a favourable outcome for them on every occasion.

Sub-continental Indians, too, would need to re-define their attitude to the overseas Indians. They are not children of some lesser gods, culturally deficient and deformed, who inhabit the remote, unlovely fringes of Indian culture and civilization. They are a people with a distinct cultural identity which derives from India, but is not confined to it. Their culture is a confluence of many influences. Overseas Indians cherish the Indian part of their heritage, they want to nurture it, nourish it with new inputs, but it can be done within the context of existing realities. They are a people caught in-between.

# Eleven

## The Suriname Lecture

I am immensely honoured to be invited to speak on this occasion marking the 135th anniversary of the arrival of Indian people in Suriname. I am pleased for many reasons. This is my first visit to this part of the world [the Netherlands where the lecture was delivered]. In books we read at school many years ago, we saw beautiful pictures of your country, its canals and windmills, the magical tulip gardens and the neatly manicured flat green fields stretching into the distance as far as the eye could see, its great seaports and magnificent churches, its ancient centres of learning. To now physically see them with my own eyes is a childhood dream fulfilled. So, thank you for the invitation.

Like you—or many of you—I, too, am a descendant of an indentured labourer. My grandfather, from Bahraich district in eastern Uttar Pradesh, went as a *girmitiya* to Fiji in 1908. Girmit comes from the Agreement, and those who went under the Agreement became known as *girmitiyas*, just as your forebears who went to Suriname under the Contract system became known as *Kontrakis*. My grandfather was one of 60,000 who crossed the *kala pani* to that remote Pacific archipelago, almost twice the number who went to your country in the Caribbean. Our forebears were a part of the massive migration of Indian indentured labour which began with Mauritius in 1834 and continued until the early years of the 20th century. By then, over a million had crossed the oceans to the 'King Sugar' colonies scattered around the globe. So I share with you a common historical experience of migration and displacement.

Like most of you, I, too, am a part of the diaspora of the 'Twice Banished,' in your case from India to Suriname and then to the Netherlands, and in my case from India to Fiji to Australia. For a variety of reasons—personal choice, racial discrimination, political marginalisation, economic hardship, a deep desire for personal betterment—over 120,000 of my people have left Fiji for other lands since the military coups of 1987, and more will leave as the opportunity arises. We, too, have crossed out own *kala pani*. So your story of migration and re-migration, of starting from scratch in foreign lands is familiar to me, with all its pains and joys of adapting to new situations.

## The Suriname Lecture

I have been to Suriname, so places like Nikeri and Paramaribo are not just idle, exotic names on a map, but places with faces and memories. I have eaten *dhallbhari roti* and duck curry at Roopram's Roti shop in the capital city. And who can forget the *masquita* and *macchari* of Nikeri! I was overwhelmed by the warm hospitality of the Surnami Indian community. I knew something about the Surinami Indians before I went to Surinam. In 1995, Ram Soekhoe, working for one of the television stations here, went to Fiji to make a documentary on the situation of the Indian community there. He interviewed many people, including me, but was especially keen on meeting some local community leaders. We took him to a small town called Nausori to meet with Mr Bal Dev. Ram laughed out loud when he heard the name. Why we wondered, puzzled. He said in Suriname, the name referred to someone of few means, without a fixed abode, harmless, who lives on free feed by telling people: '*Hamaar naam Baldev, hum khaaye pi ke chal deb*'!

Like so many of you in post-war Suriname I, too, grew up in the countryside in rural Fiji. I, too, was brought up on the *Ramchatramanas*, the story of Sarvan Kumar, *Allha Khand*, the *Birhas* and the *Bidesias* and the *Baithak Gana*, the *Lehnga ke naach* (what you call *Ahirwa ke naach*). A few days ago, I listened to the songs of Ramdew Chaitoe and Andre Mohan. The evocative words about love and loss and impermanence, the melancholy mood of the music, the rustic musical instruments, took me back to my childhood, bringing back memories long forgotten. I remembered how, amidst all the poverty and destitution and hopelessness in the aftermath of indenture, songs and music, elementary stuff, nothing fancy or sophisticated (just *dandtaal, dholak, majira* and harmonium) kept our culture alive, our collective soul intact. Apparently, it was the same in your part of the world. And I am so delighted that fragments from that fractured past still survive in the Netherlands.

And the names too: Ramdev, Mohan, Nanhoe, Chaitoe, Soekhlal. These, too, were familiar to me. They were common enough in rural Fiji in the post-war years. They could easily have been the names of uncles and older cousins. Names are strange things, aren't they? Why do we give certain names and not others? As I thought about this, I realised the important role naming plays in the way in which we negotiate issues of culture and identity and find our place in the world. Let me share with you the Fiji experience. Indentured labourers from rural India were named after events, calamities, days, after flowers and birds. So: Mangal, Bhola, Dukhia, Genda, Budhai, Sanicharee, Bipti, Sukkhu, Garib, and so on. If you knew the Indian cultural code, you could roughly tell a person's station in life by his or her name. When the time came for the *girmitiyas* to name their children, they began naming them after gods and goddesses and with words having religious connotations, to erase distinctions based on caste and class: Ram Charan, Shiu Wati, Mahadeo, Latchman, Dharam Raji, Ram Jattan, Suruj Bali, Janki Devi. Who could tell whether Ram Charan was a chamar or a kurmi or something else? Our parents went further, naming their children Mahendra, Satendra, Vijay, Rajesh, Satish, Maya, Padma, and so on, with absolutely no cultural or religious connotation whatsoever, at least not any that I can recognise. Inventive names erased hierarchies based on caste and ritual purity. Such were the silent, subtle processes of cultural change and transformation in Fiji.

The isolated, self-contained world of my childhood has now almost vanished beyond recall. My children think that I am hallucinating when I tell them that I was born on my father's farm, delivered by an illiterate Indo-Fijian mid-wife, and grew up without piped water, paved roads, electricity and regular newspapers. Radio came late to the village, in the late 1950s. There was no television then, of course, no internet, no mobile phones. I sometimes wonder how we managed to survive through those difficult times. Not only survive but actually triumph (although I have to admit to being a Luddite when it comes to even the most basic of modern technologies!). From that kind of background to this has been a remarkable journey of exploration and unexpected discoveries. In this regard, too, I share much in common with you.

For more than a century, people of Indian indentured diaspora lived in complete isolation and ignorance of each other. Given the vast distance that separated us—you were in the Atlantic Ocean while we were in the Pacific—this is not surprising. There was simply no way of knowing. We lacked education, and the colonial education that we did receive focused our intellectual attention squarely on the cultural and technological accomplishments of our colonial masters. For the most part, we were preoccupied with eking out an existence, often without a helping hand and frequently in circumstances on the outer edges of desperation. Those who wrote about us were outsiders, who had little inkling of the deeper impulses of our lives, what made us tick. Some, though well meaning, were actually apologists for the colonial government and the plantocracy, which saw our forebears simply as units of labour to be exploited for profit. For them to accord us a measure of humanity would have undermined their project of economic exploitation; it would have been morally indefensible for one group of human beings in good conscience to oppress another. Our colonial masters saw us as potentially troublesome subjects to be controlled and managed. But we must also accept a part of the blame, for we saw our own history with a certain degree of embarrassment and shame. We saw our past as covered in silent darkness and loathed being reminded of our humble origins, especially by those who wanted us to know our place in the larger scheme of things so that we didn't grow too big for our boots. The past, for us, was truly past; that was then; we had moved on.

But things have been changing in the last two decades or so as the grandchildren and great-grandchildren of indentured labourers have themselves undertaken the task of understanding and interpreting their past, to comprehend the truth of their historical experience in all its maddening complexity and variety. I have devoted a very large part of my professional life as a historian, now spanning some thirty years, trying to rescue our history from the enormous condescension of posterity. In my first book, *Girmitiyas: The Origins of the Fiji Indians* (first published in 1983), I tried to understand the background of the indentured who went to Fiji (and to other places across the globe), who they were, where they came from, their social and caste status, their economic circumstances, the reason they might have left their homes for strange, unknown places. Much, cruelly, was assumed about the *girmitiyas*, but very little actually known.

To find out, I did two things. I went through each and every one of the 45,000 Emigration Passes of all those who embarked for Fiji from the port of Calcutta. It had to be done, the whole thing; there was no way around it, no short cuts. I suppose in some inexplicable sense, it was my way of paying homage to those who had undertaken the journey. I coded and transcribed the data (on the district of origin and registration, caste, sex, next-of-kin, age, date of recruitment and embarkation, and so on: a horrendously tedious task that I would not wish even upon my worst enemy) and analysed it using the computer (in those prehistoric days of the late 1970s!). And I spent more than six months travelling through and living in the impoverished villages of eastern UP districts of Basti, Faizabad, Gorakhpur, Gonda, Bahraich, and many others from where the *girmitiyas* had come. I wanted to understand the place of migration in popular culture of the region. I travelled in rickety, overcrowded buses carrying sheep and goat besides people, slept in foul smelling, bug-infested beds, ate greasy food from sooty *dhabas,* drank tea from mud cups, and did other strange, blush-inducing things (out of necessity, of course!) which are now best left un-recalled. All I will say is that it is not an experience I would recommend to the finicky or the faint-hearted.

I proved conclusively, statistically, that the indentured labourers were not all low caste riff raff, but represented a fair cross-section of rural Indian society, including higher, middling and lower castes, and coming from sections of society which, in the late 19th century, were under great stress because of recurring natural calamities (droughts and famines) and the cruel effects of British revenue policy which caused crippling indebtedness, fragmented land holdings and scattered families. I showed, too, that while many were deceived into emigrating—fraudulence is present in most forms of labour recruitment, even in our own age—many came from an already uprooted mass of humanity on the move—to the Calcutta jute mills, Assam tea gardens, the Bihar coal mines, Bombay textile mills—in search of employment. I argued that migration to the colonies was an extension of the process of displacement already underway on the subcontinent. I suggested that indentured migration was a complex, multilayered narrative, susceptible to multiple readings, but the whips-and-chains version full of violence and brutality is usually given prominence in popular renditions of indenture. That, alas, is the way things will remain. Some matters of popular belief will always remain impervious to reason or reasoned research.

In my later work, I looked at the experience of the indentured labourers on the plantations in Fiji. There can be no argument that indenture was a harsh, brutalising experience, which broke many and left others by the wayside. Pain and suffering and violence were an integral part of the indenture experience. All this is clear from the historical record, but it is by no means the full story. The plantation was not everywhere the 'total institution' it was alleged to be. In some places, indenture was a life sentence, in others it was a limited detention of five or at most ten years. For some men and women, it was an enslaving experience, for others it was liberation from the vicious cycle of poverty and destitution at home, from which there was no possibility of emancipation in this life, or the next or the one after the next: actually, never. We must accord some measure of humanity and agency to our forebears. They were simple people from simple backgrounds, but they were not simpletons.

What we are celebrating on this occasion is the triumph of the human spirit over life's great adversities. For, from the debris of indenture emerged a community of people, at once resilient and resourceful, determined to build a better future for themselves and their children. From the remembered fragments of their motherland, they established new communities, built *pathshalas* and *mandirs* and *mazjids* and social and cultural institutions. A new lingua franca emerged—Fiji Baat, Sarnami Hindi—and a new composite culture combining the new and the old, pragmatic and utilitarian in approach and world view, more egalitarian and less respectful of oppressive and moribund traditions and rituals which sanctioned hierarchy and difference. It is this wonderful story of change and adaption, resourcefulness and creativity, which we are celebrating today. When you come to think of it, we of the Indian indentured diaspora—whether in Suriname, Guyana, Mauritius or Fiji—have a lesson to teach the world, especially Mother India. We have demonstrated how, in certain circumstances and under certain conditions, apparently divinely ordained social and cultural institutions and practices deemed immutable can, in fact, change. The way the caste system has broken down in the Indian indentured diaspora is a good example. Religious tolerance is another. *Hum pragti aur parivartan ke jeete jaagte udharan hain.*

I don't know about Suriname, but one institution of migration and indenture which acquired a particular significance in the life of the indentured labourers in Fiji was *jahajibhai*, the brotherhood of the crossing. It was close to real kinship, just as real as the brotherhood of blood, a pillar upon which many a community was built. I suspect a new kind of *jahajibhai* relationship is being forged now. It is the *jahajibhai* of the cyberspace. The internet has shrunk our world, brought us closer. We email each other, visit each other's websites. Hardly a week goes by when I don't receive a request for help with this project or that, often from complete strangers, mostly descendants of indentured labourers in various parts of the world. Just a few weeks back, I received an email from Nalini Mohabir, a Canadian of Indo-Guyanese descent doing a doctorate in Geography at Leeds University, who wants to visit Fiji for research, and sought my advice about where to go, who to see and talk to. She is one among hundreds of children of the Indian diaspora who are now expressing an interest in knowing about their past.

There are many reasons for this. It is a natural human phenomenon to know who you are and where you have come from. It is not peculiar to the people of Indian origin. 'Roots' and 'Identity' are big subjects in universities around the world. The desire to know is also sharpened by the levelling forces of globalisation, making us want to hang on to something that is uniquely ours, that gives a particular sense of identity and belonging. I detect an awakening sense of the past among our people, and a desire, too, to pay homage to the sacrifices and struggles of our forebears. In time, the *Girmit Divas* and the '5th of June' may become important secular celebrations of great symbolic significance.

There is a gathering sense of pride in our collective achievements in so many diverse fields. When a haunting novel about a struggling man of unfulfilled literary ambition, humbled and humiliated in his own extended family—I am, of course, referring to *House for Mr Biswas*—helps VS Naipaul win the Nobel Prize for literature, we all feel a vicarious sense of pride in his great personal achievement. When Vijay Singh, the son of an airport worker in Fiji, scales the greatest heights of world golf, we applaud. It gives us immense pleasure to know that a great-grandson of an indentured labourer in Fiji, Anand Satyanand, is the Governor General of New Zealand, or that Jai Ram Reddy, again from Fiji, sits as a Permanent Judge of the International Criminal Court for Rwanda. The list goes on and on. We appreciate the accomplishments of the children of the indentured diaspora more than most because we know how very difficult and unpredictable the journey has been.

Travel and technology have complicated grounded, ethnographic notions of citizenship which too has played its part in fostering a new, overarching sense of identity for us. There was a time, not too long ago, when questions of identity and citizenship were one-way traffic. You were either this or that, but never both. Dual attachment was considered to be disloyalty. But that zero-sum game, that ideology of complete assimilation into the social and cultural fabric of the host society now mercifully lies buried in the graveyards of discarded history. Now, we celebrate pluralism and diversity. That is why, Fatima Meer, the distinguished South African intellectual and activist, can claim herself to be a proud South African as well as a child of India. That is why Lord Dholakia is a proud British peer as well as proud son of Gujarat. I am a proud Indo-Fijian as well as a proud Australian. This openness and flexibility enables us, without apology, to cherish and celebrate the various multicultural strands of our particular identity and heritage.

India itself has played a large part in the last decade or so to foster a greater consciousness of an Indian diaspora. This resulted from a massive increase in the size of the Indian diaspora in recent decades. It is now some twenty million strong, and increasing daily. India's effort to harness the diaspora's immense intellectual and financial resources to promote the subcontinent's economic modernisation program—much in the same manner as China had done earlier with its own large diaspora—has played an important role. The annual *Pravasi Bhartiye Divas* symbolises this effort. So far the main focus has been economic, specifically, how the diaspora can help India. I hope that with time, this relationship will become less one-sided and more mutually beneficial. We know what India wants: it wants our goodwill, support and, very important, naturally, our dollars.

There is a puzzle here. India reminds us incessantly to be loyal to our countries of birth (and this started with Jawaharlal Nehru's speech at Bandung in 1954 and was repeated by Minister Vyala Ravi this evening), but it would also like us to commit 'fiscal treason' (if that's not too strong a word) to our countries of birth by asking us to invest our resources in the ancestral homeland of our forebears. India's position is understandable. It is on its way to becoming a superpower of the 21st century. We, from the Old Diaspora, need to ask what is it that we want from India, what the terms of relationship should be from the perspective of our needs and aspirations. We should have a *MAD* relationship with India, asking for 'Mutually Acceptable Development', and not being content with having a one-sided, self seeking one.

I should now like to correct myself. I have so far spoken of the Indian diaspora in the singular, but it is, of course, the result of many causes and countless crossings over many centuries. We can distinguish at least three distinct phases. First, in the era before the emergence of European dominance, was the 'Age of Merchants,' when enterprising Indian traders travelled over land and sea to central Asia and east Africa. The memory of their journeys and explorations now survives in grand monuments and ancient artefacts of history. The second phase was the 'Age of Colonial Capital' of the 19th and 20th centuries of which we, the descendants of the indentured diaspora, are the products. And the third phase, 'The Age of Globalisation,' is essentially a product of the post-World War II era. Given our diverse origins and circumstance of migration, it is understandable that our attachment to, and feeling for, India will vary considerably. The 'Dollar Diaspora' and the 'Desperate Diaspora' will see things differently.

An obvious point, you might say, but it is not always appreciated. Sometimes we are all classified under the category NRI. Now, the standard interpretation of NRI is, as you all know, *Non-Resident Indian*. That is fine, but there are other meanings as well. For instance, *Newly-Rich Indians*, in whom India is interested for their wealth and expertise. Then there are the *Never-Returning Indians*, who turn their backs on the place of their birth and wash off their hands completely. We all know a few *Non-Reliable Indians*! And then there are NRIs like myself: *Not Really Indian*! The point I want to make is that we are not all peas in the same pod. We converge and diverge as members of an amorphous Indian diaspora, depending on need and circumstance. We share many things in common— food, faith, fashion—but we are also acutely aware of the different historical and cultural influences which have shaped our unique identities and our perceptions of things around us. Thus I am not an 'Indian Overseas' nor an 'Overseas Indian,' but a Fijian, of Indian descent. I am an Indo-Fijian whose soul is nourished by three distinct cultural and civilizational influences: Indian, Western and Pacific (Fijian). Without any one of these, I will be the poorer.

Earlier, I spoke of the diaspora of the Twice Banished. This developing diaspora needs more study. It is a complex phenomenon. It presents challenges as well as opportunities. Questions of homeland and territoriality, of belonging and attachment, become more complex and contested. Our civilizational home is India, but we were born in Suriname or Fiji. And we now live in the Netherlands and Australia. As new identities get formed and transformed, how do we balance within our inner lives influences which have made us what we are? Let me put this more directly. As you make new homes in the Netherlands, what aspects of Sarnami culture do you still carry with you in your daily lives and which you will transmit to the next generation? What are the Sarnami ties that bind? Or will Suriname gradually recede from the intellectual and cultural horizons of the new generations growing up here and remembered, if remembered at all, as a temporary stopover for a people destined to wander the globe? I don't have any answers, but I think the question is worth asking.

I salute the achievements of the Sarnami community both here and in Suriname. We are all *jahajibhais* in this journey begun by our forebears over a century ago who, I have no doubt, will be looking on our achievements with immense pride. Indenture in the remote corners of the globe was the destination of our grandparents and great-grandparents. Through their hard work and sacrifice, they ensured that it wasn't going to become our destiny. We pay respectful homage to this beautiful legacy they bequeathed us. *Garva se kaho ke aap kontracki ke santaan ho.*

# Twelve

## A Hundred Years in a Lifetime

*All memories are finally about loss. We don't write of the past except when we've been ejected from it*

Carol Joyce Oates

Florida, Utah, Montana, Louisiana, Gladstone, Victoria, Eve, Plato, Jacob. Names of esoteric places and famous people, you might say. That they are. But they are also the names of the first Indian children born in Fiji. They were born not in Rewa or Rakiraki or Raralevu, later to become important centres of Indo-Fijian settlement on Fiji's main island of Viti Levu, but on the remote, tiny island of Rabi, on planter John Hill's estate, the biggest employer of the first batch of Indian indentured labourers to arrive in Fiji. The new migrants were sent there because other European employers who were expected to recruit them were angry with the government for prohibiting the employment of Fijian labour and so they refused to have anything to do with the new migrants. Sir Arthur Gordon, Fiji's first governor and the chief architect of the indenture scheme—he had seen its operation in Mauritius and Trinidad where he had been governor before coming to Fiji—was disappointed but not despairing. By the 1880s, the prospects in the nascent colony brightened considerably with the expansion of the recently arrived Australian-owned Colonial Sugar Refining Company (CSR), which would go on to dominate not only the industry but also Fiji's economy for nearly a century until its departure in 1973.

Between *Leonidas*' inaugural voyage in 1879 and *Sutlej V*'s last in 1916, 87 ships, especially designed to carry human cargo in difficult conditions over long distances, ferried some 60,000 men, women and children from Calcutta and Madras to Fiji. They had such magical names after rivers and classical figures: *Danube, Elbe, Ganges, Jamuna, Rhine, Avon, Syria, Pericles, Leonidas*.

Remarkably, only one of the ships, the *Syria* in 1884, perished through negligent navigation, on the reefs at Nasilai, claiming 59 lives, though the journey itself—three months by sailing ship and one by steamship—broke many land-locked lives and disrupted irreparably the settled habits, practices and thoughts of ancient village India. The voyage across the *kala pani*, the dark dreaded seas, was a great leveller of hierarchy and protocol. But the destruction also contained within it seeds for rejuvenation, for from the fragments of a common past and a mutual predicament, a shared destiny and a common destination, emerged other bonds. None was more emotionally powerful than the bond of *jahajibhai*, brotherhood of the crossing, as intimate and comforting as real blood kinship which men cherished well into their twilight years as a mark of solidarity against the uncertainties of the outside world.

In the end, some 24,000 of the indentured migrants and their families (some born in Fiji) returned to India at the conclusion of their indenture, but the majority stayed on, attracted by the promise of possibilities in their new homeland and the fear of reception they might receive in India having broken taboos—marrying across caste lines, eating food cooked by unknown hands, doing work considered ritually polluting—taboos still sacrosanct at home. Many talked well into their old age of one day returning, but the day of decision never came as memories of the past frayed and faded and the realities of life in a new place took hold. The *girmitiyas* and their descendants faced these new realities with resilience, often on their own, without a helping hand. In time, their labour laid the foundations of the Fijian economy, illiterate thumb-prints seen most visibly in the undulating seas of green cane fields across vast, often inhospitable, stretches of previously untamed terrain, in the damp paddy fields of the Rewa and Navua deltas, in the slowly emerging market towns in the cane belt, precursors to modern urban centres, in rudimentary structures on their way to becoming ground-breaking primary and secondary schools, in the steady stream of school children leaving the village environment to enter the world of the professions beyond the imagined horizons of their parents and grandparents.

My direct link with Fiji begins in 1908. That was the year my grandfather came to Fiji as a *girmitiya*. *Aja* (grandfather) was lucky in one respect: he arrived in Fiji when the worst abuses of *girmit* were over—the heart-rending infant mortality rates of the 1890s, the excessive over-tasking, the physical violence on the plantations, an uncertain life on the raw edges of extreme vulnerability. In 1907, there were 30,920 Indians living in Fiji, of whom only 11,689 were under indenture. The freed population—*Khula*—were cultivating 17,204 acres of land on their own, 5,586 devoted to cane and 9,347 planted with rice. In time, sugar cane cultivation would become the principal occupation of the Indian population. By 1911, of the 40,286 Indians, 27 per cent had been born in the colony, the Fiji-born proportion of the population increasing rapidly with time, until, by 1946, they became outright majority of the population, spawning the threat of 'Indian domination' that would bedevil the country's complex political negotiations as it lurched towards independence in the 1960s.

As young children, we heard stories about indenture from *Aja* and other *girmitiyas*—the hard work from the break of dawn, about overseers good and bad and indifferent, the fractured family life in the estate lines, the cultural confusions and transgressions that pervaded plantation life, the ways in which they attempted to make sense of their predicament. I heard these stories long before I read scholarly accounts of the indenture experience at university. These accounts, most famously Hugh Tinker's *A New System of Slavery*, captured our imagination. I read it in the final year of my university undergraduate studies. That book, with its catchy, memorable title, emotionally appealing but intellectually suspect, set the tone of the new historiography. *Girmit* was slavery by another name, nothing more, nothing less, the book informed us. The indentured labourers themselves were gullible simpletons from impoverished rural backgrounds, hoodwinked into migrating by unscrupulous recruiters (*arkatis*), and brutalised by the unrelenting pace of work on the plantations, their sufferings ignored, their women molested by the overseers and *sirdars* (Indian foremen), their families separated, their dignity in tatters.

This rendition of *girmit* was reinforced for me by the centenary celebrations of 1979 marking the arrival of Indian people in Fiji. I was then a graduate student at The Australian National University. The overall tone was understandably grim. Until then, the word *girmit* had not been a part of the general vocabulary of the Indo-Fijian community. For most people, the word was synonymous with shame and slavery. The word acquired a new vitality during the celebrations as people used it to pry open a past about which much was quietly assumed but little actually known. But that past was viewed through the lens of a troubled present in which Indo-Fijians were increasingly being marginalised from the mainstream public discourse through the vagaries of racial politics. Consequently, a complex and contested history was pressed into the service of an ideology designed to portray Indians as victims of history, without voice, without agency. The 'whips-and-chains' story is still a dominant part of the public discourse and understanding of *girmit* even though the new indenture historiography casts serious doubts about its explanatory value. There is of course undeniable truth in the indenture-as-slavery thesis. Many *girmitiyas* were broken by work, claimed by disease or wrecked by human violence and greed. Suffering and pain were an integral part of indenture. All this is abundantly clear from the historical record. But it is not the whole story. It is possible to acknowledge hardship while granting *girmitiyas* agency as a people who had a hand in shaping their history.

A central plank of the slavery thesis is that deception and fraudulence played a key role in the recruitment process. Migration was not an integral part of Indian society or psyche, the argument went, and no one in their right minds would therefore ever leave their home for places unknown or unheard of. The Indian peasant was a landlubber, bound to home and hearth by strict codes of ritually-authorised behaviour, not an intrepid explorer of unknown, pollution-threatening worlds. That view is archaic, for even in medieval times, as Irfan Habib and others have shown, peasants moved about in search of better opportunities and to escape the depredations of predatory landlords.[1] In the 19th century, rural India was in the throes of profound change caused by, among other things, the introduction of new notions of private ownership of property, increasing fragmentation of land holdings, deepening indebtedness among the peasantry, the effects of natural calamities. Places in eastern Uttar Pradesh, which furnished 45,000 of Fiji's 60,000 migrants—the remainder came from South India after 1903 when sources in the North had begun to dry up—were particularly adversely affected. As employment opportunities there diminished, people moved about in search of a better life elsewhere. It was the natural thing to do.

And so, large numbers left—for the Assam tea gardens, the Calcutta jute mills and factories, the Bihar coal mines and the Bombay textile mills. Between 1891 and 1911, many districts in the Indo-Gangetic plain—Faizabad, Gonda, Allahabad, Azamgargh, Benares—experienced population decline, which officials attributed partly to emigration. In Gonda, migration had become 'a natural way out of the difficulties with which the population did not know how to grapple;' in Sultanpur was being used to restore 'fallen fortunes or ease off a redundant population which have long been familiar to the inhabitants of the district;' and in Ghazipur, 'immense numbers of people leave their homes every year to find employment in or near Calcutta and in the various centres of industry in Bengal and Assam, while many weavers and others report to the mills of Bombay. The extent of this migration is astonishing and its economic influence is of the highest importance since these labourers earn high wages and remit or bring back with them large sums of money to their homes.'

The indentured labourers to Fiji and to other places came from this uprooted mass of peasantry. Most of them were registered in their own provinces rather than in large distant cities as critics alleged. But not all those who registered migrated. In Gonda and Basti, two of the largest indentured emigration districts, nearly 50 per cent did not migrate, while elsewhere, nearly a third remained behind either because they were rejected or because they refused to enlist. The high failure rate gives some agency to the recruited. This is not to say by any means that the unscrupulous recruiters did not snare the gullible and the greedy and the unwary into their nets. They did, but perhaps not to the extent the slavery thesis alleges. Migration to the colonies was, I would argue, an extension of the massive movement of people within India. I vividly remember *Aja* telling us how he happened to come to Fiji. He was up and about, a young man in his early 20s, when a friend told him about golden opportunities awaiting him in the *tapus* (islands). What opportunities, he did not ask. He was footloose and free, and the lure of adventure attracted him. He eventually ended up in Calcutta, in the batch bound for Guyana (Demerara). That ship was full, so he took—or was put on—the next one to Fiji. I have no doubt that he had no idea what or where Fiji was, but that somehow did not seem to matter to him. He knew that he would be back one day soon, after he had earned enough to get started on his own. As it happened, the break for him was permanent.

Fiji was spared the massive cultural dislocation that accompanied slavery (and even indenture) in the Caribbean and elsewhere. Fiji was, after Surinam, the last major importer of Indian indentured labour. By the late 1870s, the darkest period of indentured emigration was over, the period of an almost complete break from India a thing of the past. Fiji was lucky to escape the horrors of its sister colonies in the Caribbean. The *girmitiyas* never completely lost touch with their cultural roots. As early as the 1890s, only a decade after the beginning of indentured emigration, the basic texts of popular Hinduism and folk culture were circulating in the main areas of Indian settlement in the sugar belts of Fiji. These included *Ramchritramanas, Satya Narayan ki Katha, Surya Purana, Devi Bhagat, Danlila, Durga Saptshati, Indra Sabha* as well as stories from *Baital Pachisi, Salinga Sadabrij* and *Alaha Khand*. The texts were recited communally at social functions and other occasions when people got together to celebrate life or mourn its passing. From very early on, *Holi* (*Phagua*) and *Tazia* (*Mohurram*) were observed as public holidays on most plantations. Religious leaders, both Hindu and Muslim, established centres for spiritual instruction (*kutis* and *dharamshalas* and *madarasas*). Informal gatherings of like-minded men later materialised as cultural and social associations which made enduring contributions to the growth and development of the Indo-Fijian community.

Religion became both an instrument of survival as well as a tool of resistance. Despite their best efforts, Christian missionaries, associated in the *girmitiya* minds with the excesses of the CSR overseers and the racially discriminatory practices of the colonial government, never made much headway in the Indo-Fijian community.[2] They refused to convert because they saw their own religion as superior. This was in marked contrast to the Indian experience in the Caribbean where Christian missions, especially Presbyterians, enjoyed far greater success among the Indians, providing them, through education, a powerful vehicle for self-improvement and upward mobility. In the Caribbean, an immigrant culture weakened by long separation from its ancestral roots and almost total dependence on the plantation system, fell easy prey to external temptations; in Fiji the roots, though frayed and planted in a shallower soil, were allowed—through indifference as much as anything else—to nurture themselves unhindered.[3]

There was another important contrast with the Caribbean. Whereas the indentured labourers and their descendants there lived on the plantations for generations—and reminders of the dominant influence of the plantation system are still visible in Guyana—in Fiji, the period of dependence was limited to five, or at most ten, years. The point to underline is that in Fiji, *girmit* was a limited detention, not a life sentence for several generations, that it was in parts of the Caribbean and in the case of slavery. Those freed from indenture from the mid-1880s onwards began to establish free settlements, mostly around the sugar mills on the two main islands of Viti Levu and Vanua Levu. These places remain the principal centres of Indian settlement in Fiji even today, still dependent in one way or another on the sugar industry as growers, casual labourers, mill workers. Besides providing the former *girmitiyas* with individual opportunities, the free settlements were also symbolically important as beacons of hope for those still under indenture, a visible reminder of the reality of freedom that lay so near. The rapid growth of free settlements meant that the period of complete isolation for those under indenture was limited, and with time the boundaries, both physical as well as emotional between the indentured and the free, became porous.

For many immigrants, indenture, for all its hardships, still represented an improvement of their condition in India. This was particularly so with the lower castes who were permanently consigned to the fringes of rural Indian society as untouchables, tenants-at-will, and landless labourers with little hope of betterment in this life—or the next. The routine of relentless work on the plantations was nothing new to them as strenuous physical labour was their permanent lot in India. In Fiji, at least, their individual identity was recognised and their effort rewarded on the basis of achievement rather than a preordained status. For them, the levelling tendencies of the plantation system heralded a welcome change from an oppressive past and promised a future in which they and their children had a chance. Others, perhaps those who were victims of natural calamities, such as famines, floods and droughts, or of exploitative landlords, welcomed the peace and security that the new environment offered them. Reflecting on his indenture days, one labourer told the anthropologist Adrian Mayer in the 1950s: 'The time of indenture was better than now. You did your task, and knew that this was all. You knew you will get food everyday. I had shipmates with me, and we weren't badly off when there was a good sirdar and overseer. Of course, if they were bad men, then you had to be careful. But now what do I do? I have cane land, bullocks and a home. Yet every night I am awake, listening to see if someone is not trying to burn my cane, or steal my animals. In indenture lines, we slept well, we did not worry.' [4] Both oral evidence as well as archival records indicate some lower caste labourers, especially *sirdars*, taking revenge against their high caste compatriots for the social oppression they had experienced in India. So, at one level, the *girmitiyas* were all peas in the same pod, but they were also a socially differentiated group from diverse backgrounds and with divergent experiences and expectations of what life was all about, what it had to offer. *Girmit*, then, was a simultaneously enslaving as well as a liberating experience.

*Aja* became a free man in 1913, after serving his indenture as a stable hand for the CSR at Tua Tua in Labasa. Like most other freed *girmitiyas*, he continued as a mill hand for the CSR for a few years more before eloping with his best friend's wife, leasing a ten acre piece of land and starting on his own in the newly opened settlement at Tabia. He planted rice, lentils, maize, beans, eggplants, watermelon, pumpkin, and peanuts until sugar cane arrived in the late 1930s. It was on that sugar cane farm, raw, without paved roads, running water or electricity, that we were all born and raised. Now the farm is gone, taken back by the Fijian landowners. This has ruptured my sense of the place of my birth, diminished the intensity of my association with it, reminding me of the temporariness of things, the transience of life itself. *Aja* went to Tabia not because he had friends or family or fellow caste members or *jahajibhais* there but because land was available for lease. Geography, the availability of productive agricultural land and its proximity to markets and roads and other facilities, determined the pattern of territorially and socially scattered Indian settlements in Fiji, rather than caste brotherhood or religious affiliation or some other criteria. This meant that the pattern of village India, with socially ranked clusters of houses with clear caste-based rules defining access to common facilities, formulating and enforcing rules of appropriate behaviour, could not be reproduced in Fiji. The fragmentation of the Indian village world, begun in the depots of Calcutta and Madras, and accelerated on the plantations, was completed in the post-indenture period.

I knew *Aja* as an old man of perhaps around eighty, although he reckoned he was well over a hundred in the way most old men do. Some things I can say about his life with absolute certainty, from personal experience, while others I deduce from my own reading and research. *Aja* spoke his own language (a mixture of *Bhojpuri* and *Awadhi*) with other surviving *girmitiyas*. He spoke Fiji

Hindi with a distinct provincial Indian accent. My Fiji Hindi, incorporating more English and Fijian words, would be incomprehensible to him. He always wore Indian clothes—*dhoti* and *kurta* and *pagri*. The Indian garment would disappear with him and his generation, replaced by western clothes of shorts and shirt that became the standard for my father's generation. Women's jewellery and finery—*bichwa* (toe-ring), *payal* (anklet), *jhumka* (earing), *nathini* (nose-ring), *bajuband* (armlet) would also disappear with the *girmitiya* women, replaced by a single string of gold sovereigns—*mohur*—which women displayed as a sign of status and prosperity. In rural areas of Fiji, they still do.

*Aja's* world was full of ghosts and demons and evil forces—*bhoot* and *shaitan*, and *jadu tona*—which had to be pacified through a variety of precise ritual performances, that would disappear with him. He continued to invoke, in (to me) incomprehensible language, the names of village and clan or caste deities—*gram devtas* and *kul devtas*—for some blessing or to ward off an evil or impending misfortune. To cure headache, jaundice, fever or dog bite, he consulted the local magic man; he had faith in him; that after all was how things were done in India. He knew nothing about western medicine, which was expensive and inaccessible anyway. He still remembered *bhajans*, devotional songs, which he and other *girmitiyas* sang with great fervour on special occasions. And although caste as a basis or determinant of social relationship had been jolted in the crowded depots of Calcutta and in the crowded cabins of the immigrant ships, finally crashing on the plantations[5]—because work rewarded productivity, not caste status, because sanctions could not be imposed for breaches of behaviour, because paucity of women necessitated cross-caste, even cross-religious marriages and because the plantation management was intolerant of caste restrictions which interfered with the deployment of labour—despite all these, *Aja* continued to practice some minor customs from his childhood, perhaps to retain a vanishing connection with a remembered past. So, he never shaved himself but waited every Sunday for a *hajam*, a professional barber by caste, a fellow *girmitiya*, to shave him and collect his fees in kind, usually some rice and lentils.[6] That practice died gradually as the *girmitiyas* moved on and as new forces of change (education, improved communication) entered the community. So, too, did the practice of seeking marriage partners for children from roughly comparable castes.

Life in Fiji must have been very different for *Aja* and others like him, in some ways a complete contrast to what they had left behind. The physical landscape of an island surrounded by sea, cris-crossed by rivers and streams, full of forbidding forests and brooding mountains, and inhabited by a people who looked strange, must have been alien to a land-locked people from the flat, settled Indo-Gangetic plains. Perhaps the pace of work on the plantations may not have been new to those who came from labouring and farming backgrounds, though its relentless pace, in the absence of a vibrant, organic community, must have taken its toll. Within the domestic sphere, traditional notions of proper relations between men and women were re-negotiated, as they had to be, as women worked alongside men in the fields and assumed other responsibilities they would not have countenanced in India. Caste, minus its minor ritualistic aspects, had gone, and boundaries of social and cultural inclusion and exclusion were drawn more flexibly. New, pragmatic, cross-caste and cross-religious relationships had to be established in a new environment. In that new environment, the *girmitiyas* were more on their own, more alone, making their way by adapting the metaphors and strategies of a remembered, evanescent, past. My enduring memory of *Aja* is of an old man lying on a string bed in the shade of the mandarin tree behind the thatched house where he slept, looking vacantly into the distance, his near-blind eyes focussed on some imaginary point, always talking about the world of his childhood, sometimes crying, wandering aloud about what his friends and family might be doing back home, hankering hopelessly for a past that was truly past, but unable—perhaps not knowing how—to embrace the new world that was his home. He died in 1962.

My father was born around 1918. No one knew the precise date; that did not seem to matter. Whenever asked about it, he would say he was born during the *Badi Beemari*, the Influenza Epidemic of 1918. That rough approximation served the purpose. His generation grew up in the shadow of indenture. They were formed and deformed by the experience of poverty and uncertainty on the unformed edges of a slowly evolving community, still uncertain of its identity and character but making strenuous efforts to establish and enforce standards recalled from a remembered past. They grew up in a largely enclosed and culturally self-sufficient world. Once indentures had expired, Indians had ceased to be of much concern to the colonial administration. Left to their own devices, the Indian community developed its own voluntary associations and self-help projects—forming settlement committees to harvest cane, establish temples and mosques, build schools, construct cemeteries, start annual festivals, organise *Ramayan* recital through village *mandalis*. *Panchayats*—a five men council of village elders—were started in the early 1930s with official encouragement to maintain a semblance of order in village life. They resolved petty issues—settling land boundary disputes, adjudicating fines for damage caused by stray cattle, intervening in family quarrels, punishing extra-marital relationships—and enforced community standards. Suspicion of alien legal institutions and practices, the cost of court cases, fear of social disapproval and ostracism—a mixture of all these—forced people to resort to time-tested ways. The *panchayats* worked effectively for a while when the village world was still isolated, but lost their authority and rationale in the post-war years as joint families cracked, education and income increased, and improved communication connected the village to the outside world. Now, they are a distant memory. Litigation became a prominent, fractious feature of Indo-Fijian life. As it still is.

The self-absorption of the Indo-Fijian community came from the particular circumstances it encountered in the post-indenture period—the scattered settlements, the hard struggle on the cane farm, the absence of outside helping hands, the indifference of the colonial state—but it also resulted from a colonial policy which restricted contact with others, most notably and damagingly, within the indigenous community. Sir Arthur Gordon's 'Native Policy' as it came to be known, created a separate system of administration—in effect a state within a state—which curtailed Fijian mobility and limited opportunities for employment outside the authorised chief-dominated order in order ostensibly to shield the indigenous community from the corrosive effect of contact with the outside world.[7] When Indians transgressed village boundaries and established *de facto* relationships, Fijians were reprimanded and often fined, and Indians expelled from the vicinity of the *koros* (villages).

Deliberate colonial policy designed to keep the two communities in separate compartments compounded the problem of cultural disrespect and suspicion that resulted from racial prejudice and cultural difference. There were some exceptions in some parts of Fiji, but separate development and compartmentalised existence for the two communities became the norm. There was a Fijian *koro* on the outer fringes of our settlement: a row of brooding bures surrounding a neatly manicured *rara* (open green), but we never entered it for fear—of what I cannot say. There was a Fijian woman who had somehow adopted my father as her younger brother and was openly playful with my mother, her *bhauji*. We called her *phua*, father's sister, and treated her like a member of the extended family. But that was about it. We children had no Fijian friends. In the absence of any meaningful contact, we continued to view things Fijian through the prism of prejudice. The Fijians reciprocated our ignorance.

My father's world, like that of most of his contemporaries, centred upon a ten acre plot of land leased from the Native Land Trust Board. It was only a lease, so obvious in hindsight, but we never thought that the land wasn't our own, that it wouldn't always remain our own. The notion that it might revert to the owners—as it has now done—never once entered our minds. The ten acre plot was the CSR's idea when, facing labour shortage after the end of indenture, it decided to get out of cane growing to concentrate on milling.[8] The CSR was clever. It wanted to relinquish cane farming, but not control over the industry.

It reasoned that with careful husbandry, the limited acreage could be made big enough to be economically viable, but certainly not big enough to make us too big for our boots. On that ten acre farm, we grew sugar cane and rice, had a cow or two, some goats and chicken for meat and vegetables for domestic use or for selling to neighbours to raise cash. That was about it. Like other people in the village, we did not get anywhere very far, but we got by. J.W Coulter, the American geographer who carried out field research in Laqere, the village across the river from our own, captures the daily routine of farm life in the late 1930s and early 1940s accurately:

> The regular work of Indian farmers in Fiji is in contrast to the irregular, easy going life of the Fijians. The Oriental rises at half-past five, harnesses his oxen, and plows from six to eight. He breakfasts at home or in the field on roti and milk and tea (roti is bread made from flour and fried in ghee). He resumes plowing until ten; at that time his oxen are unhitched to lie in the shade during the heat of the day. Shortly after ten he milks his cow, and from ten-thirty to twelve hoes weeds or cuts fodder along the ditches or road-side. At noon he lunches on rice, dal or rice curry, and milk. In the early afternoon he hoes again, cuts more grass, or does odd jobs about the house. From three to five he plows. Supper at six consists of rice curry and chutney and milk. There is smoking and conversation by a kerosene lamp until bedtime at eight. In the evenings groups of Indians who have been working in the fields all day trudge home in the dusk, carrying lunch pails.[9]

The details might vary from place to place and from time to time, but the overall picture will be familiar to anyone of my generation who grew up on an Indo-Fijian farm in the post-war years. WEH Stanner, who closely observed the Indian community in the mid-1940s, also captures the problems and aspirations of the community accurately. Thousands of families suffered 'under a crushing burden of private debt,' he writes. 'Peasants and labourers lived frugally, worked long hours for extremely low wages or incomes, and saved with desperate application to keep alive, to repay loans and mortgages, to buy freehold land, to remit funds to India, to discharge customary social obligations requiring expensive outlays, and to acquire a competence for old age or return to India.'[10] On the social side, Stanner notes, caste barriers had almost disappeared. 'High and low castes might sit together at school or in other assemblies or live together in unsegregated neighbourhoods. Restriction on vocation and occupation had greatly modified.

European dress was widespread among men except in rural areas. Women no longer veiled and their costume, too, had altered. The *purdah* was unknown. Religious ceremonial had simplified and shortened, especially the ritual purification, Hindu-Muslim separatism had so far weakened that members of the two religious communities sat together in amity on public committees, often took the same line of policy, co-operated politically (especially on educational matters) and mingled fairly freely socially.'

Some old customs, observed by our grandparents' generation, were on the way out. Stanner has noted the diminishing relevance of caste in everyday life. There were others. Polyandrous relationships were not rare during indenture because women were few and competition for them was intense. But as the sex-ratio improved and the community stabilised, monogamous marriage became the strict rule, the breach of which often led to violence, occasionally murders. During indenture, again because of the shortage of women, Hindu-Muslim marriages were not uncommon—and tolerated—but this practice, too, ended in the post-indenture period as the two groups began to establish 'morally correct' behaviour for their followers and as debate about religious identity engulfed the community. Inter-religious marriages are rare today. The practice of child marriage, common in my grandfather's generation, and continued from village India, also ceased. The legal age of marriage for boys was increased in 1961 from 16 to 18, and for girls from 13 to 14, though in practice most marriages took place later than the stipulated legal age. Girls' education was still frowned upon. In 1940, only 11 percent of the girls (1,430)—compared to 20 per cent of the boys (3,607) attended primary school. This situation changed within a decade. In 1959, for example, of the 77,000 pupils in primary schools, 20,000 were Indian boys and 15,000 Indian girls. The remaining gender barriers would crumble soon as the value of education, even if it was not for a career, became entrenched in the community and as the expectations of the women's role in the home and in the community at large expanded.

The leased farm was the only property our parents had, but it was clear that there was no future on it for all the children, six boys and two girls. We were encouraged to seek alternatives. Education was the key to that quest. Our parents started community schools—nothing fancy, just rudimentary structures of thatched bures of bamboo walls and cow dung-plastered floor on a piece of land donated by some generous villager. By 1956, there were 154 Indian schools in Fiji, of which 129 were run by non-denominational settlement committees. Some partially literate village elders assumed the role of instructors in Hindi and elementary arithmetic in return for help with house and farm work. The spectacle of poor parents with nothing, making sure that the life of their children was better than theirs, is moving. Things improved with time and government assistance. By the early 1970s, over 500 primary and secondary schools were run by Indo-Fijian settlement and denominational bodies.

I have for some years been interested in the colonial texts which instructed our fathers' generation, to see the kinds of ideals and ethos the colonial officialdom tried to instil in them, its conception of the ideal colonial subject. I recently came across a copy of texts which were used in Fiji Indian primary schools in the 1930s. They are instructive. Here is just one example from the *School Journal, 1930*. There are stories and anecdotes in it from Indian history: about Siddhartha, Rama, Harish Chandra, Tulsi Das, Guru Nanak and other figures of legend and myth. The emphasis on things Indian is important; it was a marker of our collective cultural reference point. The government was keen for the Indian population to retain its links with its cultural heritage (and then complain that the Indians did not assimilate into the mainstream colonial society!). The *Journal* also carried stories about Fiji, excerpts from the governor's addresses, announcements about coming events, but these were brief, dry and uninteresting. Much more interesting were the stories about the Empire, Our Empire, marked by red patches on the *Clarion* atlas. The geography of Samoa and Hawaii featured in some of the texts as did items on Casablanca and the Ford Motor Factory at Detroit, the White Cockatoo. And then there were tips on how to be good citizens, law abiding, respectful of authority, appreciative of the great things that the 'Mother Country' was doing for its children in the colonies. Items on the best way to cultivate maize, banana and tobacco, the precautions to take during hurricanes and floods, the importance of keeping wells clean, were designed to teach people about clean, healthy, hygienic living.

If you were training to be an Indian primary school teacher in 1930, you would be expected to know, among other things, two virtues for which the Chinese are famous, why ANZAC was celebrated, what things the people of Nigeria and Fiji had in common, how the Union Jack came into existence, the names of some of the finest buildings in Auckland, where the missionary John Williams was born, what religious festivals Rumanians enjoyed most and how they celebrated it, how David Livingston got his education, what Florence Nightingale's favourite game as a child was, what pupils knew about the children of Labrador, the importance of the Chrysler Building in New York, the number of talons or claws a cat had. If you were sitting your Primary School Leaving Certificate Examination in 1936, you would be expected to know, among other things, the name of one of the best known governors of Roman Britain who encouraged the building of houses, towns and markets, the name of the British General who captured Jerusalem in 1917, the name of the brave French Commander who was killed in the same battle as General Wolfe, the name of the Roman Empire revived by Charles the Great, the name of the highest mountain in Australia, the chief export of New Zealand, the capital of Fiji before Suva, two ways in which disease could be spread. Highly relevant, dry and topical things like that! This sort of education was for the chosen elite of the community, the primary school teachers. The idea was not to 'educate' the populace but to train cogs for the colonial bureaucratic wheel. Apart from the court clerks and assistants and interpreters in the district administration, primary school teachers were people of respect and status in the community. Most people of my father's generation aspired to know just enough to read and write letters or sign their names to official documents.

Besides education, the earlier generations devised other ingenious means to erase barriers to social mobility and obliterate marks of social differentiation based on caste or some other such criteria. One way of doing this was the names people gave to their children. *Girmitiyas* had names which a careful observer could use to decipher a person's social status. The lower and middle castes were named after objects, days and months, a particular emotion or event or state of affairs in the household or the village at the time the child was born. Thus such names as Dukhia and Bipati (sadness/hardship), Gendia and Phulbasia (after flowers), Hansa (a mythical bird), Bhola, Bhullar and Jokhu (simple ones), Mangal, Budhai, Sanicharee, Mangru, Somai, Sukkhu (after days of the week), Gulab and Gulabi (after a colour), Bahadur, Shera (brave one), Sundar (pretty one). Other names with no particular connotation that I can decipher included Kalpi, Bisun, Tahull, Jaitoo, Jhinul, Chagun, Aleemoolah, Ulfat, Chaitu, Umrai. The *girmitiyas* named their children after gods and goddesses and great mythical figures, which threw the old patterns into confusion, making it difficult to establish one's caste from the names. These names were common in my father's generation: Ram Prasad, Ram Saran, Ram Autar, Arjun, Hari Prasad, Ram Piyari, Bhola Nath, Bihari Prasad, Ganga Din, Jamuna Prasad, Sukh Raji, Suruj Pati, Shiv Lal, Mata Prasad, Tota Ram. No one could tell whether Ram Prasad was a Chamar (a tanner) or a Kurmi (cultivator). The higher castes maintained their caste surnames—Sharma, Singh, Mishra, although oral evidence suggests that these names were sometimes appropriated by those below them in social hierarchy. Sanskritisation was clearly at work here. Our parents named their children after film stars and famous personalities—Rajendra Prasad, Raj Kumar, Jawahar Lal, Vijay Singh, Rajesh Chandra, Mahendra Kumar, Satish Chand, Surendra Prasad, Sunil Kumar, Biman Prasad—thus obliterating the last vestiges of caste distinction.

In some areas, though, distinctions and differences were being institutionalised. This was particularly so in the fields of cultural and religious identity.

With the end of indenture in 1920, a number of religious and cultural associations emerged to provide a semblance of order and regularity to a rapidly stabilising Indo-Fijian community. Arya Samaj and Sanatan Dharam had been established at the beginning of the 20th century, but Muslim League and Sangam, the umbrella organisation of the South Indian community, came in 1926. As the community began to set down roots, the different groups engaged in an intense effort to 'define' the proper code of religious conduct, the proper observance of rituals and ceremonies. Conflict erupted. Samajis, followers of Swami Dayanand Saraswati's reformist branch of Hinduism, clashed with the more orthodox, ritual-observing, idol-worshipping Sanatanis.[11] Shia and Sunni Muslims clashed over whether the appropriate successor to Prophet Mohammed were members of his own family (his son-in-law Ali and his sons Hussein and Hassan) or the Caliphs. Hindu-Muslim tensions, reflecting the political developments on the subcontinent in the inter-war period, were visible but restrained, though as the divisions hardened and pressure mounted to conform to strictly prescribed codes in food and dress and prayer and worship—not least because of the arrival of religious teachers from India—the more relaxed interaction and easy friendships of earlier years 'when we were all brothers' suffered. Faith became an important marker of identity in time, erasing and superseding other markers such as regional origin. And so it has remained.

The enclosed and socially isolated world of my father's generation began to fracture when my generation arrived in the post-war period. The values and practices which had enthralled my father's generation, embroiled them in acrimonious debates with other sections of the community, defined their sense of identity and place, gave them meaning and purpose, had less relevance for my generation. Arranged marriages were, for us, a thing of the past, as were large families (a baker's dozen was not uncommon in many families). Daylight marriages of short duration became the norm for us, but were unheard of in the past. Our conceptions of women's role in public and private life would have been alien to the earlier generations. Compulsory shaving of head and facial hair as a public sign of bereavement was observed, but not enforced. Strict rules about diet—little beer but definitely no beef—were beginning to be observed in the breach. Village moneylenders—*mahajans*—who had exercised such a baleful influence in the past became a distant memory for us as banks spread their tentacles around the country. The great debates of the late 1940s about whether prohibition should continue to be imposed on the Indo-Fijian community—an issue that deeply polarised people and wrecked political careers—meant nothing to us. Whether the meat you ate was *halal* or *jhatk*a, an issue that had strained Hindu-Muslim relations in the past, had no relevance for us. Similarly, whether

Sanatanis greeting Arya Samajis with a *Namaste* rather than the customary *Ram-Ram* would be seen as a sign of defeat or subservience, seemed petty to my generation. Christmas—*Bada Din* (Big Day)—became for my generation an excuse for exuberant, drunken celebration, eating fresh goat meat and drinking rum—only the poorest of the poor ate chicken or duck on that day—a much anticipated feature of our annual calendar.

We spoke a 'new language.' Words and concepts used during my father's generation were forgotten: *kakkus* (toilet), *bhuccahd* (silly, stupid), *chachundar* (loose woman, a flirt), *bhong* (dumb), *behuda* (fool), *jahua* (con man), *lokum* (gaol), *bailup* (place for cattle), *Black Maria* (police van), *bagrap* (buggered up), *lifafa* (envelope). We had no idea what *tanzeb*, *nainsukh*, *motia*, once the pride of female jewellery, looked like. *Lehanga naach* (male dancers dressed as female) which was performed during marriage ceremonies to lighten the mood, *gutka* (stick dance) done during festivals, *tassa*, *hudda*, *nagara* (all folk musical instruments) were for us a part of a vanishing past. Unlike our parents, we did not require permission from the colonial officialdom to drink alcohol. Aubrey Parke, who was district commissioner in Labasa when I was completing my primary schooling in the 1960s, tells me about the distinct categories of permission you required: one which allowed you to drink beer only, one which permitted the consumption of both beer and spirit in a pub, one which entitled you to buy a dozen bottles of beer a month and, if you were really somebody, you had the permission to buy a dozen bottles of beer and a bottle of spirit—Dozen and One—a month. That world was gone when we were teenagers. The older generation mourned the passing of a culturally-ordered world which had been built from the memory of a remembered past, but there was little they could do about it.

Improving communication—better roads, bridges and regular public transport—joined us to an expanding world beyond the village horizon. Radio came in the 1950s and Hindi newspapers—*Jagriti, Jai Fiji, Shanti Dut, Kisan Mitra*. And films: *Alam Ara, Anarkali, Baiju Bawra, Awara, Shree 420, Jagte Raho, Pyasa, Mother India, Ganga Jamuna*. Films had been coming to Fiji since the late 1930s—eight of the ten cinema houses were run by Indo-Fijians in the 1940s—but they were viewed mostly by people in the urban areas.[12] Going to movies was a major social event of the week, an occasion to display the latest fashion in clothes and jewellery, to meet the elite of society, to know who was who in the community. The Hindi newspapers, Hindi movies, the religious functions we performed with mundane regularity, kept us intact as a community, gave us purpose and cohesion. We in the villages, closer to our cultural roots, thought ourselves superior to the urban dwellers who had, so it appeared to us, drifted away and embraced western ways.

Expectation of what life was—or what it could be—had risen for our generation. By the early 1960s, for instance, primary education was within the reach of most children who wanted it, and secondary education, too, for those who passed their entrance examination. We now could, if we were any good—and our 'goodness' was judged solely on the basis of our performance in external examinations—contemplate a lowly career in the public service, in the banking sector, in the sugar industry as trainee overseers and in the teaching profession, possibilities that were beyond even the imagined horizon of our parents. In the early 1960s, university education was restricted to a select few—perhaps ten a year—who were sent on government scholarship to New Zealand (rarely to Australia) to train as high school teachers, administrators and economists. They were the cream of the crop, who returned from overseas after few years, proclaiming themselves culturally disoriented, social misfits, unable to speak their language, ill at ease among their own people, even embarrassed about their past. For all their idiosyncrasies, though, they made a huge impression on our youthful minds, representing possibilities that could be ours if only we tried hard enough. Many became our role models.

But all this changed with the founding of the University of the South Pacific in 1968. That event must be counted as one of the turning points in the modern history of the Pacific islands. It opened up opportunities for higher education to thousands of children from poor homes who would almost certainly have otherwise missed out. It brought us into contact with people from other parts of Fiji and from other parts of the Pacific, which had, until then, remained forbidding names on paper, nothing more. A new generation had come of age at a critical time in the region's history as islands were on the eve of independence. We were trained—and destined—to play an important part in our countries' and our region's future.

Our world was more diverse than our parents'. Those who went to Christian or urban schools lost the Hindi language, were more exposed to modern influences, were more at home in cross-cultural friendships. Those of us who went to rural schools or schools run by various Indo-Fijian cultural organisations, retained firmer links with our culture and language. This, I now realise, had its obvious advantages, but it also imposed limitations that dawned upon me much later. Just as we went to predominantly Indian schools, Fijian children went to predominantly Fijian schools—Queen Victoria and Ratu Kadavulevu. In 1960, when I was in grade two, there were only 88 non-Fijians in the colony's 325 Fijian primary schools, and only 53 non-Indians in Indian primary schools. We thus grew up engrossed in the ethos of our own society, untouched by cross-cultural influences, completely ignorant of the values, interests and concerns of the Fijians, blind to the complex, inner impulses of their society. And yet, we were a part of the generation which was called upon to play an important role in national life in the post-colonial era—as teachers, administrators, politicians. No wonder Fiji has faltered so often in its recent postcolonial journey.

We were the last generation of Fiji school children to complete high school before independence. We were the last to study the colonial curriculum. Senior Cambridge was the exam high school children sat until New Zealand Entrance came in the late 1960s. Once again, the emphasis was on learning other peoples' pasts and experiences. So in geography lessons, we had lessons on Burma, Central China, Malaya, Singapore, Manchuria, East Anglia, the Midland Valley of Scotland, about Brittany, Denmark and the Mediterranean coastlines of France, about California, the Canadian maritime provinces, the corn belt of the United States, Florida and the St Lawrence Valley, about the Snowy River Scheme, irrigation faming in Renmark, South Australia, the transport problems of the Cook Islands—they had transport problems there?—the relief maps and the sheep industry in New Zealand and Australia. I did not do well in geography because, among other things, I did not the name of the highest mountain in Australia. I knew that it began with a 'K' but wasn't sure whether it was Kosciusko or Kilimanjaro. Coolgardie and Kalgoorlie confused me. And try as we might, we could not spell Murrumbidgee. What kind of name was that?

In history in the lower grades, we studied the rise of the Liberal Party in New Zealand, the importance of the refrigeration industry to New Zealand agriculture, the Wakefield scheme, the Maori Wars (as they were then called), about John Macarthur, the merino sheep and squatters, the effects of the Victorian gold rushes and the rapidly expanding wool industry, topics like that. In higher grades, we left the Antipodes to focus on the grand themes of modern history. So we studied the unification of Italy and Germany, the Crimean crisis and the First World War, the Bolshevik Revolution, the rise of Adolf Hitler and Mussolini, the emergence of the trade union movement in Great Britain and, briefly, the rise of new nations in Asia. Pupils ahead of us by a few years studied the causes of the 1929 Depression, the Partition of Africa, the social reform policies of Gladstone and Disraeli, the significance of the 'Import Duties Act of 1931,' the Gold Standard, the Abdication crisis, the Irish Free State.

In our English classes at secondary school, we studied both literature as well as language. Language was dry, antiquarian, but literature was something else, good, solid, untrendy stuff that would be dismissed today as hugely Eurocentric: novels, short stories, poems and plays by John Steinbeck (*The Pearl*), William Golding (*Lord of the Flies*), Emily Bronte (*Wuthering Heights*), Joseph Conrad (*Lord Jim*), William Wordsworth (*Daffodils*), Samuel Taylor Coleridge (*Ancient*

*Mariner*), Edgar Alan Poe (*Raven*), DH Lawrence (*The Snake*), William Shakespeare (*Hamlet, Macbeth, Merchant of Venice, Romeo and Juliet*), TS Eliot (*Love Song of J Alfred Prufrock*). The list does not end there. Reading, broadening our imaginative horizon was fun, but writing short composition pieces could be tricky. For instance a long meaningful paragraph on modern art, the astronauts, western films, the bottle drive of collecting for Corso, about the main stand at a flower show, the case for or against television (when we had no idea what this creature was), a climbing adventure, baby sitting or, of all things, a winter morning. In hot, humid Tabia of all places! A few years back, I met a man in Brisbane who had sat the Senior Cambridge in the mid-1960s. There was an essay question on the 'Phenomena of the Beatles', the musical group. Not paying heed to the spelling, he proceeded to write a long and (he thought) a meaningful paragraph on the 'Phenomena of the Rhinoceros Beetles!' With misunderstandings like this, it was a miracle that we passed external exams, and with good marks too.

We were introduced to the global sweep of the human experience in history and literature, to the creative genius of the great minds of the world, but I am not at all sure we understood what we were reading. The subject matter was alien. We read to set standards; cramming was what was required of us to pass exams, not free-ranging exploration of new worlds the books were opening before us. We were taught to learn, not question, the value of colonial education. Still, for all their cultural biases, the western texts opened up new worlds for us. They awakened our imagination, emphasised our common humanity across boundaries of culture and race, and sowed the seeds of future possibilities. The idea of the fundamental oneness of humanity has remained with me. So, I don't cringe at the colonial texts we learnt parrot-fashion; I am grateful for the windows they opened.

The metaphors of our own culture and allusion to our own past had no place in the higher colonial learning, although in primary school we learnt Hindi and learnt about our ancestral culture and history, about various gods and goddesses and the heroes and heroines of Indian history. We had enough of the language to read the *Ramayana* and Hindi newspapers to our unlettered parents. The language connected us to our cultural roots. Indian school children played an important part in keeping the culture alive. There was no Hindi in high school in the late 1960s. I regret that now, but it did not seem to matter then. And I have, through private effort, continued to read, write and speak Hindi. But the sense of loss is palpable among those who have no Hindi at all. Some, now in middle age, are making an effort to learn the language.

More regrettable, for me, was the complete absence of Fijian culture and history in the curriculum. We heard occasional hair-raising anecdotes about the notorious cannibal Udre Udre who reportedly ate one hundred humans, marking each feast with a stone heaped in a pile, or about Maa'fu, the mercurial Tongan, who nearly colonised Fiji and Cakobau who so gracefully ceded the islands to Great Britain. But that was about it. Fijians remained for most of us objects of fear and suspicion, their names invoked by mothers to send unruly children to bed. 'If you don't go to bed, Timoci will take you away.' We all had a Timoci in our families. To us, all Fijians were peas in the same pod. I did not, until quite late in life, know about the inner configuration of Fijian society, its rituals and ranking systems and precise protocols, its political divisions and rivalries. I am sure it was the same with the Fijians who saw Indo-Fijians as *Kai Idia*, an undifferentiated group descended from an enslaved past. For many of them, Gujaratis and *girmitiyas*, the *Kurbis* and the *Madrasis*, were one and the same thing. That said, the post-colonial generation is becoming more aware of things Fijian, thanks to an increasing number of multi-ethnic primary and secondary schools, the multi-ethnic university campus in Suva, and broader social interaction in the workplace and in the community at large. In their attitudes and relationships, their habits and moods, the Indo-Fijians, while retaining their 'Indian-ness' are becoming more conscious of the 'Fijian-ness' in their hyphenated identity.

There was nothing in primary or secondary education about Fiji history, so that generations of children grew up knowing virtually nothing about their past. History—and the Humanities generally—was for no-hopers; bright students did the hard sciences. But there is, I think another reason for the absence of Fiji from the curriculum. There was no shared understanding of the country's past, no consensus on its commonalities. Thanks to colonialism's stratagem, there was not one Fiji but three, each with its own distinct place in the colonial compartment. While one group lauded colonial rule, the other castigated it. One demanded primordiality as the basis of political culture, the other espoused secular, egalitarian ideology as the principle of political relationships. One asserted paramountcy as the principle of political representation, the other wanted parity. One owned the land, the other was landless. And so the divisions went. No wonder the educators edited local history out from the text books. Learning someone else's history was safer. Fiji has paid a heavy price for the ignorance of its history.

For Indo-Fijian children, education became a profound agent of social change, just as indenture had been for the *girmitiyas*. The classroom was a great leveller of hierarchy. Before the Second World War, education, especially higher education, was largely the prerogative of the wealthy and the well-connected in the Indo-Fijian community. Wealth, status and power came from owning property or proximity to officialdom. The early generation of leaders came from this privileged background: lawyers, landowners, businessmen such as Badri Maharaj, the Grant family, the Deokis, the Ramrakhas, the Mishras, the Singhs of Ba, the Sahu Khans, the Tikarams. But the expansion of educational opportunities opened up the field to children from poor, nondescript backgrounds. Talent and merit became the markers of success and ladders to power, and that has remained the case. The old, well established families, whose names were once synonymous with status and sophistication and fame and fortune, have gone and are now largely forgotten.

As we grew up, the world of our parents began to recede into a vanishing past—joint families, proper and periodic observance of rituals and ceremonies, the comforting bonds of a cohesive community, family solidarity, respect for age and authority, politeness in the presence of pandits, extreme carefulness in the management of money, healthy fear of the unknown. The gap widened with time in much the same way as it had done when our parents moved away from their parents' world. The change was inevitable—and liberating. And it continues unabated. As mobility increases and modernity touches nearly every aspect of life, the Indo-Fijians are becoming more aware of their complex and confusing identity. Living in a society corroded by the ravages of racial politics, they continue to nurture the roots of the Indian cultural heritage as a matter of pride and choice, though perhaps not with the reverence and understanding of their parents and grandparents. Indian music, dress, food, and art are being interpreted and re-interpreted through a different and distinct lenses, touched by modernity and the inevitable forces of globalization that would have been feared and forbidding to the earlier generation. Western cultural values, alien and alienating to our forebears, also continue to be embraced and incorporated, not the least because it opens up doors to other opportunities.

Perhaps what will surprise the earlier generations most, as they peer down the corridors of time—surprising in view of the prejudices and stereotypes and entrenched attitudes that had to be overcome—is the way in which their descendants have accommodated themselves to the ethos and mores of a society, deeply informed by its indigenous past, in ways they could not, or were perhaps unable and unwilling to. They will be surprised at the extent to which their children and grandchildren have taken to drinking *kava*, enjoying Sevens Rugby, eating *lovo* food, wearing the *sulu*, conversing in the Fijian language and being familiar with Fijian cultural protocols. They will be disbelieving of the depth of inter-racial friendships in the community. They will, I am sure, marvel at the long, troubled, unpredictable, confusing, depressing and exhilarating journey from being an Indian to being an Indo-Fijian.

# Thirteen

## One Life, Three Worlds

To be an Indian from Fiji is to be a complex bundle of contradictions. It is to be formed and re-formed by a unique mix of social, cultural and historical experiences. Although the Fijian constitution defines us as 'Indian,' we are, in fact, marked by a confluence of three quite distinct cultural influences: South Asian, Western and Oceanic. Generalizations in these matters are always risky, but the truth will be obvious to people of my age, the post-world war two generation growing up in Fiji. Our food and our religious and spiritual traditions, our dietary habits and general aesthetic sense (in music and cinema, for instance) is unmistakeably South Asian. Our language of work and business and general public discourse, our educational system and legal and judicial traditions, our sense of individual and human rights, is derived from our Western heritage. And our sense of people and place, our sense of humour, our less charged, 'she'll be alright,' 'tomorrow is another day,' attitude to life in general, comes from our Oceanic background.

A century of enforced living in a confined island space has produced overlapping and inseparable connections. The precise contribution of one influence over another on us, our world view, on the general shapes of our thought and action, would vary from time to time and from place to place. It would depend on our educational background, the degree of exposure we have had to external influences, the family circumstance and our network of relationships. There will be variation and diversity. We will accentuate or suppress a particular aspect of our heritage depending on the company, context and perhaps acceptance: more English here, less Indian there. Nonetheless, every Indian person from Fiji will carry within them the traces of the three primary influences which have shaped them.

Most Indo-Fijian people of my age would have three—sometimes more—languages: Fiji-Hindi, Hindi[1], English, and Fijian. Proficiency in the last three would vary. A person growing up near a Fijian village, or with extensive interaction with Fijians at work or play, would speak Fijian more fluently than one who grew up in a remote, culturally self-enclosed Indo-Fijian settlement. Likewise, a person from a rural area is likely to be more fluent in standard Hindi than his or her urban cousin who did not have the opportunity to learn the language formally in primary school. And someone who grew up in a town or city and went to a government or Christian school is likely to be more at home in English than a person from the country.

But every Indo-Fijian person, without exception, would be able to speak Fiji-Hindi with no prior preparation. That is the language that comes naturally to us. It is the mother tongue of the Indo-Fijian community, the language of spontaneous communication among ourselves. It is the language that connects us to time and place, to our childhood. It was the language through which we first learned about our past and about ourselves. It was the language that took us into the deepest secrets, stories and experiences of our people. Our most intimate conversation takes place in Fiji-Hindi. Our thigh-slapping sense of humour, earthy and rough and entirely bereft of subtlety or irony, finds its most resonant voice in that language. And its influence persists.

Whenever we Indo-Fijians meet, even or perhaps especially in Australia, we are very likely to begin our conversation by asking *Tab Kaise*, 'How Are You.' This is less an enquiry than an effort to establish an emotional connection. Yet, the irony is that we do not accord Fiji-Hindi the respect that it deserves. Purists tell us that it is broken Hindi, a kind of plantation pidgin, with no recognisable grammatical pattern, full of words with rough edges and a vocabulary of limited range incapable of accommodating complex thoughts and literary expression.[2] We are slightly embarrassed about its humble origins and apologetic to outsiders, especially from the subcontinent. Its use is properly confined to the domestic sphere. It is not the language we use in public discourse. There is little Fiji-Hindi on Fiji radios, there is nothing in the newspapers. The media uses—has always used—standard Hindi. That is what hurts: the continued calculated neglect and the sniggering put-down of the language by the Indo-Fijian cultural elite. The startling gap between the reality of our private experience and the pretensions of our public performance could not be greater.

I cannot comment on the deeper structures and origins of the language, but common knowledge and popular understanding suggest that Fiji-Hindi is 'cobbled together'—as the critics would put it dismissively—from the dialects and languages of northeast India, principally Avadhi and Bhojpuri[3]. Formal Hindi was not the mother tongue of the immigrant population; these two languages were, which then merged into Fiji-Hindi, with subsequent words, metaphors, images from South Indian languages, and Fijian and English.[4] This was the new *lingua franca* which emerged on the plantations. The plantation system was a great leveller of hierarchy and social status. The caste system gradually disintegrated, and with it the finely-regulated cultural order that the immigrants had known in India.⁵ The new regime rewarded initiative and enterprise, and individual labour. The living conditions on the plantations produced new cross-caste, cross-religious marriages. People of all ranks and social and religious backgrounds lived and worked together, celebrated life and mourned its passing communally. They had no other choice.

From that cloistered, culturally chaotic environment emerged a new more egalitarian social order, and a new language, Fiji-Hindi. Old ways had to give way and they did. New vocabulary and grammar had to be mastered, new ways of looking at the world acquired. The Indian calendar—*Pus, Bhadon, Asarh, Kartik*—was, or began to be, replaced with the Roman calendar. English words entered the new vocabulary, names of institutions (town for *shahar*, school for *pathshala*, *binjin* for benzene, *kirasin* for kerosene, *kantaap* for cane top, bull for the Hindi word *baile*, *phulawa* for plough. And in areas near Fijian villages, Fijian words entered the language as well. This humble new language, levelling, unique, unadorned, a subaltern language of resistance, drawing strands from a large variety of sources, is the language that comes to me naturally.

Yet it is not the language that I would speak on a formal occasion, while giving a public talk in Fiji or an interview to a Hindi radio station in Australia. I am expected to use formal Hindi in public discourse. Everyone expects this of a cultural or political leader. It confers dignity and status on him, earns him (for it is rarely her) the people's trust and acceptance. To be able to use Hindi fluently is to be seen as someone who has not lost touch with the people, is still connected to his roots, can be trusted not to betray the interests of the community. Over the years, I have given dozens of public addresses in Hindi. People express genuine appreciation that I am still able to speak the language, after being away from Fiji for most of my adult life. 'Look,' they say to the supposedly wayward younger generation losing touch with their cultural roots, 'he lives in Australia but still speaks our language. He hasn't forgotten his roots. And nor should you!' Notice that Indo-Fijian identity in this quote is tied with Hindi. The same people who applaud me for speaking in Hindi would talk to me in Fiji-Hindi in private; to speak in formal Hindi with them in private, informal situations, would be the height of pretension. It is all *tamasha*, theatre.

I am glad I am still able to read and write Hindi. I would be the poorer without it, but for me it is a learned language all the same, with all the limitation learned languages bring with them. Those who hear me speak the language fluently have no idea of the amount of effort I put into preparing my speeches. Although I don't actually read the text in order better to connect with the audience (as all good teachers know), each word is written down, in *Devanagri* script, the speech rehearsed line by line several times over, virtually committed to memory.

Proper imagery and metaphors have to be chosen with the help of a bilingual Hindi-English dictionary, because what is clear to me in English is often obscure in Hindi, and the forms of address are different. The disparity between the private, painful effort of preparation and the appearance of a polished public performance is deep.

For years, I unthinkingly accepted the need to speak formal Hindi. It was the expected thing to do. No other alternative, certainly not Fiji-Hindi, was conceivable. I could speak in English to Indo-Fijian audiences, but that would be pointless, talking over their often unlettered heads. I felt curiously elated that I could read and write and speak the language better than many of my contemporaries; it was my badge of honour and pride, my way of demonstrating that I could still connect with my people. But I now realise the futility of my action: a reluctance to acknowledge the 'game' I was playing, thinking that Hindi was my mother tongue. When it clearly was not.

Hindi was the medium of instruction in most Indo-Fijian community schools from the very beginning, and an examinable subject for the Senior Cambridge School Certificate in the post-war years. From the start, the colonial government was keen on Hindi. It encouraged the spread of English because it was the 'official and business language of the colony,' but Hindi—or Hindustani—could not be ignored. 'Hindus and Muslims alike will need it in different forms as the key to knowledge of their religions and literature and as the means of communication with their relatives and co-religionists in India. And for a considerable section too busy with their own affairs to undergo much schooling, and imperfectly equipped to use a foreign language as a vehicle of thought without danger to their practical relations with their environment, their 'mother tongue' must remain both their sole means of communicating with others and the sole means of expressing their thoughts and feelings.' Hindustani was important for administrative purposes, too, because 'an adequate knowledge of Hindustani must be needed by the European community in touch with the Indians, the more so because without it, it is, and will be, impossible for the European official or man of affairs to get into close touch with just those classes which to a large extent depend on him for help and guidance.' And finally, there was the broader consideration 'that Hindustani is the *lingua franca* of probably a larger number of inhabitants of the Empire than English itself and is spoken in a number of colonies besides Fiji.'[7]

The government's agenda is understandable, but it is not entirely certain that Hindustani *was* the 'mother tongue' of the indentured migrants, who came principally from the Avadhi-Bhojpuri speaking areas of north-eastern India and Telugu, Tamil and Malyali speaking regions of the south. For the South Indians, Hindustani was not the mother tongue at all, and in the north, Hindustani or

Urdu was the language of business and administration and the cultural elite, a legacy of the Mogul era of Indian history; it was not the language of the mass of the peasantry. And it is not at all certain that Hindustani was the language spoken in other colonies whose immigrants, too, had derived from the same regions as the immigrants in Fiji. For administrative convenience, then, Hindustani was imposed as the 'mother tongue' of the Indo-Fijian community.

The government's position was supported by the Hindi-favouring Indo-Fijian cultural elite, although many of them preferred not Hindustani—which was a mixture of Hindi and Urdu—but a purer form of formal Hindi, and wished for an extension of English in primary schools.[8] The preference for Hindi or Hindustani (but not Fiji-Hindi), reflected a wider process of Sanskritisation taking place in the community in the post-indenture period. For many Indo-Fijians, indenture or *girmit* (from the agreement under which the immigrants had come to Fiji) was viewed as a period of unspeakable shame and degradation. That ended upon the abolition of indenture in 1920.[9] Community leaders sought to establish voluntary social and cultural organisations to erase the memory of a dark period in their lives, and to impart correct moral and spiritual values to their people.

This was evident in virtually every aspect of Indo-Fijian life.[10] The Fiji-born discarded rural Indian peasant dress of *dhoti* (loin cloth) and *kurta* (long flowing shirt) and *pagri* (turban) for western-style shirt and shorts and slacks. In religion, animal sacrifice and other practices of animism of rural India gradually gave way to cleaner forms of Brahmincal Hinduism.[11] The caste system, with all the ritual practices associated with it, slowly disintegrated. Hindu children were given names after gods and goddesses—Ram Autar, Shiv Kumari, Saha Deo, Ram Piyari, Latchman—to erase caste distinction. All these represented a conscious, deliberate dissociation from a past understood as painful, embarrassing and degrading.[12] The public embracing of Hindustani as the *lingua franca* was a part of that effort.

Both Hindustani and Indian history and culture were promoted in the colonial curriculum, and published in the *School Journal* edited by A W MacMillan.[13] Stories of great men and women, of kings and queens, historical events of great antiquity appeared, all designed to make the Indo-Fijian children proud of their ancestral heritage, of their 'motherland': stories about Siddharata (Buddha), Rabindranath Tagore, Emperor Akbar, Pandita Ramabai, Raja Harishchandra, figures like that. The *Journal* also highlighted the great achievements of the British Empire, and published pieces on important places and peoples in it. There was nothing—or very little—on Fiji and the Pacific, little beyond some amusing anecdotes about the Fijian people. So not only the language, but the mind and soul of the Indo-Fijians was nourished by stories from our two 'motherlands': India and England. The actual 'motherland,' Fiji, was left undiscussed, disregarded, confined to the fringes of the humorous anecdotes. Our immediate past was ignored not only because it seemed mundane but also because it was the site of deep contestation. Indenture was an indictment of the government, whom the labourers saw as having a complicit role in the atrocities which they endured on the plantations. India was safer. The emphasis on India and things Indian, hero-worshipping and frankly romantic, continued in the post-war years in the specially composed school texts, *Hindi pothis*, by the India-born Ami Chandra.[14]

English was the second language taught in the Indo-Fijian primary schools. The aim was to give school children an elementary knowledge of grammar and vocabulary, the sort of rudimentary knowledge required to understand official instructions and notices, and occasional snippets from the great texts of English literature. The texts used in the post-war years were the *New Method Readers*, *Caribbean Readers*, *The Oxford English Readers for Africa* and University of London's *Reading for Meaning*. There was nothing in these texts about Fiji or the Pacific Islands. Here is the Table of Contents of *The Oxford English Readers for Africa, Book Six* for the last year of primary education: The Story that Letters Tell, How Messages are Sent, *The Island*, by Cecil Fox Smith, Farmer's Work, The Arctic Wastes, *I Vow to Thee, My country*, by Cecil Spring-Rice, Sound and Light, Different Kinds of Buildings, *The Bees* by William Shakespeare, The Fight Against Disease, The Work of the Post Office, *The Discovery*, by JC Squire, The Men Who Made the World Larger, A Wonderful Little Builder, *Bete Humaine* by Francis Brett Young, Napoleon, Some Stories of Famous Men, Bridges and bridge-Building, Good Citizenship, A Famous Speech from Shakespeare, *On Mercy* by William Shakespeare and, finally, Some Business Letters.[15]

The list needs no commentary: it is Anglo-centric and its intellectual orientation and purpose self-evident. Much the same trend continued in secondary schools where English texts and examples were replaced with examples from Australia and New Zealand.[16] I suppose the intention of the texts was to inculcate in us a deep pride in the British empire (upon which the sun never set, we were taught to remember, and to remember, too, that Britannia ruled the waves, that 'we' had won the great wars of the 20th century, that London was the cultural centre of the world, that the best literature, the best of everything—the Bedford trucks, the Austin and Cambridge and Morris Minor cars—came from England), to appreciate the good fortune of being its member, to be grateful for what little tender mercies came our way because we had nothing, we were nothing.

I recognise the cultural bias of the texts now, and it is easy enough to be critical of their colonising purpose. But these large and troubling issues did not matter to us or to anyone else then. I recall the thrill, on a remote sugar cane farm with no electricity, no running water, no paved roads, of reading about faraway places and peoples as an enthralling experience, making imaginary connections with African children whose neat faces we saw in glossy imperial magazines that came to our school as gifts from the British Council. An acquaintance with them reduced our sense of isolation, expanded our imaginative horizon. And it is the appreciation of that enlarging, enriching, experience that has remained with me.

While we learned a great deal about the western and the Indian world, there was nothing in books about Fijian language and culture, beyond the fear-inducing stories about a cannibal (Udre Udre) who had eaten a hundred men and marked each conquest with a stone—which was there for everyone to see. There were a few innocuous stories about Ratu Seru Cakobau, the wise and great Fijian chief, who eventually ceded Fiji to Great Britain in 1874 and the Tongan intruder and challenger to his authority, Enele Ma'afu; but that was about all. Fijians remained for us objects of fear; many an unruly child was sent to bed with the threat that Seru (or Emosi or Sakiusa or some other Fijian with similar name) would snatch us away from our parents if we did not behave properly.

The Fijian ethos, as we understood it, often through the prism of prejudice, inspired no great respect. We valued individual initiative and enterprise, their culture, we were told, quelled it. We saved for tomorrow, they lived for now. We were the products of status-shattering egalitarian inheritance; Fijian society was governed by strict protocol. They ate beef; we revered the cow as mother incarnate. Our schools were separate. Fijians went to exclusively Fijian schools (provincial primary ones and then to the Queen Victoria or Ratu Kadavulevu), while we attended primarily Indo-Fijian schools. For all practical purposes, we inhabited two distinct worlds, the world of the *Kai Idia* and the world of the *Kai Viti*.[17] Fiji has paid a very large price for its myopic educational policy.

This, then, is my inheritance, and the inheritance of my generation: complex, chaotic, contradictory. I have lived with it all my life and throughout the course of my university education in different countries over the past three decades. It enriches me even as it incapacitates me, complicates the way I do and see things, the way I relate to people around me, the way I see myself. There have been many moments of sheer agonising desperation over the years when confusion reigned in my linguistically fractured mind, when I could not find words in any language to convey precisely what I wanted to say, how I felt about a particular place or person, when I felt hobbled and helpless, like the washerman's donkey, belonging neither here nor there: *Na ghar ke na ghat ke.*

English is the language of my work. I am not closely familiar with its deeper grammatical structures and rules of engagement and composition: alpha, beta and coordinate clauses, auxiliary, infinitives and intransitive verbs, prepositions and subordinate conjunctions—these things confuse me even now. And its classical allusions to Greek and Roman mythology—Pandora's Box, Achilles Heel, Trojan Horse, Crossing the Rubicon, Cleopatra's nose, Ulysses, Cyclades and Cyclopes, Medusa's Head; its references to the stories and people of the Old and New Testaments, to Job, John, Matthew and Abraham, the Wisdom of Solomon, to quotations from the *Book of Ecclesiastes* and *Ezekiel*; its borrowing of words and phrases from European literature—it was years after high school that I realised that the phrase 'to cultivate your garden' came from Voltaire's *Candide*, what TS Eliot meant by 'Hollow Men' and why 'April is the cruellest month,' what Heathcliff's windswept moors looked like—all this knowledge had to be acquired through surreptitious reading; they remain beyond my easy reach even now.

Yet, my professional competence in the language is taken for granted. The journals and academic presses to which I send my work for publication make no concession to my chequered linguistic background. That is the way the game is played in academia.[18] It has taken many years of learning and un-learning, many years of doubt and desperation, to acquire some proficiency in the language. I try to write as simply as I can, which leads some colleagues, *au fait* with the lexicon of post-modern scholarly extravaganza, to equate simple writing with simplistic thought! I have sometimes been accused of writing fluently, but only if the readers knew the effort, the revision after revision and the deliberate thought that has gone into the writing. I recognise good writing when I see it; I envy the effortless fluency of writers who produce words as if they owned them. Essays and reviews in *The New Yorker,* for instance, with their wonderfully engaging prose, the breathtaking quality of images and metaphors, invariably provoke admiration in me. I readily accept my limitations, my inability to produce with words meanings and miracles like those for whom English is the mother tongue. That is the way it is, and always will be.

Some colleagues in the Pacific islands, non-native speakers of English, are more adventurous, less accepting of the conventions of the language, who are prepared to flout its rules, play with it in unconventional ways, bend it to meet their needs.[19] They have 'indigenised' the language in interesting ways, encouraged, I suppose, by the liberating tenets of post-colonial and cultural studies. So what appears to me to be badly mangled English in need of a sharp, ruthless, editorial pen is avant-garde poetry for them. In an appealingly rebellious kind of way, they are unapologetic, defiant in their defence of idiosyncrasy. Clearly scholarly conventions, styles and expectations have changed in the last two decades or so. The diversity tolerated—perhaps even encouraged?—now would have been unthinkable when I was learning the alphabets of the academe. I recognise, as I see the younger generation, that I am trapped by a different past and different expectations. I am sometimes accused of being a part of the 'assimilationist' generation which paid scant regard to local modes of expression, local idioms, but slavishly embraced the ethical and intellectual premises of colonial and colonizing education and the English language. I suppose we are all products of our own particular histories.

Writing formal academic English is one thing, speaking it colloquially quite another. To be reasonably effective, one has to have some knowledge of the locally familiar idioms and metaphors, a grasp of the local lingo, as they say. These are not as easy to acquire for someone who came to Australia half-formed. I have had to educate myself on the side about Australian society and culture and history and its special vocabulary. This has not been easy in an academic life filled with pressure to create a refereed paper trail that government bureaucrats can see and understand (and, most importantly, reward). The task is made all the more difficult because we had nothing about Australia in school beyond the most elementary lessons about Lachlan Macquarie, John MacArthur and the merino sheep, the gold rushes of the 19th century, the convict settlement and the squattocracy, cramming exercises in geography (which was the longest river in Australia, its highest mountain, its capital city, its tallest building: that sort of thing) and the occasional novel (*Voss* and *To the Islands*) in high school. Not surprisingly, Australia remained for us remote and inaccessible, the *sahib's* country, a place to dream about, a land from where all the good things we so admired came: the Holden car, the refrigerator, the tram engine, the canned fruit, the bottled jam and the refined white sugar, so pure and so good, that we used it as an offering to the gods in our *pujas*.

Seeing Australia as a student from a distance was one thing; living in it, trying to get a handle on the texture of the daily lived life, was another. Its sheer size and variety: the hot, red featureless plains merging into the shrubbery desert in the distance, the remote, rural, one-street towns on the western fringes of the eastern states, dry, desolate spaces along highways littered with the decaying remains of dead animals and the rusting hulks of long-abandoned vehicles, places that lie beyond the certitude of maps, at the back of beyond, as they say. I had to get used to the idea that golden brown, not deep green, was the natural colour of Australia, that its flora and fauna were unique.

New words and phrases I had never heard before had to be learned and used their proper context: Dorothy Dixer, Gallah, Apeshit, Blind Freddy, Rels, Bulldust, Coat-hanger, Dingbat, Wanker, Drongo, Tall Poppy, Scorcher, Ripper, Ratbag, Ocker, My Oath, Knockers, Bludger, Dinky Di, Fair Dinkum, Perv,

Spitting the Dummy, words which locals use effortlessly, but which are strange to newcomers. Nothing can be more embarrassing than using a wrong word at the wrong time, or committing a *faux pas*, in the company of people who assume you are equally knowledgeable about the local lingo as them. At a party in Canberra many years ago, I used the word 'fanny' in what context I do not remember. In the United States, where I had lived for a decade, it means female buttock, but here it meant something quite different (you know what I mean!) Pin drop silence greeted my remark, to use that tired cliche.

Beyond vocabulary, I also felt as a new migrant that I should equip myself with the basic knowledge of this country's history. One cannot be a university academic in Australia and remain ignorant of its history, especially when I live in Canberra and have as neighbours colleagues who have had a large hand in shaping the way we see Australia: Ken Inglis, Bill Gammage, Hank Nelson, John Molony, Ian Hancock, Barry Smith. But it is more than the desire simply to be 'one of the boys,' 'to be in the know.' When new migrants enter a country, they enter not only its physical space but also its history with all the obligations and responsibilities they entail; to be effective and responsible citizens, they need to understand the inextinguishable link between the country's past and its present.

So I had to bone up on Australian history and folklore: Gallipoli, Eureka Stockade, Ned Kelly, the Anzac Tradition, the debate about Terra Nullius, the Great Dismissal, the Bodyline Series and Bradman's Invincibles, about Phar Lap, Mabo, Bob Santamaria and Archbishop Daniel Mannix, Dame Edna Everidge, Simpson and his Donkey, Kokoda Trail, Patrick White, Gough Whitlam, 'Pig Iron' Bob, 'The Australian Legend,' 'The Rush That Never Ended.' I now know the names of most Australian prime ministers in roughly chronological order. I am passionate about cricket. My summer begins the moment the first ball is bowled in a cricket test match, and ends when the cricket season is over (and when the agapanthus die out). And I read Australian literature and follow Australian politics as a hobby. Gaps remain, of course. There is much catching up to do. I wish, as I write this, that I—and the Indo-Fijian community generally—had made half as much effort to understand the culture, language, traditions, the inner world of the Fijian people, among whom we have lived for well over a century, but about whom we know so little. Sadly, the ignorance is mutual.

The curiosity and the thirst for new knowledge I have about this country, its past and its present, its vast parched landscape, is not matched, with few exceptions, by my colleagues and friends in Australia about *me* and *my* background, my history and heritage, the cultural baggage I bring to this country. I have sought to educate myself about the Judeo-Christian tradition, about the meaning and significance of Lent and Resurrection and the Last Judgement, for instance, or about the Sale of Indulgences, the Reformation, about Yahweh and the *Torah*. And I know a few Christmas Carols too ('*On the twelfth day of Christmas...*'). But my Australian friends, perhaps understandably, have no idea about my religious and cultural heritage, about the *Ramayana* and the *Bhagvad Gita*, about the festivals we celebrate: *Diwali* and *Holi* and *Ram Naumi*, about our ritual observances to mark life's journey or mourn its passing. It is not that they are incurious: they simply don't know. My inner world remains a mystery to them. I regret very much not being able to share my cultural life more fully, more meaningfully, with people whose friendship I genuinely value.

The process of understanding is a one-way street, I often feel. Perhaps they have no incentive to know about me; it is I who have the greater need to know. I am the one who is the outsider here, not them. Perhaps things will change when—it is no longer a question of if—multiculturalism takes deeper roots, when the public face of Australia truly shows its diverse character, when more of us become more visible in the public arena rather than remain as cartoon characters propped up for public display on suitably ceremonial occasions. The contrast with the United Kingdom is huge in this respect. There, as I discovered in my two extended trips there in recent years, multiculturalism is a publicly accepted and proudly proclaimed fact, in popular culture, in the universities, in the media. Multiculturalism is just starting its journey here. In Australia, in my experience, the primary line of demarcation is gender, not cultural identity. When we advertise positions, we are asked to make special effort to alert women candidates to potential employment opportunities. Universities require adherence to the principle of gender balance on committees. Few colleagues ask: why are there so few Pacific and Asian academics in my Research School of Pacific and Asian Studies? Many would remark on the gender imbalance in it. But I digress.

English is my language of work, but it is inadequate in expressing my inner feelings, in capturing the intricate texture of social relationships which are an integral part of my community. There are simply no English words for certain kinds of relationships and the cultural assumptions and understandings which go with them. The English word 'Uncle' denotes a particular relationship which most native speakers would understand. When finer distinctions are required, the words maternal and paternal are added. But it is still inadequate for me. We have different words for different kinds of uncles. A father's younger brother is *Kaka*.[20] His elder brother is *Dada*. Mother's brother is *Mama*. Father's sister's husband is *Phuffa*. They are all uncles in English usage. But in Hindi, each has its own place, its own distinctive set of obligations. We can joke with *Kaka*, be playful with him, but our relationship with *Dada* is more formal and distant. A *Dada* can be relied upon to talk sense to one's father, with some authority and effect; a *Kaka*, knowing his proper place in the order of things, cannot, at least not normally. Brother-in-law in English is pretty generic, but not in Hindi. Sister's husband is *Jeeja* or *Bahnoi*, but wife's brother is *Sala*. We have a joking relationship with the latter—he is fair game—but not with the former. Your sister's welfare is always paramount in your mind. A troubled relationship with *Jeeja* could have terrible consequences for her. Older brother's wife is *Bhabhi*, and younger brother's spouse *Chotki*. *Bhabhi* is treated with a mixture of respect and affection, more like a mother. With *Chotki* we have an avoidance relationship, and keep all conversation to the bare minimum. We don't call *Bhabhi* and *Chotki* by their names. Ever.[21] And it would be unthinkable for them to call you by your name either. We relate to each other not as individuals, but as social actors with culturally prescribed roles.

Some of the cultural protocols and restrictions governing family relationships have inevitably broken down in Australia, and even in urban Fiji, succumbing to forces of modernity and the culturally corrosive effects of accelerated mobility. You have no choice but to speak to *Chotki* if she is the one who picks up the phone. But my younger sisters-in-law still do not address me by my name, not because this is something I myself prefer. On the contrary. I am still addressed respectfully as *Bhaiya,* as cultural protocol, or memory of cultural protocol, demands. And I take care not to be a part of loose talk in their presence. All the children invariably call me *Dada*. It would be unthinkable for them to call me by my name. It is the same with my children when addressing their uncles and aunties. Even Indo-Fijian community elders and my friends would be called uncles and aunties though this convention or practice would not apply, on the whole, to my Australian friends. So, in denoting the complex maze of domestic relationships we have, I find English inadequate.

English has made greater inroads and makes more sense in other day-to-day activities though. When shopping for groceries, I often use English names. Watermelon, for example, not *Tarbuj,* Bananas, not *Kela,* Rice, not *Chawal,* Onion, not *Piyaz,* Potatoes, not *Aloo*. But some vegetables I can only properly identify with the names I used as a child: I always use *Dhania*, not Coriander, *Haldi*, not Turmeric, *Karela*, not Bitter Gourd, *Kaddu*, not Pumpkin, *Dhall*, not Lentils . I wish I knew why some names have remained and others have gone from memory.

I was once a fairly fluent reader and speaker in Hindi, although now the more difficult sanskritised variety is becoming harder to understand. It takes longer to read the script and decipher its meaning. Listening to the news, on SBS Hindi radio for instance, I get the meaning but miss the nuances; painfully, the gap increases with each passing year. My Hindi, now more stilted than ever, is restricted to the occasional conversation with people from South Asian background, from India, Pakistan and even Bangladesh. There is an expectation on the part of many South Asians that I would—should—know Hindi because I look Indian and have a very North Indian name.

It is not an unreasonable assumption. And I use it, as best I can, to establish rapport with them, to acknowledge our common ancestral and cultural heritage, to establish a point of contact, to define our difference from mainstream Anglo-Australia. I cannot deny the enjoyment this gives me. Many weekend taxi drivers in Canberra are Pakistani university students keen to bolster their meagre incomes. When I travel with them, they—or I—would ask the obligatory question: Where you from? The taxi drivers would reply in English. *Achha,* okay, or *Theek hai*, that's fine, I am likely to say. If there is chemistry (about cricket, for example) we will continue in English-interspersed Hindustani. When words fail, or are unable to carry a conversation forward, we revert to English, but the connection has been made. That is the important point; that is what matters.

Hindi comes in handy in my private cultural life. The music that fills my house, to the bemused tolerance of my children—Dad is playing *his* music again!—is Hindustani or, more appropriately, Urdu: *ghazals*, romantic songs, by Mehndi Hassan, Jagjit Singh, Pankaj Udhas, Talat Aziz, Ghulam Ali, and sweet-syrupy songs from Hindi films of yesteryears by Talat Mehmood, Mohammed Rafi, Lata Mangeshkar and Mukesh. This is the music that arouses the deepest emotion in me, takes me to another world, can reduce me to tears. An even faltering knowledge of the language, often with the assistance of a bi-lingual dictionary, enriches my appreciation of the words in the songs.

It is the same with movies, though the language of the screen, designed to reach the masses and denuded of flowery literary allusions, is much more accessible. Most Hindi videos these days are dubbed in English to reach the non-Hindi speaking world (especially the Middle East and Southeast Asia) or young children of the diaspora who have no Hindi, but the pleasure is not the same as listening to and understanding the dialogue in the original language. Hindi enables me to enter a wider culture and connects me to people and places that would otherwise remain inaccessible. In that sense it is like English, minus the fluency.

I am glad I still retain some small knowledge of the language. But things of the heart, which give me meaning and deep pleasure, enrich my life, I cannot share with most of my Australian friends. The gulf is too wide; we are too different. Nor, to be fair, can I, try as I might, understand or truly enjoy the deepest aspects of their cultural and aesthetic life. I was on a remote pre-historic farm, beyond the reach of radio, when the Beatles were taking on the world! And the sporting heroes of Australia, with whom they grew up, are unknown to me.

In everyday life, though, I do not use formal Hindi at all. To do so would be considered silly and pretentious. At home with my wife, and sometimes with my children, I speak Fiji-Hindi. It is my natural language. There are no standard conventions which I have to follow. Its loose grammatical structure enables me to improvise, to incorporate into the vocabulary English words of ordinary usage. That freedom is exhilarating. I use Fiji-Hindi when talking to other Indo-Fijians, not necessarily to converse at length in it, but to establish a point of recognition. The nature and depth of the conversation would depend on the closeness I have with the speaker. With most Indo-Fijian men, I would have no hesitation using Fiji-Hindi. I would be more reserved with Indo-Fijian women though, so as not to give any signal or hint of intimacy. Indian cultural protocol even today demands a degree of distance between men and women who are not close friends or family: hugging, giving someone a peck on the cheek and other western forms of showing affection are out of bounds and considered improper. English would for me be the most comfortable medium of communication with them, neutral. It is the same with my wife when talking to Indo-Fijian men. With children of friends and family, I normally speak in English, conscious that they might not— and many don't—have Hindi or Fiji-Hindi.

The Fiji-Hindi I speak now is not the one I spoke as a child. Then, it had few foreign words. But now, my Fiji-Hindi is increasingly filled with English words and phrases. I suspect it is the same in many urban parts of Fiji too. *Drinks aur Dinner hai*: it is a drinks and dinner party. *Kafi late hoi gaye hai*: it is getting quite late. *Lunch kar liha*: have you had lunch. *Kutch trouble nahi*: no trouble. *Bada bad hoi gaye*, does not look good, *Us ke support karo*, support him, *Report likho*, write a report, *Walk pe chale ga,* will you join me for a walk, *Telephone maro*, ring. My Fiji-Hindi would sound strange, unfamiliar, to people of my father's generation back in rural Fiji. My children's precariously limited, English-accented Fiji-Hindi would be incomprehensible to them, just as their language, full of rustic references and vanished metaphors and words would appear vaguely strange to us.

There is some sadness in this perhaps inevitable change. It is the price we pay for 'progress,' I suppose, for living away from our place of birth. Fiji-Hindi was the language of my childhood. It was the only language of communication between me and my parents, both of whom were unlettered and are now dead. It was the language through which I saw the world once, through which I learned about our past and ourselves, told stories and shared experiences. That Indo-Fijian world, and my mother tongue, will go with me.

Fiji-Hindi is my mother tongue, not my children's, who have grown up in Australia. They have some faltering familiarity with it, but that will go with time.

It is the same with other children—or young adults—of their age. There will be little opportunity or incentive for them to continue with the language. Fiji is their parents' country, they say, not theirs. For most of them, English will effectively become the only language they have. Some Indo-Fijian families in Australia and elsewhere, traumatised by the coups and the ravages of ethnic politics, have actively sought to erase their memories of Fiji and things Fijian, even Indo-Fijian. The rejection of Fiji-Hindi is a part of that process of denying the past. Others have sought actively to embrace aspects of Indian subcontinental culture. Their children learn Hindi or Urdu in community-sponsored language classes. They attend temples and mosques to learn the basics of their faith and celebrate all the most important festivals of the Hindu or Muslim calender. Classical dance and music classes flourish in many Indo-Fijian communities in Australia.

Hindi or Urdu, I suspect, rather than Fiji-Hindi, will be the second language of choice for the new generation. Born or brought up in Australia, they will have their own contradictions and confusions to deal with. Their problems and preoccupations will be different from mine. I admire the way they are adapting to their new homeland in ways that I know I could not, did not have the skills to. Confident and resourceful and inventive, they are completely at home in cross-cultural situations. The cultural gulf between their world and that of their Australian friends in music, film and general aspects of popular culture will never be as great as it is for me and people of my generation. My fears and phobias, my confused and confusing cultural inheritance, won't be theirs. Mercifully, their destinies won't be hobbled by mine.

# Fourteen

## Primary Texts

'Mr Joe builds a house.' That is the first sentence from the *Caribbean Readers Introductory Book One*. It is also the first text in English that I ever read or, rather, recited in chorus in grade one at age seven in Tabia Sanatan Dharam Primary School. Mr Joe, a black farmer in neat white shirt and long pants and a light hat, had gathered on his farm an unforgettable array of characters: Miss Tibs the Cat, Mr Dan the Dog, Mr Grumps the Goat, Master Willy the Pig, Mrs Cuddy the Cow, Miss Peg the Donkey, Mother Hen and Percy the chick. Fun-loving and loveable, they colluded and connived and spoke a language we all knew well. Mr Grumps, big-horned, was averse to work: 'What! Me! Work! No.' From a farming background ourselves, where house and farm work were a dreaded part of our daily routine, we understood him perfectly well. Master Willy, with a perpetually puzzled look, endeared himself to everyone by finding Mr Joe's lost shoes. Ms Tibs, sniffy, did not like Master Willy. 'No, he must go. We do not like him,' she tells her friends haughtily. Mr Joe intervenes. 'Let him stay here now and work.' 'Work?' Master Willy, expecting to have a good time, expresses surprise. 'Oh!' And so things rolled along on Mr Joe's Caribbean farm. We, of course, had no idea what or where the Caribbean was, but that did not matter. First experiences often etch indelible imprints on our memories, and Mr Joe's family has remained with me, like yesterday's warmly-remembered songs.

In the years after, we left our Caribbean friends behind and switched to the Oxford *English Readers for Africa* and the University of London series, *Reading for Meaning*. There we met John and Jane at a big railway station in London. John is leaving for a school in Oxford and Jane wants to cry but she cannot cry in a railway station 'in front of all the people'. That seemed strange to me, not to cry when something sad happened, such as farewelling your own brother. I learnt about the English stiff upper lip much later. We also met our African friends Luka and Rota, about our age, neat in their crisp new clothes, having a fun-filled holiday near Lake Victoria somewhere in Africa, learning to row, sail and fish. They loved travelling, they said, 'because we see so many new things

How we envied them. We never went anywhere because we couldn't afford to. Besides, there was nowhere exciting to go anyway. We dreaded school holidays because they meant hard field work, planting paddy or hoeing cane, often on our own farm, but sometimes as hired hands on our neighbours.' Holidays cut us off completely from the world. We could not talk about the wonderful new world we were exploring, a world of words and books and pictures beyond even the imagined horizon of our parents. But it was still magical to think about the happy and carefree life of Luka and Rota and John and Jane, and to hope that someday we could be like them, too. That thought, the remote possibility of one day leaving the deadening routine of village life for something more interesting in some place far away, alleviated our anxieties.

We learnt about the history and geography of strange places: Oxford, Bournemouth, Yorkshire, Southampton, Dundee, Constantinople and Cairo, the Great Arctic Waste, the Lake of Galilee (a 'sheet of water shaped like a harp'). What was a harp? We had no idea. And Italy, where the 'march of the seasons is a constant pageantry of beauty and colour.' Pageantry of colour: that confounded us. The only colours we knew in our tropical world were brown (earth) and green (grass) and blue (sea). Reference to life during an English winter left us completely bewildered, as did the piece on the power of Babylon under the great Nebuchadnezzar, the son of Nabopolassar, and Herodotus' stories about the 'enormous extent of the royal city and the massiveness of its walls,' its remaining bits and pieces 'eloquent of its magnificence.' Big words sent us scurrying to the school's single well-thumbed dictionary. We learnt the names of strange trees: oak, aspen, poplar, pear, sycamore, willow, fir, beech, when the only ones we knew were coconut, mango and tamarind. Flowers: daffodils, crocuses and tulips, when all we had around us was hibiscus, frangipani and marigold. We learnt about various forms of landscape: Lakeland, savanna, steppe, desert and delta; about monsoon rains on the Tsana Plateau (wherever that was); about historical figures and events; Napoleon Bonaparte, the 'emperor of the French who was a strange man', but who was also 'one of the cleverest soldiers the world has seen'; Isaac Newton, who was 'often so deep in his thoughts that he would forget to eat his own dinner unless reminded to do so;' Oliver Goldsmith, 'the writer of delightful essays and stories,' about the *Armada:* ' Night sank upon the dusky beach, and on the purple sea/ Such night in England ne'er had been, nor e'er again shall be;' about the East India Company, which built 'goodly ships of such burthen as never were formerly used in merchandise. In later years, we read about the origins of writing ('Writing is a kind of drawing, for each letter is made up of straight lines or curves just as a picture is drawn by putting straight and curved lines in different positions;') about the importance of farming (reinforced by a piece of Chinese wisdom: 'The happiness of a nation is like a tree. Farming is its root, manufacture and commerce are its branches and leaves. If the root is harmed, the branches break off, the leaves fall and the tree dies.') As children of farmers, we found these words reassuring. Some things, though, escaped us, such as the advice on 'How to Repair China': 'Put the white of an egg (after slightly beating it) on the edges of the broken pieces of china, using a fine paintbrush. Immediately dust one edge of the china with the powered lime, and put the two broken pieces together instantly.' We had no idea what china was. Nor, I suspect, did our teachers. But that somehow did not really matter. It was the pleasure of encountering the exotic that engaged us.

Then there were enchanting stories which taught us to be self-reliant, cautious, wary of strangers bearing gifts, to have your wits about you. Stories such as 'The Monkey and the Shark'. This was my favourite; it was everyone's favourite. The monkey and the shark were good friends. One day, the shark tells his friend that his family wants to meet him. The monkey, flattered, jumps on to the shark's back as he swims out to sea. Far away from land, the shark tells the monkey the real purpose of the invitation. 'I did not explain why I wanted you to come with me,' he says slyly. 'I did not ask you to come with me because I want you to see our home. I asked because our king is ill and the doctor says he will only get better if he eats the heart of a monkey. So I am taking you to him.' The monkey, his eyes bulging with fear, remained cool. He tells the shark that he had left his heart in the tree. 'You see, we monkeys are not like other animals. We don't always carry our hearts with us. I left mine up in the tree. It isn't here, but if you take me back, I will get it.' The shark, trusting, turns back. Once safely up in the tree, the monkey says he is not coming down, he won't be fooled again. 'Do you think I am like the washerman's donkey?' 'The washerman's donkey?' the shark asks. 'I have never heard about her.' Monkey: 'What do you mean?' 'Please tell me about her.' 'I'll explain,' says the monkey. And so we move to the next story, and the next about 'Kintu and his Cow', 'The Hare and the Tortoise', 'The Blind Men and the Elephant.' Well-written, amply illustrated stories with a strong moral underpinning.

Our parents, themselves illiterate, asked us to read the stories to them as we sat cross-legged around the dim light of the kerosene lamp in our crowded, dung-plastered thatched hut after dinner: the radio had not yet arrived, television came decades later. We, in turn, listened to stories our *girmitiya* grandparents had told our parents, stories from the *Panchatantra* and *Baitaal Pachisi* about ghosts and goblins and frightening goings-on in the underworld, which terrified us in the unlit stillness of the night.

My favourite were the exchanges between Emperor Akbar and his quick-witted prime minister Birbal. There was no question that Birbal could not answer, no embarrassing situation from which he could not extricate himself. One star-lit night, Akbar and Birbal were sitting on the lawn outside the palace. Looking up at the sky, Akbar thought of a question which he thought Birbal would never be able to answer. 'Birbal, tell me how many stars are there in the sky?' the Emperor asked. 'Huzur [Your Majesty]', replied Birbal, 'I will answer that question if you can tell me how much water there is in the ocean.' Akbar knew at once what a foolish question he had asked. Once Akbar thought of a prank to embarrass Birbal. The two were eating dates and throwing the seeds under their chairs. When Birbal left the room momentarily, Akbar pushed his heap of seeds under Birbal's chair. When Birbal returned, Akbar said loudly, 'Birbal, I did not know you were so greedy, eating so many dates.' Birbal noticed the large heap of seeds under his chair, but nothing under Akbar's. He immediately knew Akbar's trick. Unflustered, Birbal replied, 'Huzur, I admit I am greedy. But I ate only the fruit and threw the seeds away. You have eaten the fruit as well as the seeds.' As usual, Birbal had the last laugh.

Stories such as these kept us engrossed, connected us to the world beyond the village, beyond the immediate, unremarkable experience of our daily life. The characters were unique in their own way; they sometimes had strange names (such as Sokoloko Bengosay!), and spoke a language we were just the beginning to learn. But, for all the difference of time and place and history and culture, they were accessible. We understood their predicaments; they were universal.

There was the story about some children from a poor home somewhere in Africa pleading with the headmaster to admit them to his school. 'Please, sir,' the children say, 'we have come from a village very far away. We have often heard about your school. We have no school in our village. So we have never been to school before. We have never read any books. We have never written with pens. We have never even written on slates. We have not learned any English yet. Please, sir, we have never learned any lessons before, but we do want to learn now. We want to come to your school. We have washed our clothes very carefully. We have just bathed in the river. We have made our bodies nice and clean.'

We probably used different words, but the spirit of supplication was instantly recognizable. For us, growing .up in post-war Fiji, education was not necessarily a birthright, but an act of goodwill, a gift from a neighbour or a kind-hearted relative: books had to be purchased, school fees paid, school uniform sewn, and cash was always in short supply. What was given could also be taken away. That fear haunted us. We were taught to be grateful for the small mercies that came our way. Picking up crumbs from the table was no shame for children from poor homes. One step at a time: that was the motto of my generation. Our primary school was started by our parents to give us the education they themselves had missed. We were taught in Hindi and English. English took over in time, but Hindi remained one of the subjects we studied, alongside arithmetic and general knowledge. The English texts alerted us to the magical lives of children in other parts of the world, the Hindi texts enriched our understanding of our own culture. These texts, used in primary schools in the post-war years, were written by Pandit Ami Chandra, an India-born educationalist who had migrated to Fiji. His short books, pothis, as they were called, did for Hindi what the Caribbean and Oxford readers did for English. We were introduced to the alphabets, to picture stories and poems and then to complex subjects:

Each *pothi* began with a Hindu prayer, which we recited every morning before classes began, palms joined, heads bowed, eyes closed: *Dono kar jod nava kar sheesh, Vinay hum karte hain Jagdish, Dijiye hum ko vidyadaan, Karen jisse hum sab ka kalyan.* 'Our palms joined in prayer, we beg, 0 Lord, for Your blessing so that we can work for the betterment of humanity.' Muslim students prayed at the mosque across the road. In the Hindi books, we also learned about flowers, plants, fruits and animals (but those which were familiar to us), about the importance of being honest, respectful of parents and teachers and village elders, the value of good hygiene and sports and good husbandry. Here, too, we encountered Columbus, Magellan, Captain Cook, and great historical events such as the rounding of the Cape of Good Hope, the coronation of Queen Elizabeth and the arrival of Charles Kingsford Smith and the Southern Cross in Suva (which terrified Fijians, who scattered hurriedly shouting *'Sobo, Sobo,'* Oh God, Oh God).

These books, too, had their morality tales. Such as the story about the goat and the fox. Once, a fox fell into a well. A goat walked up to the well and asked what the fox was doing inside. 'Sister,' the fox replied, 'I am having a cool, fresh drink.' 'I'm thirsty, too,' the goat said. 'Join me,' the fox replied. After a while, the fox told the goat that she wanted to get out. Could she stand on the goat's shoulder to get out of the well? 'Yes, sister,' said the goat. When the fox was safely outside, the goat asked her to help her get out, too. 'You should have thought about that before you jumped in. Goodbye.' The lesson: look before you leap.

The *pothis* had bits and *pieces* about Fiji. We came across Tailevu and the Yasawas, the wreck of the *Syria* in 1884, the arrival of Indian indentured labourers. But that was about it. The Fiji stories bored us, they lacked romance and adventure. The stories that did catch our imagination were from Indian history: Mogul emperors (Jahangir and Akbar and Aurangzeb), the Taj Mahal and Ganga, the Nobel Laureate, Rabindranath Tagore, with his brooding eyes and white flowing beard, the fiercely anti-British Queen of Jhansi resplendent in white sari, riding a white horse and carrying a sword in her right hand, and Mahatma Gandhi, the slight, sparsely clad, toothless 'Uncrowned King of India.'

## INTERSECTIONS

We read stories from the *Mahabharata* about the epic battle between the Kauravs and the Pandavas, and we recited them to our parents. We felt proud of our cultural heritage, proud to proclaim our cultural identity untainted by other, lesser influences. We were 'true' Indians, we liked to think, unlike those in the towns who had drifted away from their roots. Our main cultural reference point was India. We celebrated festivals and performed ritual and ceremonies that our grandparents had brought from India. The stories, which we shared with our parents and others in the evenings, kept the memories of the ancestral land alive. We didn't know it then, but we children preserved a vital link between our past and our present.

Knowledge of Hindi enabled us to read aloud to our parents and other villagers weeklies such as *Jagriti* (The New Age), *Fiji Samachar* (The News of Fiji) and *Shanti Dut* (The Messenger of Peace). Radio was slowly making inroads into the more well-to-do households, but the newspapers were the real window on the convulsing outside world. We heard vague talk about our becoming independent from Great Britain someday, and news reports about a new party being formed to protect 'our' interests and our moral duty to support it. Still, for all the commotion, national politics were for most of us a distant, abstract proposition. The future of the sugar industry, caught in a devastating strike in 1960, was different. It was our lifeline. We had no sugar left at home; the crop was flowering in the fields, the cane-cutters were idle, and cash was in short supply. Everyone was trying to influence us one way or the other. We were told not to trust the radio news. We didn't. We relied on the Hindi newspapers, especially *Jagriti*. Father listened intently to every word. For him, sugar cane was his lifeblood.

We could read the *Ramayana*, the basic text for us orthodox (*Sanatani*) Hindus. Written in accessible language, it told the story of a virtuous prince, Rama, forced into exile for 14 years for no fault of his own. Wandering the forests, he encountered personal tragedies (his chaste wife Sita was abducted by the evil king, Ravana), conquered evil and eventually returned triumphant to his kingdom of Ayodhya. Good had conquered evil. In that story, our parents saw a rendition of their own predicament. They, too, had suffered much through no fault of their own. They, too, hoped that one day their poverty and petty humiliations in life would end. Reading the *Ramayana* to the accompaniment of *dholak, dandtaal, majira* and harmonium lightened our otherwise dreary evenings and bonded the scattered and fractured community and nourished its collective soul. In some way, the story also soothed the pain of poverty. It is easy enough now to criticize our people for shoring up fragments of their ancestral culture, but that was all they had. Without it, they would have been nothing, allowed to become nothing. The Hindi films, the Hindi music, the religious texts, the ceremonies and the rituals we performed with mundane regularity kept us intact as a community.

Hindi has remained with me all these years. Some of the fluency has gone with the passage of time and long stretches spent away from home, but I am grateful for what remains, especially when I think of the sadness that the absence of the language has caused our Indo-Caribbean cousins. Their sense of loss, of creolization and alienation, is deep and painful. Hindi is the language of my emotion and prayer. I use it to connect with my past and my people, my cultural roots, my inner self. English is the language of my work. Acquiring it has not been easy, and many gaps remain. I am completely ignorant of its complex history and only passingly familiar with its deeper signs, metaphors and allusions. It took a long time to understand what 'Crossing the Rubicon' meant, or 'Opening the Pandora's Box' or 'Achilles' Heel.'

The metaphors of our own culture and allusions to our past had no place in this new learning. I regret that now, but it did not seem to matter then. We were taught to learn, not question, the values of colonial education. Still, for all their cultural biases, the books opened new imaginative horizons for us, leveled hierarchy based on economic wealth and social status, connected us to other worlds and pasts, awakened our imagination, emphasized our common humanity across boundaries of culture and race, and sowed the seeds of future possibilities.

Word, the power of the written word, word as the carrier of information and the vehicle of knowledge, word as the tool of thought and creativity: those, for me, are the enduring legacies of the texts. For me still, knowledge comes from reading. Words I read in primary school about the importance of books have remained with me. Books were a 'very wonderful thing. Some kinds of books were worth more than gold and silver because they brought to us knowledge which was gained by clever men who died long ago.' 'A person who owns some good books can see more and travel farther than the richest man in the world, for the rich man who just travels about may forget much that he sees, but the person who has the books need never forget. His books will be with him all his life.' We were told to treat books with respect. 'When we have read a book, we should keep it carefully, for our memory of what is in it may fail, and then we may want to read it again. Books are the storehouses of all the knowledge in the world.' These words lodged deep in my consciousness. The printed word still retains its magic. A well-crafted sentence or paragraph, unexpected imagery or vivid metaphor, cause admiration and pleasure. The unique smell of a new book, its crisp, untouched pages promising adventure and discovery of unknown, unexplored worlds, still captivates me. Reading for me is synonymous with living. Come to think of it, it is life itself.

# Fifteen

## Blurred Lines

Reshmi, my cousin, was always the feisty one in the family. A 'tomboy,' she was rebellious and a risk-taker. Uncle and auntie worried about her. 'Why can't you be more like Geeta,' they would say, much to my embarrassment. Truth is, I wanted to be a free spirit like Reshmi. *Arre pyari laadli beti*, Reshmi would reproach me playfully, the dearly loved one, 'why don't we switch sides. Then you can be their *Sati Savitri*, the irreproachable one, and I will be left alone.' But nothing came, or could come, between us. Reshmi has remained my best friend.

After Vatuwaqa High, Reshmi went to the local university but didn't finish her undergraduate course. No surprises there. Life outside was far too interesting to restrain her various enthusiasms, which included movies and the night club scene. She was also a great one for causes, from the rights of the squatters and market vendors and beggars to more toilets in public places. Civic pride was big with her. 'A city's hospitality is measured by the number of public toilets it has,' she once said to me rather mystifyingly. I thought it was theatres and restaurants. We lost touch for a while when I left for Australia in 1995. My parents had arranged my marriage to a distantly related divorcee accountant in Sydney. As the eldest one in the family, I was to be their passport, their 'exit strategy.' It is a common enough practice among our people desperate to get out through any means and at any cost. There is no shame in sham marriages. 'Don't do this *yaar*,' Reshmi pleaded with me. 'Sacrificial bloody lamb we should not be. This is the 21st century, man,' she said. 'They can't buy and sell us like cheap meat.'

'You can afford the luxury, *bahini*' I replied. 'Bright and beautiful and all. Being the only child does not hurt either. *Eklauti beti*. And boys will give their left arm to get you,' I said. 'What? Not the left ball, you mean?' Reshmi responded with a wicked laugh, putting her arm around my shoulder. I was serious. 'Me? Who is going to come for me?' 'There is nothing wrong with you Geeta. If I were a boy, you know.' '*Bas, yaar*.' Enough. We both knew there was no point arguing. The decision was made, and that was that.

Reshmi was protective of me, and promised to keep in touch. 'If he ever lifts his finger at you, tell him that I will bust his balls. I may be small, but I am not weak.' She meant it too. We kept in touch through emails and regular phone calls exchanging gossip and news about family matters. As I had expected, Reshmi got involved in community activism, talking to women's groups about their rights, stressing the importance of educating girls, organising neighbourhood watch schemes, facilitating parent-teacher meetings. Then in 2004, she stood for the Samabula Ward for the Suva City Council as an independent, and won. 'This is a man's world, baby,' she had written to me, 'and I am gonna make sure I have some fun with the boys.' Typical Reshmi.

Around the same time, Reshmi also began taking evening classes at the local university, taking one unit at a time. With good luck, she would complete her undergraduate degree in about five years. Her ultimate goal was to do law. That would be her route to both personal as well as economic independence. 'I will get there, Geet,' she said to me. 'Then I will show them. Bloody lawyers, they are better at getting you into trouble than getting you out of them.'

For all her activism and public service and education, though, Reshmi was also a dutiful wife. Her husband, Jason Kumar, as sober and reserved as Reshmi was instinctive and exuberant, was a high school teacher and quietly active in the Nasinu branch of the Fiji Teachers Union. As Indian husbands go, he was unconventional. He made breakfast in the morning, did household chores, did the groceries, helped raise their two children. But there were unwritten rules which could not be breached even in this household. Reshmi could be a community activist, but she had to ensure that the evening meal was cooked. 'Saint outside, servant at home,' Reshmi said. 'You know the routine.' *Ghar grahasthi*, domestic responsibilities, always came first

In private, Reshmi's bitterness about Indian male attitudes showed. 'These fellows talk about democracy and gender equality,' she said to me once, 'but they don't practice the damn thing themselves. Hypocrites they are all.' She felt constrained, hemmed-in. In meetings, Reshmi said, they paid no attention to what she said. 'Yes, yes, and they move on. It is as if you don't exist or your views don't matter. It is so humiliating. Then why the bloody charade?' Reshmi asked. Why indeed! All the meetings were scheduled after work, around dinner time. It was a convenient time for the men folk, but not for a mother with a family to feed. 'It is an uphill battle all the way, sis,' she had written to me.

During the 2000 crisis, Reshmi had flown to Sydney to organise and participate in rallies for the incarcerated members of the Coalition government. She had developed into a punchy speaker, mixing her English speeches with Fiji-Hindi and, occasionally, Fijian, full of passion about truth and justice and fair play. And winning hearts and minds wherever she went and whoever she spoke with. At one rally, some speakers said that Fiji should not be allowed to participate in the Sydney Olympics games. Reshmi disagreed. 'We should let Mr Speight in,' she said to bemused silence in the crowd. 'Then we can put the Olympic torch up you-know-his-what!' 'His *chuttar*,' arse, someone had shouted from the crowd, to spontaneous mirthful applause.

At a rally at Martin Place, we heard stories which both of us found amusing and perplexing. One group of men held a large banner with the words '*Speight Ke Maaro Goli*,' to hell with Speight, but the literal translation would be 'Shoot Speight.' What was more intriguing was the demand by the group to take the banner to Canberra, to the parliament house in fact. Why, we wondered. 'These fellows would then get themselves photographed by all the major newspapers and use the 'evidence' to claim asylum in Australia,' a man told us. 'They wouldn't be safe in Fiji!'

There was another story from Melbourne. A soccer match was in progress between two Fiji sides. One side had many illegal overstayers, and was winning. At half time, a rumour spread that the immigration police was about to arrive. The overstayers ran for cover in every which direction, and the opposing team won the game! 'So bloody typical of our people,' Reshmi said, referring to their inventiveness in adversity. 'Well, cutting corners, seeking advantage for yourself at every opportunity, fleecing your own kind, is in our genetic makeup, sis,' I replied.

'There our leaders are about to be killed, and here these fellows think how best to advance their own personal interest. '*Kabhi nahin sudhare ga hum log*,' she said despairingly. We will never learn. 'What about principles, Geet, principles for once,' Reshmi continued, 'something more than mere bloody *pet puja*,' preoccupation with getting ahead. I detected a note of contempt in her voice. 'Get real, sis,' I said, 'welcome to the real world.' And when I told her about how some community leaders had raised funds for Fiji and then pocketed most of the money themselves, Reshmi nearly choked on the piece of blueberry muffin she was eating.

'I am better off there, Geeta,' she said, meaning Fiji. 'I am happier there. I may not have fancy cars and a big house and all like people here, but at least I will have my peace of mind and my self-respect intact. And the people are more genuine' Looking into the distance over a steaming cup of coffee, she said, 'If I can make a small difference to someone's life, I will be glad.' That was pure Reshmi: service above self. After about three weeks in Sydney, she returned to Fiji.

At the 2006 general elections, Reshmi was asked by her party to stand. Her preference was for the Samabula North Open Seat, roughly the area she represented in the Suva City Council. But the party bosses decided against it. The chances of winning it were good, and they wanted one of the senior party functionaries to contest it. Reshmi pleaded: 'I have done a lot of work there as member of the City Council; I am known, I have the networks, they are my people.' But to no avail.

Reshmi asked Jason to intervene. 'I can't, Resh,' Jason replied. 'Why not?' 'Because it would be wrong. We desperately need to win the seat, and the bloke they have chosen is good. With him, the seat is winnable.' 'And with me? Am I here to make tea for you all, cook and clean up? A doormat?' 'It's not like that, and you know it,' Jason replied meekly. 'Yes, I know,' Reshmi responded bitterly. 'You men really piss me off.' Reshmi's straight talk was her great asset, but people also feared her sharp tongue and withering humour. *Muh chutti*, people said, sniggering behind her back, loose-lipped. 'You are not keeping your kitchen in control,' someone had said to Jason. 'I wonder who wears the pants in that house,' someone else had remarked.

In the end, Reshmi accepted a seat in Koronivia. She knew it was unwinnable. The numbers were stacked against her. Campaigning so far away from home, at odd hours, in unknown territory, among people she had never met before, was arduous. And rural people were wary of city-slickers descending on them at election time only to disappear until the next election. 'Who are you to come here just before the election and ask for our vote?' hostile people asked in pocket meetings. 'Like dew, here now, gone in the morning,' an old man had said. 'What have you done for us that we should trust you?' It was a fair question, and Reshmi knew it. But she was a party faithful. A candidate had to be found for the constituency, however unwinnable, and Reshmi volunteered.

I often accompanied Reshmi on her door-to-door campaigns on dusty roads in stifling heat and drenching humidity. It was the same story everywhere: what the candidate could do for the voters. Requests for money for school fee, help with bus fares and food, contribution to the local temple, cash for a community celebration. 'These people sure know how to milk the cow,' Reshmi remarked sarcastically once. 'It's always what you can do for them. All the time. *Koi sharm nahin hai*,' no shame. They have no thought for the country, or for anyone else.' 'Yes, but what can you expect from these desperate people?' I replied. 'The voter owns the vote, and there is a price on everything, even your vote.' Reshmi shook her head in dismay. 'It's come to that, hasn't it? I sometimes wonder why I am busting my arse for them.' 'Because you are you,' I said, as I hugged her. Reshmi's eyes were watery from the exhaustion of the campaign.

The result was predictable. Reshmi lost badly. She knew she was gone from the start, when the first few ballot boxes were counted, but the landslide defeat still hurt, especially the deceptiveness of her own people. 'They came to my shed, drank our grog, ate our *pulau*, said 'we are all the way with you sister,' and then this? *Is se aur kitna gira insane hoy sake haye*. Is there anyone as low down as these people? But life had to go on, now a little poorer for all the money spent on the campaign. Reshmi was down, but not defeated. 'That's life,' she said, throwing her hands up in the air. I couldn't help admire her sense of balance and equanimity amidst all the chicanery of her own people.

But soon after the elections, things began to turn sour. There was squabble about participating in the multi-party government and fuss about the allocation of cabinet portfolios. 'All part of the teething problems,' Reshmi said in her emails, and we left it at that. 'This is too important an opportunity to miss, sis,' she said. The sweet irony of the result was not lost on her. It was a balanced cabinet composed of Fijians and Indo-Fijians, with a Part-European as the Leader of the Opposition. 'Isn't this what we have been waiting for all these years: Indians and Fijians in power and Europeans in Opposition?'

Jason was less sanguine. The talk around the grog bowl was that there was trouble brewing. The power-sharing arrangement in the constitution was fine on paper but unworkable in practice, his friends were saying. 'They will co-opt and then destroy us,' Jason told Reshmi. The party would lose its identity. The people who had joined the cabinet were self-seekers, and might even join the other side. There were rumours of palms being greased. 'They are not serious,' Jason said. 'Leopards don't change their spots.' 'Yes, yes, nor Zebras their stripes,' Reshmi retorted. 'But we must not let this opportunity pass, Jason. Don't these fellows see that? It may not come again.' 'Try telling that to the grog swipers,' Jason said. 'What would they know?' 'More than you and I Resh,' Jason replied. 'They have their ears and eyes close to the ground.' 'Frogs in a well, if you ask me,' Reshmi said dismissively.

After a few months of relative quiet, the military reared it head again and began to make demands on the government in words full of threat and intimidation. The war drums were beating louder and louder. Reshmi was alarmed. The price of everything was rising, and continued confrontation between the government and the military would only make matters worse. 'When elephants fight, it is the grass that gets trampled upon,' she said in an email to me. She talked about the mushrooming squatter settlements near major urban centres and the destitution and desperation that stared the poor people daily in the eye. 'Where will they go? What will happen to them,' she kept asking.

At the office, morning teatime talk turned tense as the army repeated its threats to remove the government. Reshmi's close friend, Emily Vunileba, was the first one to speak up, more in regret than in anger. 'This is not the way things were supposed to turn out,' she said to Reshmi. 'We have learned nothing.' 'Well, it looks like a fight among your own people,' Reshmi said. 'Who would have ever thought a day will come when a Fijian army would turn against a Fijian government. It was supposed to be our final back up. That's the really frightening part, Reshmi. It will be one vanua against another.'

Looking at Reshmi sitting across the coffee table, Emily said, musing to herself really, 'At last things were coming right. We had the numbers on our side and a Fijian-dominated democratically elected government, which is what our people wanted all along. Fijians on top, but through proper means. The vanua will bleed before all this ends,' Emily said sadly, quoting her local pastor. 'When Fijians get rattled, they rattle the country. There will be no peace until the spirit of the land is pacified.'

Jason had dismissed the alarmist rhetoric about death and destruction and retribution and revenge. The talk around his grog bowl was that Fijians will eventually accept whatever the army decided. 'They are a pragmatic people,' he said to Reshmi. 'They will quickly shift to wherever the power lies. That is in their nature. Fijians are much more astute than we realise. They understand political machinations far better than we do.' Warfare and shifting alliances, political cunning and conniving were an integral part of Fijian cultural heritage. '*Jis ki lathi, usi ka bhains*,' whoever wields the club wields the power.

Over the weeks and months, as the rhetoric heated up and the military began to sound more belligerent, the tension everywhere in the civil service and in schools—began to increase. Fijian and Indian teachers ate lunches separately, talking in their own languages. They walked past each in the corridor without words where warm greetings were exchanged in the past. Ashwin, their son in Form Six at Samabula High, told Reshmi one day how his Fijian friends were becoming more reserved, even resentful towards him. The laughter and the gaiety were gone. 'They don't look me in the eye any more,' he said. Many were children of Fijian politicians in the deposed government. The Indo-Fijian children remained quieter than usual. They knew that in any physical confrontation, they would come second best for sure.

As the military takeover became imminent, Reshmi and Jason began preparing for the worst. 'Ash and Asha will go to Lautoka to stay with Reshmi's mum and dad until things calmed down,' they both decided jointly. They talked to a few neighbours to form a neighbourhood watch group. This was the one lesson they had learnt after the mayhem of 2000 when Speight hooligans had terrorised the street. Stones and sticks were stored discreetly in parts of the compound to fight the attackers. Emergency food supplies were stocked. The car was tanked up with fuel. Clothes were packed in bags in case they had to leave quickly. Mobile telephone numbers were exchanged with the neighbours. No one knew how long the stalemate between the military and the government would last.

Months of mounting tension came to a head on 5 December. The commander, in battle green dress and wearing a beret, looking visibly nervous and sipping a glass of water, read out his wooden coup speech on television at six in the evening. 'We consider that Fiji has reached a crossroads and that the government and all those empowered to make decisions in our constitutional democracy are unable to make these decisions to save our people from destruction.' Then he retreated to the barracks, surrounded by his armed security guards.

Jason froze as he heard the words, for the sentiments were exactly the same as those Rabuka had expressed when he staged the first military coup in 1987. Then, he had said, Jason recalled as clearly as if the words were uttered yesterday: 'The Royal Military Forces has taken control of the Fiji Government to prevent any further disturbance and bloodshed in the country.' And he recalled how the words were repeated throughout the day amidst amber, funeral Hind music.

Reshmi looked at Jason: she too remembered the words. They embraced. 'They all say that, don't they,' she said as Bainimarama's words sunk in. 'Knights in shining armour, selfless servants of the people, risking their reputations and even their lives to save the nation.' Jason nodded in agreement. 'You just watch, this man will also cling to power with his dear life. They all do.' 'Once the troops are out of the barracks, they seldom go back,' Jason remarked. 'Just watch how quickly the bees will gather around this honey pot.' 'Or flies around you-know-what,' Reshmi said, spitting the words.

As dusk descended on an eerily quiet Suva, and the city cowered in the gathering darkness, Jason and Reshmi took a quiet ride into the city along the Queen Elizabeth Drive. This was what they had done in 1987. On the night of the 14th of May, they had written a one-page condemnation of the coup, made thousands of copies and dropped them at strategic places around the city, including the Suva bus depot. But now that youthful vigour and activism was gone, replaced by tired resignation.

'It all comes back Jase,' Reshmi remarked as they drove past the Vuya Road separating the Pacific Theological Collage and the Suva Grammar playgrounds, the site of mayhem during 2000. 'The soldiers, the armed trucks, the silence, the same fear,' Jason remarked. 'I suppose they are right,' he said as they crossed the Nasese bridge, 'the only thing we learn from history is that we don't learn from history.' Reshmi nodded. 'Yes, but there is a difference this time around, have you noticed?' Jason looked at her. 'This time, the soldiers are not wearing masks and balaclavas.' 'Yes, last time the soldiers hid their faces in shame and in fear of retribution,' Jason said. 'But now, they are proud of what they are doing.'

'What is there to be proud about, Jase?' Reshmi sighed. 'As that man, doctor something, said on television the other night, 'violence does not solve problems, it merely compounds them.' 'Yes, but tell that to someone who is convinced he is right and who has gun in his hands. Soldiers don't ask 'why' when their commander tells them to jump. They ask 'how high.' Where will all these unemployable fellows go, what will they do, without the military? They have no other home. Bainimarama is their paramount chief, and they will do as they are told.'

'We'll be alright,' Jason said to Reshmi, holding her hands. 'Ash and Asha will go to the Hamilton Polytechnic to complete their forms six and seven. We have enough saved for that. And we two will stick around. It's not garden of roses on the other side.' That he knew when he visited his relatives in Australia and New Zealand soon after the 1987 coup. Then, well-to-do people had sold their homes, given them away more like it, given up secure, well-paying jobs, and fled, only to encounter the harsh reality of starting all over again in strange places, among compete strangers and invariably at levels lower than their Fiji positions. Having left in anger and bitterness, there was no turning back for them. And they had remained embittered all these years.

'You worry too much for nothing,' one of Reshmi's cousins, Radha, a lawyer in the Director of Public Prosecutions, said to her one day while having coffee at the Dolphins Plaza. 'This is our coup.' 'Meaning?' Reshmi asked incredulously. 'Well, the army is with us this time,' Radha replied. 'It is against all those corrupt people who have been suppressing us all these years. Remember the glass ceiling in the public service, the racist affirmative action policies, the burning of temples and mosques? We have suffered long enough. It is time to show spine. It is time we stood up for our rights.'

'But a coup is a coup, Radha,' Reshmi retorted. 'You know nothing good can come out of it except more suffering.' 'No, Resh, there are good coups and there are bad coups. This is a good coup. It is about ridding the country of corruption. It is a clean-up campaign, remember.' 'You know very well there no such thing as a good coup. A coup is a rape of democracy, and do you really think there is such a thing as a good rape?' 'You take things too seriously, sis,' Radha remarked. 'Sometimes, to protect the law, we have to go outside it,' she said, quoting from a newspaper article. 'Cheer up, sis. This is not the end of the world.' 'It is the end of the world as we have known it, Radha,' Reshmi replied.

Reshmi's circle of non-Indian friends began to shrink. Jemima, one of her best friends, a cousin of a minister in the deposed government, began to distance herself, avoiding eye contact and saying the briefest of hi's when they crossed each other on Victoria Parade. One day, when Reshmi met her in the MH supermarket in Flagstaff, she asked her pointedly, 'Why are you avoiding me, Jem.' 'You know why,' she replied. 'Well I am not personally responsible for what has happened.' 'Look at your people shouting from the roof tops. Good coup. Godsend. Necessary Evil.' 'I don't support that,' Reshmi replied. 'Why hold me responsible for other people's views?' 'They are not other people. They are your people. What are you doing about it?' Jemima said icily before heading off to the car park.

'May be we are wrong,' Jason said one day quite out of the blue.' 'Maybe we are too self-righteous.' He mentioned the names of religious groups and businessmen, men of standing in the community, who were supporting the interim regime. 'They all can't be wrong.' Reshmi had noticed how Jason had gone quiet the past few months, but thought this was due to coup-fatigue. She looked at him, stunned. 'Who says so, your *talanoa* grog group?' 'Actually, yes.' 'What have they ever stood up for?' 'For their self-respect, Reshmi,' Jason replied. 'We have always been apologetic about ourselves, always taking the back seat as if we don't belong here, always getting kicks up our backside and then asking for more.' This was Radha all over again, Reshmi thought to herself.

'This is not about us versus them, Jason,' Reshmi replied, 'we are all in the same boat. We will sink or swim together.' She continued, 'An eye for an eye: you know what Gandhiji said.' 'Yes, the whole world will go blind.' 'Then what?' Reshmi asked. 'This place is so rotten that something had to be done. All the *ghoos-khori*, corruption and bribery, the greasing of palms. You have to break the egg to make an omelette.' 'Yes, that's the excuse they all use to get on to the gravy train,' Reshmi shot back. 'The egg is broken so I might as well make an omelette. But you know what, you will never be able to eat that omelette in peace as long as the curse of coups hangs over this land.'

Jason changed metaphors, repeating something he had picked up during one of his grog sessions. 'My house is on fire, Resh, and we have to do something. We can't just stand on the sidelines and carp. That luxury is reserved for bloody academics and television talking heads, the chattering classes. They have nothing to lose.' Reshmi replied without missing a beat. 'Yes, our house is on fire, Jase. In that case, we must join the fire fighters, not the arsonists.' Reshmi's withering repartee was on full display.

'Go out there, talk to the people, see things for yourself in the squatter settlements in Nasinu and Kinoya,' Jason told Reshmi. 'I will take you there myself. Talk to the people. Listen to what they have to say.' It was a depressing drive through the Kinoya-Tacirua stretch, areas full of wretched tin shacks, soot and filth and stench of dog shit from the overgrown drains, barely clad children wandering aimlessly on the roads. 'Go and talk principle to people here and see the response you get. *Pet* (livelihood) before principles.'

'How will the coup solve the problems of these people,' Reshmi wondered. 'Things will get much worse before they get better.' *E khandak se nikalna bahut mushkil hoi*. It would be very difficult to get out of the wilderness. These squatter settlements were a recent phenomenon, the result of non-renewals of leases on farming land. The mood the Fijians were now in, more leases will not be renewed. The politics of revenge and retribution will tear this place apart, Reshmi thought to herself and it's the poorest of the poor who will suffer the most. Desperation would only compound their misery and make them more vulnerable to the demagoguery of their leaders.

'Why can't our leaders talk truth to these people, real truth,' Reshmi asked Jason. 'Tell them that this coup is wrong, that it will fail, that things won't become normal anytime soon.' 'No, we have to convince the rest of the world that this coup is not wrong,' Jason countered. He was a complete convert to 'the cause.' 'Our white neighbours don't understand what is going on here. They never have. We are doing what they want us to do: practice good governance.' Then he added, 'They came around in the past, and they will come around again. It's just a matter of time. We are simply too important for them to ignore us.'

'This is not about good governance, Jason.' Reshmi said sharply. 'This is about greed, people getting into power through the back door on the barrel of the gun.' She rattled off the names of ministers who had lost in the last general elections. 'Go to China and India as much as you want,' Reshmi continued, 'but it is Australia and New Zealand that we will have to live with. We can't escape the truth of our history and geography.' She reminded Jason of a similar but failed attempt soon after the first coup. 'We should honour history, but not be held hostage to it,' Jason remarked. *Itihas ke manyata do, uske ke zanzeer men nahin bandho.* 'China and India are the emerging superpowers, and these fellows better recognise that quick-fast. The white men's empire is ending.'

'How you have changed, Jason,' Reshmi said to him one day. 'Before, you and I marched, risked arrest and beatings, and begged our neighbours to help us restore democracy.' She reminded him how they were among the founding members of the 'Back to May Movement' in 1987. 'Now you want them to look the other way.' 'No, Reshmi, we want them to see it our way, the way we see it. We have drawn a line in the sand and we won't retreat.' Looking at Reshmi, he said, 'We will keep this saga before the courts for a long time. There will be appeal upon appeal until we get what we want.' 'So that's what courts are for, are they?' Reshmi asked. 'And here I was thinking they were about dispensing justice.' 'Think again, Reshmi,' Jason said. 'This is the real world of real men and real politics.'

'Maybe democracy doesn't work here,' Jason said when they had another argument. 'What has democracy done for this country for the last thirty years? Elections and rigged elections, more divisions among our people, corrupt politicians getting fatter on the gravy train, our people taken for a ride.' Then he responded to something Reshmi had said earlier about people power. 'People are stupid,' Jason said. 'They don't know what is good for them. You give them the vote and they send in crooks.' *Ek dam lucca log ke* 'They are so easy to buy with a few cheap promises.'

'Whose fault is it?' Reshmi asked sharply. 'We go out and tell people to vote for the leader, vote for the party, don't worry about the local candidate. The team is important. It is only the leader who matters. Trust him as you trust your doctor. He knows what is wrong. He knows what the cure is. With that kind of mentality, we will of course suffer.' She reminded Jason how embarrassing it was to see politicians on television unable properly to read speeches written for them, and making a botch of things. 'We kick up dust and then complain we can't see.'

'It is not a question of fault, Reshmi,' Jason said. 'Most of our best and brightest have left. Many have parked their families overseas. We are left with the *chakka panji*, the hoi polloi. They have nothing to lose, nowhere to go.' There was contempt in his voice. 'These fellows care for little beyond their immediate family needs. Give them grog and they will be happy. Why should we trust the future of our country, your and my future, to these bumpkins? These *chutias*, arseholes.'

'So these unelected do-gooders know what is best for us?' Reshmi countered. 'They are in it for themselves, believe you me.' She reminded Jason of the names of relations of prominent people in the government getting appointments to statutory bodies and boards of public companies.' Coups within coups,' Reshmi said, 'people settling old scores, setting themselves for the future.' 'We are perfect at playing the victim,' Reshmi continued. 'Place yourself on a perch, place the garb of victimhood on your head, blame everyone for your misfortune and denounce anyone who disagrees. Well, that won't do me. We condemn others for their petty bigotry. Are we any better?'

Jason reminded Reshmi how people in the crowded areas of the Suva-Nausori corridor were grateful for the military presence on the roads. 'They feel secure. Look at how armed robberies have gone down, there is no trashing of temples. People can walk freely at night. So what if sometimes solders go too far? So what if a few heads are cracked? Par for the course, I say.' 'The guns give us an illusion of security, no more, Jason,' Reshmi replied. 'The coup has ripped race relations apart in this country. Who will save us when the Fijians turn on us? Remember blood is thicker than water.'

'By then, we will be gone,' Jason said. Reshmi had forgotten that they had applied for a migration visa to New Zealand about a year ago, especially for the sake of Ash and Asha and their education. The plan was to settle them in Waikato and then return to Fiji. The coup had changed everything. Jason had decided that he would migrate too. 'This place is finished, Resh,' Jason said. *Khalas*. 'We have to think of our future. No one else will.'

'I can't go, not now,' Reshmi told Jason firmly. There were her elderly parents in Lautoka to look after. No country would have them because of their age and fragile health. Besides, something deep had stirred in her. The coup had unleased a passion for political justice and human rights that she did not know she had. The haunted look on the faces of children in the squatter settlements and roadside stalls pained her deeply. 'I can leave, but where will they go?'

# Sixteen

## Frequent Flyers

One by one they all went, selling their dream houses on Vale Levu Street in Tamavua's fashionable Namadi Heights. Once the pride of the most desired suburb of Suva, the place now looked deserted, unkempt, full of household rubbish on the side of streets and stray dogs wandering aimlessly looking for food. Soon after 1987, Ram and his wife Sashi had migrated to Vancouver, Anish and Chitra left for Auckland and Ravi and Vikashni for Canberra. 'This trickle will turn to a torrent, you just wait, Bro', Ram had said to me one day. And he was right too. It was not before too long after May that long queues formed in front of Australian, New Zealand and American embassies. Anyone who could leave was leaving. 'Immigration to Emigration, that should be the title of your next tome, Doc,' Anish had said.

Ram, Anish and Krishna were my school mates from Labasa Secondary, sons of struggling cane farmers, like myself, but who had all done well. They had finished their commerce and law degrees in Auckland and Wellington, and were steadily climbing up the local corporate ladder. Getting ahead in the quickest possible time was their main preoccupation. They felt genuinely sorry for me and my choice of a career as a historian. 'Why history when you could have done anything you liked?' Ram had wondered aloud once. 'Do law, Bro,' Ravi advised me. 'It is not too late yet.' 'And what, become a liar?' I had responded half in jest. 'Well, better a rich liar than a pious pauper,' he replied with a chuckle. 'Making a difference is what life should be about,' I had added, somewhat pompously. 'Yes, Mahatmaji. Making a fast buck will do me,' Anish had said, tapping me gently on the shoulder.

True to their vocation and ambition, the three bought the best blocks on the street and built their dream homes modelled on architectural designs imported from Sydney and Auckland, double storey structures with polished hardwood (*dakua* and *damanu*) floors, impressive barbeque sets, liquor cupboards full of the best imported spirits and wines, framed Monet and Picasso prints on the walls and the best local handcraft strategically displayed in the living room. It was their version of high living with class. What really upset them most about Rabuka's coup was that it so rudely disrupted their dreams of living long and well in this part of town. 'Fuck Fiji,' Ram had said when he was leaving. 'It is losing this house that really pisses me off.' 'And to see some bloody Fijian living in it,' Ravi had spat out bitterly.

For a while, we lost touch with each other as we all went our different ways. A few years after migrating, I heard that Ram had died in a horrible road accident while driving from Vancouver to Edmonton. I did not know Sashi well. Anish is doing well in Auckland and we meet every so often, but he has made a new start and Fiji is falling off his mental map. 'Why hanker for something that will never be yours,' he once wrote to me. I knew many migrants who felt that way about Fiji. Ravi remained close because we lived in the same town for a while when I returned to Canberra after a spell in Hawaii before he moved to the western Sydney suburb of Newlands. A slight idealistic streak in him appealed to me when Fiji was full of lawyers with no conscience or public-mindedness. Vikashni was distantly related, the eldest daughter of Uncle Shiu Prasad of Waiqele, and that kept the link alive. Shared anxieties about starting afresh in a new place, the lurking fears of failure and losing face, the common demands of raising a young family in an unfamiliar cultural environment, had cemented the bonds.

Ravi and Vikashni and their two young children lived in Canberra South, in one of the outer affordable suburbs of the town where many young, starting families had homes. Nappy Valley, they called it. Vicki had no difficulty finding a job as a nurse at the local hospital, and the two children were enrolled in Duffy Primary. Ravi was less lucky. He found it difficult to break into the fairly close knit Australian legal profession. The leading law firms were full, so he was told, and there was no vacancy at the office of the Director of Public Prosecutions where migrant lawyers tended to get a start. He did odd jobs as a consultant, which in truth meant menial, mind-numbing work most lawyers passed on to their lowly subordinates. But mostly he stayed at home, picking up kids from the school and doing odd jobs around the house. Once a week he stuffed junk mail in the neighbourhood mail boxes. On weekends, he worked at the Jamieson Shopping Centre as a trolley collector, meeting and swapping stories with men from similar backgrounds from different parts of the world: Sudan, Croatia, Turkey, Ethiopia. Meeting these men, Ravi knew that he was not alone in his depression and desperation. Although from different parts of the world, they all shared similar experiences: frustration at not having their qualifications recognized, difficulties with children's expectation of parents, trying simply to survive with dignity.

Ravi was always on the quiet, almost withdrawn side, but there was no hiding his unhappiness. In Fiji he was an up-and-coming lawyer, someone people looked up to, a figure of respect in the community, a trustee of many community schools, with a career in politics in the offing. In Australia, he had gone from being a little somebody to a big nobody, and prospects for improvement in the immediate future looked dim. But he had his family to think of. Abhay and Apeksha had no future in Fiji, and he had no right to stand in their way either. At least Vicki was employed. And Ravi tried to console himself that he was not alone in his predicament.

Vicki could see that Ravi was unsettled, and that disturbed her deeply. The last thing she wanted was to see him unhappy. She knew the sacrifices his family had made to see him through the law school. He was the first one in the family to finish secondary school. His parents had borrowed money to send him overseas, hoping that a foreign degree might give him a head start. In the typical Indian way, it was expected that after completing his law degree, Ravi would help out with the education of his younger brothers, all bright boys with the potential to go places. That was the way things were done in Labasa, people getting out of the unending rural misery by standing on the shoulders of those who had gone before them. But after 1987, it was thought best for Ravi to migrate so that he could one day sponsor all of them. Everyone was thinking that way.

Soon after Ravi had migrated, his father died of heart attack he suffered when told one day that his lease would not be renewed and that he would have to vacate his ten acre plot (to be leased out, it was later learnt, on a share-cropping basis, to the ever avaricious neighbour Mr Ram Jattan who had quietly instigated the non-renewal proceedings). Ravi knew then that his plans to settle down permanently in Australia would have to be deferred for a while. Uppermost in his mind was the welfare of his elderly mother, Auntie Sukhdei. There were no close relations nearby to look after her. Migration papers would take a long time to be processed. Even if she did manage to leave, what would she do in Australia, someone illiterate in English and unfamiliar with Western culture, cooped up in a suburban home with no Indo-Fijians in the neighbourhood? Ravi had seen some elderly lost-looking people passing time in shopping malls during winter, lonely, objects of pity, gawking vacantly at the passing human traffic. 'Waiting to die,' one of them had said to him one day.

'Maybe, you should return to Fiji for a while, Rav,' Vicki volunteered to Ravi one day. Ravi just looked at her somewhat startled by the suggestion. 'I mean, for a short while till Mum is settled down. I will manage things here.' 'But what about Abbie and Apes?' Ravi asked. 'Oh, they will be fine. They are like their father strong, or maybe I should say stubborn like a mule,' she said as she planted a kiss on his cheek. 'Oh Vick,' was all Ravi could manage. It was brave and heartfelt gesture of support, but Ravi knew how hard it would be for Vicki raising two kids all by herself, running a household and working fulltime. But he also knew in his heart that Vicki made sense.

A week or so later, Ravi rang Daven, his former law partner in Suva, to see if there was still a place for him there. 'Just for a short while till things settle down. May be a year or two at the most.' 'For as long as you want, Bro,' Daven said encouragingly. 'The business is down, but we could do with a good litigator. And you were just about the best we had.' 'Flattery will get you somewhere big one day,' Ravi replied, relieved.

Ravi returned, rented a flat in Augustin Street and started where he had left off. The office staff welcomed him back warmly because they admired his kindly and compassionate ways. There was sympathy for him, perhaps more like pity. Soon life set into a routine. But charm and the excitement which had so animated life on the Vale Levu Street appeared to have deserted the city. Many of his close friends had left, were leaving, or making plans to. Real Estate prices were plummeting, the streets looked forlorn, full of potholes and filth, houses unpainted and covered with soot, shops full of shoddy goods. His former suburb was a ghost of its earlier self, the promise of the early years disappearing without a trace. The old moral order seemed to be collapsing too. Incest cases had increased dramatically, the newspapers regularly carried horror stories about the sexual abuse of children, prostitution, suicide cases because of failure in exams or because of tangled love affairs, increasing divorce rates and domestic violence. Something in society was snapping, the sense of order and purpose and cohesiveness. Everyone seemed to be for themselves. Perhaps these had always existed, but they were becoming more visible now. Ravi found the sight of young girls and women from broken homes congregating at The Triangle or at the Post Office early in the evenings distressing.

Days were easy to pass, while occupied in the office or appearing in the courts. And there was the ever present tanoa bowl and regular lunches at The Cottage. Nights were a nightmare for Ravi. It was not as if Augustin Street did not have nocturnal attractions of its own. It was full of men, like Ravi, early-to-middle-age, whose families were safely 'parked' outside the country but who had returned to resume their old jobs. There was plenty of duty free liquor around, and boozy dinner parties were a regular feature of the street. Women were in plentiful supply too, single mothers, girls from desperately poor homes, university students earning much-needed cash on the side. 'Buyers market,' everyone said. Some men were secretly glad to have their wives out of the way for them to indulge their perverted sexual fantasies. But this was not Ravi's way. He was a light drinker, and he missed his family. In an old fashioned way, he believed sex outside marriage was sinful. He resolved that he would try and visit Vicki and the kids once every six to eight weeks.

These reunions were in the beginning joyous occasions. The kids enquired enthusiastically about 'relos' back home: Nana, Nani, about the neighbours and the kids, about Tipu their dog, and Rani the cat. Vicki cooked food that Ravi liked: spicy lamb and crab curry, various varieties of dhal. They frequented the Belconnen and Fyshwick markets for fish and fresh fruits and vegetables. Ravi went to Abhay's soccer matches and to Apeksha's musical performances. They hiked in the Brindabellas, had picnics at the Cotter Dam. Occasionally, they drove to Sydney for the weekend, and kids enjoyed Darling Harbour. Vicki introduced Ravi to her friends, most of who were working at the hospital. 'The mystery man,' they would joke. 'Here today, gone tomorrow.' An elderly man had said to him, 'Be careful young man, Vicki is a real head turner.' Vicki blushed, but Ravi never doubted her fidelity. Time flew. Before they knew it, it was time to return home. The goodbyes were heart-wrenching. Then the routine returned.

Both Ravi and Vicki knew that they would have to find ways of occupying themselves apart from work. Ravi joined the Rotary Club, Suva East Branch. Rotarians were progressive people doing good things, helping raise funds for scholarships, buying computers for schools and organizing book bins for the community libraries. There was regular fellowship, which kept Ravi informed and connected. Periodic forays into the countryside, whether it was a drive to Rakiraki through Monasavu, or exploring the lush, craggy mountain ranges of the Serua-Namosi hinterland, opened up new areas which had remained hidden to him, and to most people in Fiji. Some Rotarians were from Australia on various assignments in Fiji, and they brought along Australian newspapers and magazines to the 'make-up' sessions which kept Ravi reasonably well informed about events in Australia.

Vicki, too, was keen to escape the ever-threatening loop of loneliness, and in this she was encouraged by her friends at work. She cut her hair short and began wearing skirt and pants rather than the traditional salwar kamiz which had been the cornerstone of her sartorial repertoire in Fiji, attracting disapproving looks from some of her Fiji friends. She began to take cooking lessons at a friend's house in Garran, both out of choice as well as necessity. Abhay and Apeksha complained that their friends at school always made funny faces at them at lunch time. They did not like the smell of curry and roti. Some had called them 'curry munchers.' 'Why can't you be like other mums, for a change,' Abhay had once snapped at her, more in frustration than anger. 'Pasta would be good for a start.' Vicki was hurt, but not surprised. After all, they were the ones who had come to this country, and they should adjust and not always insist on hanging on to the old ways. And so she had a go at Italian, Greek and Lebanese cuisine.

She also joined the 'Mums for Duffy Soccer Club,' for which Abhay played. The Club prepared sandwiches and coffee and tea for the weekend matches and little munchies for the boys. Sometimes she would accompany the team at their weekend retreats at Cooper's Creek. She became a member of the Duffy Parents Association and helped out at the weekend fetes. Then there was the Duffy Mothers' Book Club which met the first Tuesday of every month. All the weekend activities were exhausting, but Vicki didn't complain. As things fell into a pattern, she actually looked forward to her various activities.

A new world was beginning to open up to her, expanding her horizon in unanticipated ways. She had a new and widening circle of friends, mostly Australians. That she found refreshing because most Fiji women had few interests outside home and most were caught in the 'Keeping Up with the Jones's' world. Vicki found her Australian friends curious about Fiji. Several of them had visited the country and wanted to know more. Mrs Swinstead, the wife of the former Westpac manager at Lautoka, asked Vicki to give talks about Fiji to her friends in the 'University of the Third Age.' At first self conscious, she quickly read up on whatever she could find in the Woden library, and shared her thoughts and experiences, gaining confidence each time she gave public addresses. She talked about the Indo-Fijians, how they got there, the Colonial Sugar Refining Company, the coup. She helped her friends' kids with their school assignments about Indian religion and culture, about which she briefed herself surreptitiously. Vicki was what you might call your model migrant: sensitive to the local environment, eager to learn new ways, to contribute whatever and wherever she could, ever ready to 'have a go.'

Abhay and Apeksha too were adapting in their own ways. At first they were shy. Their English was not fluent, and they had a lot to learn about Australian culture and ways of doing things. But in no time, they had mastered the lingo and the local dress code, including pierced ears, trendily-torn jeans and spiky hairstyle. Abhay was a natural at sports, good at soccer, as most Fiji boys are, but getting better at cricket too. Apeksha took to popular culture like duck to water. She caught up on shows like 'Home and Away,' and 'Shortland Street.' She went over to her friends' place for sleepovers, and boys came to Abhay's place, drinking coke and eating ordered pizzas, lying about on the floor watching video and playing Nintendo. Vicki bought a second-hand billiard table which kept the boys at home within her earshot.

Ravi's visit was still looked forward to, but not with the same anticipation of the first visits. Fiji was weighing Ravi down, sometimes against his own will. The daily news of harassment somewhere, the religious bigotry, the glass ceiling in the public service, the increase in incidents of violent burglaries, the regular interrupted water supply and electricity, the palpable sense of despair among his people. In the courts, he did cases involving incest, rape, attempted suicide, domestic violence, all on the rise. It was all coming apart at the seams right in front of his eyes. So much promise, he thought to himself, so much of it gone to waste so quickly. When visiting Canberra, he continued worrying about events back home. But the children, and latterly Vicki too, had been showing less and less interest in what happened in Fiji.

When Ravi mentioned this to Vicki one day, she replied, 'Well, Rav, sometimes to move forward, we have to switch the lights off, shut the door and move on.' It was not that she did not care about Fiji, but now there were so many other things to think about. The children, for example. 'Do they care about anything?' Ravi asked. They seemed to him to be obsessed with mundane trivia. 'They do, Rav, but it is not easy being a teenager in this society.' Vicki knew about the drug problems and teenage pregnancies plaguing the local schools, and was thankful her children were safe in the company of good clean friends. She was watchful and observant. Nothing escaped her. When Ravi mentioned seeing Abhay with a stubby in his room, Vicki said, 'Count your blessings if the worst they are doing is beer.'

There were many things that upset Ravi, but he realized there was no point raising them. Kids were staying up regularly till long past midnight watching television. Their rooms were a health hazard, with clothes, empty Coke cans, junk food wrappers and magazines lying around. There was never any offer of help with housework or in the kitchen. Ravi dreaded talking to his children, fearing their sharp, snappy responses. Once he asked Abhay about his school work, and he had replied, 'Not that shit again, Dad.' 'But that's why we came here, Abbie, for you guys.' 'Don't put the guilt trip on me, man. Look, school is not the end of the world. If I stuff up, so what? There's heaps of other things I can do.' Apeksha lived in a world of her own and knowing her temper tantrums, Ravi thought it best to leave her alone. This was no way to live family life, but he seemed helpless.

When Ravi mentioned his conversation with Abhay to Vicki, she felt genuinely sorry for her husband. This was no way to talk to their father, she agreed. 'I will talk to him,' she promised. But there was a deeper point lurking in Ravi's head. What hurt him most was that he could not talk to his own son in a language that he could understand about things that really mattered to him. He simply could not enter his son's world, try as he might. All he had was his own experience to go by. 'That's all I know, Vick,' he said one day. 'All we can do is to be here for them when they need us,' Vicki replied. 'That's all, and hope that things will come good.' 'Thank God, we at least have each other,' Ravi said.

When Ravi came over in the early days, Vicki would adjust whatever she had on her calendar to suit Ravi's schedule. His happiness and satisfaction were her priority. But now she had her own routine which she was loathe to breaking. Thursday evenings would be her Yoga classes. On Fridays she went to the gym. Then there were regular outings with her friends. On these occasions, Ravi would have to make do with whatever was left over in the fridge or order a pizza for himself. Cooking was never his forte. In Suva, his house girl took care of all his domestic chores. All he had to do was to issue the order for the day. His grocery shopping was done for him. His clothes were washed and ironed, shoes polished. But in Australia, all these chores he had to do by himself.

Small things magnified the growing difference. Vicki, very health conscious, would have a light dinner of salad and soup, perhaps, or even Asian noodles, whereas Ravi had gotten used to home-cooked roti and spicy curry. He was indifferent about breakfast and lunch, but dinner had to be taken in the traditional Indian style, eaten with fingers. He really couldn't ask Vicki to cook every evening for him, and yet he missed his routine. Vicki had her own favourite television programs, soapies and serials, which she watched religiously, asking friends to tape the ones she missed for some reason. Every night before bed, Vicki would watch some mindless programme on television to relax, while all that Ravi wanted was silence and solitude before switching off. Vicki would try to get Ravi involved by telling him about the various plots and how they were connected, but they had little meaning for him. Once or twice he thought to himself: 'The world is going to the dogs, half of humanity is mired in desperate poverty and here everyone is glued to meaningless, juvenile love entanglements.' Whenever he tried to switch on to the news channels, he felt that his family was merely tolerating him. 'I have had a hard day,' Vicki would say, a cue to watch something light before retiring to bed.

Local stories which stirred public opinion and filled the airwaves meant little to Ravi. Kangaroo culling was big news, which had been picked by animal liberation people in many places, including Japan, as did passionate stories about the closure of primary schools in emptying suburbs, the construction of jails and roads close to inhabited areas, stories about the wayward ways of local and national politicians, about refugees and boat people and asylum seekers. What mattered most to him, Fiji, was hardly ever mentioned in the news and yet Ravi knew that Fiji was churning.

In the early days, Ravi could talk to Vicki about Fiji, but now her interests were captured by things closer to home. She cared deeply about what happened in the neighbourhood about which Ravi could not care less. For Vicki, Fiji was beginning to fade from her mental radar, just when it was beginning to imprison Ravi. Family connections too were becoming tenuous. Many of both Ravi's and Vicki's family and friends had already migrated, or were planning to. Vicki saw little point in hanging on to the memories of a place which had caused so much rupture and anguish in their lives.

Vicki gradually became aware of Ravi's restlessness and tried to introduce him to her friends from work. Once or twice she organized barbeques at home. She invited him to after-work drinks, to the occasional Sunday picnics at Cotter. They were decent, well-meaning people but with limited experience. They asked simple questions about Fiji and told him about people from there they had met. The outings were nice, but they only temporarily alleviated Ravi's growing sense of isolation. 'Pity about Fiji, mate. It didn't have to be a four letter word,' a man once said to him. It was a cue to change the subject.

Re-establishing links with the Fiji people might help, Vicki thought, and on several occasions they drove to Sydney to participate in festivals, musical evenings and fund raisers for various causes. Ravi knew some of the people, but they had all moved on. Some of them talked about house prices, playing the share market, golf, and overseas holidays. Full of pretension, living well for them was the best form of revenge. Fiji was furthest from their minds. Others remembered the trauma surrounding their departure from Fiji and said, and hoped, that things would never improve there. Revenge and retribution was what they wanted. For Ravi, there were few points of contact and exploration.

One day, about two years ago, Ravi distinctly sensed that his visits were not as warmly welcomed as they once had been. The children now barely acknowledged his presence. Fiji was fast becoming another country to them. They were losing the language and whatever they had learned of traditional Indian culture. They now only vaguely recalled the names of their younger cousins and extended family members. They lived in a virtual world of their own. And Vicki had created a network of friends and associates who were a vital source of support and encouragement for her. They were almost like a family, perhaps even closer than the family she had back in Fiji.

Now sometimes, the kids asked, 'When are you returning to Fiji, Dad?' The question spoke not of concern but of relief at the return of routine unhindered by the presence of a vanishing figure in their lives. Ravi realized sadly that he was a guest in his own home. 'We can't go on like this, Vicki,' he said one day. 'This is no way to live a family life. I seem to have become a stranger to my own children.' The growing distance between Ravi and Abhay and Apeksha had not escaped Vicki. And she understood, although it was unspoken, that Ravi would prefer Vicki to live with him in Fiji. 'This is home now, Ravi,' she said to him. 'We have nothing back in Fiji.'

'But what will I do here,' Ravi asked, not really expecting an answer, wondering aloud. He had a job in Fiji, a lifestyle he liked, some friends with whom he had shared much over the years. Despite everything that had happened, he still had a presence in the community. People looked up to him, and he liked helping out whenever he could: filling forms, witnessing documents, giving free legal advice to community and charitable organizations. Life had a purpose and a meaning beyond simply the act of living.

'It's always about you, isn't it? Vicki said. 'Always. 'What will I do?' Have you thought about us, me and the children? What will *we* do *there*? Abbie and Apes are still in high school. I can't simply abandon them just like that. They are too young to be left alone.' And they had other obligations to meet as well. They had just renovated their house, with a big loan from the bank. The new car had to be paid off. Apeksha was preparing to spend an exchange year in Japan, and money would be needed for that as well. And Vicki had a secure, satisfying job, which she was grateful to have.

Ravi knew that Vicki was sensible and rational. Why would anyone give up a secure job to return to uncertainty? They talk about bloodless coups, Ravi thought to himself, but some things are worse than death. He was exaggerating, but only just. The thought of rupturing his relationship with Vicki never once entered his mind, despite all the turbulence and uncertainty of recent years, nor did the thought of keeping two kitchens, as the expression goes, ever enter his mind. 'You play the hand you are dealt' was almost his motto. He thought he would remain a commuter, a frequent flyer for the foreseeable future.

**Postscript**

But then, two years later, fate intervened in the form of George Speight. The fraudulent Fijian nationalist overthrew another democratically elected government, derailing the process of reconciliation that had promised to restore hope and opportunity to an ill-fated Fiji. 'Indians are different,' he told the world with a smirk. 'They act different, they eat different and they smell different. They are heathens.' 'They will reduce this place to rubble,' Daven, Ravi's law partner, said of the coup makers, 'and finally claim this country as their own. Fiji for the Fijians, finally.' 'Democracy *is* indeed a foreign flower here. We have no place in it,' he said ruefully on another occasion. 'We will never belong, Bro, never be invited to belong.' He was selling his law practice to relocate to Auckland. 'Life is too short for this shit.'

Labasa was emptying, reverting to bush, as people were moving to the mushrooming squatter settlements around Suva. Joining the exodus were Ravi's own brothers and nieces and nephews, embarking on the first step of a journey that would eventually take them to foreign shores. Auntie Sukhdei's death finally settled the issue for Ravi. Fiji, with its unending saga of violence and treachery and racial hatreds, lost its hold on his soul. It no longer felt like home anymore. There was nothing left for him in Fiji. I'd rather be a little no body in Australia than a big somebody over here, Ravi finally resolved. Life would not be a bed of roses there, he would have to learn and listen hard again, re-connect with his family, re-enter their world on their terms, not his own. 'I will always have my memories,' Ravi thought to himself, as he packed up, thinking about his childhood, chasing his cousin around the cane fields, meeting Vicki, the birth of his children. He knew of the long and lonely road ahead, full of unpredictable twists and turns, but he was glad to give up the life of a frequent flyer. He was finally going home.

> *Dil naa ummid to nahin naakaam hi to hai*
> *Lambi hai gam ki shaam magar shaam hi to hai*
>
> *Don't let your heart despair; to do so is utterly useless,*
> *Grief's evening is long, but it is only an evening.*

## Waituri To Nelspruit and Other Places in Between

*Ye safar bahut hai kathin magar*
*Na udas ho mere ham safar*

*This journey is exceedingly hard, but*
*Don't despair, my fellow traveller.*

*Ye sitam ki raat hai dhalne ko*
*Hai andhera gam ka pighalne ko*

*This night of tyranny will pass*
*These dark sorrows will melt away*

Waituri. The name is unfamiliar to me. It is, in fact, an Indo-Fijian settlement in the flat, damp, water-logged Nausori hinterland a short distance from the local airport. From the late 19th to about the middle of the 20th century, it was a sugar cane growing area, one among several on the Rewa delta and among the first to be settled by Indian indentured workers. When cane production was abandoned due to the perennially wet weather and low sugar content, Waituri became a rice settlement in the late 1950s. But that phase too came to an end, in the 1980s and 1990s, when the economy collapsed after the 1987 coups and the local rice mill was closed down. For a decade or so, the place was abandoned and left to revert to bush, all the memories of the early days of toil and hope erased.

In the last five years or so, the place has again begun to come to life, from an unexpected source—Labasa. At first there were a few hastily erected tin shacks housing a few stray families. Then, as news spread of the opportunities the place offered, more people arrived, families and friends, escapees from Vanua Levu. The place now has the look of a new settlement in the making. Some homes have power, there is running water and the rudimentary roads are serviceable.

INTERSECTIONS

A massive internal dislocation is underway in Fiji, caused by the expiry of sugar cane leases under the Agricultural Landlord and Tenant Act. Whole areas of Vanua Levu have emptied: Daku, Wainikoro, Lagalaga, Nagigi, once the vibrant heartland of the cane country on the island, but now overgrown and desolate. Places like Waituri offer these desperate people the hope of a new beginning.

Among the new migrants in Waituri are my own extended family of nieces and nephews and distantly-related cousins. My older sister and her husband arrived there about six months ago to join their daughter and her family who had relocated a few years back. She died last week, after a long battle with debilitating diabetes and general undiagnosed ill-health so common in the neglected rural areas of Fiji.

I arrive from Australia in time to attend her funeral. It is a strange sensation. My sister got married when I was very young. We saw her infrequently over the years. Once married, Indo-Fijian women were seen as a permanent part of their husband's family. Any lingering attachment to their natal family was discouraged as a sign of disloyalty to her new relations. We had no understanding of my sister's married life, the difficulties she might have encountered in her new home about which there were a few quiet whispers, the ways in which she might have tried to adapt and change. For all practical purposes, she had become a stranger, her inner world unknown to us. The story of her journey is now lost forever.

It was this stranger's passing that I had come to mourn. My brothers, who had also flown from Australia to attend the funeral, and I talked about our distant youthful days for the week we were in Suva together. We recalled stories and incidents from our childhood, the pranks we played on unsuspecting strangers, the things we did to amuse ourselves during the vacations, the furious soccer matches played with ball made of rolled up newspaper in dry paddy fields, the surreptitious activities which, when caught, could lead us into real trouble (such as pouring boiling water on pumpkin plants to kill them because we were so fed up of eating pumpkin curry day in and day out), but, sadly, our sister's life was not, could not be, among our recollections.

Slowly over several days, the details emerged as long forgotten memories were revived around the grog bowl. Our sister had several girls, all married now, and two boys, the older of whom died tragically a few years ago, crushed by the cane tractor he was driving. My sister never fully recovered from that tragedy. She had become a lost soul, people said, forlorn, given to sudden emotional eruptions when old memories of happier days returned to haunt her, which they did frequently. There is something unnatural about children going before their parents. As if all this was not enough suffering, her favourite grandchild died when the car she was in on her way to school plunged into the local river, drowning everyone in it. From then on, her grip on life began to weaken markedly, people said, her zest for life gone. She was just waiting to die.

My sister's daughters, none of whom had gone beyond high school, were bright kids but economic circumstances and social traditions had circumscribed their opportunities. That was the way things were then. They were lucky in having good, caring husbands, who had cleared the bush in Waituri, leased several parcels of land, and were growing vegetables for the local market.

They were doing well by local standards, and had plans for future expansion. Their spirit and endurance commanded respect. They had gone through so much hardship, and yet they remained undaunted, their spirit unflagging. The transition from being cane growers to vegetable farmers could not have been easy. The rhythm and pace of life is different, there is no established and dependable community network to lean on for advice and assistance, but they are coping well, in fact, more than well.

Surprisingly, they don't regret leaving Labasa. The constant uncertainty of temporary leases, the absence of ready cash income to meet the daily needs, the unending grind amid diminishing opportunities, had taken their toll. In Waituri, the cash income, although small, is regular. There is a new future to look forward to. And there are more openings for children in Viti Levu.

The future of children weighs heavily with most Indo-Fijian parents. It has always been so. I recall my own childhood in Tabia. We were told by our parents that there was no future on the farm for all the six boys, that we had to look for other alternatives. We did. All of us eventually left the farm for other professions. We all now live overseas.

One of my nieces has two boys. One is in form four and the other in form six, both at Vunimono High School a few kilometres away. They are shy and deferential, eyeing me respectfully from a distance, avoiding direct eye contact. I am a name to them, nothing more, a stranger who was a member of the family who had gone places, but whom they had never met except through images on the television and pictures in the newspapers. The older one tells me that he wants to become a doctor. That kind of ambition, in this kind of place, seems strangely incongruous. But, then, who would have thought that a boy from a primitive Tabia would one day become a professor in Australia. The boy is a straight A student in school, and I have no doubt that he will realize his ambition. He has that steely determination, that hunger.

He, and others like him, will leave Waituri one day, just as his parents left Labasa. This place where they are growing up will some day come to be seen as a stopover in a long journey of displacement. This is where they will start, but not where they will end up. I wonder if these children, growing up with so much disruption and dislocation, will ever know the joys and satisfactions of growing up in a settled, cohesive community, ever experience the sustaining love that comes from belonging and attachment to a larger intimate group.

In the evenings, people gather at my niece's place where my sister spent her last days. A *Bhagvata katha* is held every evening for thirteen days, the traditional mourning period for orthodox Hindu families. After the *puja,* people sing *bhajans,* devotional songs. They are poignant, cathartic and often heart-rending: about the purpose of our life on earth, its impermanence, about the futility of mourning for a soul which has escaped its earthly form to reunite with the universal, indestructible soul. We all join in, tears flowing freely, without embarrassment. *Koi Thagwa Nagariya Lootal Ho:* How some thief has ransacked our community (taken a beloved soul away).

People who come in the evenings are mostly from Labasa and a few from other parts of Fiji whom the family has befriended. They are all migrants, facing similar predicaments, seeking solace and support in each other's company against the demands and disillusions of the outside world. A sense of community is evolving out of need and necessity, and from a shared sense of being unwanted, unwelcome strangers in this place.

The Nausori-Suva corridor is full of displaced Labasa people, I learn. They are contemptuously called 'Labasians.' Their rustic speech is derided, their willingness to work for a pittance scorned. They are seen as snatchers of other people's jobs. It hurts, a man says to me, to be called names, to be looked down upon, but what can we do? We have to feed our families and send our children to school. The very spirit of enterprise and the ethos of hard work, which are and have long been the hallmark of our community, helped us escape poverty and destitution, are now being spat upon. We will put our head down and keep to ourselves, a man says. Yes, I say to myself: this too will pass. We all live in perpetual hope.

Talk turns to politics as people ask me about my views on what is happening in the country. But I am here to listen and deflect questions. I realize, as I listen, that the goings on in Suva have little relevance in Waituri. No one reads the newspapers here. Television news is watched, but people's poor English prevents a full comprehension of current events. Television is valued especially for the entertainment it provides. Radio is more common as a vehicle for the news of community events than for hard news. Death notices and religious programs instructing on the proper way to conduct important rituals and ceremonies, are a special favourite.

Opinion about the coup is divided. Those who have more contact with the outside world are hoping for the best. The Qarase government's racially motivated policies are talked about. They didn't care about us, a man says. Everything was done for the Fijians as if we did not matter. But what has Bainimarama done, a man asks? The price of everything is going up: fuel, food, bus fares. We have no say in this government. Things will get much worse before they get better, seems to be the consensus. I detect a tone of despair and helplessness in the conversation. These are innocent, helpless victims of other peoples' ambitions and agendas, caught in circumstances not of their making and completely beyond their control.

So what's the way out, I ask? Work hard, mind your own business, educate the children and hope they will migrate. That's the only way out. There is no future for us here. It all sounds so depressingly familiar. I am reminded of an old Mohammed Rafi song: *Chal chal re musafir chal, tu us dunyia men chal:* Go traveller, go to that other world…

History has a strange way of repeating itself. More than a century ago, our forbearers left their homeland in unhappy circumstances to build a better life for themselves and their children. But somehow, somewhere, things went horribly wrong. A century later, fear and insecurity continue to stalk the life of the Indo-Fijian community. People are on the move again.

For many Indo-Fijians, Waituri, and places like it throughout Fiji, will be a temporary stopover in a long and unpredictable journey ahead. It is their temporary destination, but not their final destiny.

## Labasa Lelo Lelo

The National Stadium is humming at over eight thousand strong as the Inter-District Soccer Competition gets underway. This is my first attendance at this milestone sporting event in almost thirty years. Everything has changed. I have changed. Nothing is familiar. I am seated in the second-to-last row of the pavilion in the company of soccer-crazy nephews from Labasa, who now live in various parts of Fiji and overseas. This is the main sporting event in their annual calendar. They have been following the build up over the season. They know the names of all the main players, their strengths and weaknesses.

Roy Krishna is the man to watch, I am advised. Roy is the present boy wonder of Labasa and Fiji soccer, a slip of a lad, just nineteen, grandson, I am told, of a proud Fijian grandmother (on his father's side). On the field, he is agile, strategically positioning himself, opportunistic and most pleasing of all, unselfish. He has a fine soccer sense.

He reminds me of the Labasa soccer genius of my days, Anand Sami. The maestro played for Labasa and for Fiji in the seventies and eighties, his soccer skills universally admired and warmly recalled decades later. The Sami brothers were the soccer princes of Fiji. Anand now lives in Brisbane, like so many of his generation, such a huge, irreplaceable loss for Fiji.

Radio personality Anirudh Diwakar is sitting next to me. I had run into him earlier in the day and was pleased to see him again. He is a soccer enthusiast, and recalls the names of great players of yesteryears, household names in their days but now lost to memory. He mentions Chandra Bhan Singh, the magical midfielder for Lautoka in the 1960s, the cunning field marshal who deployed his troops on the park with masterly precision. He is probably the greatest midfielder Fiji has ever had. And Mike Thoman, the charismatic fullback, who would nonchalantly swipe a bowl of grog on the sidelines when the ball was at the other end of the ground.

In Rewa, there was the volatile, explosive, hot-tempered Johnny Bakridi who was known for never completing a game because he would be sent off for punching or kicking an opposing player. The poor fellow did not know that riling him up was one of the tactics his opponents always employed! He invariably fell into the trap. And Satish Datta, the stylish, handsome mid-fielder. In Suva, there was the inimitable Chotka, the bow-legged midfield general who was the city's backbone for nearly a decade, who later migrated to Sydney and became a taxi driver there, and the sleek striker Munlal, the younger brother of the legendary John Lal, a sometime Fiji coach, who had played professional soccer in Australia in the 1960s. And from the Friendly North came Brian Simmons, the left midfielder who went on to play for Fiji, Gordon Lee Wai, whose sister, Jenny, was in my class at Labasa Secondary, the Zoing and Sami brothers. Boys from Ba, a most fearsome, imperious lot dressed in black, were in a class of their own: Esala Masi, Josetaki, Bale Raniga, Farooq Janeman. They exemplified the indomitable, boisterous spirit of their big province.

All names from ancient memory, completely unfamiliar to the present generation. Soccer was our passion, the only game in town. There was no television then, so we followed the matches on radio, re-living its thrilling moments long after the matches had ended, wondering whether we would one day actually witness a real tournament ourselves. For us in Tabia, this was a glorious but distant dream.

Soccer was an 'Indian' game well into the early sixties, the game of choice for the children of the *girmitiyas*. It was inexpensive, easy to organize and involved the entire community. The Colonial Sugar Refining Company encouraged it, with the tacit support of the colonial government keen to keep things compartmentalised. From humble, haphazard beginnings, it gained institutional support in the post-war years as the population increased and demands for leisure activity gained momentum. The Lloyd Farebrother Trophy provided the impetus for an annual get-together, and so started the inter-district competition. The teams are multiracial now. In some cases, the majority of the players in a team are Fijian although the majority of the supporters and team management are Indo-Fijian.

On the playing field, ethnicity does not matter. The district does. How wonderfully refreshing; this loyalty to a region that transcends ethnicity, religion, class and other man-made barriers. If we can achieve this common identity on the soccer field, I think to myself, why can't we achieve a similar feat in the field of politics? Why do we insist on having ourselves represented in parliament by one of our own kind? We grow up going to school together, playing together, mixing socially on myriad occasions, yet are compelled to follow the ethnically exclusive furrows in matters of political representation.

The antics of a player from Tavua catches our attention and we all laugh uproariously. The No 2 Tavua fullback is full of wild passion, completely engrossed in the game, gesticulates to his players, argues with the referee, thumps his foot on the ground and throws his arms up in the air to indicate disapproval about something. Every time he touches the ball, we giggle loudly in anticipation of some fireworks, and explode if he does something funny. I think he is aware that he is playing up to a packed gallery. Yes, soccer is good theatre as well, the cause of much thigh-slapping laughter.

Murgi Chor,' Poultry (Paltry!) Thief, someone says when the referee gives a decision he does not like. This is an old expression familiar to me, and so uniquely Fijian, so harmless and yet so vivid. I ask Anirudh about new additions to our soccer vocabulary. 'Aawe, Aawe,' he says, is one, 'He's coming, He's coming.' In other words, watch out, take quick evasive action. 'Lelo, Lelo,' is another, 'Take it, Take it,' 'E Nahin Jaai,' 'This won't go in.' And so it goes.

I am served a bowl of grog while the match is in progress. This is new to me. In my day, you sauntered down to the basement of the stadium for a *bilo*. But now, people bring their own with them. My nephews have brought theirs in several large lemonade plastic bottles. They take yaqona wherever they go. They seem unable to function without it. This is common throughout Fiji. I recall with particular horror a sign I had seen at the Raralevu Crematorium just a few meters away from the pyre saying 'Kava Sold Here,' for the benefit of those waiting for the cremation ceremony to begin.

The Stadium becomes tense as the Labasa-Rewa game starts. Labasa is at the top of the ladder and expected to win easily over a lowly-ranked Rewa. But Rewa, in red, is no walkover, as the match ends in a draw. Throughout the match, the support for Labasa is intense and the cheers loud. I realize that the Stadium is packed with Labasa supporters. They are desperate for a Labasa win. I wonder why when suddenly the reason dawns on me. The Suva-Nausori corridor is clogged with displaced Labasa people, especially the mushrooming squatter settlements. These simple people from rustic background are derided here, the butt of jokes. I recall a letter in the press from a Labasa girl pleading for sympathy from Viti Levu people, saying that for many from Labasa, coming to Suva was like going to New York or London. These simple, simple-hearted, people needed sympathy and tolerance, not condescension, she seemed to be saying.

There is a glue that binds us Labasans. Everyone thinks we are country bumpkins, inferior, lacking in social graces, but we know the truth, we say quietly to ourselves. Look at the number of doctorates Labasa has produced, someone had remarked to me, per capita the highest in Fiji; I don't know if it is true, but it is good to hear it anyway. We are all proud of Roy Krishna, our golden boy whose boots carry the hopes and dreams of so many Labasans. Wouldn't it be wonderful if we could show these Viti Levu fellas who is the champion on the soccer field? That is why we are all desperate for a Labasa win.

For sixty minutes or so, every Labasan in the audience is one, passionately cheering for their team. Differences dissolve. The person on my right is a very senior police officer. The fellow in front is a mechanic and on my left is a secondary school teacher, who now lives in Nasinu. We drink grog from the same bowl, slap each other on the shoulders excitedly as Labasa makes a good move, and sigh in disappointment when things don't go right. We are a mob. For a few magical moments, we become boys again, oblivious to the troubles plaguing the country, recklessly heckling the supporters of our opponents on the field, uncaring about what happens to Suva or Tavua or Lautoka, or anyone else, united in our love for the team from the Friendly North.

I had gone to the National Stadium not to watch soccer but to spend some time with my nephews whom I have grown to love deeply, who are mischievously playful with me, for whom I am nothing more or less than simply an aging, slightly eccentric uncle, not a pandit of local politics or a professor of history whom they occasionally see on the local television news. That is the beauty of this deepening, unaffected human bond, a wonderful reminder of what, in the end, life is all about.

But there is something about the evening that has touched me in an indefinable way. It brought back distant, fading memories of youthful passions: soccer matches in dry paddy fields, the fierce inter-village competitions and the fistfights which often broke out afterwards as rivals challenged and taunted each other, the black magic which some ardent supporters used to boost the chances of their teams, the dissecting of the day's developments deep into a kava-lubricated night. Many people of my childhood have either migrated or moved on. I returned home a renewed Labasan from the Friendly North, or LA, as they proudly say these days.

## Chuuk

'I am off to Chuuk,' I tell a colleague. 'Chuuk, eh!' he responded. 'Yes, Chuuk in the FSM.' 'FSM? Er, Fiji School of Medicine, perhaps?' 'No, the Federated States of Micronesia.' 'I see,' he said. He had no idea.

I had some idea of its geography, but not much, even though I had taught about Micronesia as a part of my larger Pacific History courses for decades. This was my first, much longed for, trip to this part of the world.

I am part of a 25-strong Election Observer Mission, co-ordinated by the East West Centre in Honolulu, on behalf of the Asia Pacific Democratic Partnership in Washington DC. There are representatives from various parts of the world: Korea, Thailand, Indonesia, India, Palau, Philippines, New Zealand Australia and the United States.

Chuuk is having two sets of elections, one National (President and Vice President of the FSM) and the other for the local House of Representatives. The role of the Observer Mission would be to observe, naturally, but not to intrude, to learn and to advise on any improvements to the electoral process.

Getting to Chuuk is quite an effort: from Sydney to Manila, from there to Guam and then, finally, an hour and half later, to the island itself. For some unknown reason, I had thought of Chuuk as a flat atoll, perhaps like the Marshall Islands.

But I am disabused of that notion as I look down from the window of my Continental's Air Micronesia (Air Mike) to see a string of verdant islands protruding sharply from an endless, brilliantly blue ocean. There are many islands in the Chuuk Lagoon, all beguilingly beautiful in their own way.

Micronesia has had a long and tragic colonial history. First came the Spaniards from the time of Magellan in the 16th century onwards. From the middle of the 19th came the Germans. Their empire ended in 1914, to be usurped by the Japanese who ruled it until the Second World War. Then the Americans took over the islands as a 'Strategic Trusteeship.'

What that meant was that the trusteeship partnership could not be terminated unilaterally by either party. And second, matters relating to the trusteeship would have to be discussed in the Security Council, where the United States of course had veto power.

This 'double insurance' gave the United States complete hold over the islands. The islands were important strategic assets. It was from Saipan and Tinian that the B52 Bombers took off for Vietnam in the 1960s. The Missile Range at the Kwajalein Atoll in the Marshall Islands is still active and important.

When independence came in the 1980s, the different islands chose different routes. Marshalls and Palau became republics and the Northern Marianas became a commonwealth of the United States. The smaller islands of Yap, Chuuk, Pohnpei and Kosrae formed the Federated States of Micronesia.

All formed a 'Compact of Free Association' with the United States which provided various packages of financial assistance in return for free, unhindered passage of the American military through the waters of Micronesia. Chuuk, like other smaller islands, survives on the American largesse. The Spaniards came for God, it is said, the Germans came for Gold and the Americans came for Good.

The tragic reminders of Chuuk's colonial past are everywhere. Chuuk lagoon was the headquarters of the Japanese Imperial Navy in Micronesia. Most of the ships were sunk by the Americans during the Second World War, and the Lagoon, I am told, is full of about one hundred wrecks: a veritable marine graveyard of rusting hulks. It is divers' haven, though, attracting enthusiasts from all over the world. Diving is an important source of the island's economy.

On the other islands in the Lagoon, we see long abandoned jetties, bombed airfields now over grown beyond recognition, air raid shelters covered with vine, rusting buildings. The region's premier high school, the Jesuit-run Xavier College, is housed in a Japanese building built to withstand bombs. The building is still impressive in it concrete solidity. The Japanese obviously thought they would be in the islands forever. Things were built to last

And people talk warmly of the Japanese period, our guide tells us. There was economic growth then, development, the building of infrastructure, and discipline. All that is gone now, and former productive rice farms and other food gardens have reverted to lush bush. The main road in the capital, Moen, is an endless series of potholes.

We get our briefings from election officials about voting procedures and polling stations. WE have our checklist of things to look for. There are no political parties in Chuuk. Clans and extended families play an important role in choosing candidates. But there are campaigns, everyone votes, and the ballot is secret.

It is difficult to get a sense of the campaigning that has gone on before the polling day. There is no newspaper in Chuuk, and the radio is in Chuukese, which does not help me. Television is of no use, full of American soap opera and the ubiquitous CNN updates. We talk to some candidates to get a sense of things, but our (or at least my) understanding of the dynamics of the local politics is rudimentary.

We are split into groups of two to tour the different far-flung islands. My partner is a young lady from Korea, Soonjung Yee. Early on the day of polling at around 7am, we head off to our respective boats which have been hired for us and then across a slightly rough passage to our specific destination.

We visit six polling stations scattered across the island. Everywhere without exception, polling opened sharp at 7. The crowd is small in some places, large in others. We are talking here about small communities. The polling officials are organised, the booth hidden behind a cloth curtain in some places or placed at a discreet distance in a corner in others. The effort to preserve privacy is obvious.

We jot down notes of our conversation with election officials and of our own observations. Early next morning, we gather at our hotel for several hours and the various teams compare notes and prepare a preliminary report. The full report will come later. We are pleased with what we have observed but we also have suggestions for changes and improvements. Beyond that, I am unable to say much now.

Many things impress me. The first is how we are received in the different places. We had no idea about how people would see us. But everywhere, there is a warm welcome, a sense of gratitude that we had travelled such long distances to witness their polling. The world was watching, and people were impressed.

I observe with my Fijian experience. In Fiji, as we know, people expect to be transported to the polling booth, fed many bowls of grog and even food. We are all familiar with the ubiquitous tanoa and the pulau pot. In Chuuk there is none of that at all. People come to the booth of their own volition, vote, hang around for a while, and then leave. In Fiji we have compulsory voting; in Chuuk voting is non-obligatory.

And I am moved by the patience people show. They stand in the queues for their turn to vote. They do their sacred duty, and then move on. The way we used to do it in Fiji all those years ago. The *tamasha*, the sideshows, the *hulla gulla*, the hustle bustle, the majestic madness of democracy in action.

There is an expression in Chuuk, 'Chuuk You.' It means, so I am told, that you have been smitten by the haunting beauty of the islands, and that you will return one day. Yes, 'Chuuk You'. I am already 'Chuuked'.

## Bougainville

September 11. The world is remembering a day of terror, and talking the language of revenge and retribution. A rumour of war is in the air. But not in Buka, now the unofficial capital of Bougainville. There, the Bougainville Constitutional Commission is meeting for the first time. I have been invited to participate in its proceedings. It is an honour and privilege to be here. It is also a poignant reminder of the intense anticipation as we ourselves began our new constitutional review journey more than seven years ago.

The meeting is an historic event for this strife-ridden island of 200,000 people some 1000 kilometres east of Port Moresby. The 24 member-Commission consists of a wide cross-section of the community, representing church, women's, trade union and community groups, representatives of the Bougainville Revolutionary Army and the Bougainville Resistance Force (both now called Ex-Combatants) and of the North, Central, South and Atoll regions of the province. Few of the commissioners have had previous political experience at the provincial level—or at any formal level. Most are 'ordinary' citizens called to perform an extraordinary task for their people.

The Commission is chaired by Joseph Kabui, a thickly-bearded, experienced politician of mild, thoughtful disposition and a distinguished presence. Around the table are men who were once sworn enemies. Ismael Toroama, a lightly built man with sharp, darting eyes, fierce-looking and sporting visible battlefield scars, was once the most feared field commander of the BRA, and on the most-wanted list of the Papua New Guinea Defence Forces. Opposite him is Hilary Masiria, the formidable leader of the BRF leading the fight against the BRA. And there is diminutive Damien Damen, the feisty representative of 'indigenous' political and religious groups, the founder of the 50-toea resistance movement, in the same room as Rev. Matthew Tagak of the Uniting Church.

It is as unlikely and as incongruous a gathering as you are ever likely to see under one roof. They represent divergent, sometimes diametrically opposed, agendas, and eye their colleagues with a certain understandable wariness. But as the talks proceed, suspicion dissolves. People talk of making a new beginning for a new, united Bougainville. Francis Ona, the legendary founder of the BRA, is not there, though his looming shadow is. He is not a part of the peace process but neither, people say, has he actively opposed it. That they see, hopefully, as a silver lining. There is also a sense that Ona is no longer the force he once was, and his absence, therefore, not as destabilizing as it could have been.

The Commission has been appointed to draft a new constitution for an autonomous Bougainville in six months, autonomous, for the time being, within the political framework of a united Papua New Guinea. It is a direct result of the Bougainville Peace Agreement signed at Arawa on 30 August 2001. That agreement provided for three related processes to achieve peace on the island. The first was Autonomy. Bougainville will have a 'home-grown' constitution which will enable its people to manage their own affairs with diminishing intervention from the national government in Moresby. The island will have its own court and administration personnel in time and make decisions about how to manage and harvest its resources. That was one of the demands of the separatists.

The second part of the Arawa accord was a 'Weapons Disposal Plan.' During the ten-year conflict from 1989 to 1999, an unknown number of weapons were smuggled into the country, through nefarious means, from the Solomon Islands and elsewhere. No one, including the United Nations Observer Mission on Bougainville, knows the number of illegal arms floating about in the countryside, but it is in the hundreds, they concede. The hope is that through a sustained effort of dialogue with the participants, the arms will be retrieved. But what incentive is there for people to return their arms, I ask? Peace is the answer, officials say. People want peace. They are fed up with war. One certainly hopes so.

The third step in the peace making process is a referendum on the future of the island. Independence from Papua New Guinea was the demand of the BRA and other separatist groups. But people agreed to delay the referendum on independence for ten to fifteen years, enough time, participants say, to allow for tempers to cool down, reconciliation to take place and for a considered decision about the island's future to be made. The new constitution is optimistically expected to be completed by early next year, paving the way for elections to be held for an autonomous Bougainvillian government. The road ahead is long, but at least things are moving in the right direction. That is no mean achievement.

The conflict in Bougainville erupted into the open in 1988 when landowners, angry at the horrendous environmental damage the Panguna copper mines had caused, began destroying mine property. The mine, operated by an Australian company, had contributed mightily to the coffers of the national government, but local people felt cheated of what they considered a just share of the revenue. And so localised raids gained momentum, escalating into a broad-based ethnonationalist movement demanding independence from Papua New Guinea. Bougainvillians, who felt themselves different and distinct, had attempted to secede from PNG at the time of independence in 1975. Their secessionist efforts had been contained through constitutional guarantees of greater autonomy and through provincial decentralisation.

By the late 1980s, these were not enough to meet a growing, broad-based Bougainvillian demand for political autonomy. In 1990, Bougainville declared independence from PNG. State apparatus collapsed, law and order broke down, and violence was rampant. As Anthony Regan, now the constitutional advisor to various Bougainvillian parties puts it, 'Most non-Bougainvillians left Bougainville during 1989 and early 1990, many fearing for their lives in a process that was in some respects a form of ethnic cleansing.' But declaration of independence brought in its wake other problems, among them the escalation of intra-Bougainvillian tensions. Bougainville, like most of Melanesia, has enormous cultural, linguistic and social diversity—there are some 21 distinct languages and 39 dialects spoken on the island—and these came to the fore as various factions manoeuvred for political control.

The social and economic consequences of the conflict were appalling for the island. Estimates vary of how many people died during the decade-long conflict, but some people conservatively put the figure at ten thousand. Ismael Toroama puts it closer to twenty thousand. Ten or twenty, the figure is horrendously high, higher by far than in any other conflict in post-war Pacific. The economy, once flourishing, ground to a halt, the infrastructure collapsed, investment vanished, and people once in the vanguard of entrepreneurial activity left the island. The sad legacy of the past is visible today, in the aimless wandering of unemployed youth in the dusty, pot-holed main street of Buka, the erratic power supply, the bare shops.

As the conflict continued, so, too, did efforts to find peace, both among Bougainvillians themselves and between Bougainville and Papua New Guinea. These bore fruit. The conflict ended in 1997, and leaders returned to the negotiating table. The Arawa accord of August 2001 marked the culmination of that process. The road ahead is tough, but everyone assures me that they have turned the corner. There is no other alternative to peace. I certainly hope so. What remains with me more than anything else as I leave the island is the determination I saw in peoples' eyes to leave behind a fraught and fractured past to create a new future for themselves. Few have any precise idea of what that future might look like and how they might get there, but they do know what they do not want.

The words of one of the Commissioners still rings in my ears: 'The journey of a thousand miles begins with the first step.'

### The Caribbean

14 May 1998. The date marks the 117th anniversary of the arrival of Indian indentured labourers in Fiji as well as the 11th anniversary of the coups there to depose a month-old government in which the Indo-Fijian community, for the first time, had more than token representation. But my thoughts are elsewhere as my American Airlines jet cruises high above the Atlantic. I am on my way to the Caribbean, to Trinidad, Guyana and Suriname, on an inaugural journey of diasporic exploration.

The Caribbean lies at the other end of the world. I am embarrassed, as I look at the maps in the in-flight magazine, at my ignorance about this part of the world. I have heard of Caracas, but Curacao? Antigua, yes, but Anguilla? Our ignorance is mutual. People in the Caribbean have heard of Fiji but don't know its precise location. Is it near Guam, someone asks. No. Then Mauritius, perhaps, or Java or the Andaman Islands. Tahiti is the best they can do. Ms Boodhea, a young desk attendant at the Park Hotel in Georgetown, is staggered to know the distance I have travelled to come to her part of the world. She herself is dreaming of leaving one day. 'But you are on the other side of midnight,' she says, amazed.

Our ignorance underlines the enormous geographical spread of the Indian indentured diaspora. It is remarkable, when you come to think of it, that so many hundreds of immigrant sailing ships, loaded with miserable human cargo and aided only by primitive navigational technology, travelled such great distances through so many islands and so much reef-ridden unchartered water and found their precise destination with such little casualty.

Among the million *girmitiyas* who crossed the *kala pani* was my own indentured grandfather. He was in fact recruited for Demerara, he told us, but when he reached the depot, he found his ship full. The next available vessel took him to Fiji. A century later, I am undertaking a journey my *girmitiya* grandfather was drafted to make. Trinidad is my first stop. It is hot little, feisty little island with an attitude, riding the boom of oil-fuelled prosperity. About two thousand square miles in size, it is crowded with over one million people, forty percent black and Indian each. It is easily the most prosperous of the Caribbean islands.

The contrast with Guyana is stark. After years of massive and frequently violent misrule, the country's infrastructure is in tatters, its economy floundering, its people deeply divided and drifting. Guyana is a big country of eighty three thousand square miles, but with a population of only seven hundred thousand, living mostly in a thin strip along the Atlantic coast. Like Trinidad, Guyana is bi-racial, and locked in a deadly game of ethnic rivalry, visible and invisible.

Suriname lies across the Coryntine River from Guyana. Once a Dutch colony, its population is about a third each black and Indian, and the rest made up of Javanese, Creole and Ameri-Indians. Although Suriname shares with Trinidad and Guyana the history of Indian settlement, its soul is unmistakeably Dutch. The Netherlands is its spiritual home. The game of cricket, the passion of the British Caribbean, has no meaning here, nor does the English language. Suriname, like Guyana, is flat along the coast, and cris-crossed with canals, now stagnant, neglected and overgrown. The Dutch imprint is clearly visible. Its weather, like much of the Caribbean, is clammy. The low lying clouds are ever pregnant with rain. The countryside is lush green.

Each place has its own cultural peculiarity, but it is the similarities that startle me. In Guyana I was taken to meet the chairman of a local municipality. It was around mid-day Sunday, but by then he had already nearly gone through a bottle of cheap rum. The Caribbean generally is a place of hard drinking men. He shook my hand, looked at me quizzically, assessing, and said, 'You are a coolie-maan from Fiji?' The words took me by surprise at first, but I knew what he meant. It was a term of recognition, a reference to our shared history of indentured servitude. I was one of them. I was welcome.

There is something distinctive about us (old) diasporic Indians that binds us together: our essential egalitarianism, our openness and adaptability, our zest for living here and now, our impatience with ritual, protocol and hierarchy, and, importantly, our complex, problematic relationship with India. We do not regard ourselves as the children of a lesser god, banished into exile for some misdeed in previous life. We are not *naqli*, fake, Indians. We rejoice in the myriad influences which define our identity. Our shared prejudices cement friendships.

Everywhere, I am reminded of the contribution Indian people have made to the economic and social development of the countries where they live: in agriculture, commerce, the professions. People recite the story of success proudly, and with good reason. The statistical evidence of achievement is impressive. And the point is often made to underline the under-achievement of other communities, their dependent mentality.

Yet Indians in all three countries have a deep sense of ambivalence and alienation. Even after a century many do not feel fully accepted as part of the region. The situation varies from country to country, but it is a difference of degree, not of substance. The most obvious marker of uncertainty is the emigration of large numbers of Indians to North America and Europe. In Guyana and Suriname, most Indians would leave if that were possible, I was told. The same in Fiji. People talk about commitment and belonging. A t-shirt proclaims: 'I live in another country but I am 100% Guyanese.' This is tourist talk. The reality is different. As in Fiji, the wealthy and the well-connected are living well, their children and financial investment safely put away somewhere else.

Indian intellectuals are contesting the long-held view of Caribbean identity being essentially black, especially in Guyana and Trinidad. The defiant expression of Indian cultural and religious identity at the popular level is also striking. Temples and mosques dot the landscape. Some places have been re-named: Benares, Faizabad. Hindu homes fly multiple *jhandis*, flags, to proclaim their religious identity. Indian food is the fast food of the Caribbean, at least in these three places: bus-up shut (roti) and double (deep fried roti stuffed with vegetables), aloo paratha, dhalpuri, delicious curries, popular among both Indians as well as blacks. The most popular restaurant in Paramaribo is Roopram's Roti Shop.

A hundred years' of isolation from India has resulted in many changes. In Trinidad and Guyana, and to a lessor extent in Suriname, Hindustani or Bhojpuri has been lost, and there is deep regret about this. We miss Hindi 'bad-bad,' a man says to me in Trinidad. He is culturally stranded, helpless. He sings melodious Hindi songs well. He has mastered the rhythm but does not understand the words he is singing. They are mostly sad, sentimental songs of love and loss: Rafi, Hemant Kumar, Mukesh, singers of yesteryears. He is genuinely moved when I explain the meaning of the words to him. So am I, at our shared diasporic loss.

In all three places, the ideology of cultural assimilation, of the melting pot, is being rejected in favour of cultural retention and pluralism. Religious texts are translated into English or Dutch, and recited. Pujas are done regularly. Hindu and Muslim festivals are celebrated. Indian music and Hindi films form a part of the Indo-Caribbean culture. There are inner tensions and conflicts among the different groups but these are muted. The shared sense of deprivation and neglect during a long period of black rule has produced a degree of cultural and ethnic solidarity.

Indo-Caribbean people are returning to their primordial roots, a scholar tells me in Trinidad. I meet several people who are using the documents of indenture to trace their Indian roots. Creative writing is flourishing here as in few other Indian diasporas. Poems, novels and short stories deal with the violence and chaos of the post-indenture period. The drunken violence against women, depicted in the literature, is especially striking. Understandably, much of this imaginative reconstruction, mostly by expatriate Indo-Caribbeans, is tinged with romance and full of anger at the outside world. Still the emotional and intellectual engagement with the past is impressive.

My month in the Caribbean is over quickly. It is an exhilarating, learning, enriching experience. I have struck friendships which will endure. I have memories of people, of places, of sights and sounds, which will remain with me. I remind myself, as I travel in the region, that had the ship not been full, my grandfather would have gone to Demerara. And I wonder where I would have been: perhaps somewhere in that part of the world, on the other side of midnight.

**To London**

*Pussy Cat, Pussy Cat, Where have you been?*
*I have been to London to see the Queen*

I was walking towards Camden Market on a grey London afternoon in mid-May when I felt a tap on my shoulder. 'Any pubs around here, sir?' an old, bedraggled man asked me. 'I am sorry, but I am new to this place,' I responded. 'Where you from?' 'Australia.' 'But you don't look Australian.' 'What's an Australian supposed to look like then?,' I confronted him directly 'No offence, guv,' the old man replied somewhat apologetically. 'I thought you was from India.' Before I could recite my genealogy, he said, 'Great country, India. My dad and uncle were in the Indian Army. I was born there. Was *pukka badmaash*, too, I was,' a real rascal. The old fellow, lonely and wandering, was in a mood to offload, but I was in a hurry. 'Good luck,' I say as I walk on.

On my way back, I stop at a shop in Euston to pick up a bottle of Australian red, one of life's minor weaknesses. The dark South Asian-looking man at the counter was pleasant enough. 'Where you from?' I couldn't help asking that perennial question immigrants of colour automatically ask each other everywhere. 'Sri Lanka,' he replied. 'Murali is a genius,' I venture to start a conversation. Muralitharan, the ace Sri Lankan spinner. 'I don't like cricket. Englishman's game,' he replied sullenly. That peeved me. Cricket is the game God plays, and it is plain knowledge that God is not an Englishman. And, I thought, if English are so bad, what are you doing here in their country? But there was no point arguing. 'You are hailing from where?' he asks me as I begin to leave. 'Fiji,' I replied. He gave me a blank, unknowing look. 'Fiji,' I repeated. Still no reaction. 'Fiji Islands,' I said. 'In the South Pacific.' 'In Gujarat?' I gave up.

A few days later, I was on the tube — English for underground train — when a chubby young woman with shaved head and wobbly, jelly-like stomach, thrust a bottle of coke into my hands as she prepared to take her seat. I pretended not to notice her. The first rule of the tube is not to look strangers in the eye or strike up conversation with them. Who knows who you are talking to, and where that conversation might lead. The woman sneered at me. 'You don't speak English, do ya?' She must have thought I was a refugee, or worse. 'I do,' I said somewhat defensively, 'but I don't get your accent.' The noise from the moving train had made hearing worse. 'I am from West Caardiff, that's waaii.' That's why indeed.

London is like that, full of people weird and wonderful. This mother of all cities is a haven now, as it has always been, for wannabee revolutionaries, renaissance seekers and, increasingly, refugees from eastern Europe and north Africa. This city, I remind myself as I pound its pavements, was the home of the Bloomsbury group. This is where Karl Marx wrote the *Das Kapital* and Charles Darwin his *Origin of the Species*. For years, I had avoided London. The colonial hang-up, I suppose. When colleagues sang praises of London, I swooned about Labasa. But the city has grown on me since my last visit there several years ago. This is my third extended visit and most certainly not the last. Let me admit it: this is where I would love to live, if I could afford it—and if the weather could be improved.

For a student of modern history, London is mecca. Relics and reminders of Britain's vanished imperial glory abound. My flat is in Russell Square, named after the Secretary of State for India who reluctantly sanctioned indentured emigration in the 1840s, fearing it would become a new system of slavery. Whitehall, whose policies defined our destiny, is within walking distance, as is Marlborough House, the site of the penultimate conference on Fiji's independence, and Downing Street, the Houses of Parliament. And there are other monuments that children of my generation, now reaching middle age, read about in primary school texts: Big

Ben, the Tower of London, St Pauls' Cathedral, the London Bridge, Buckingham Palace, Hyde Park, Piccadilly Circus. Old ditties from primary school come back: *Georgie Pogie Pudding and pie, Kissed the girls and made them cry. When the girls came out to play, Georgie Podgie ran away.* And *London Bridge is Falling down, falling down, falling down.* Reflecting on their cultural significance in our young lives revives vanishing memories of another era. We were once so innocently proud of belonging to an empire on which the sun never set, when Britannia ruled the waves, remembering those large patches in our atlases covered in red whose names we memorised for our entrance exam geography questions (the longest river in Africa, the highest mountain in Australia, the capital of Rhodesia).

What surprises me most about London is its cacophonous multiculturalism. It is open, upfront and defiantly visible. Its signs and signatures are everywhere, in sports (Nasser Hussain is the England cricket captain), in journalism (Black and Asian television reporters speak in distinct Oxbridge accent), in food (curry is now more popular than fish and chips), in public life (the House of Lords has Lords Desai and Patel and Parekh and other high and mighty). This is not to say by any means that London is friction-free. There are seething cultural and ethnic tensions in the more depressed areas of the city in the east end. There is complaint in the media about white Oxbridge bias. Supercilious affectations of pedigree and self-importance show in public affairs. Who you are rather than what you know matters hugely. And people still worship an old lady, born to fabulous, unearned wealth and privilege, whose only known passion is for horses and dogs.

But at least there is open public debate about these issues and, it seems to me, a genuine desire to get things right. England is an island but in the physical sense alone. The media leads and shapes public debate. For me, one of the glories of England is its newspapers: there can't be many in the world which are better than *The Independent, The Guardian* and *The Times*. Reading and re-reading them consumes all my spare time during weekends, and even then there are bits and pieces left over for the following week. Such style and flair, such intrepid reporting.

I am in London to prepare a detailed documentary history of how Fiji became independent. As an editor of the 'British Documents on the End of Empire' series, I have been given full access to all the Fiji records at the Public Records Office at Kew Gardens. This is both a privilege and an honour, and a huge responsibility. Working at the PRO I am the happiest I have been in years, away from the drone of daily routine (the emails, the telephone, the blinking computer screen) to indulge my enduring passion for historical research. The book will be finished late next year[1].

The 1960s was Fiji's decade of decolonisation. By the early 1960s, independence was firmly on the horizon. Harold Macmillan's 'Winds of Change' were blowing upon our shores. It was not a question of if but when Fiji would become independent. Its timing became a matter of intense and passionate debate in the Legislative Council. The Fijian leaders, their people caught in a ferment of unprecedented social and economic change, preferred to retain the 'special' link with the British monarchy for a very long time. Frankly, they could not see why it needed to end. Indo-Fijian leaders wanted the cord severed quickly. They saw no virtue in continued colonial rule.

The most bitter debate throughout the 1960s focussed on the method of election. Fijian and European leaders preferred the communal roll; indeed, they were adamant about it. Indo-Fijians stuck firmly to their demand for the common roll. The same issue continues to haunt Fiji forty years later. Should Fijian interests be paramount? What did paramountcy mean in practical, political terms? Did it mean a few extra Fijian seats in the Legislative Council? How should the lease problem be resolved? Should merit and seniority or the principle of racial parity determine appointment and promotion in the civil service? Should Fiji become a Christian State? Should minority communities receive separate political representation? These issues are still with us today. The cast of characters has changed, but not the character of the problems.

It is fashionable these days to berate the British for practising the politics of divide and rule. But the blame game, so easy and so politically expedient, takes us only so far, and no further. The truth is that we were active participants in making our own history, not passive victims of it. The pace of change towards internal self-government was determined not in London, but in Fiji. London prodded us to move on; we procrastinated. The Colonial Office was acutely embarrassed by European over-representation in the Legislative Council and wanted it reduced drastically, but Fijian adamance won the day. London went along, reluctantly, so as to keep the Fijians on side.

There was intellectual sympathy for the position of political equality espoused by the Federation Party, but it was the plea of the Fijian leaders that London heeded—and needed to heed. Governor Derek Jakeway said it openly in Sydney that the United Kingdom government could not envisage a day when it would place independence in the hands of an 'immigrant community' over the objections of the indigenous people. And at the Colonial Office, people were open about devising a constitutional solution that would keep Fijians in power for a long time after independence. The introduction of cross-voting (called national seats after independence) was a means to that end.

The personalities who dominated the political debate stand out in the records. Ratu Mara, as he then was, was easily the Fijian leader of the moment, complex and conflicted, negotiating the competing claims of Fijian nationalism on the one hand with the demands of a multiracial society on the other. The tension showed. AD Patel was recognised in Suva and London as a principled political leader of rare intellect, a Gandhian at heart, but whose relentless advocacy of a non-racial Fiji was doomed to fail at the altar of ethnically compartmentalised politics. There was Mr Apisai Tora, the charismatic firebrand of the 1960s, petitioning the Colonial Office about his various pet peeves of the moment: the chiefs, the Indians and the local sahibs. And then there was Sairusi Nabogibogi, jail bird, messiah, writer of fiction and hero of the Fijian underworld, about whom more elsewhere in this volume.

Visiting the past, talking about people long dead or gone from public life is my profession, my passion, my pastime. But I read shelves upon shelves of Fiji files with a deep sense of anguish. We seem as a nation to be moving round in circles, without resolving any of the deep-seated problems facing our people. We don't seem to have learnt from our past mistakes. Hobbled by a failed past, we are unable to grasp our beckoning future. The experience of reading the files is akin, I imagine, to seeing how sausage is actually made: it is enough to make one a vegetarian.

I leave you with the words of Gary Younge, a black columnist for *The Guardian*. In them, he describes what his ideal nation should be:

> It is a nation where citizenship is not undermined by the happenstance of race or choice of faith but is understood as a common purpose and sense of belonging. A country that celebrates diversity because it understands the distinction between discriminating between people and discriminating against them. It is a place where people are not demonised collectively because of who they are but judged individually by what they have done. A land, like any other, where the poison of racism will always be present but where the antidote of anti-racism will be always available for those who wish to use it.

My sentiments exactly; I wish the words were mine too.

## Nelspruit

Nelspruit. The name is unfamiliar to me. World geography was never my strength in school. It is, in fact, the name of the capital of Mpumalanga province of South Africa, a tree-lined, well stocked, formerly all-white city at the edge of the great Kruger National Park. As Padma and I travel across the length and breadth of South Africa over three weeks, other exotic places with alluring names we had once rote-learned in primary school come to life: Cape of Good Hope,

Pretoria, Durban, Johannesburg, the Phoenix Farm, Port Elizabeth, and many, many more. As did phrases we had picked up in books all those years ago: a pride of lions, a journey of giraffes, a dazzle of zebras.

As we gawked and clicked at the animals in the wild at close range from the safety of our safari vehicles, I realized for the first time how beautifully apt the descriptions were and, conversely, how utterly ill-equipped we were culturally to appreciate them. Africa was not a Dark Continent for people of my generation growing up in post-World War II Fiji. We were a part of the British Empire (how could we ever be allowed to forget it?) upon which, we proudly proclaimed, the sun never set. We looked at all the red patches on our much-thumbed Clarion Atlas and felt curiously proud to be connected to all those remote places around the globe. That knowledge somehow lessened our sense of isolation and nurtured our curiosity about distant places and pasts.

That passion to know about the world has persisted with me. I still get a special thrill when I can recite the name of the President of Botswana or the capital of Upper Volta, much to the puzzled amusement of my children. Our primary school curriculum emphasized our common colonial British heritage, captured most powerfully in the Senior (and Junior) Cambridge examinations which children across the Empire took. By the mid-sixties, Cambridge exams were on their way out, replaced by the New Zealand Certificate and University Entrance exams. Still, in our early primary school, we studied the *Oxford African Readers* and the University of London's *Reading for Meaning* books. In them, we came across the fun-filled experiences of 'our cousins,' young African children, such as Luka and Rota, having a holiday, about Sokoloko Bengosay, a fat woman desperately trying various tricks to become thin and pretty (until her doctor told her that she was soon going to die, upon which she stopped being a glutton, which then reduced her weight and made her look thin and pretty again!), and parables and morality tales about the importance of prudence, caution, obedience to authority, honesty and the virtues of good citizenship. We learned our lessons well, too well I now realize, about being dutiful and diligent.

The occasional glossy magazines that found their way into our tiny library from the discarded collection of the British Council branch office in Labasa, introduced us to the pictures of people and animals in other parts of the Empire, especially Africa. It was such a thrill, on this trip, for me then to see the lion, the hippopotamus, the zebra, the giraffe, the elephant, the rhinoceros, the leopard, the cheetah and other animals in the wild. I thought of my unlettered father as we toured the Kruger because I had acquired much of my fascination about wild animals from the stories he told us (which he had picked up from his indentured father). And to see with our own eyes the physical features of the countryside we had studied in school. We had learned about the savannah grasslands in our geography lessons, but had no idea what they were, what they looked like, until we drove through the former Transvaal region.

For me, the monuments and historic places had their own intrinsic fascination: the sites commemorating the Great Trek and the Boer War, Robben Island where Nelson Mandela and other anti-apartheid activists were incarcerated, the Phoenix Farm on the outskirts of Durban where Mahatma Gandhi had perfected his weapon of *Satyagraha* (Truth Force), the life of the Indian community in Natal, the Cape of Good Hope (so named by King John II of Portugal, we had learned in school and which the plaques now confirmed) which was first circumnavigated by Vasco da Gama in 1497 (circumcised some one had written in an exam paper: the ever mischievous Liaquat Ali perhaps?). Some facts we had learned in school were clearly wrong, I discovered. Cape Point (Kaarpunt in Afrikaan) was not the southern most point of the African continent, Point Aghalus was. And so it went.

These remote places of romance and adventure on the African continent turned into places of turmoil and violence in the sixties. We did not know it then, of course, (the topic was too dangerous and too close to home to be discussed at school) but Africa was in the throes of decolonization. In our General Knowledge class, we memorized the names of famous African nationalists such as Kwame Nkrurmah and Jomo Kenyata in preparation for such exam questions as 'Who is the most famous leader of Ghana?' or 'So-and-so is the president of which country?' We heard news on the radio about the terrible conflicts in Congo, about the never ending Biafaran civil war. I recall my father listening to the regular Hindi world news bulletin on our recently bought Telefunken radio set and wondering what or where these places were and why there was so much violence there.

In the 1970s, Africa was nothing but bad news. It was a place where nothing ever seemed to go right. Colonial rule had ended, but colonialism's legacy had not. National boundaries drawn up by the colonial rulers were being aggressively transgressed by bellicose nationalists, and arrangements for power sharing among the different ethnic groups and notions of non-racial citizenship were being questioned and eroded. Nothing for us symbolized more the violence and treachery of the continent, of promises gone awry, than the expulsion of the Indian settlers of Uganda by its demonic (and in hindsight quite farcical) president-for-life, Field Marshall Idi Amin Dada, his megalomania brilliantly captured in the film *The Last King of Scotland*. With the expulsion of the enterprising Indian business community—there was no Indian indentured migration to East Africa—the country descended into chaos and poverty.

And so things remain there, although I heard in South Africa that some of the Indians were beginning to return, but their wealth and family safely 'parked' in Europe and North America.

The Ugandan experience aroused deep fears among our own people in Fiji at the time. If the long-settled Indians could be expelled from Uganda, just like that, couldn't a similar thing happen here? We had achieved our independence without strife, but none of the deep-seated fears of the different communities about their place in the broader scheme of things had been addressed. These were postponed for a later generation, with what consequences we now know only too well. In 1975, Fijian nationalist firebrand, Sakeasi Butadroka, opened the floodgates with his motion in parliament to have the Fiji Indians repatriated to India. The motion was defeated after a bitter and acrimonious debate. For the Indo-Fijians, though, the writing was visible on the wall. Many began looking for greener pastures elsewhere. In time, what began as a tickle turned into torrent. Within the next decade or so, with emigration proceeding apace, there will be more Indo-Fijians living outside than in Fiji.

Within a short span for my generation, Africa has been transformed from a place of romance and exploration and adventure into a place of grinding poverty and mindless violence. Africa is in the news again, bad news, as we prepare for our journey. Drought and disease are creating havoc across the continent, as they have done for some time. Our television screens are full of pleas for assistance in cash and kind as emaciated babies with bloated stomachs and buzzed by flies look pleadingly into the camera. Tribal violence is tearing many countries apart. Tutsis and Tutsis have been at each other's throats for some time. The President of Sudan is being cited for crimes against humanity. In Zimbabwe, the octogenarian dictator Robert Mugabe's reluctance to respect the verdict of the ballot box and concede defeat to his rival Moran Tsvangirai, is arousing worldwide condemnation, though so far to little outward effect. Africa seems full of tin-pot dictators unwilling to relinquish power. Yesterday's democrats have over-night become today's dictators.

South Africa is in the news for another reason; for the so-called 'xenophobic' violence. This is black violence against fellow black Africans from neighbouring countries (principally Zimbabwe, but also Mozambique, Botswana, Namibia) fleeing their desperately poor, violence-ridden countries to seek a livelihood somewhere else. The television images are arresting, disturbing, of young men and women fleeing from their South African pursuers armed with sticks and stones into dusty hovels scattered across a desolate landscape. Be careful, friends urge us, stay away from the trouble spots, meaning black areas on the outskirts of major urban centres.

But television images are misleading. Without context and perspective, relying only on brief images and urgent sound bites, it is all too easy to assume that xenophobic violence is a pervasive feature of South African society. It is not. The violence is confined by and large to the so-called 'informal settlements,' a euphemism for wretched tin shacks on the outskirts of major towns and cities where the desperately poor working class black Africans live in hope and despair. But 'xenophobic' is a misleading description of the problem. Xenophobia in its strict sense of course means a 'fear of strangers.' Here, the fear is of 'black' Africans from neighbouring countries, not whites or coloureds. The violence is class-based and rampant in the most marginalized areas of the country. The distinguished South African psychologist Don Foster suggests that the fear has deeper roots and the present violence against black 'aliens' (as they are called) stems from it. It is the fear of invasion from the north where the aliens are blamed for all the ills afflicting African society: crime, disease, AIDS, poverty, when many black South Africans feel dispossessed, disconnected and deeply discontented with their lot. 'Thwarted masculinity' is the phrase Foster uses to describe the condition of the South African youth for whom vulnerable outsiders become easy targets, giving them the illusion of power and authority. Open borders and free trade and other benefits of globalization are fine on paper, he says, but their social and economic consequences on the coalface of life is another

South Africa embarked on a new non-racial, post-apartheid journey with the release from prison of its most celebrated political prisoner, Nelson Mandela, after twenty odd years in incarceration, over dozen of them on the notorious Robben island (which we visit and which fills us with horror about the conditions the inmates had to endure there: backbreaking work in the quarries, solitary detention, institutional violence, naked racism). Mandela is a truly exceptional figure, one of the genuine giants of modern history, alongside Mahatma Gandhi and Martin Luther King, a man of immeasurable courage, personal dignity and grace. He became post-apartheid South Africa's first president in 1994, forming a 'Rainbow Coalition' in his culturally, linguistically and geographically diverse and fragmented (and potentially explosive) nation. If providing a smooth transition from one fraught era to another at a time of great anxiety and tension when things could easily have gone awry were Mandela's only legacy, that would be a momentous achievement in itself. But perhaps Mandela's greatest achievement, certainly in the African context and in light of the experience of many developing countries, has been his voluntary relinquishment of power to the new generation when he could have, like so many other leaders on the continent, clung to it for as long as he wanted, such was his aura and authority.

'Mandela is a man of history,' Daan, our elderly Afrikaan tour guide and a retired teacher tells us. He echoes a widely held view. 'The first five years of the post-apartheid era were golden years for our country,' he says, even though he quietly rues the way in which aspects of his own Afrikaan past are being systematically erased from the public view: street names changed, public monuments neglected, heroes of the Afrikaan past uncelebrated. His past is vanishing before his eyes. Daan acknowledges that the euphoria of those early years is now largely a vanishing memory, the promise of hope and of rapid betterment postponed. 'Far from being a society in the advanced stages of recovery from our terrible past,' writes the commentator and author Heidi Holland, 'South Africa is a gigantic psychiatric unit. With so many of us, whites as well as blacks, failing to acknowledge let alone wrestle with our wounded psyches, we are not so much a nation in decline following great expectations, but a traumatized people constantly hovering between depression and delusion.' South Africa still is the most developed country in the continent, thanks in no small part ironically to the architects of its apartheid past, but the gulf between the early rhetoric and the current reality is stark. Blacks and Afrikaan speaking blacks and coloureds are still largely absent from the private sector. Few of them find places at leading institutions of learning.

To redress the balance, the Mbeki government has enacted the Black Economic Empowerment program to increase black presence in the economic sector through affirmative action and reserved quotas. There is some progress, but also much abuse. The well-to-do and the well-connected benefit, I am told, but that is the reality everywhere. Behind many successful black businessmen is some white or Indian person, people remark. Some coloured leaders are calling for an end to the racially oriented affirmative action programs. Alan Boesak, the anti-apartheid activist who fell from grace during the dying days of apartheid, is another one of them: Such programs are entrenching divisions and institutionalizing racism he says, and warns the country of the dangers of 'flirting with ethnicity.' 'The ANC,' he says, 'has succumbed to the subtle but pernicious temptations of ethnic thinking, has brought back the language of ethnicity into the speech of the movement and has as government brought back the hated system of racial categorization.'

That may all be true, but the political reality (numbers alone) demands active engagement with black issues and concerns, however contentious these might be. Not to do so would be political suicide. The political mathematics is really as simple as that. The stark reality is that black poverty stares you squarely in the face in hundreds upon hundreds of informal black settlements throughout the country; rotting, overcrowded corrugated tin shacks often without running water, electricity or other amenities. South Africa will have to pay penance for the neglect and abuse of the past for a very long time, and minority communities will have to sacrifice their share for national reconciliation and healing if they are to live with honour and security in the emerging new order. Aspiring black leaders are already demanding greater black empowerment.

The past has a palpable presence in South Africa's present. Parts of the country are pure first world where the supermarkets are well stocked with goods and gadgets of all kinds, the kind available in western supermarkets anywhere in the world. The roads are wide and clean, homes have swimming pools and well manicured lawns maintained by black servants. Travelling through parts of Pretoria or Cape Town, you could be excused for thinking you were in Sydney or Melbourne. These are your former exclusively white areas. But other areas, especially in the suburbs and outskirts of cities, would be replicas of the most squalid areas of human habitation found in the poorest countries of the developing world: roads narrow and pot-holed and strewn with rubbish, foul smell from overgrown drains, houses of tin shacks.

The contrast between black and white in wealth and opportunity is deeply confronting, but the disparity is no accident of history. It is, in fact, a deliberate product of the apartheid regime which was born when South Africa declared itself a republic in 1948. A cornerstone of the apartheid system was the Group Areas Act which stipulated complete residential segregation of the different races, purely on the grounds of race, nothing else. On paper, the proposal may have looked only mildly offensive: people asked to live with their own kind in their own designated areas; but in practice, the system was nothing but pernicious. The whites got the best, most developed areas, with the best infrastructure, schools, hospitals, public service and the like, and they fought for its complete retention. The non-whites, especially blacks and Indians, were uprooted from urban areas where they had lived for generations and sent to completely new and often inhospitable places to start afresh. And they started with a huge handicap. Their newly established schools and hospitals were under-staffed and under-funded; employment opportunities were few and far between, and poverty hovered around the edges. There has been some improvement in recent years, but the markers of South Africa's iniquitous past are still visible.

It may not be true now, but for a long time, South Africa had the largest Indian population outside South Asia. At nearly a million strong, it is certainly the world's largest Indian community descended from Indian indentured migration. About 160,000 Indian indentured labourers went to South Africa (Natal) between 1860 and 1911, a part of nearly one million who crossed the *kala pani* (the dark, dreaded ocean) to work in the 'King Sugar' colonies across the globe. But unlike other sugar colonies, the majority of South Africa's indentured came from South India (which traditionally supplied labour to the neighbouring areas in Southeast Asia). Today, the South Indians constitute the majority of the Indian population. In Fiji, being late comers and a minority, the South Indians had to adjust themselves to the dominant north Indian culture, bearing the brunt of their cultural prejudices about colour and caste. Their darker skin, food habits and language all provoked derisive comment from the northerners who called them *khatta pani*, eaters of sour (inferior) food. In Natal, I am amused to learn, the Southern Indians have taken their revenge, referring to their northern compatriots derisively as *roti*, people not up to much good! The shoe was firmly on the other foot.

My introduction to the Indian community in Natal came during my first year at university through Hilda Kuper's wonderful book, *Indians in Natal*. It was the first book on another overseas Indian community I had read, and it made a deep impression on me: black and white pictures of men and women wearing familiar dress and with familiar names (Chinsami, Gangamma), performing rituals and ceremonies which seemed vaguely similar to our own, men working on the sugar estates that resembled our own CSR farms. Kuper led me to other ethnographers of that golden age of overseas Indian anthropology: Arthur and Juanita Niehoff, Morton Klass, Burton Benedict, Chandra Jayawardena and Raymond Smith. The great Adrian Mayer, the author of the incomparable *Peasants in the Pacific* about our own community, I already knew but, after Kuper, in a renewed kind of a way.

The South African Indian community is at the back of my mind as we plan our African trip. It is, in fact, the principal reason for our visit to Durban where most of them still live. The contrast with Fiji is unmistakable. Sugar dominated our life and determined our patterns of occupation and residence for nearly a century. Large numbers of our people still variously depend on the industry and many families continue to live in the sugar belt. In South Africa, few renewed their indentures once these had expired. Most escaped to urban centres as soon as they could to secure sources of livelihood other than agriculture. They were replaced on the sugar estates by black Africans. And so it remains. Indenture for South African Indians, as for the Fiji Indians, was a limited detention and not a life sentence, although poverty and insecurity are still the constant companions for many.

Among the urban Indians, the vernacular languages are gone, especially Hindi; Tamil and Telugu and Gujarati are spoken by the older generation, but the language will go with them. English is for all practical purposes the main language of both public and private communication. I note the fluency and flair with which many on the radio and television speak it, the legacy no doubt of good English education at the country's elite schools. There is a Radio

Mirchi, like the one in Fiji, but the announcers speak English and the songs are modern re-mixes which are completely unknown to me. Food has changed, but not unrecognizably so. Every town and city has its 'Indian' restaurants serving generic Indian food of the type available anywhere else in the world. There is some creative reckoning with the past through novels and poems, but nothing compared to the output in the Caribbean, or even Fiji. The apartheid regime crippled the creative spirit. But with the liberation has come a new confidence· which may yet translate into something. Ashwin Desai and Goolam Vahed have made a brilliant start with their *Inside Indenture*, a pioneering study of the lived indenture experience in South Africa, an original work of singular importance.

Amidst all the unfamiliarity of the surroundings, though, there are some pleasant discoveries. I am on the lookout for South African Indian music. In Holland a month earlier, I had picked up a dozen or so compact discs of Sarnami songs (*Baithak Gana*: rustic songs sung to the accompaniment of elementary musical instruments) which had reminded me of the music of my childhood. I wondered if I could make a similar discovery in Natal. I did indeed. In a rundown Indian shopping area in one of the outer suburbs of Durban, I came across a shop selling local music. I was particularly intrigued by the *Pachara* songs. At first, the words and the rhythmic tune seemed vaguely familiar; but then, suddenly, it all came to me. *Pacharas*, I remembered, were songs of trance sung by *ojhas* (spirit men) in the village to recall village or family deities (*gram* and *kul devtas*) to identify the cause of some misfortune in the family or to get some sense of impending events which might being harm. It was all very mysterious and fear-inducing: fear of what I cannot now say, but I recall with particular horror the most notorious spirit man of all, Sibda Badal from Wainikoro, a hunchback with the power, so people said, to bring whole families down, to cause the death of animals and people, just like that. Listening to the songs brought back memories of childhood which until then I had completely forgotten.

The Indian community in South Africa is as divided by class, culture and historical experience, as it is elsewhere. The descendants of Indian indentured labourers still live principally in the KwaZulu Natal region. Johannesburg has a large and moderately prosperous cluster of Gujaratis who came as artisans and traders later, as happened in Fiji. An overarching, and in truth an artificial, sense of 'Indianness' was imposed by the apartheid regime which treated all Indians as a homogenous group for administrative purposes. Under the Group Areas Act, they were all without exception banished segregated residential settlements on the outer fringes of white-dominated urban areas. I had assumed that such enforced relocation, a sudden rupture of communities and relationships established over long period, would be a traumatic experience for those affected by it.

That it was in many places, but I heard a different story in Johannesburg. There, the Indians were removed from the city precincts to a newly opened Indian settlement called Len Asia. In the city, Vivek, our elderly Gujarati guide, tells us, Indians ran their businesses on rented properties and the women folk stayed at home to look after the family. But in the new settlement, homes had to be built or bought, and everyone had to work to make ends meet. One result of the increased pressure was that more Gujarati girls completed school and more women joined the workforce, as they had to. In a curious and unpredictable way, segregation had led to the Gujarati women's liberation! I was inclined to see the South African Gujarati experience through my Fijian lenses, but was soon disabused of my preconceptions. The Gujarati community in Fiji is still pretty self-contained and generally inward looking, though less now than before. People play at caste, and marriage within one's caste is still considered desirable. In South Africa, caste plays little role in social affairs, and marriages outside the community are common, or at least not a topic of disapproving comment. This greater openness of the community came about in a curious and not altogether voluntary way. During the apartheid years, immigration from India was prohibited because of India's position on the apartheid regime, so marriages perforce had to be arranged within the community in South Africa. And the marriage circle widened as the range of choices within the community diminished and as education and employment opportunities expanded, making caste a largely irrelevant factor. This is beginning to take place in Fiji, too, but so far in a small way.

In Durban, we saw the darker side of enforced racial segregation under the Group Areas Act. We were taken to Chatsworth, a forty-year old Indian settlement on the unlovely outer fringes of Durban by Ashwin and Goolam. With a population of over three hundred thousand, Chatsworth is still predominantly Indian, but now also with a sprinkling of blacks. Chatsworth would have to be one of the most depressing areas I have ever seen in my life: and I have seen a fair bit. In dreary blocks of low cost housing of the type we have in Fiji (Raiwaqa), entire families live together in single and double room flats with few amenities and very little privacy. How they manage to make do in such small, cramped space is beyond my comprehension. There is drug trafficking here, Ashwin tells us, sexual abuse, domestic violence and, as we can see, unimaginable poverty. We meet brave women, such as Girlie Arnod, who have struggled all their lives to keep their family life intact. But the struggle has taken its toll, and many have given up hope. A single issue of the Chatsworth tabloid carries headlines which capture the grim reality of this place: 'Tragedy Hits New Trade School as Roof Collapses on Labourers,' 'Police Crack Down on Robbers in Chats,' 'Drug Addiction Grows Among Scholars,' 'Drive By Suspect Threatens Witness From Prison Court.'

Chatsworth is not a site of liberation as Len Asia marginally was. In Len Asia, the people have at least built a semblance of a community. In Chatsworth, the housing scheme allowed only for nuclear families with the result that extended families and communities built up over generations were sundered. Gone at a stroke of the pen were bonds 'based on trust, friendship, sociability, obligation and mutual support overlaid with a framework of kinship and religious norms,' writes Ashwin Desai. This site of abject desperation offers little hope. We are told that the younger generation of Chatsworth has no hope of finding employment. They will forever remain on the margins of society, living on the meagre charity provided by the state and the crumbs they pick from the table. As we leave the settlement, a young man sitting on a wooden crate and flipping through the pages of the local daily (advertising goods that will remain outside the reach of the people here) looks up at Padma and says forlornly: 'Please find me a job, any job.' That haunting image remains with her. It is not so much the poverty as the absence of opportunity, any opportunity, which is the real bane of life in Chatsworth.

Apartheid is gone, but the hope its end spawned has failed to materialize. The 'multitude that brought down the apartheid regime,' writes Ashwin, 'had a millennial faith in the exiled and imprisoned leadership of the ANC. The multitude that brought the ANC to power with millions of acts of rebellion, from strikes to burning barricades to refusing to stay and pay and obey, became (just slightly fractious) people under the ANC. This may seem a harsh indictment, but this certainly seems to be the lot of the people of Chatsworth and the hundreds of informal black settlements mushrooming across the length and breadth of South Africa.

I am interested in how the Indians see their future in South Africa. There is no clear-cur answer. Among the older generation, there is some nostalgia for the peace and order that existed during the apartheid regime. Referring to the bourgeoning crime rate in urban areas (Johannesburg is the crime capital of the world, I learn), a man says to me: 'Then they were in and we were out. Now, they are out and we are in.' He means the criminals are freely roaming the streets while ordinary law abiding citizens live barricaded behind bars. Nearly everyone talks about the rampant corruption being a pervasive feature of South African public life. 'In the old days, they stole from the till,' Vivek says to me, 'but now they are stealing the till itself.'

Vivek is disillusioned, but not embittered. A retired primary school teacher in his seventies, he lived through the horrors of the darkest days of apartheid and does not mourn its passing. 'At least we are free now,' he says, 'free to do whatever we want, including making mistakes.' Jaya, a graceful old Gujarati lady who has travelled the world and who speaks beautiful English, says proudly,

'This is my country, the best place in the world. I will live nowhere else.' There is something deeply touching about this enduring fondness for one's place of birth and childhood memories.

Vivek's and Jaya's attachment is understandable. They have been a part of South Africa's history. Vivek lives in Mayfair, a formerly all-white area within a stone's throw of the central business district of Johannesburg. He points out to us the infamous police stations and magistrates' courts where generations of blacks and anti-apartheid activists were incarcerated. He talks wistfully about the contribution the Indians made to the anti-apartheid cause. The names of the most illustrious ones are legion: Mac Maharaj, Ahmed Kathrada, Dullah Omar, Fatima Meer, and many others. Mahatma Gandhi was, of course, the first Indian to challenge the racial order of the white colonial empire in South Africa. But all that seems to belong to another era now: maybe not obliterated, but overshadowed by the emphasis on black power, black struggle and black contribution. 'Once we were not white enough,' a man says to me, referring to the privileges denied to them because of their less than fair (brown) skin. 'And now we are not black enough.' These words powerfully underline the Indian ambivalence in contemporary South Africa.

It is reinforced by a report we read in *Sunday Times* of a former police cell in the northern KwaZulu town of Dundee where the Mahatma was detained in 1913 being converted into toilets and a storeroom, Superintendent Gail De Mork says she was not aware that 'this was a site of such importance.' Businessman Dharam Maharaj wants action, for his people to 'take a stand against this arid come together as a community to restore this site,' but nothing is likely to happen. Gandhi's Phoenix Farm, the place where the Mahatma launched some of his great human experiments with Truth, us he put it, now lies in a slum of heart-breaking poverty and destitution, and looked after by a black caretaker. When I raise the issue with Vivek, he tells me what young people are saying: 'What did Gandhi do for us?' The younger generation of Indians in cities like Johannesburg and Durban are carving a niche for themselves in the professions and in the public sector. Politics is left alone. It is too corrupt, they say, too remote to their daily concerns which centre around their families' welfare and future above everything else. They have little awareness of their past, of the sacrifices and struggles of their forebears. But the South African Indians are not alone in this. This ignorance and amnesia is global, and by no means confined to Indians alone.

As we leave South Africa, I have the distinct sense that for many young Indians, while South Africa will be the home of their parents and grandparents, it won't be the home for their children. They are already talking of London and

Perth and Melbourne, and a dozen other Western cities, as the destinations of choice for the next generation. Many have made plans to move one day, as has happened in other places with substantial Indian populations, such as Fiji, Guyana and Surinam, South Africa, too, will empty of its Indian population. It appears inevitable that the Indian presence will gradually vanish from the collective consciousness into the margins of a distantly remembered past. 'From Immigration to Emigration' may in time also become the epitaph of the South Africa's Indian community, as it has of so many countries of the *girmit* diaspora.

# Eighteen

## Sairusi, Tom, Mr Bechu Prasad, Sir Paul Reeves

Sairusi Nabogibogi. The name will mean little to the present generation of Fijians. But to those of us marching lock, stock and barrel into niggling middle age, the name was synonymous with violence, terror and unspeakable criminality. It was fearsome enough to send unruly children into blanket-wrapped silence in the menacing darkness of their thatched houses. Sairusi was a man of many parts: a charismatic criminal, a serial prison escapist, a proto-Fijian nationalist fiercely opposed to colonial rule and European dominance, a self-confessed admirer of Mahatma Gandhi and Kenneth Kaunda of Zambia, a fiction writer of talent, a self-proclaimed messiah and divinely ordained saviour of his people, in short a man of destiny. He was the undoubted hero of the Fijian underworld of the 1950s and 60s, much as Apolosi Nawai had been at the beginning of the 20th century. Now this once feared man and all that he claimed to stand for survives only in the fading memories of a passing generation.

Sairusi Nabogibogi, 5ft 8in tall, built a bit like the heavyweight boxer Sonny Liston with the 'same air of brooding menace,' as reporter Matt Wilson put it, was born on 2 September 1932 at Nakawakawa, Wainunu, Bua, son of Miriama Kadrudru of Nakawakawa and Josefa Nabogibogi from Nayavutoka, Ra. When he was only three, his father saw a vision of Sairusi as a returning messiah marked for great things. But his early career was unremarkable. He was educated at Ratu Kadavaulevu School and the Queen Victoria School, where Apisai Tora was among his contemporaries and with whom he formed a life-long, but not trouble-free, association. From high school, Sairusi went to the Nasinu Training College, but was expelled in 1949 for allegedly loitering around the women's dormitory. Sairusi protested the drastic sentence, especially, he said, when other similar offenders were let off lightly or went unpunished. But as Sairusi was Sairusi, his fate was sealed. He told the Controller of Prisons later that 'it was at this point he made up his mind deliberately to become Fiji's worst-ever criminal.' I am not sure if Sairusi used the word 'criminal' to describe himself—probably not—but that is what the records report.

Sairusi's first serious brush with the law came in 1951 when he was charged with criminal trespass and larceny. He pleaded guilty and was sentenced to nine months imprisonment. Released from prison on 10 May 1952, Sairusi returned to his old ways, becoming a 'confirmed and expert burglar,' in the words of the Fiji Intelligence Service which described him as the 'smartest Fijian criminal in Suva.' Throughout the 1950s, Sairusi continued to tempt fate and live dangerously at the edge. But his luck ran out when he was charged for a series of sexual assaults on European women in Suva. He denied the charge before the Suva Magistrate's Court, claiming that he was being framed for his political beliefs, but he was convicted and committed to the Supreme Court for sentence. On 21 July 1958, Chief Justice Sir George Lowe, who would later chair the inquiry into the 1959 riots in Suva, sentenced Sairusi to eight years' imprisonment and ordered that he, Sairusi, be kept under police surveillance for five years after his release. Sairusi appealed his sentence, without success. That embittered him deeply. He felt that 'he had been savagely treated' without being given a chance to reform. It was not only what Sairusi allegedly did that terrified the establishment; it was what it represented in the closed world of colonial society—a potent mix of race and sex and violence, a fear of the other, the crossing of sacrosanct boundaries—that perhaps weighed even more heavily on the minds of the officialdom. An example had to be made of him to deter others.

Incarcerated, Sairusi decided that he would not be a 'normal' prison inmate. He was sent to Suva Gaol but accused of trying to organise a breakout among the prisoners, was transferred to the Natabua Prison in Lautoka in April 1959. The transfer did not help. Sairusi quickly established himself as 'the acknowledged leader of the prisoners,' who was 'virtually in charge of the gaol.' How did this come about? Because Sairusi became a champion of racial equality. 'When I went there [to prison], Fijians and Indians had a piece of sack to sleep on and one blanket, that's all,' he recalled in 1972, while European and Part-European inmates had mattresses, pillows and bed sheets. 'We were all prisoners and we should all have had the same facilities.' His agitation paid dividends, which endeared him to his inmates. He continued to break out almost at will, under the nose of the prison wardens, and return to his cell with cigarettes, books, and liquor. His cell, 7ft by 8ft, with a wooden bed and nothing else, became his sanctuary. 'I did not listen to the radio,' he recalled. 'Sometimes I read all night.' He refused release from solitary confinement half way through his sentence because 'I wanted to be by myself and think and read.'

While in prison, Sairusi even managed to acquire a revolver and ammunition, though police also suspected someone else (his name I withhold) of being his accomplice. On 21 September, Sairusi appeared before the Senior Magistrate in

Lautoka on two counts of burglary and one of causing actual bodily harm, and sentenced to four years imprisonment. Sairusi, ever determined to be his own man, railing at the world around him, did not mend his ways. Perhaps he could not. He kept breaking out, flouting prison regulation. Rules and regulations and prison walls were for lesser mortals, not for him. Living dangerously, he paid the price. On 19 January 1960, Sairusi was sentenced to a further year's imprisonment for breaking out of prison (and meeting other known criminals at the Lautoka Cemetery at night). Soon afterwards, he escaped from Natabua Gaol altogether.

On the run, Sairusi met up with an Indo-Fijian, let's call him Bhaggu, a notorious Lautoka-born criminal operating in the Sabeto area, a kind of Al Capone, the police said, a 'truly wicked man [who] operated an extremely profitable murder racket.' Together, Bhaggu and Sairusi wreaked havoc in the cane belt, breaking-in, threatening violence, cowering people into submission on behalf of whoever paid them. Bhaggu, the hired gun, was convicted of gun running in 1963, and sentenced to eight years imprisonment (reduced on appeal to four years). Released in 1966, he was murdered by a young neighbour. Those who live by the sword die by the sword, you might say. On 12 July 1960, the Commissioner Western, Mr McAlpine, was shot while getting out of his car at his house in Lautoka. The police reported that the would-be assassin fired one round from a single-barrelled shot gun at point blank range hitting McAlpine in the stomach. As he lay doubled over, he fired another hurried shot missing him, and then ran away. McAlpine survived but had to be invalided out of colonial service. All fingers pointed to Sairusi as the suspected assailant, though probably the incident was masterminded by Bhaggu himself. No evidence linked Sairusi to the shooting, nor to the shooting of a Sabeto farmer, Varun Deo (not his real name) as he held his one year daughter in his hands. In the post-war years, Sabeto had the reputation as one of the most murderous places in Fiji, and especially dangerous during the bitter sugar cane strike of 1960. McAlpine's shooting was, I suspect, linked to it.

Meanwhile, Sairusi's reputation for performing mysterious deeds escalated. Many thought he was a magician. As the police reported, 'it was even rumoured that he had a cloak which, when he put it on, rendered him invisible.' Some even believed that 'he could walk through walls as and when he wishes.' At any rate, he was deemed a sufficient enough menace to be befriended (though probably not bought) by some Lautoka businessmen, as well as some prominent Fijians in the civil service who shared Sairusi's anti-European views, including Apisai Tora and Ratu Mosese Varasikete. Even SM Koya, who often represented criminals in court in the1960s, was reported credibly to have been in touch with Sairusi.

On 4 October 1960, at Apisai Tora's request, Ratu Penaia Ganilau, then Deputy Secretary for Fijian Affairs, flew over to Lautoka to meet Sairusi. Sairusi had sought an audience with the high chief to deny any involvement in the shooting of McAlpine and Bhaggu and to demand a retrial of the 1958 court case against him. Nothing came of the meeting, which soured Sairusi's attitude towards the Fijian hierarchy even further. He was convinced that he was more wronged against than wrong.

Sairusi then escaped to Suva, crashing through a police barrier at Lami. Once there, he again found himself in the familiar company of looters and criminals. 'I really suffered during those ten months,' he recalled. 'Being an escaper is like living in a glass house. Everyone is watching you.' His run ended on 31 March 1961, when acting on information, the police captured him at his father's house in Raiwai. Although armed with a .22 rifle, Sairusi surrendered without a struggle. He pleaded guilty to unlawful escape from custody before the Acting Senior Magistrate on 22 May, but insisted that he had been punished for crimes he had not committed in the first place. 'All sons of Fiji should get the same treatment whether red, black, white or yellow,' he told the court. 'My chiefs have let me down and this should stand as a guide for the future generations that they should not rely on any one person but only on the Almighty God.' His reference to chiefs perhaps recalled his fruitless meeting with Ratu Sir Penaia.

Sairusi was sentenced and sent to the Suva Gaol under maximum security. He was mellower now, not the daredevil of his younger days. But his resentment at alleged unfair treatment remained. On 15 July 1962, a Minister taking a Sunday service in the prison, convinced that Sairusi was on the mend, asked him to lead the prisoners in prayer. Grabbing the opportunity, Sairusi 'gave a vehement plea to the Almighty to deliver the Fijians from European bondage.' From then on, there were no more sermons for Sairusi. A letter he wrote to the Visiting Justice of Prison on 17 May 1965 indicates that revenge was very much on Sairusi's mind:

> A prisoner will never forget the person who began the whole procedure that brought his disgrace and captivity. And that person in most cases is the policeman. In his heart, the prisoner shall be nursing his hatred while at the same time he is thinking of ways and means for revenge. He will be hoping some day, somehow, somewhere, he will have a chance to give the policeman what he deserves.

Mercifully, Sairusi was never again given that chance. Soon after writing the letter, Sairusi was examined by the government psychiatrist, Dr D.F. MacGregor.

Was Sairusi mad, delusional? No, Dr MacGregor concluded. Instead of suffering from mental or nervous illness, Sairusi believed 'himself to be a righteous man pursuing righteous causes and that he is for these reasons above the law.' He 'regards the law of this land as something imposed by arbitrary action upon a reluctant people and does not regard it as binding upon him.' Sairusi, MacGregor said, was no ordinary man. On the contrary, he found him to be 'sane, highly intelligent, forceful, charming, ruthless and utterly without regard for the law or for the rights of others if these conflict with his own wishes.' Dr. Macgregor continued: 'There is a field of human abnormality in which a person is not quite like others and yet suffers from no actual disease of mind; he might be regarded as falling within this category but medical science is powerless to influence such people and I have no medical recommendations to make.' Sairusi recalled Macgregor telling him that if he, Sairusi, did not end up in St. Giles, he would end up as president of Fiji one day. 'Interesting, isn't it,' he laughed.

Sairusi occupied his restless mind with other things. While in the Suva Gaol, he wrote a novel, *Tawa Cava* (Immortal) set during World War Two. Those who read it saw in the novel Sairusi's 'deep pride in his own race and considerable anti-government and anti-European feeling.' In 1967, Sairusi entered a short story under the nom de plum 'Viti Viti Kabasi' to the Fiji Arts Council Literary Award, and won the second prize. The nom de plum, Sairusi said, meant 'the sound of the snapping twig is like a compass which points one as to which direction the object of the noise is.' He received visitors—Meli Baleilakeba, GO Parr, and Sir Maurice Scott—and kept abreast of political developments outside the prison walls. He told a police constable early in 1968 that the Alliance Party under Ratu Mara (as he then was) had let Fijians down. Some in the Federation Party tried to entice him to their fold, but Sairusi would have no truck with them either, unlike Apisai Tora—with whom Sairusi had fallen out at the end—who had joined an 'Indian' political party he had once pilloried.

Released from prison in 1969 under a compulsory supervision order, Sairusi Nabogibogi returned to his father's village Nayavutoka in Ra. He contested the 1972 general elections on a nationalist platform (anticipating Sakeasi Butadroka's ideas by several years), for the Ba-East-Ra seat, but lost, winning only 1300 votes of some 9500 votes cast. In 1977, he stood for the Ra-Samabula-Suva Fijian communal constituency for his party, the Fijian Conservative Party, but was equally unsuccessful, collecting only 1862 of the 7540 of the Fijian votes cast. Sairusi was concerned about the future of his people. 'In 100 years there may not be any full-blooded Fijians left,' he said, 'I hope my chiefs are worrying about the same thing too and do something about it. I hope they do, from the bottom of my heart.' Racial miscegenation was a real worry to him. He wanted Fijian chiefs to forbid 'Fijians marrying other races,' stop them dressing like the other races. 'The more we inter-marry, the quicker we are gone,' he said. And lack of Fijian economic progress caused pain as well. 'I am ashamed when I come to Suva. It does not belong to the Fijians. Does anything belong to the Fijians in the city? Does any business house belong to any Fijian? I walk in the streets here and I bend my head down. I am ashamed that I have nothing in this town.' Sairusi spoke words which many Fijians would have recognised, expressing a sentiment many would have shared.

Aside from politics, Sairusi focussed his energy on establishing a communitarian self-help movement—the Messiah Movement—at Salemi, Nakorotubu in coastal Ra. Sairusi himself was the Messiah, the King. Salemi from Jerusalem. His own separate compound was called 'Salaam,' the Arabic word for peace. Accounts vary about what the Movement stood for, but it was broadly akin to the kibbutz: all for one and one for all, share and care altogether. It sought to instil discipline and a strict work ethic among the youth (Cauravou ni Salemi). Labour was strictly supervised, responsibilities carefully apportioned, a planned program of daily routine observed, people held accountable for the performance of their duties. Classes were held and attended by young and old. English was taught, but Fijian culture and tradition received special emphasis, because, Sairusi believed, they were in danger of being lost, corrupted by alien influences. The individual work ethic, with all that it entailed, was not for him or his people. Indeed, everything done at Salemi was done within the framework of Fijian culture, or a particular version of it, under Sairusi's presiding genius. He had many followers across the country who were enticed by his vision for a pristine pastoral community, hypnotised by his charismatic personality. Sairusi's hold on his followers was such that they refused to believe that he had died. They kept his body erect against the wall for several days before they finally buried him. Some still believe, to this day, that he will return as their messiah.

It is tempting to view Sairusi Nabogibogi as a maverick, an odd ball, albeit a dangerous one. He was probably that, and more—and less. Sairusi was no saint. That he himself would admit. He was a complex, conflicted character. Viewed historically, he belongs to a long list of dissident Fijians swimming against the currents of their time and the tenets of their own society. His deeds and thoughts bring to mind the name of Apolosi Nawai at the turn of the 20th century, a strong-willed person convinced of his own righteousness and manifest destiny, railing against a world he was convinced was out to get him, and determined to set things right by his own light. The fire he tried to light flickered for a while. Now it is part of a past vanishing beyond recall.

INTERSECTIONS

### Tomasi Rayalu Vakatora

I received the news of Mr Tomasi Vakatora's passing away on Tuesday evening in Lautoka while on a lecturing assignment there. It saddened me immensely. Tom—as he insisted on being called- was a wise and trusted friend and my 'partner-in-crime' on the Reeves Commission. In his passing, Fiji has lost one of its truly illustrious sons.

Tom Vakatora was no ordinary Fijian. He was a distinguished member of that greatest generation of Fijian civil servants ever to have worked for Fiji. Coming of age in the post-war era, they played an invaluable role in effecting Fiji's smooth transition from colony to independence.

Their names are legion: Semesa Sikivou, Josefata and Esiteri Kamikamica, Filipe Bole and Taufa Vakatale, Savenaca and Suliana Siwatibau, Mosese Qionibaravi, Isireli Lasaqa, Rusiate Nayacakalou. The list is long, and I apologise for omissions.

Tom Vakatora's range of accomplishments was awe-inspiring. He was born on 18 September 1926 at Naivalaca, Noco in Rewa, and educated the Noco District School, Suva Methodist Boy's School, Lelean Memorial School, Nasinu Teachers Training College and briefly at Ruskin College, Oxford and the London School of Economics. With more encouragement and support from officialdom, he could have gone on to complete his university degree. He regretted the missed opportunity.

He began his career as a primary school teacher in 1948, resigning to join the Labour Department in 1955. There he rose rapidly, reaching the rank of Permanent Secretary and Commissioner of Labour in 1969, one of the very few locals to attain such distinction then. He retired from the civil service as Permanent Secretary of Works and Tourism in 1974.

A brief stint in the Senate was followed by his election to the House of Representatives in April 1976. There over the years, he served in a range of ministries before being appointed Speaker of the House from 1982-1987. After the coups, he served in Ratu Mara's interim administration, becoming Deputy Prime Minister and Minister of Finance and Economic Development in 1992.

Tom's cv would be the envy of almost everyone, but his greatest achievement was yet to come—as member of the three-person Fiji Constitution Review Commission headed by Sir Paul Reeves. For his enormous contribution to that mammoth task, his place is secure in the history books.

I first met Tom Vakatora in March 1995 at the VIP House at Berkeley Crescent, on our way to being sworn in as commissioners at the Government House. He was formal and forbidding, as I had been warned he might be. A man of explosive temper, people had said, hard to get along with. 'Mr Vakatora,' I said as I extended my arm for a handshake. 'Tom,' he said firmly.

The next day, after the first formal and largely friendly session of the Commission's proceedings, I said to Tom sitting across the table: 'Well, Tom, there is no blood on the floor.' 'Not yet,' he replied with a straight face. My goodness me, I said to myself, what have I let myself into. When I mentioned this episode to him many months later, he laughed and said that was his way of assessing me, testing my strength.

Tom's vast experience assisted the Commission's early planning work. He insisted, and we all readily agreed, that we disregard the advice of many political leaders that the Commission should not hold wide-ranging consultations throughout the country but peruse submissions made to previous commissions and make recommendations on that basis. We were proved right. The public consultations provided a great forum for soul searching national dialogue on the political future of the country.

As we travelled and talked, both Tom and I realized that there were more things that united the different and diverse communities of Fiji than those which divided them. Make no mistake: he was a very proud Fijian, unmistakably, unapologetically so; but he also realized that the destinies of our people were inseparably intertwined. He wanted to find a solution to our political difficulties that would address the concerns of all communities.

We were lucky in having Sir Paul Reeves as our chairman. A graceful, generous man, he said to Tom and me that if we came up with a united position on any issue, he would not stand in our way. He encouraged us to talk among ourselves. We did. Tom treated with complete respect even though I was much younger than him. He had a huge respect for protocol and the rules of engagement.

One long weekend, Tom and I spent long hours at *The Fijian* exploring together the fears, interests and aspirations of the communities we represented on the Commission. Out of that prolonged, sometimes tense (but never acrimonious) discussion emerged a consensus, committed to paper, which laid the foundation for our future thinking on the most important issues we had to resolve. The only thing Tom regretted about that weekend was that I did not play golf. But I was forgiven, because I was his friend.

Some Fijian leaders said harsh, hurtful things about Tom after the Commission had finished its work, that he had somehow, somewhere, sold out the Fijian people, that he was asleep on the job, clueless. But Tom was unfazed, convinced in his soul that he had done the right thing. His conscience was clear. His, and the Commission's, vision stands vindicated. His critics now acknowledge their error of judgment.

Tom was a strong man, but a large part of his inner strength came from two things he cherished most in his life: his family and his faith. He was a loving father and an indulgent grandfather. And he could not have found a more companionable and supportive partner than Wai. Despite all his achievements, Tom never forgot his roots, nor his near and distant relatives whom he visited in Noco whenever he could. He was a large, enduring presence in their lives.

I have many memories of Tom: happy on good red, celebrating Diwali at our home in Canberra; of him teaching my then tiny son how to tie a fish hook and then watching him fish from the banks of Lake Burly Griffin; of the thigh-slapping stories he told with his impish sense of humour, of introducing me to the cultural complexities of his people, of fondly introducing Padma to a group from his village as 'vuniwai ni tiri tiri,' because her dissertation was on Fiji mangroves, of him and Filipe Bole, fuelled by ample amber liquid, singing Fijian songs late into the night at his home.

But my most enduring memory is of the day before we submitted our report when he skippered a boat to the Nasilai Reef, with Wai, Padma and me in it, to the place where the Syria was wrecked in 1884, causing the death of 59 girmitiyas. He asked a man from his village who had joined us to retrieve two pieces from the rusting wreckage. He gave me one and kept the other for himself. 'My people saved your people then,' he said. 'Now, you and I can save all our people together.' A wonderful but daunting sentiment.

To that endeavour of saving his deeply divided nation, he made a distinguished contribution. And for that, he will be honoured for as long as people remember.

### Mr Bechu Prasad

Mr Bechu Prasad's death has touched the nation. There is universal sadness that he is no longer with us. Babuji, as he was known affectionately, touched our hearts not only because he was the oldest living person in Fiji. That was certainly a part of the reason for the huge popularity he enjoyed in all our communities.

But he had other qualities that caused admiration. He was a true son of the soil. He was a dedicated farmer, and a man of immense discipline. Farming was for him a way of life of which he was proud. He belonged to that generation of farmers who looked to Mother Earth not only for what it could give them, but what they could back in return. Babuji was a model farmer who could well serve as an inspiration for our and future generation. The sad irony, he once said, was that while he liked farming, the younger generation did not like farm work.

Babuji never gave up. In 1984, Cyclone Eric destroyed his home, his prized possessions scattered around the village. But instead of feeling sorry for himself, Babuji helped government officials distribute ration and other assistance to the people. His concern always was for his fellow human beings.

His love for Sabeto was well known. But beyond that was his enduring love for Fiji. Once a young reporter asked him about Fiji. This is what he said: 'This is my mother country. The same place you live in, the same place I live in. You must think about that. My mother and father came to this country. They work hard here. Where can we go? Tell me. We must stay here and die here. No other place. That's the important part. We must remember that.' In his passionate, unquestioning love for the land of his birth, Babuji could also act as an inspiration for the younger generation.

Babuji lived a long and bountiful life. He was born during the *girmit* era. His parents were indentured labourers. At small age, he witnessed their suffering, their hardship at first hand. Then, as a young man, he saw his people pick up the pieces and start life as independent farmers on small plots of land. He lived through the era of the CSR and Colonial Rule. He saw Fiji become independent. And he saw us falter. But his faith in this country and all its people did not diminish. He believed right to the end that with enough goodwill, we could overcome the adversities we face and make this land of ours a paradise for all. In this respect, too, he taught us a lesson.

Babuji was proud of his heritage. But he was not blinded by it. His circle of friends extended across our multiethnic communities. He regarded Ratu Sir Lala Sukuna as a father figure, a great model for leaders. Ratu Sir Lala visited him often whenever he was in the west. Ratu Sir Kamisese Mara listened respectfully to his views about the problems of the farming community. In fact, he was only one of two men in the Indo-Fijian community—the other was Swami Rudrananda—who could 'lecture' to the Prime Minister without giving offense. Such was the affection and trust he inspired in people. Only Babuji could tell Prince Charles to his face that when he sat down in his house, there should be no talk of politics!

Babuji was a man of the people. He gave selflessly to all who needed his help. He was president and manager of Sabeto Indian School for 70 years. He served as Lautoka Indian Advisory Council chairman from 1937 to the late 1990s. He was a member of the Liquor Board and Indian Advisor to the Native Land Trust Board. He served as a member of the Nadi Hospital Board and as Cane Growers Councillor for the Natova Sector in the first Council elected in 1985. The list is extensive and impressive.

It is no wonder that Babuji received many awards and honours for his community service: The Coronation Medal (1953), the Justice of the Peace Medal in 1956, Certificate of Honour in 1959, the Independence Medal in 1970, the MBE in 1973 and the 25th Anniversary of Independence Medal in 1996. He appreciated these awards, but they did not affect his work or inflate his ego. He continued to work for the greater good of the community.

Prejudice and narrow-mindedness were alien to his nature. That is why our people feel that they have lost someone near and dear, a family member. But as we mourn Babuji's passing away, we also celebrate his long and distinguished innings, his passionate love for Fiji, his deep faith in his fellow human beings, his life of service. Babuji, we salute you and are proud of you.

### Sir Paul Reeves and Fiji

Two weeks before he died, Sir Paul Reeves wrote to me to say that he had cancer and might not be able to overcome it. But characteristically he did not dwell on his ailment. Instead, he talked about Fiji. 'Our work in Fiji was among the most satisfying that I have done, and sometime it will have its day.' He concluded: 'I have dear memories of you, Tom and myself, an incongruous team that did great things.'

Sir Paul had good reason to be proud of his Fiji work. He was called upon to help Fiji in its moment of great need, and he rose to the challenge as few others could have done. The post-1987 years were the most fraught in Fiji's modern history. The military coup of that year had ruptured race relations, torn up the constitution, severed the cherished links with the British Crown, and plunged the country into an abyss of darkness. The two major communities, Fijians and Indo-Fijians, had diametrically opposed views about the country's problems and the best way to resolve them. Fijian nationalists were adamant in their demand for complete political paramountcy and the Indo-Fijians insistent on genuine political partnership.

Into this tense and seemingly irreconcilable situation entered Sir Paul Reeves as Chair of the Fiji Constitution Review Commission. The task of the Commission was to review the racially-lopsided 1990 constitution and to make recommendations for a new one which, to use the language of the Terms of Reference, took 'into account internationally recognized principles and standards of individual and group rights, guarantee full protection and promotion of the rights, interests and concerns of the indigenous Fijian and Rotuman people, and have full regard for the rights, interests and concerns of all ethnic groups in Fiji.' In other words, square the circle.

No one really gave the Commission any chance of success. There was a great deal of scepticism about Sitiveni Rabuka's motives. Would a person who had carried out the coup really change the constitution to accommodate the interests of other communities? Hardly likely, most people thought. The review, many felt, was a ruse to keep the international community at bay while the coup supporters entrenched their position in the country. And the Fijian nationalists, led by Inoke Kubuabola, Apisai Tora, Taniela Veitata, and others, demanded the full retention of the 1990 Constitution.

Sir Paul knew the tough task that awaited him in Fiji. He made one early decision that had a huge impact on the work of the Commission. He hired Alison Quentin-Baxter as its chief legal counsel (ably assisted by Jon Apted). Alison was the complete professional of unimpeachable integrity and an enviable tenacity of purpose. Nothing escaped her notice. She left no stone unturned. She kept the Commission on an even keel, educating us on arcane matters of international law and conventions, alerting us to alternatives. Alison has not received the kudos that she so richly deserves.

Sir Paul met the rest of the 'incongruous team' in Fiji. He was understandably concerned to establish early rapport between the three Commissioners. The task was not easy. Tom Vakatora was the Government's nominee, a tough, formidable man of explosive temper. He had been a part of the Cabinet Sub-Committee which had approved the 1990 Constitution, the very document we were supposed to review. His presence on the Commission simply reinforced among Coalition supporters the sense the review would be nothing but a charade. The early days were difficult, but in time, Tom proved to be a character completely different to his public persona: warm, companionable and extremely hard working. Beneath a gruff exterior beat a kindly heart. He became my lifelong friend.

I was the Coalition's nominee. I did not know of Sir Paul I am ashamed to admit, even though I had his daughter Jane in my class at the University of Hawaii. But I established early rapport with him. My first impression of Sir Paul was that he was a warm human being, a man of grace who did not stand on protocol as some other local dignitaries did, always reaching out. There was little paper trail behind him so I did not know where he stood on some of the critical issues we were asked to consider. I therefore kept an open mind and my powder dry, just in case.

Early on in the piece, Sir Paul said to Tom and myself, 'If you two reach consensus, I will not stand in your way.' He encouraged the two of us to talk among ourselves, to break down barriers and to establish trust. This we did, to great effect, I would like to think. It was during a one-on-one meeting between Tom and myself at The Fijian one long weekend, that we reached provisional consensus on some difficult issues, as the papers of the Commission will one day show. The credit belongs to Sir Paul for having confidence in himself to allow the two of us talk and explore consensus.

Then there was Sir Paul himself. He was a man of grace and gravitas—a former Anglican Archbishop of New Zealand and its Governor General, a man proud of his indigenous Maori heritage but not imprisoned by it, a man of deep spirituality and integrity, of solid convictions but always willing to listen carefully to contrary points of view. He easily put people at ease with his humour and infectious laughter. He was the ideal ambassador for the Commission. He won the confidence and trust of the major political leaders who were so recently at loggerheads. They saw him accurately as a man of peace, a fair mediator. That was no mean achievement in the circumstances.

The work of the Commission was a collective effort, so it would be invidious to isolate the input of the individual Commissioners. Opinions will vary and recollections will differ. Sir Paul's principal contribution lay in moderating discussion and in playing the role of the fair cop and in giving us the space to be ourselves. For me, Sir Paul's unique interventions lay in two areas. One was the relationship between Church and State. Methodist Church was adamant that Fiji should be declared a Christian State. Christianity was an integral part of indigenous Fijian identity, and recognizing the special role of the church was a part of the larger agenda of entrenching the principle of Fijian paramountcy. Very often, the demand was backed up by some obscure passage from the Bible. This was completely foreign to me and frequently left me nonplussed. But not Sir Paul. He could with ease recall some appropriate chapter and verse from the Bible to diffuse the issue or contradict it outright! This left some of the submitters perplexed, this deep knowledge of the scriptures on his part. Isn't it better to be a good Christian than to insist on a Christian State, he would ask? I remember one person saying to me, 'The falla too good, eh. He a talatala [preacher] or what?'

The other area in which I watched Sir Paul's intervention with great interest was on the question of indigenous rights. Many an indigenous presenter tried to make out that Fijians were like oppressed indigenous communities elsewhere in the world, including New Zealand. That did not wash with Sir Paul although he listened respectfully to their views. Where Fijian interests and institutions needed to be protected, they should be, was Sir Paul's view. One provision of the Compact says that 'To the extent that the interests of different communities are seen to conflict, all the interested parties should enter into negotiations in good faith in an endeavour to reach agreement.' In that effort, 'the paramountcy of Fijian interests as a protective principle should continue to apply, so as to ensure that the interests of the Fijian community are not subordinated to the interests of other communities.' That was a sensible position to adopt. To those who invoked various international conventions on the protection of indigenous nights, the Commission took the view that these instruments were designed to ensure the full participation of the indigenous communities in the management and governance of their societies, not enshrining the principle of paramountcy. Sir Paul's experience as the Anglican Observer at the United Nations came in handy.

One aspect of the 1997 Constitution that has received much criticism is its racially-based electoral system. In this regard, the Constitution is completely at variance with the recommendations of the Reeves Commission. The Commission recommended that Fiji move away gradually but decisively from a racial electoral system to a non-racial one. To that end, it recommended that two thirds of the seats in Parliament (46) be elected from open, non-racial rolls and one third (25) from racially reserved rolls (but only for a short period as a transitional measure). The Parliament reversed the order at the insistence of the SVT, especially its hardline representative on the Parliamentary Select Committee, Inoke Kubuabola, who wanted the full retention of the 1990 Constitution and would not budge an inch. .Now Kubuabola is presenting himself as the champion of non-racialism. Such are the processes of personal transformations in contemporary Fiji.

There were other recommendations designed to heal the wounds of the past and to unite the nation. The Senate should be elected from the provinces, not nominated by political leaders, so that it could act as a true house of review of the people and in the process encourage loyalty to one's province of origin rather than to one's ethnicity. The President and the Vice President should be elected by a joint sitting of the two houses of parliament as an Electoral College for the purpose. In the allocation of public resources, the principle of need rather than ethnicity should be observed along with the principle of proportionality. I know that Sir Paul was very proud of the human rights provisions of the report.

As I have said, no one gave the Commission much chance of success when we began our work, but by the time we finished, we had managed to re-start a remarkable national conversation about reconciliation and nation-building. In this effort, Sir Paul's role was crucial. He had earned everyone's trust and confidence, and that made the Commission's work all that much easier. The healing process that began with the Commission's work was continued, and resulted in the promulgation of the much-praised 1997 Constitution.

In the covering letter to the President, Sir Paul personally inserted a few sentences that spoke to the way in which he envisaged the task of nation building. The report, he said, 'stresses that the unity of this nation is a continuous process of discovery and enrichment.' A continuous, not a fossilized, process admitting of change and adaptation. He said that progress in a multi-ethnic society is achieved 'when citizens realise that what is good for their neighbour must ultimately be good for them as well.' Finally, he hoped that the Commission's report 'will be the touchstone against which the people will measure progress towards a strong and united future for themselves and for generations to come.'

That hope now seems forlorn, but who knows? Someday perhaps, Sir Paul's vision of Fiji as a vibrant multi-ethnic nation, united by a common purpose and a shared sense of collective destiny, confident about the future and at peace with itself might 'have its day.'

Sir Paul Reeves will occupy an honoured place in the galaxy of leaders who have had a hand in shaping Fiji's destiny. He will not be forgotten. Moce Maca, Sir, Fare Well.

# Nineteen

## Caught in the Web

Visit the fijilive website of 20 and 21 August 2008 and you will find the following animated and often acrimonious posts on me. One says that 'Dr Brij Lal is a man of the past. He is no longer relevant. He is one person who should be blamed for giving Fiji a lousy Constitution which is race-based.' Another says that 'Brij Lal was an architect of a constitution that has made a mockery of Fiji legal rights. Brij Lal is a scholar who is still in a colonial country. Can he live in Fiji under this Constitution? No. He is frightened for his life and that of his family.' A person who identifies himself simply as Sharma adds that 'It's time for Brij Lal to shut up. His comments are of no value to the current govt. Commodore Bainimarama has people much experienced in his team to clean up Fiji and make it a better nation for all people of Fiji.' For Vikash Ram, 'Only people living and working in Fiji should have a deeper say in its governance not people living abroad and working overseas who used to call Fiji home. It's easy to say many things from a distance.' Tui Viti says that since I have no interest in Fiji, I should not be allowed back in to Fiji.

On the other side of the divide are these. From Emosi: 'I think Dr Lal is right. Let truth and justice prevail. No one is above the law.' From 'Some One Away,' 'Finally someone is willing to stand up and tell the truth! Dr Lal, Fiji needs more people like you.' Finau Mere adds: 'Get them to face the consequences. Brij, thank you for your contribution. It is valued by the majority who dislike the illegal behaviour we the people of Fiji are victims of.' Finally, Diana Moqolaki says, 'I am not surprised about the comments on Dr Brij Lal because these are the same people who condemn the previous coups and they see it fit to embarrass [embrace] this 2006 coup because it suits them and their agendas. All coups are wrong whether it suits you or not. They must be condemned and held accountable to the law.'

I have reproduced the comments generously to give the reader a sense of the tone and temperature of the responses one normally finds on Fiji websites post-2006. They are simple, often simplistic, direct and confrontational, full of passion and erupting anger, but also short-lived. The need to express their opinion satisfied, people move on. Another day, another topic, another set of responses.

I brought the wrath of the cyberspace warriors upon myself with some comments I was invited to make on a Radio Fiji news program, which were published, without my permission, on fijilive. Before I knew it, my views were carried by the major newswire services reporting on or from Fiji. Comments made in a telephone interview, taken out of context, became a major news item. That is the nature of the beast, I realise. We live in a borderless world, its component parts connected with mind-boggling speed.

I am not a 'media tart,' to use a popular Australian characterisation of former Queensland premier Peter Beattie. Most academics are not. In fact, most exhibit an instinctive aversion to media exposure and to the sound bites that reduce complex issues to simple declarations without nuance, qualification or shaded meanings. But I have not been able to escape the media ever since serving on the commission to review the Fijian constitution a decade ago. Since then, I have been hounded for comment and analysis on Fiji politics. It is an obligation and a responsibility I cannot escape, although fulfilling them while doing intense scholarly unrelated to the field of Fijian politics does take its toll.

The unfolding events since the December 2006 coup have been the source of much confusion among the public, and the media has understandably sought comment and clarification from experts and others intimately associated with events in Fiji. For many in Fiji, I am in that category. My views were sought on a number of issues. One important issue facing Fiji was the threat of sanctions from the European Union if Fiji did not honour its undertaking to hold parliamentary elections before the mutually agreed date of March 2009. Will elections be held by that date, I was asked. My response was no, or very unlikely. If elections were held in that time frame, Laisenia Qarase's party would be returned to power with a thumping Fijian majority, an outcome totally unpalatable to the military and to the Interim Administration. Moreover, Commodore Bainimarama has promised not to relinquish power until his so-called 'Clean Up Campaign' is completed and the President's flawed, in truth unconstitutional, mandate achieved. The Fiji Labour Party, which is part of the Interim Administration, has endorsed that position (until its leader was unceremoniously dumped from the Cabinet in early 2008).

What about the constitutionality of the President's Mandate, I am asked. My response is forthright. The President has no mandate of his own to give in the first instance. In the Westminster system adopted in Fiji, the executive acts on the advice of the elected government. His powers are carefully circumscribed in the constitution. If the President has one important responsibility after he has assumed executive power in a situation of emergency when the elected government is unable to discharge its responsibilities, it is to return the deposed government to power as expeditiously as possible. He cannot use his 'reserved' powers to authorise an extra-constitutional rule for an unspecified period of time. He cannot play God with the politics of the country.

I am asked about the purported suspension of the Great Council of Chiefs. The GCC, I respond, is a constitutionally recognized body, and it cannot be suspended, as an institution, so long as the constitution is still in place. Its membership can be reviewed, but that is a secondary matter. What are my views about the Interim Administration's claim that the GCC is an 'arm of the government,' as Fijian Affairs Minister Ratu Epeli Ganilau asserts. That it is not, nor should it be. Instead, the GCC should have as much fiscal and administrative autonomy as possible so that it can become, as it wants to, the guardian of the national and not only Fijian interests. The autonomy of the GCC is constitutionally guaranteed. And so it went. These comments, offered within the span of a few days, invited the above comments.

What do they tell us about the current state of affairs in Fiji and about wider trends in public communication in the electronic age? There are several things to note. The comments come from those with access to the internet. I suspect they are the professional types (civil servants, people in private employment, university students), and so their views may not necessarily be representative of a wider cross section of the public opinion. But for the purposes of this essay, let us assume they are. We don't know whether the cyberspace warriors live in Fiji or overseas. Cyberspace has no precise physical location, no singular identity. That is its strength as well as its limitation.

Clearly opinion is divided. There are, on the one hand, those who wish Fiji to be left alone to manage its affairs without external interference. They quietly support the coup, or at least its stated aims. 'Give chance to the army to do something which never happened. Things will be better for Fiji,' says one writer (Anand). It is a view shared by a fairly large cross-section of the community, especially by those who were victims of the Qarase government's racially motivated affirmative action and other discriminatory policies. They resent any suggestion that the prospects might not be as bright as they hope, that the road ahead might be rockier than anyone expects. If things are not going to be as rosy, they don't want to know. Their mind is made up; it is no use confusing them with facts. Nothing is rotten in the State of Denmark.

On the other side of the divide are those for whom a military coup against a democratically elected government is unacceptable at any cost, a heinous crime that ought to be universally, unequivocally condemned. This view is expressed by many (but by no means all) academics and public intellectuals, human rights activists, lawyers and, of course, members and supporters of the deposed Qarase government. Mere Samisoni is prominent in the newspapers, and Rewa chief

Ro Teimumu Kepa is shouting for democracy from the sidelines. There are many recent, opportunistic, converts to democracy. In 2000, they were safely and quite publicly ensconced in the George Speight camp. They welcome any support they can get from whatever source.

The battle is broadly divided into these two diametrically opposed camps. There is no concession to the opponent's viewpoint, no admission of doubt. There is no common ground. Privately, individuals may concede a point or two. Some may say they approve the outcome but not the method used to achieve it. Yet others may concede that, in hindsight, certain policies of the deposed government might have been misconceived or misguided, but to admit it publicly in the heat of the battlefield is to concede ground: a risky proposition.

Then there is the related matter of who should be 'allowed' to comment on the current affairs of Fiji. Many feel that outsiders should refrain, or be forced to refrain, from commenting on public matters. They left the country, their commitment to Fiji is suspect, and they want to have the best of both the worlds. Most of those who espouse this position are on the side of the Interim Administration. The irony is that these very same people were among the most vocal seeking outside intervention at the time of the previous coups. On the other hand are those, members and supporters of the deposed government, who are more interested in the message, not the place of residence of the messenger.

The anti-foreign angst is understandable. Foreign commentators with little commitment to principle or place can wreak havoc without bearing any responsibility for their actions or utterances. Their loyalty to their place of birth is doubted, their motives questioned. I cannot nor should be counted in that category, having spent my entire professional life working on Fiji in a range of capacities, including as member of the Fiji Constitution Review Commission whose report forms the basis of Fiji's barely-surviving (but now abrogated) 1997 constitution. But foreign voices cannot be shut out. Nor should they be.

There was a time when physical boundaries were real, when ideas travelled slowly, and when it was possible to control or restrict access to unpalatable information. That was the case in 1987, for instance, when the military could ban the publication of newspapers and shut down communication with the outside world. That was then. The world of communication has been revolutionised since. The boundaries have become porous place beyon belief. They can be crossed with the click of the button and cherished sovereignty breached in myriad ways.

The internet is a great leveller of hierarchy. Anyone who has access to a computer can roam the world for information. Chat sites enable free, open and anonymous dialogue in the cyberspace. Personal blogs post information which may not find its way into the mainstream media, and often does not, because its source cannot be verified or because the material is inflammatory or defamatory, or worse. Newspapers have their own online reader-response sites which enable instantaneous reaction with unimaginable speed. Should it really matter in that case where the writer lives? What I write in Canberra can be posted on any website anywhere in the world and openly available to anyone except those without access to the computer.

Location and residence aside, opponents of 'free speech' invoke other spurious grounds for limiting commentary. Some invoke the archaic, almost sophomoric, notion that disciplinary qualification is necessary for commenting on contemporary events. In this view, a historian has no business commenting on politics or constitutional matters, which should remain the domain of political scientists and constitutional lawyers. I say archaic because the notion, in these post-modern times, of artificial disciplinary boundaries limiting or constricting the expression of human thought is too naïve to require comment. The thrust of contemporary intellectual life is the transgression of boundaries. No one dismisses Noam Chomsky's critique of American foreign policy because he is by profession a linguistic theorist, or Edward Said's advocacy of Palestinian issues because he was a professor of English and comparative literature. EP Thompson was a great Marxist historian who played a pivotal role in the disarmament debate in Europe. I am no Chomsky, Said or Thompson, but the principle is the same.

Then there are those who seek to restrict comment on cultural grounds. A 'non-native' should have no business commenting on 'native' affairs. I accept some limitations within bounds, but reject the authority of self-appointed gatekeepers to determine the limits and limitations of debate. Readers of this journal [*Fijian Studies*] will recall the controversy it generated over its name when it was first launched. Some Fijian nationalists argued that it was an inappropriate expropriation of the name Fijian, which they contended belonged, and should properly belong, solely to the indigenous community. I am glad the publisher persisted. Nor should we accept ethnic groups and categories as homogenous entities. They are intersected in various ways that defy simple categorisation. And then there is a larger question which must be asked: What becomes of a person's human right to comment on issues pertaining to other nationalities or ethnic groups? Why shouldn't western feminists be allowed to comment on issues of concern to their third world counterparts? The horrors of Rwanda, Cambodia or Kosovo are not 'national' problems but blot on the conscience of humanity

My own position is clear. There are issues that transcend national boundaries about which we cannot remain silent. A military coup against a democratically elected government is never, in my books, an 'internal matter' for a country. It breaches principles and values which humanity has embraced as its own and for which people in their millions over the centuries have sacrificed their lives. There are certain principles worth defending anywhere, anytime. If the world had remained silent about apartheid in South Africa, to take only one example, that abhorrent regime might still be in place. Indigeneity or national sovereignty should never be allowed to kill genuine debate about issues of concern to all humanity.

In Fiji's case, there is a further consideration. Now, remittance from Fiji's former citizens and workers living in foreign countries is one of the largest sources of the national income, exceeding that of sugar and gold and timber, and matching the income from tourism. As emigration continues, as it will without doubt do, the importance of this source of much needed revenue will increase. It seems hypocritical to seek financial support from abroad but deny former citizens the right to express an opinion on the ongoing events in the country. The Interim Administration in Fiji wants the international community to assist in rehabilitating the country to parliamentary democracy, but bristles when it is asked to specify a time frame within which that process will take place. It breaches international conventions and condones treason, but then condemns its neighbours for the principled stance against its actions.

The internet facilitates unmediated free flow of information. It is free-for-all in the cyberspace. Misinformation or simply blatant errors of fact get broadcast and people's characters gets maligned, their reputations impugned. 'Brij Lal should be blamed for giving Fiji a race-based constitution,' says a correspondent. 'Brij Lal was the architect of a constitution that makes a mockery of Fiji's legal rights,' says another. Comments like these appear regularly on many web and chat sites, often stated as incontestable, self-evident facts. Uncorrected, they assume the mantle of truth.

Although flattering to the ego, I am not 'the' architect of the constitution as critics assert. I was one among several who contributed ideas that went into the report which then formed the basis of Fiji's constitution. My fellow commissioners, Sir Paul Reeves and the late Tomasi Vakatora, contributed as much, if not more, as I did. It is hurtful that their contribution is demeaned and devalued for the sole purpose of attacking me. The actual constitution was drafted by a select committee of the Fijian parliament and it was the parliament which finally approved the document. It was endorsed unanimously by the Great Council of Chiefs. To lay the blame for the constitution's alleged failures at my door is manifestly unfair, not to say mischievous.

How does the constitution make a mockery of Fiji's legal rights? This assertion makes no sense to me, and yet it gets published and circulated in the name of free speech. I am blamed for Fiji's race-based constitution whereas, in fact, I have been a public critic of this aspect of the constitution. I firmly believe, as the Reeves Commission recommended, that Fiji needs to move away from its race-based politics to embrace a non-racial future. To that end, the Commission recommended that two thirds of the seats in parliament should be contested on an open, non-racial basis and one third on a racially-reserved basis but only for a period of time before that is jettisoned. The parliament reversed our recommendation. So the politicians and not I should be held responsible for the constitution's racially orientated electoral system. Having said that, I can understand the logic that underpins the consciationalist 1997 constitution.

In a more conventional forum, such as a book or a journal article, I would have the opportunity to present a considered response. But this is not possible when dealing with the cyberspace. The window of opportunity is limited to a day or two at most. Then, discussion moves to other current topics of the day and interest in the controversy is lost. It has been suggested that I should have a website of my own to publish my ideas and respond to debates. But I have neither the time nor the skill nor, to be perfectly honest, the taste for this. I am a product of my time and age whose facility and fascination with technology is limited.

Uncorrected and unrefuted, the internet exchanges are archived, though for how long and in what condition it is difficult to say. What use or sense will future researchers make of the mass of conflicting, controversial information? How will the history of the present be written fifty years hence? In the past or even at present, historians could look to the archives for traces of the past in documents. But under-funded and poorly resourced, many archives are simply unable to perform their essential function of preserving records. Certainly, they are unequipped to archive electronic information, which includes much of the cyberspace material. The transitory nature of the electronic data is a source of concern as is the publication of material of dubious veracity.

The public expects responsibility and a degree of accountability from its public intellectuals. But do those cyber hosts who broadcast information of the type I have mentioned have a responsibility too, especially to those who are the targets of venomous but anonymous criticism? I have been accused on a website of running a Fijian Studies Department at the Australian National University whose intention is to dispossess indigenous Fijians of their cultural identity. I was alerted to this post long after it had appeared on the website. The damage was done; there was nothing I could do to remedy the situation. Should the host have demanded verification from the writer, or asked me for a response? On another website, my professional work was being discredited by a former academic with hardly any publications at all. I was being called names, challenged on this point or that, and I was not even aware of what was going on. I accept that a cyber host has a responsibility to broadcast information and comment freely, but he or she should also have the responsibility to protect the reputation of innocent parties caught in the cyberspace crossfire. At the very least, the identity and purpose of the websites should be clearly labelled so that readers are made aware of their true function. A gossip site should be clearly differentiated from a site for the scholarly exchange of views.

What, finally, should be the role of public intellectuals at a time of grave crisis, such as that facing Fiji at the moment? Should they accept the strictures imposed on them on the basis of gender, ethnicity or place of residence and refrain from commenting on contemporary political events? My firm answer is no. Put simply, it is the message that is important, not the identity of the messenger. Killing the messenger will not make the problem disappear. This is so self-evident yet so overlooked.

Further, whatever else may be the case, the reality of globalisation must be confronted. As I have said many times before, Fiji is an island, but an island in the physical sense alone. Fiji cannot breach international norms of human rights and expect to escape with impunity. A military coup against a democratically elected government cannot be an internal matter for a country, as I have already said, just as genocide and other heinous crimes against humanity are not. Any breach of international norms will bring swift retribution. If Fiji does not hold elections before a stipulated date, March 2009, the European Union will withhold the much needed funds for the re-structure of the country's ailing sugar industry. This is the truth, whether it is spoken from Canberra or Korovou.

Public intellectuals not only have a right but, perhaps more important, a moral and ethical responsibility to speak up when guns curtail the freedom of speech and induce a sense of self-censorship among citizens. They should do so with sensitivity and care, but without fear or favour. We must be true to our calling. We should freely transgress the increasingly porous boundaries of academic disciplines and the nation-state, not bow to the strictures they impose and demands they make. We should be the conscience of the oppressed and the voiceless. Nothing human should be alien to us.

*Twenty*

# From the Sideline:

## An Interview with Vilsoni Hereniko

The following interview was tape-recorded at the Australian National University on 21 September 2000.

*VH*: How long have you been here at the ANU (Australian National University) and why are you here instead of Fiji?

*BL*: I've been here since 1990. Before that, I was at the University of Hawaii (UH). I left Fiji in 1983. The reason why I am at ANU and not at the University of Hawaii has nothing to do with professional satisfaction, because UH was intellectually stimulating, with wonderful colleagues, especially at the Center for Pacific Islands Studies. But I came here in 1990 to write a book [*Broken Waves: A history of the Fiji Islands in the 20th* century] and my family decided that this is where they wanted to be. All of a sudden I discovered the joys of discovering the familiar contours of Anglo-Australasian culture with which I had grown up—the kind of texts we had read, the kind of people we had met. So this was a more familiar cultural surrounding to me than the United States was. And the family liked it too. Also, of course, Australia has cricket and rugby, and those things began to matter. Why not Fiji? I've always wanted to go back to Fiji, but the opportunity never came. Certainly if the Rabuka-Reddy Coalition had won the elections, I would have been there and given up an academic career. From time to time, I've also wanted to return to the University of the South Pacific, but the continued political upheaval in Fiji and all that it entails for academic freedom dissuades me from returning.

*VH*: Let's go way back to your childhood. Tell me, where did you grow up, what school did you go to, and what inspired you to be the kind of person you are today?

*BL*: I grew up on a small ten acre cane farm on leased native land. Both my parents were unlettered. We came from a big family of six boys and two girls. From very early on, it was very clear to us that there was no future on the farm for all six of us; our parents said, well, you'd better get educated and become a clerk or cash earner in some capacity. The incentive to do well was always there, propelled by economic circumstances. My interest in history started very early. My grandfather was an indentured labourer and it just happened I was his favourite grandson. I used to sleep in his bed and take him around to do his ablutions, and so on. I heard stories about India, about his experiences on the plantations. Many of these were romanticized, but reinforced by the kind of cultural environment in which I was growing up: essentially Indian and devout orthodox Hindu. My curiosity about distant people and distant places started very early on. I was curious about these people; who were they, how did they come to Fiji? They spoke a funny language, they dressed differently. And then at primary school, I did reasonably well. I went to secondary school where I had some very fine teachers. All of them have done very, very, well indeed in their later careers: Vijay Mishra, professor of literature in Perth; Subramani, a professor at the university in Fiji; Krishna Dutt, my history teacher, who is a prominent public figure in Fiji; all of these people freshly graduated had a kind of dynamism. They took teaching seriously. They took you seriously, because in a sense your success reflected their own success as teachers or mentors. My parents were supportive, partly out of necessity, economic necessity. My teachers were encouraging, interesting, interested. I suppose I had a natural curiosity; I wanted to become an English teacher. In high school we had novels I've mentioned in my books, English texts—Dickens, Bronte, Hardy, and so on. That imaginative world appealed to me. I suppose it was a form of escapism, from the dreary realities of poor life in the rural countryside. Then at university I met people who were extremely encouraging. One, whose political views I have often disagreed with, was Ron Crocombe. But Ron was a very stimulating kind of person. He provoked you, he took you seriously as a scholar. My favourite teacher though was a lady by the name of June Cook, a chain-smoking English woman who came to Fiji after a stint as part of the United Kingdom delegation at the United Nations. She was a professional historian. She read her lectures as a don would read a lecture at Oxford or Cambridge, and we took her seriously. I think the University of the South Pacific in the early days, let's say until about from the early-to-mid-seventies, was an interesting place to be at because we were experimenting with a regional project. There was also a deep concern among both staff and students to prove ourselves, that we were a first-rate academic institution. Just because we happened to be in the third world didn't mean that we were third rate. This eagerness to prove our intellectual prowess, if you will, made a very exciting atmosphere and after USP I knew that I was hooked on the humanities and I haven't looked back.

*VH*: So where did you go after USP?

*BL*: I finished my USP degree in 1974, before my allotted three years. Then I applied to Walter Johnson, who was from the University of Hawai'i but teaching at USP, a very distinguished professor of history, former chairman at Chicago History Department. He taught a course on recent American history. He saw some potential in me and asked me to apply to go to UH to become his teaching assistant in the World Civilization program. But UH rejected me. They rejected me because they said you only have a three-year degree and we have four years; we don't know about the calibre of teaching at USP. Besides, English is your second or third language, and so they rejected me as a teaching assistant. As it happened, the chairman of the history department of the University of British Columbia (UBC), Margaret Prang, was visiting USP. Ron Crocombe talked to her about me, and Margaret Prang said we'd like to have him and flew me over to UBC as a teaching assistant. Within about three weeks they gave me a graduate fellowship to complete my master's, which was in Chinese and Indian history. As it happened, at the end of my MA, when I graduated they gave me a prize for the most outstanding student in history. I remember very distinctly people at USP elated with my success because this was proof that the kind of graduates they were producing locally could do well outside. After that I went back to Fiji in 1976 and taught there for two years and then applied to get a scholarship to come to ANU, which I did. I arrived here in 1977 and finished my PhD in 1980, on the history of indenture, and then I went back to Fiji for a couple of years. For six months I was unemployed because there was no job for me at USP; people there didn't want me. It was a very frustrating, depressing time for me. After that I decided I wanted to leave Fiji because I was not happy with the dull intellectual atmosphere there. I mean, having done a PhD at a university like ANU, which is rigorous and intellectually exciting, I felt that I was called on to play the role of a public figure, as one of the few local doctorates at USP. I found that socially satisfying, but intellectually very, very shallow. I felt that if I wanted to make a success of myself as an academic, I'd have to get away from USP. Maybe it was narrow-minded thinking on my part at that time, but I felt I needed to prove myself somewhere else. And so I went to Hawaii, and after that I came to ANU.

*VH:* You say you joined the history departments in Hawaii and ANU? When did your interest in politics begin?

*BL*: When I went back to Fiji after finishing my PhD, Fiji had its fourth general election since independence in 1982; it was a very tense period. There was a real possibility of a change of government because the Western United Front with Ratu Osea Gavidi had joined up with the National Federation Party. They were looking for someone to chair radio broadcasts, but no one would touch them, because it was so sensitive, and Fiji is such a small place. So they asked me. At first I hesitated, but I accepted the responsibility and I chaired those sessions, the panel discussions. I commented on the elections, and my interest in electoral politics started from there. But at the same time, I suppose, living in my own country, I couldn't really escape my responsibility to understand what was happening. I was a historian working on the nineteenth century, but I was living in the present. There was a need there for me to understand what was happening and also a responsibility and obligation to articulate it as I saw it. I think there's a tension in my life: I inhabit the interface between scholarship and practical action. I can't be one or the other; I have to be emotionally engaged with something to be intellectually engaged with it. Those are the two things I have been doing. After I did the elections, a book came of out of it, and I began to do both history and politics. I suppose living in Hawai'i meant that I could write without looking over my shoulder to see who was approving or disapproving of what I was writing. There was no internal censorship. I wrote honestly and as objectively as I could, without any fear of persecution. I suppose if I were living in Fiji, subconsciously I would be aware of what I was writing. Being away from Fiji meant I was not aligned to any faction within different political parties. Over time people began to read what I wrote. Some agreed, some disagreed, but at least they didn't question my integrity or my credibility. Then in 1995 the constitution review exercise came. I think that was partly out of respect for what I was doing.

*VH:* Who approached you?

*BL:* I was approached by Mr Jai Ram Reddy, Leader of the Opposition, whom I had known a little bit but not much. I later found out that he had asked a number of people who might be the best candidate to represent the opposition. I understand that my name was mentioned by many people, but they felt that while I had the intellectual strength and the ability, I wasn't political enough. I didn't understand politics. Mr Reddy's position was that this was precisely the kind of person they wanted, who could at least try to understand things from the other side as well. To give them some fresh ideas; they didn't want a puppet there. They wanted someone who could be critical of who we were, what we had done, as well as understand and engage with issues of concern to other communities. It's a fact that a number of my former colleagues advised me against taking up the appointment because they said it was a farce, that nothing was going to come of it. 'Do you think that the man who had done the coup would turn around and change the constitution?' There was cynicism, there was doubt, and for good reason too, given what had happened in the past. But I thought it was a challenge that I had to take up. I'm glad I did because five years later I have no regrets about what I did, or the recommendations we made.

*VH*: It was a huge responsibility put on your shoulders to be one of the architects of this constitution. Did you find that daunting at all?

*BL:* Yes! I was overwhelmed at times. The fact that I lived by myself for sixteen months, cooped up in a small apartment simply intensified the pressure. I could not talk to anybody because the protocol required I keep my distance. I deliberately kept away. I never talked to any political leaders because it was not the right thing to do; I couldn't have done it anyway. So, I knew the history, I knew something about the task, but I wasn't fully aware of the enormity of what was there and the huge expectations. Everyone expected me to fail. Also there were many new areas I had to read about that I had never read before. International conventions, couched in legalistic terms about indigenous rights, political rights, and civil rights. Sometimes my interpretation of a document conflicted with somebody else's interpretation. The enormous amount of reading was exhausting. But I think the good thing about that exercise was that there were only three of us. There was no fallback. Sir Paul said to us that if you two agree among yourselves I won't stand in your way, and this is what happened. Mr Vakatora and I agreed on many things. We had to talk to each other, get to know each other, explore each other's fears and concerns with communities and the groups we represented. I think that promoted intense dialogue; if it had been a larger committee, people could have passed the buck. In this case there was no passing the buck, there were just two of us.

*VH*: Tell us very briefly about the other two on the committee, Mr Vakatora and Sir Paul.

*BL:* Mr Vakatora was a former Speaker of the House of Representatives, a Cabinet Minister, and a very senior public servant at the time of independence. A very, very hard politician, highly intelligent, he had been involved in the cabinet's draft, which laid the basis for the 1990 constitution. So he had been involved in this process before. A lot of people told me that with him on the Commission, it was a sure sign that we would fail because of his undeserved reputation for being very hard, an obstructionist. In the end we worked very hard and we became lifelong friends. I have the deepest admiration for him as a man, his intellect, and his integrity. Sir Paul didn't know Fiji, but he brought with him a wealth of goodwill, and his public persona was reassuring. He was a very good leader in the sense of not being frightened of receiving ideas from others. The fact that he was part- Maori, the fact that he was a man of the cloth, the fact that he was a former Governor General, the fact that he had the confidence of both sides of politics, certainly helped the process. Of course we had our legal counsel, who basically translated our thoughts into acceptable legalistic terms.

*VH:* During this time of working on the constitution, what would you say were the most important insights that you gained?

*BL:* There are many things. I think that one insight I gained was that people were not as far apart as was often made out to be. When we went to rural areas, right across Viti Levu from Sigatoka to Rakiraki, and other places in Vanua Levu as well, we often heard Fijians and Indians telling us that at the village level people got along very well. They had lived together for a hundred years. They knew each other; they spoke each other's languages. A number of times Indo-Fijians came to us and wanted to make a submission in their 'own dialect.' The problem, they said, was that in Suva politicians stood up and, for whatever reason, espoused all kinds of extremist rhetoric and that eventually filtered down to the grassroots level. With proper leadership, people at grassroots level can work together very well. I wish there were some kind of administrative mechanism to bring them together instead of having a provincial council for Fijians and advisory councils for Indo-Fijians. That's the first insight.

The second insight I got was that there is a deep respect for certain Fijian institutions among Indo-Fijians. The Great Council of Chiefs is one. Many people asked, 'What's wrong with having a Fijian as a president?' Nothing. We celebrate that. A lot of people said we wouldn't be able to sell that idea to the Indian community, but I was able to because that's something that I myself support. I'm quite content with the Fijian side of my heritage and I think, as you can see, everyone else approves of that in parliament.

The third insight came from what people said in private, not necessarily in public. From the Prime Minister down, including the Methodist Church in its formal presentation, people said that elections shouldn't take place from provincial constituencies because this accentuates provincialism. It's destructive, it's divisive, and it's counterproductive as far as Fijians are concerned. They want to go back to the constituency-based system of the 1970 constitution, because that provided more unity of focus and activity and so on. The impression I got was that there's a fear of provincialism resurfacing as well as of increasing fragmentation of Fijian society, which is what happened in the 1999 election. So many Fijian political parties, and now with confederacy politics, have accepted provincial representation, so we are again going down that route. There was a great deal of understanding and tolerance, whether it was what people were just saying to us I don't know, but the sense I got was that with proper leadership we could have crossed the bridge.

*VH:* It seems to me that one of the main problems with the present situation is this crisis in leadership. One of the things you touched on is the separation between the chiefs and the common people. I think what has happened over the years is that the Fijian chiefs, many of them, have lost touch with the common people. At present in Fiji, there's no one person who stands out as being capable of leading the country, navigating the canoe through treacherous waters at this point in time. Would you say that is the problem?

*BL:* That is definitely a major problem. There are two problems here. Let's talk for the moment about Fijian community. The Fijian community is far more complex and divided now than it was in the past. Some 40-45 per cent of the Fijian people are living in urban or peri-urban areas, where their interests and concerns and aspirations are different from those of their counterparts in rural areas. There's a sizable Fijian middle class, particularly after 1987, that has its own needs and agendas. The rural chiefs are unable to come to terms with this new reality caused by urbanization, migration, modern education, travel, the new horizons opening, and also interactions with the multiracial world of other communities. So you're talking about a complex, fluid society that's changing very, very rapidly. An institution that filled a particular need at a particular point in time, is finding it very difficult now.

But something else, which you touched on, which I think is very important, concerns leadership: Among Fijians, all the way through the twentieth century, you had Ratu Joni Madraiwiwi, then you had his son Ratu Sir Lala Sukuna, then you had the four greats: Ratu Penaia Ganilau, Ratu George Cakobau, Ratu Edward Cakobau, Ratu Sir Kamisese Mara, people who were tutored by the British to take over national leadership in the course of time, when Fiji eventually became independent. These were chiefs who had an overarching kind of mana and influence right across the Fijian community and nationally. Even though Ratu Mara came from Lau, he was seen as a national leader. With his departure, we see the end of an era in Fijian leadership. What you'll find is that now people will gain their influence, their authority, and their mana from the provinces. Because of the resurgence of provincialism and confederacy politics, their larger influences seem to me to be more circumscribed. You may have a paramount chief from this area or that, but I don't see anyone on the horizon who has the makings of a truly national leader.

The second thing is, you have commoners, not necessarily high chiefs, who will rise to the top. Their success in politics-Rabuka, Qarase, Filipe Bole, Kamikamica, whoever it is—will also bring a new dynamic to Fijian leadership. The question is not whether it's Fijians who are at the helm, but which Fijian, what kind of Fijian. These questions will be asked more and more now than in the past. In the past the Fijian interest was very clear. We knew who the Fijian leaders were. But not today. I think more questions are being asked and the answers contested, more so than in the past. On the Indo-Fijian side, there's also a dearth of leadership. From 1929 to 1969 we had A D Patel, Vishnu Deo, S M Koya, and a few others. After the mid-1970s to 1999 we had Jai Ram Reddy and Mahendra Chaudhry. But these are people in their sixties, and they are on their way out, eventually, in the next four, five, ten years. The best and the brightest of the Indo-Fijian community are leaving in the thousands. So what you have in Fiji is basically people who can't migrate, won't go, and that affects the kind of people who are thrown up as leaders. I think as far as leadership is concerned this is going to be an issue that people of Fiji will have to grapple with in the future.

*VH:* What is the ideal profile for a new leader for Fiji, one that may be able to grapple with the realities and the complexities of the present situation? What should be the characteristics of this Leader?

*BL:* That's a question that is almost impossible to answer. I suppose one would need to have somebody who has the confidence of his or her own community, but has a larger vision that encompasses others, one who is inclusive. But maybe time has moved on for one person as a single leader to be at the helm. Maybe time is now opportune for a collective kind of leadership—people with strengths in different areas. I don't think you're likely to see another Ratu Mara in your lifetime, that kind of experience and background. I don't know, the situation is so politicized, so fraught. The logic of politics in an ethnically divided society dictates that to win votes you have to take an extreme position, which is what happened in 1999. Rabuka and Reddy were seen to be trying to move to the centre. They were outflanked on the one hand by other Fijian parties, and on the other, by Chaudhry. In an ethnically divided society, when you have moderate leaders coming together to forge a common ground, they will always be outflanked by racial extremists. That is a real challenge for leadership. People need to understand that in a society like Fiji we have to make progress cautiously. We must always be sensitive to many divergent interests and needs and different forms of discourse. The Fijian form of political discourse is indirect, illusive; the Indo-Fijian's based on a long tradition of robust democratic debate. And the two clash. What we need is a leader who understands some of the inner logic and inner dynamics of the other community, as well as his or her own.

*VH:* I think it was Rabuka who said that democracy is a foreign flower. It seems to me that the democratic process is one that doesn't suit Fiji. Thus, it's not very productive when everyone focuses on democratic principles. History seems to have shown us that if democracy is to work something has to be modified, to take into account the Fijian chiefly system, its hierarchical nature. For example, supposing there's a council of leaders consisting of conflicting factions, including members of the Indian community-something that seems rather attractive in the present situation. Is anyone considering alternatives?

*BL*: I think we need to have dialogue between representatives of the different communities. I think the Great Council of Chiefs missed a golden opportunity. For the first time, in the 1997 constitution the Great Council of Chiefs was constitutionally recognized. The expectation was that it would be representative not only of indigenous Fijian interests but also of national interests. That was our idea Council of Chiefs for all of Fiji. But not all Fijian chiefs were interested in that approach. So when the test came they failed. When George Speight's coup took place, they listened to Speight and his demands for political control and supremacy, but there was no place at their table for any representative of the democratic voice. At the least, they should have said, 'We want to hear the other side as well before we make a final decision.' I think that's one thing that's disappointing. The other thing is, of course, that the Great Council of Chiefs was in some senses hijacked by younger chiefs and others with private political agendas and motivations of their own. Some of the chiefs from rural areas did not have a full understanding of the complexities of what was happening. In a way, George Speight put a gun at the head of the Great Council of Chiefs. 'You'll decide this, you'll appoint this person as the vice president and this person as the president.' Then, when appointing the president, they were told, 'Now you must appoint so and so as the prime minister.' That, I think, undermined in a serious way the sanctity of the Great Council of Chiefs. I think they haven't come out of this crisis very well. I certainly hope that the Indo-Fijians will be able to get together and form a group of elders who are above party politics, to be able to deliberate on issues at the national level and in some sense create a liaison with the Great Council of Chiefs at an informal level. I think that's important, that kind of dialogue at the grassroots level, the provincial level, and the national level, outside the political arena. That's very important.

When you talk about democracy as a foreign flower, I would say several things. One is that Fiji has never had democracy in the sense that we properly understand the term. There are many models of democracy. For example, in Fiji the president is nominated by the Great Council of Chiefs. Half the senate is nominated by the Great Council of Chiefs. So many other things: landownership and so on are outside the arena of politics. So Fiji's democracy has always grappled with and tried to accommodate special interests within a broadly overarching democratic polity. There are many models of democracy. If democracy is a foreign flower, then there are many other foreign flowers as well. For example, Christianity is a foreign flower. In Fiji it is now a part of the indigenous culture. The truth is that democracy was fine as long as they were winning—from 1966 to 1987. It failed when they failed to win. That's the second thing.

The third thing is: What would you put in place of democracy? Theocracy? Ethnocracy? I think that the way forward for Fiji is to do two things. One is to acknowledge the sanctity, the authority, and the power of certain indigenous Fijian things. That's absolutely vital, and that's what we did in our report. We have got to acknowledge that. Sometimes it comes very close to breaching international conventions, but we said no, the president should be a Fijian, and everyone should accept that. This is an explicit acknowledgment of Fijians' special place and control over those institutions by Fijians. All of this should happen within the broadly overarching framework of equal citizenship. There must be respect for individual rights. You see, I come back to the point that indigenous Fijians are divided and diverse in their lifestyles, their orientations, their ideologies, and their values. In the long run, democracy will be good for them. Democracy here means the right to exercise individual choice to vote. Given the enormous diversity, and given increasing urbanization and other factors, the Indo-Fijian population is likely to decline significantly. Already we are in the 40 percent range; in the next ten years we are likely to be in the 30s. So the Indo-Fijian presence wouldn't be a big factor in the way it was in Fiji politics for much of the twentieth century. While we must have institutions and organizations at different levels to facilitate discourse outside the arena of active politics, at the same time, I don't know what would be a better alternative to democracy, the ballot box, the parliament, and all of that.

*VH:* We have to take into account that people like Rabuka or George Speight, acting on their own accord or as pawns of other interests, were able to walk into parliament and wrest control of power. On the other hand, the majority of people appear happy to deal with their own grievances within the constitution, but once you've got someone like Rabuka or George Speight taking over parliament, then all the repressed or sup-pressed feelings of people come to the surface and the response becomes a very emotional rather than a rational one. So yes, I think the democratic process can work for most people, but how do we take care of people like Rabuka or Speight? How do we prevent anything like that ever happening again?

*BL:* No constitution can prevent a coup. That's a given. I think there's no guarantee that coups won't take place in Fiji or elsewhere. What's happened in Fiji, and this is my judgment, is that there was dissatisfaction right across the country, especially among the Fijians, with the style of Chaudhry's administration. It was seen as confrontational; it was seen as doing too many things too quickly. People felt rushed; Chaudhry was in a rush to deliver, having made those costly promises during the campaign. Chaudhry is a strong trade union leader, and a trade union has its own culture of dealing with problems. For instance, the end is really the important thing, the means is neither here nor there. Dissatisfaction was wide-spread. I also have the sense that many people were saying, well let's give him a chance and see. Some people were unwilling to wait, including a number of groups—one is diehard nationalists who basically believed that Fiji should always be run by Fijians, the Butadroka group. Another group comprises people who were defeated at the polls, who sought revenge. They will use any excuse; I am thinking of Apisai Tora, for example; he will support any cause that will support Tora. So there's the politics of revenge. There are also people who were fast-tracked to promotion, or benefited from racially oriented affirmative action programs, and they wanted to reach the top right away. There were well-connected businessmen and others who felt their ambitions thwarted by this new government with its own network and its own clientele. All these people supported the coups, but at the end of the day I have a sense that they had their own agendas and they exploited the confused and innocent emotions of people. There was already a kind of substratum of dissatisfaction-somehow things were not right-and they tapped into that.

*VH:* Do you think there's something that's very particular or specific to Fijian culture that makes it seem so easy, during times of tension in Fiji, not to follow the rule of law, but somehow resort to something very primal?

BL: We are a multiethnic society. We've practised the politics of communalism for nearly a century. So we've always practised compartmentalized communal politics: our group first and the nation second. That reinforces feelings of primordiality and suspicion of the other group. Way back in the 1960s you always had the cry, 'If Fijians don't unite, Indians will take their land away,' and that was enough of a rallying cry for people to come together. Race was always used as a political mobilizing tool, so when a new government comes into power that is perceived to be anti-Fijian, they go back and say, 'Fijians have had it again; this is our country.' Yet these people don't realize that Rabuka was in power in 1990 and the same people threw him out. There is now a reservoir of suspicion and mutual hostility that can be tapped into for any particular purpose. In that context the appeal for support is achieved most successfully.

*VH:* One of the things that amazed me was the initial reaction from the Fijian community once Speight had taken over parliament. You would think that the leadership would be against it immediately and denounce it. By not doing that they seemed to be endorsing Speight's actions. One way of reading that would be to say, well the majority of Fijians approve, even though they may tell us in public that they don't.

*BL*: I agree that what began as an individual action of a group of people carrying out this coup later on, through propaganda and through the media, became part of the larger rhetoric of 'This is for the Fijian interest, for the land,' and so on. I think over time it developed a momentum of its own. I mentioned the Great Council of Chiefs, who, in my judgment, failed to exercise the leadership that was expected of them and that they wanted themselves. I think that the army certainly was divided. They dithered, and the Fijian people will pay a huge price for this in the future. I've argued that the army needs more outsiders to act as a buffer, more Rotumans, maybe more Indo-Fijians in the army. I think security forces show that they did not really live up to expectations of the people. The judiciary caved in, abolishing the Supreme Court by decree. I myself think the president [Ratu Sir Kamisese Mara] failed in his leadership by tinkering with the constitution when he had no authority to do so, giving George Speight and the Great Council of Chiefs 'his personal guarantee that things would be done to their satisfaction' when he, as president, had no legal authority to do that. So the institutions collapsed, or was compromised. Maybe deep down they sided with Mr Speight and what he stood for.

Which leads me to my next point: The very same people who dithered and silently supported Speight now single him out as a traitor. They want him tried for treason. My argument always has been that while Speight must face up to the consequences of his actions, he's not the only one who is culpable. Other institutions and individuals, for whom Speight was a front man, should also be held accountable. The very same people who are benefiting from what Speight did are now turning on him saying he is the culprit, just as in 1987, they expected Rabuka to do the deed and move out. Of course he didn't. In this case, Speight has done the deed and he's now being tried by the very same people who are benefiting from his actions. There's an element of hypocrisy here, an element of trying to show the world that things are returning to normal, but of course, they're not, because singling Speight out, scapegoating, and brushing things under the carpet will not work.

*VH:* Are you suggesting then that these people should not have benefited at all, or that George Speight should not be tried? What is a better way of responding to the situation?

*BL*: I think he should be tried; there's no question in my mind about that. Rabuka went free and then we had Speight; if he goes free, there'll be somebody else. That's the lesson of our recent history. What I am suggesting is there ought to be a deep and sincere investigation, something like a Truth Commission. What happened? Why didn't things work out? Did the 1997 constitution fail? What did we do wrong? What do we need to do now to prevent such acts from happening in the future? Where have the Indians fallen short? What should they do? What more should they do to become fully accepted as part of society? Are there shortcomings within Fijian society that prevent it from dealing with the demands and realities of a modern, commercial, globalized world? Rather than focusing on simply another affirmative action policy here, more seats there, we need to grapple with those real questions. The 1997 constitution was widely approved after thorough consultation, blessed by the Great Council of Chiefs, and approved unanimously by the parliament. What went wrong? Do we need to throw the rule book out just because a team loses the game? What kinds of rules are necessary for the questions you were asking early on? Maybe we should look at alternative models. What alternative models, that our commission didn't look at, might they look at? That kind of thing is very important, but I honestly believe Mr Speight should be tried. I'm just saying that he's not the only one, and people need to understand that there's a wider network. One doesn't necessarily have to be accusatory and vindictive, but the need to understand is absolutely vital.

*VH*: Do you think there are people in Fiji who can be objective or neutral, or do you think these people will have to come from outside?

*BL:* I think there will be resistance to outsiders. It's a natural reaction to outsiders who judge us by other standards. So if there's consensus you could get some distinguished person from the region who understands the Pacific region and its cultures, someone who is trusted by people, to be a part of this exercise. I have noticed that we don't use our own people often enough. What about someone like Michael Somare from Papua New Guinea or Ieremia Tabai from Kiribati?

*VH*: I find it interesting that both those two you mention are not Fijians. Are you including them as insiders?

*BL*: What I'm saying is that if you're going to have outsiders, then get people from the region who have long experience of it, understand the situation, and can lend a helping hand. But as members of this commission or this group, the majority will have to come from Fiji itself. They must not be tokens. They must be representatives chosen by the different communities, and they must rise above politics. Look at where we went wrong, tell us. Go and look at other experiences, if you want to. This is what happened with our commission. We were put there by two different groups and yet we were able to rise above politics. It is possible. I really do think that there are people in the community, people of goodwill, and foresight who can fit the bill.

*VH:* Do you think this is being done or going to be done?

*BL:* I hope the government will do it. There is a ministry for reconciliation headed by the interim prime minister himself. I hope he will have the foresight and vision to appoint people who may not necessarily agree with him but will have the courage and independence of mind to say what they think. I think that kind of soul searching, that kind of talking through these things, is very important. The atmosphere is extremely polarized in Fiji right now. People are hurt, and the anguish is there, but I think it is important to now start the process of reconciliation. The best way to go about it is to choose respected citizens, who have the confidence of the people and let them find out where did we go wrong and how can we prevent future actions like this?

*VH:* So when you review the constitution and the work that the three of you accomplished, how do you feel about the constitution now? If you could make changes, what would you change, if anything?

*BL:* The 1997 constitution says some things that are different from the report we wrote, especially in respect of the composition of parliament and the executive.

We recommended that the president should be an indigenous Fijian, nominated by the Great Council of Chiefs, elected by both houses of parliament. I think that is a good thing. That's something that I'd like to see in the constitution. We recommended that two-thirds of the seats be national seats and be contested from three-member constituencies, and that people be forced to make alliances at that level. They reversed that by saying two-thirds should be communal and one-third open. If there is some doubt in people's minds about the system of voting, let's look at it again. Although people are critical of the 1997 constitution, one thing it recommends is compulsory power sharing. The constitution provides that any political party with more than ten per cent of seats in parliament is constitutionally entitled to be invited to be part of cabinet, which I think is a good thing. That's why the Fijian Association went into government. The Soqosoqo ni Vakuvalewa ni Taukei (SVT) is crying foul, unconvincingly, because they were invited. Instead they wanted a number of portfolios, which are the prime minister's prerogative. He invited them to participate; the allocation of portfolios is a matter of negotiation. Instead, the SVT demanded certain terms and conditions. I do not know of any other constitution for a similarly situated ethnically divided society where indigenous concerns and rights are as well protected without breaching democratic principles.

*VH:* Fiji has ethnic groups other than the Fijians and the Indians. I think we've talked quite a bit about the Fijian and Indian communities particularly, but I wonder if you have any thoughts about the Rotuma situation, particularly at this time. It seems to me that over the years, Rotuma has been treated as a colony of Fiji. Given the present climate in Fiji, maybe Rotuma might consider exploring some other kind of relationship with Fiji, one perhaps that will give it more autonomy, something akin to a compact of free association with Fiji. Do you think this is something that Rotuma should consider?

*BL:* This is an issue that came up before the Commission in 1995, when we travelled to Rotuma and received a number of submissions there. There were several concerns. One is that there was an independence movement led by Mr Gibson. There was a faction that wanted independence; not only them but Wallis and Futuna and other places like Rabi as well. So the independence option was certainly canvassed. But there are many Rotumans who didn't want it, because, they pointed out, 70 percent of Rotumans live in Fiji. They are part of the Fiji economy. Let me put it this way: we recommended that the issue of independence is for the people of Rotuma to decide. I think we also favoured the idea of some kind of compact of free association that gives Rotuma greater autonomy while maintaining a relationship with Fiji. I think we were very sensitive about that; we did not dismiss the issue out of hand. We felt that it is something the people of Rotuma should work through. Fiji's interest in this is economic, the two-hundred-mile economic zone, that's what it's all about. A lot of Fijians would say, 'Well, if Rotumans want independence, go back to Rotuma,' but most are Fiji citizens. I think that's not the issue; the issue is here's an island that is far away, in public consciousness as well as in physical distance. If they want greater autonomy, the commission certainly favoured that, and we felt that they should explore some kind of compact with Fiji, perhaps the kind of relationship Tokelau has with New Zealand, for example. We were very sympathetic.

*VH:* What are your political plans now in relation to Fiji? Do you have intentions of going back and becoming actively involved in trying to figure out where Fiji should go or how it should resolve its problems?

*BL:* I have had my opportunity. I have said what I think is appropriate. Emotionally Fiji will always be a part of me. That will always be there. I think that active politics is probably out now. The shadow lengthens and one is conscious of the small amount of time that's left. I really want to do other things. Eventually, after writing a biography of Jai Ram Reddy, a story of Fiji politics from 1970 to 1999, a period when I myself came of age and was involved in some capacity with Fiji's politics, I'll probably not go back to Fiji. I want to work on a history of Australian relations with the Pacific from 1800 to 2000, because I live here now. I'd like to explain this part of the world to people in this country because Australia has been a dominant power in this region. That's one thing I want to do. Then I'd like to write some fiction. It's difficult but I'll try. I don't see myself being in academia for very long. I've had a good run. If something better comes up I'll certainly think about it. For the time being academic life seems to be the best alternative I have.

# Twenty One

## Speaking To Power

*Nahin rahanevalli ye mushkilen*
*Ye hain aage mod pe manzilen*
*Meri baat ka tu yakin kar*
*Na udaas ho mere hamsafar*

*These difficulties will not last forever*
*Our destination is just around the corner*
*Take heed of what I am saying*
*Do not despair, my fellow traveller*

I was at home in Suva Point when our security guard came up the stairs to tell me that some people outside the gate were looking for me. As I approached them, I realised they were un-uniformed soldiers, ten of them in two twin cabs. One of them, a young man in green floral shirt and sulu, came forward and said politely that I would have to go to the barracks to be interrogated.

Padma, who had by now joined me, intervened: 'Interrogated?'

'No, ma'am.' the young man replied, correcting himself, feeling slightly embarrassed, I thought, uneasy. 'Interviewed.' At the barracks, as he led me to my cell, this young man in civilian clothes shook my hands gently as he left me to my fate. I saw tears welling up in his eyes as he left. An innocent man forced to carry out a dastardly act, knowing in his heart that what he was doing was unconscionable.

Standing at the gate I was overcome by a feeling of helplessness and impotence and palpable fear. If I had breached any law of the land, I should have been charged by the police force while affording me the full protection of the law. The military in any half decent society should have no business tormenting and terrorising its defenceless civilian population.

# INTERSECTIONS

I suppose the thought that there might be a knock on the door one day was always at the back of my mind, but when it came, it was still a surprise. I had been a vocal critic of military coups in Fiji since 1987, when the first one took place. I feel deep down in my self that there is something terribly wrong about overturning the verdict of the ballot box by the bayonet. I believe in the values of democracy and the rule of law. Democracy may not be the perfect form of government, it may not solve all our problems, but it provides the basis of legitimacy for tackling them. All this was known—it was on the record.

Things boiled over on my latest visit to Fiji during November 2009. I was asked by the Australian media about my reaction to the expulsion of the Australian High Commissioner, James Batley. I said that the expulsion was counterproductive and unnecessary, that it would deepen Fiji's isolation in the region even further, and that it came it a particularly inopportune time when there were signs of a thawing of relations between Suva and Canberra. Engagement rather than disengagement was the way forward for Fiji. Pretty self evidently unexceptionable stuff, when you come to think about it.

Soon after making these comments to Radio Australia's Geraldine Coutts, I was taken by the military from my Suva Point residence to the Queen Elizabeth Barracks, on the direct orders, I was later told, of a senior commander of the Third Fiji Infantry Battalion, the largest unit in the Fiji military. I was detained there for three hours and interrogated for about one by a Lieutenant Colonel. It is an ordeal not to be wished upon even your worst enemy. I cannot bring myself even now to recalling the traumatic details of what transpired in the military cell: the abusive language, the threat of unspeakable violence, the furious spitting in my face, the menacing shoving and slapping, the harangue about the noble aims of the military which outsiders did not understand, the arrogance of 'doctors' like myself who seem to know what was best for Fiji. I have no doubt whatsoever that my Australian citizenship saved me from further violence. I was told to leave the country within twenty four hours or face the consequences. I was left in no doubt what those consequences would be: my family might have to fetch my body from the morgue if I did not obey orders. For months afterwards, I had nightmares about the experience: the stench of urine in the cell, the blotches on the walls speaking of past acts of raw violence against the helpless incarcerated, the grilled door and the solitary window through which small rays of light filtered in to scatter the eerie darkness, the wretched blood-thirsty mosquitoes.

I had no idea of what was to come as I waited in the cell. Perhaps they might take me to another room, seat me down at a table and talk civilly about the rights and wrongs of what I was doing. Such naïveté but nothing like this had ever happened to me before. My most immediate thought was about my family, about

Padma in particular, what she might be going through not knowing precisely where I was and what was happening to me. There was no way of communicating with her. The young soldier had asked me to leave my mobile behind; that was the first thing they confiscated at the barracks. Padma is nothing if not a woman of calm common sense and immense practical resourcefulness. She rang close friends in Suva, who rallied behind her immediately, and she contacted our daughter, Yogi, in Canberra who activated her personal contacts with people in Foreign Affairs and Trade to great effect, the power and pervasive influence of the social media on full display. Within a matter of minutes, a whole transnational network of support was mobilized. Even before I had reached the barracks, the news of my impending incarceration had spread like the proverbial wild fire all around Suva.

As I stood and shuffled and waited, I also thought of friends who had 'visited' this place before me and recalled their tales of terror but also their absolute determination not to give in, to acquiesce. They were bruised and brutalized but unbowed. Their example was an inspiration for me to stand my ground. I also thought of the long and difficult struggle for democracy, social justice and equality that had gone on in Fiji and about which I had written at length. Would all that sacrifice be in vain? I was witness to a history I could not forget, would not allow myself to forget. I simply could not look the other way as a matter of moral duty when the past of which I was a part, and the country which was the place of my birth, my passion and lifelong obsession, was being assaulted by a massive force of arms. Sometimes one does not have the luxury to choose the battle one must fight.

Underlying the military's reaction was a deep sense of frustration that its narrative about events in Fiji was not getting any traction in the international media, that it was being constantly and successfully rebutted by people like myself and other colleagues in Fiji. My detention was intended, I suppose, to send out a clear message to others who were on the other side of the divide: beware if you speak out. The great American historian Arthur Schlesinger Jr. once wrote that a 'society in which the citizens cannot criticise the policy of the state is a society without the means of correcting its course.' The fundamental truth of that statement is unassailable. Dissent in a democracy should not be taken to mean disloyalty. I think it is the responsibility of every citizen, every civilised human being, to speak out against tyranny and oppression, against the subversion of democratic values and the rule of law. Scholarship must, as a matter of moral duty, speak truth to power. Silence cannot be an option. There are certain values humanity has embraced as its own which are worth standing up for and which transcend national and political boundaries.

I have long held the yew that coups don't solve problems, they merely serve to compound them. Militaries around the world have been spectacularly inept in running civilian governments. Violence as an instrument of public policy is always counterproductive. But much as we may like, we cannot turn the clock back. We must accept the reality that a coup has taken place in Fiji. The question is how do we get out of this cul-de-sac? Let us put on the table the flaws of Fijian democracy as it was practised since independence in 1970. Let the military put its cards on the table about its vision for the country. Let us engage in a broad-based inclusive dialogue process. I am convinced that common ground can be found. But there has to be a commitment to a genuine dialogue in the first place, dialogue not monologue, which is the Fiji military's preferred mode of communication and engagement.

Unless the course is corrected in a timely fashion, Fiji's problems will continue to fester. No one is going to invest in an unruly environment governed by decrees, many of which cannot be challenged in a court of law. Poverty levels are already unacceptably high. Squatter settlements around the major urban areas are mushrooming. Employment opportunities for school leavers are shrinking. The best and the brightest are leaving for other shores. But not all is lost. After the coups of 1987, the leaders of Fiji were able to sit down together and resolve the country's difficulties in a calm and constructive way. There is no reason why it cannot be done again.

It does not give me particular pleasure to say things I feel I have to say about what is happening in Fiji. I would rather be left alone to with my research and writing which truly are my abiding passion. But silence, as I have said before, is not an option for me when it comes to the subversion of the rule of law in the land of my birth, or anywhere else for that matter. I hope my intervention would be received in the constructive manner in which it is offered. And when the dust settles, I hope to return to Fiji to continue my needlessly interrupted research.

As my Qantas plane descended at Kingsford Smith the following mid-day, an announcement came over the air for me to identify myself to the ground staff at the door. I did. Three Australian Federal Police met me at the gangway. A young female officer stepped forward, shook my hand and said, 'Sir, you are home now. We will protect you.' It was at that point that all my pent up emotions, kept carefully in check until then, erupted and I broke down. The irony of the situation simply overwhelmed me: being hounded out like a common criminal from the land of your birth and being warmly embraced by the land of your adoption. Now I don't see Australia simply as the land of my adoption. It is much more than that: it is my permanent home where I will live out my last days.

Those comforting words of that young police officer at the Sydney airport will remain with me for as long as I live: 'Sir, you are home now. We will protect you.'

# Acknowledgments

Many essays included in this volume have appeared in academic and popular journals and anthologies before. They have been retained substantially as they first appeared, with a silent emendation here and there for consistency and fluency. Some documentation has been reduced for reasons of space and repetition. Readers can follow these in the originals if they so wish. As indicated at the beginning of this collection, this volume is principally for readers in Fiji, offered in the hope that it might prompt them to commit their own experience and thoughts to paper for future generations.

'Heartbreak Islands' first appeared in Sally Engle Merry and Donald Brenneis (eds.), *Law and Empire: Hawaii and Fiji* (Santa Fe 2003). 'Making History, Becoming History' and 'From the Sidelines' both appeared in *The Contemporary Pacific: A journal of island affairs*. 'While the gun is still Smoking,' appeared in Brij V Lal and Peter Hempenstall (eds), *Pacific Lives, Pacific Places: Bursting boundaries in Pacific History* (Canberra, 2001). 'Where has all the music gone?' appears in *The Contemporary Pacific* (Sept. 2011). 'Campaigns 1999 and 2006,' appeared respectively in the Canberra literary journal *Conversations*, and in Jon Fraenkel, Stewart Firth and Brij V Lal (eds), *The 2006 Military Takeover in Fiji: A coup to end all coups?* (Canberra, 2009). 'Ungiven Speech' has appeared on several blogsites but not I print. 'Road from Laucala Bay will appear in a festschrift for Ron Crocombe. 'People in Between' was presented to a seminar to the University of Hong Kong comparing the Chinese and Indian diasporas, and subsequently appeared in Brinsley Samaroo and Ann Marie Bissessar (eds), *The construction of an Indo-Caribbean Diaspora* (Port of Spain, 2004). 'The Surinam Lecture' was delivered in the Hague in 2008. 'A hundred years in a lifetime' appeared as 'Indo-Fijians: Roots and Routes,' in Rajesh Rai and Peter Reeves (eds.), *The South Asian Diaspora: Transnational networks and changing identities* (London, 2009). 'One Life, Three Worlds,' was given as a paper at Curtin University and appeared in Mary Besemeres and Anna Wierzbicka (eds), *Translating Lives: Living with two languages and cultures* (St. Lucia, 2007).'Primary Texts' appeared in Brij V Lal (ed), *BitterSweet: The Indo-Fijian Experience* (Canberra, 204). 'Blurred Lines' appeared as 'Reshmi' in Subramani (ed.), *Shifting Location: Indo-Fijian Writing from Australia* (Liverpool, Sydney, 2009). 'Waituri,' and 'Labasa Lelo Lelo,' appeared in Suva's *Turaga* magazine; 'Chuuk and Bougainville' appeared in *Fiji Times*, 'To London, to London,' in Canberra literary magazine *Conversations*, and 'Nelspruit' first appeared in New York's online *desijournal*, and subsequently in Mohit Prasad (ed.), *Dreadlocks* (2008). 'Caught in the Web,' first appeared in *Fijian Studies*. 'Sairusi' first appeared in the *Fiji Times* as did my brief profile of Tom Vakatora. A shorter version of 'Speaking to Power' appeared in *ANU Reporter* (Autumn 2010).

It is appropriate that I thank my many readers from around the world, many completely unknown to me, who have written appreciatively of my efforts over the years and encouraged me to go on. For this volume in particular, I thank David Hanlon, Vijay Mishra, Doug Munro and Goolam Vahed, valued colleagues and friends, for their words of encouragement and support. It is people like them who have enriched my life in the academy. I do want to thank Nic Halter for reading parts of the manuscript for me, and Noel Wendtman for her beautiful craftsmanship of the book. Last, but by no means the least, my family. Nothing I have done would ever have been possible without their love and support. They have been with me through each step of the way in my sometimes tumultuous journey. This volume is dedicated to the two most important people in my life: one a lifelong (and long-suffering) companion and the other taking his first tender steps into the big wide world. What a wonderful 'Intersection' to celebrate.

# Notes

## Foreword

1. Brij V. Lal, 'Pacific History Matters', *Journal de la Société des Océanistes*, 125 (2007), 199.

## Chapter Two

1. This was the metaphor used by the powerful Fijian traditional leader Ratu Sir Lala Sukuna. See *Fiji: The Three-legged Stool: Selected Writings of Ratu Sir Lala Sukuna. Edited by Deryck Scarr (Basingstoke, 1984)*.

2. See, for example, Ratu Sir Kamisese Mara, *The Pacific Way: A memoir* (Honolulu, 1997), Brij V. Lal, *A Vision for Change: AD Patel and the Politics of Fiji* (Canberra, 1997), and Robert Norton, *Race and Politics in Fiji* (St. Lucia, rev.ed, 1990).

3. See studies in Brij V. Lal (ed.), *Politics in Fiji: Studies in Contemporary History (Laie, 1986)*. Also, Ahmed Ali's brief monograph *Fiji: From Colony to Independence, 1874-1970* (Suva, 1977).

4. RG Ward, 'Native Fijian Village: A Questionable Future?' in Michael Taylor (ed), *Fiji: Future Imperfect (North Sydney, 1987), 36*. Other studies in this book deal with issues of development, population and emigration, commercial agriculture, tourism, transport and trade unions.

5. OHK Spate, *The Fijian People: Economic Problems and Prospects (Suva, 1959)*, CS Belshaw, *Under the Ivi Tree: Society and Economic Growth in Rural Fiji* (London 1964), and Ray F. Watters, *Koro: Economic Development and Social Change in Fiji* (London, 1969). My assessment of both the indigenous as well as official government reaction to these ideas is based on an exhaustive reading of the colonial archives in Fiji and London.

6. For a class perspective, see Robert T. Robertson and Akosita Tamanisau, *Fiji–Shattered Coups* (Sydney, 1988). For a racial perspective, see Deryck Scarr, *Fiji: The politics of illusion. The military coups in Fiji* (Kensington,1988). For a review of the coup literature, see Stewart Firth, 'The Contemporary History of Fiji: A review article,' in *Journal of Pacific History* (1989), 24: 242-246, and Barrie Macdonald, 'The Literature of the Fiji Coups: A review article,' in *The Contemporary Pacific: A Journal of Island Affairs* (1990) 2: 197-207.

7. See my *Power and Prejudice: The Making of the Fiji Crisis* (Wellington, 1988). Also Stephanie Lawson, *The Failure of Democratic Politics in Fiji* (Clarendon, 1992).

8. Speech reported in *The Fiji Times*, 17 November 1986.

9. Among several critiques of the 1990 constitution, see my *Broken Waves: A history of the Fiji Islands in the 20th century* (Honolulu, 1992) and Robert T. Robertson, *Multiculturalism and Reconciliation in an Indulgent Republic. Fiji After the coups: 1987-1998* (Suva, 1998).

10. This is discussed at length in my *Another Way: The politics of constitutional reform in post-coup Fiji* (Canberra, 1998).

11. See studies in my edited collection, *Fiji Before the Storm: Elections and the politics of development* (Canberra, 2000).
12. See his comments 'Provincialism not good' in *Sunday Post* 20 April 2003.
13. See my 'In George Speight's Shadow: Fiji General Elections of 2001,' *The Journal of Pacific History* (2002) 37:1, 87-101.
14. For Ravuvu's views, see his *The Facade of Democracy: Fijian Struggles for Political Control, 1830-1987* (Suva, 1991).
15. Indo-Fijian members on the committee were Joe Singh, Ben Bhagwan, Fred Achari and Joseph Kanhaiya Lal Maharaj, all Christians, when the overwhelming majority of the Indo-Fijian population is Hindu and Muslim.
16. See, interestingly, Asesela Ravuvu, *Development or Dependence*: *The Pattern* of *change in a Fijian Village* (Suva, 1988). See also Jone Dakuvula, 'Chiefs and Commoners: The Indigenous Dilemma,' in David Robbie (ed.), *Tu Galala: Social Change in the Pacific* (Wellington, 1992), 70-79.
17. According to 1996 census figures kindly supplied to me by the Fiji Bureau of Statistics.
18. See, for example Satendra Prasad, Jone Dakuvula and Darryn Snell, *Economic Development, Democracy and Ethnic Conflict in the Fiji Islands* (London, 2001), p.5. The authors report that indigenous Fijians make up 75 per cent of the police force, 75 per cent of the nurses, 90 per cent of the permanent heads of department and, of course, 99 per cent of the Fiji military forces.
19. *Towards a United Future: Report of the Fiji Constitution Review Commission* (Suva, 1996), 15.
20. Private communication.
21. Figures supplied by the Fiji Bureau of Statistics.
22. For an earlier study of this issue from an anthropological perspective, see Rusiate Nayacakalou, *Leadership in Fiji* (Melbourne, 1975).
23. For an example, see Eddie Dean with Stan Ritova, *Rabuka: No Other Way. His Own Story* (Melbourne, 1988), and John Sharpham, *Rabuka of Fiji. The authorised biography of Major-General Sitiveni Rabuka* (Rockhampton, 2000).
24. Sir Vijay R. Singh, 'Opening Address,' in *Protecting Fijian Interests and Building a Democratic Fiji: A Consultation on Fiji's Constitution Review* (Suva, 2001), 11. For a scholarly discussion, see studies in John Overton (ed.), *Rural Fiji* (Suva, 1988), and papers by RG Ward, 'Land in Fiji,' and Josefa Kamikamica, 'Fijian native land: issues and challenges,' in Brij V. Lal and Tomasi Vakatora (eds.), *Fiji In Transition. Research Papers of the Fiji Constitution Review Commission*, vol. 1 (Suva, 1997), pp.247-258 and pp.259-290 respectively.
25. Explored in Asesela Ravuvu *Vaka I Taukei: The Fijian Way of Life* (Suva, 1983), and GK Roth, *Fijian Way of Life* (Melbourne, 1973).
26. There is no proper consideration of these concepts in the published literature, but see AC Mayer, *Peasants in the Pacific: A study of Fiji Indian Rural Society* (Los Angeles, 2nd ed. 1973), KL Gillion, *The Fiji Indians: Challenge to European Dominance, 1920-1946* (Canberra, 1977), and my *Chalo Jahaji: On a journey through indenture in Fiji* (Canberra and Suva, 2000).
27. Quoted in KL Gillion, *The Fiji Indians: Challenge to European Dominance, 1920-1946* (Canberra, 1977), 138. See also my *Vision for Change*, 35-58.

28. Among others by high chief Ratu Joni Madraiwiwi, in his Parkinson Memorial Lecture published in Kim Gravelle (ed.), *Good Governance in the South Pacific* (Suva, 2002), 10-11. Ahmed Ali provides an historical outline in his 'Fijian Chiefs and Constitutional Change, 1874-1937,' in *Journal de la Societie des Oceanistes* (Sept.1976). See also studies in Tohimatsu Kawai (ed.), *Chieftainship in Oceania: Continuity and Change* (Amagasaki, Japan, 1998).

29. See, for example, Robert Norton, 'Chiefs for the Nation: Containing Ethnonationalism and Bridgning the Ethnic Divide in Fiji,' *Pacific Studies* 22:1 (March 1999), 21-50.

30. Statement reported in *Fiji Times* 14 April, 2003.

31. Among them is Adi Litia Cakobau from the powerful Cakobau family of Bau.

32. Except briefly under the leadership of Dr Ilaitia Tuwere in the mid-1990s.

33. Radio New Zealand International, Suva, 16 April 2003.

34. See Sister Bertha Hurley, 'Interfaith Search, Fiji,' in Jill Cottrell (ed.), *Educating for Multiculturalism* (Suva, 2000), pp. 92-97.

35. Former Deputy Prime Minister Taufa Vakatale has also spoken of the need 'to establish good channels of communication between various groups.' See her address, 'The Constraints and Challenges to Building Multiculturalism in Fiji,' in Jill Cottrell (ed.), *Educating for Multiculturalism* (Suva, 2000), 13.

36. *Towards a United Future: Report of the Fiji Constitution Review Commission* (Suva, 1996), 263.

37. *Daily Post* 24 April 2003.

38. See, for example, its publication, Steven Ratuva, *Participation for Peace: A Study of Inter-ethnic and Inter-Religious Perception in Fiji* (Suva, 2002). ECREA has also sponsored important studies of poverty in Fiji.

39. Among many others, besides *Protecting Fijian Interests and Building a Democratic Fiji*, are Yash Ghai, *The Implementation of Fiji Islands Constitution* (Suva, 1998), *One Nation, Diverse Peoples: Building a Just and Democratic Fiji* (Suva, 1995), Arlene Griffin (ed.), *Election Watch II: A Citizens' Review of the Fiji Islands General Election 2001* (Suva, 2002), and Jill Cottrell (ed.), *Educating for Multiculturalism* (Suva, 2000)..

40. See, for example, Manoranjan Mohanty 'Contemporary Emigration from Fiji: Some trends and issues in the post-independence era,' Mahendra Reddy, Manoranjan Mohanty and Vijay Naidu, 'Economic cost of Human Capital Loss from Fiji: Implications for Sustainable Development,' both unpublished papers (2002), Richard Bedford, 'Out of Fiji: A perspective on emigration after the coups,' in *Pacific Viewpoint* 30 (1989), 142-53, and Azmat Gani, 'Some Dimensions of Fiji's Recent Emigration,' in *Pacific Economic Bulletin* 15:1 (2000), 94-103.

41. From a Mission Statement obtained from the Department of National Reconciliation and Unity.

42. For instance, the Minister of Women and Social Welfare, Asenate Caucau likened Indo-Fijians to noxious weeds,' and refused to retract her words.

43. See also Vijay Naidu, 'Evaluating Our Past and Moulding Our Future,' in Cottrell (ed.), *Educating for Multiculturalism*, 59-64.

44. Asesela Ravuvu, *Development or Dependence: The Pattern of Change in a Fijian Village* (Suva, 1988), 171.

45. *Fiji Times*, 29 August, 1991.
46. *Islands Business*, January 1991.

## Chapter Three

1. The document was known as the 'Deed of Sovereignty.
2. See my *Another Way: the politics of constitutional reform in post-coup Fiji* (Canberra, 1998).
3. These are available at the Pacific Manuscripts Bureau, The Australian National University.
4. Brij V Lal and Tomas Vakatora (eds.), *Research Papers of the Fiji Constitution Review Commission*. Volume 1: *Fiji In transition*; Volume 2: *Fiji and the World* (Suva: University of the South Pacific, School of Social and Economic Development, 1997).
5. Quotes are from Fiji Parliament *Hansard*, 1997.
6. See my 'Rhetoric and Reality: The dilemmas of contemporary Fijian politics,' in Ron Crocombe (ed.), *Culture and Democracy in the South Pacific* (Suva: Institute of Pacific Studies, 1992), 97-99.
7. Reprinted in my *Broken Waves: A history of the Fiji Islands in the 20th century* (Honolulu, 1992), 189.
8. See studies in Brij V Lal (ed.), *Fiji Before the Storm: Elections and the dilemmas of developments* (Canberra, 2000).
9. Lal, *Broken Waves*, 232-235.

## Chapter Four

1. KS Inglis, *This is the ABC: The Australian Broadcasting Commission, 1932-1983* (Melbourne, 1983), 1
2. EH Carr, *What is History?* (Hammondsworth, 1964), 35
3. In his 'Understanding Pacific History: The participant as historian,' in Peter Munz (ed), *The Feel of Truth: Essays in New Zealand and Pacific History* (Wellington, 1969), 34.
4. See, for a typical example, David Butler, 'Instant History,' in *New Zealand Journal of History*, 2:2 (1968), 107-14
5. As opposed to, say, Jim Davidson, OHK Spate, Harry Maude, Ron Crocombe, David Stone, who were all expatriate advisors and experts.
6. OHK Spate, 'Thirty years ago: a view of the Fiji political scene. Confidential Report to the British Colonial Office,' *Journal of Pacific History*, 25 (1990), 103
7. Brij V Lal, *Power and Prejudice: The making of the Fiji crisis* (Wellington, 1988), 36.
8. Ibid., 7

9. Among the influential historians of the past who hold the hope of ultimate history is Hebert Butterfield. See his *History and Human Relations* (London, 1951), 10: 'If we consider the history of historical writing that has been issued, generation after generation, on a given body of events, we shall generally find that in the early stages of this process of reconstruction the narrative which is produced has a primitive and simple shape. As one generation of students succeeds another, however, each developing the historiography of this particular subject, the narrative passes through certain typical stages until it is brought to a high and subtle form of organisation.'

10. Lal, Deryck Scarr and Robbie Robertson.

11. Butler, 'Instant history,' 109.

12. Greg Dening, *The Bounty: An ethnographic history* (Melbourne, 1989), 109. Dening argues: 'History is a way of knowing, an act of consciousness, constantly repeated, never the same, always relative to the language in which it is expressed, always relative to the audience to whom it is given, itself a cultural artefact of an age than the one whose story it tells. History is reductionist insofar as it transforms the totality of the past into words.' See also his 'reflections on the cultural history of Marshall Sahlins and Valerio Valeri,' in *Journal of Pacific History Bibliography and Comment* (1986), 45.

13. See my *Another Way: The politics of constitutional reform in post-coup Fiji* (Canberra, 1998), 54.

14. See Ropate Qalo, *Small Business: A study of a Fijian family* (Suva, 1997), 5. See also his address to the Fijian Association Convention, 1998, and his 'The stamp of the man: initial impressions,' in *Journal of Pacific Studies*, 22 (1998), 207-12.

15. Lasaqa, *The Fijian People*, xii

16. The quotes are from David Thomson, *The Aims of History: Values of the historical attitude* (London, 1969), 27. Without meaning to be unfair to him, I have the sense that Ahmed Ali held back from searching enquiry into Fiji politics in the 1970s because he had been closely allied to the Alliance party under whose banner he would enter national politics later.

17. See his *Tandava* (Melbourne, 1992), and his poems in Arlene Griffin (ed.), *With Heart and Nerve and Sinew: Post-coup writing from Fiji* (Suva, 1997).

18. For more, see my *In the Eye of the Storm: Jai Ram Reddy and the politics of postcolonial Fiji* (Canberra, 2010).

19. See my 'The 1982 National Election and its Aftermath,' in *USP Sociological Society Newsletter*, 5 (1983), 3-17.

20. See my *A Vision for Change: AD Patel and the politics of Fiji* (Canberra, 1997), 5-6.

21. See John Sharpham, *Rabuka of Fiji: The authorized biography of Major-General Sitiveni Rabuka* (Rockhampton, 2000), 105.

22. Walter Laqueur and George L Moss (eds.), *Historians in Politics* (London, 1974).

23. Thomson, *The Aims of History*, 28. See also WH Walsh, *Philosophy of History* (New York, 1958), 112: 'There is no such thing as history free from subjective prejudice,' and 114: 'Inside any given set of presuppositions, historical work can be more or less well done. The history served by party propagandists to encourage the faithful and convert the wavering is bad history not because it is biased (all history is that), but because it is biased in the wrong way. It establishes its conclusions at the cost of neglecting those certain fundamental rules which all reputable historians recognize: scrutinize your evidence, accept conclusions only when there is good evidence for them, maintain intellectual integrity in your arguments, and so on. Historians who neglect these rules produce work which is subjective in a bad sense; those who adhere to them are in a position to attain truth and objectivity so far as these things are attainable in history.'

24. See Isaac Deutscher, 'From the Introduction (1961),' in his *Stalin: A political biography*, 2nd ed. (New York, 1966), x-xi.

25. Mark Poster, *Critical Theory and Poststructuralism: In search of a context* (Ithaca, 1989), 9-10.

26. See also Alan Ward, 'Comfortable Voyagers" Some reflections on the Pacific and its historians,' *Journal of Pacific History*, 31:2 (1996), 238.

## Chapter Five

1. Edward Said, *Culture and Imperialism* (London, 1993), xxx
2. Tony Judt, 'One Being Austere and Being Jewish,' *New York Review of Books*, 13 May 2010
3. Vincent O'Sullivan, Untitled chapter in Margaret Clark (ed), *John Mansfield Thompson: notes towards a biography* (Wellington, 1999), 165.
4. See, for example, RF Watters, *Koro: Economic Development and Social Change in Fiji* (Oxford, 1969), CS Belshaw, *Under the Ivi Tree: Society and Economic Growth in rural Fiji* (London, 1964), and OHK Spate, *The Fijian People: Economic Problems and Prospects* (Suva, 1959).
5. See my *Mr Tulsi's Store: A Fijian Journey* (Canberra, 2001).
6. See EK Fisk, *The Political Economy of Independent Fiji* (Canberra, 1970).
7. See my *In the Eye of the Storm: Jai Ram Reddy and the politics of postcolonial Fiji* (Canberra, 2010).
8. See my 'The Fiji General Elections of 1982: The Tidal Wave that Never Came,' *Journal of Pacific History* (1983), 134-157.
9. See studies in Michael Taylor (ed), *Fiji: Future Imperfect* (Sydney, 1987).
10. See my *Power and Prejudice: The Making of the Fiji Crisis* (Wellington, 1988).
11. See Padma Narsey Lal, *Ganna: Portrait of the Fiji Sugar Industry* (Lautoka, 2009).
12. See studies in Jon Fraenkel and Stewart Firth (eds), *From Elections to Coup in Fiji: The 2006 Campaign and its Aftermath* (Canberra, 2007).
13. See studies in Fraenkel, Firth and Brij V Lal (eds), *The 2006 Military Takeover in Fiji: A Coup to end all Coups?* (Canberra, 2009).
14. See, for example, *The Quantitative Analysis of Poverty in Fiji* (Suva, 2008).
15. Said, *Representations of the Intellectual* (New York, 1996), 100-101.

## Chapter Eight

1. Some of the background to this paper is in my 'Laucala Bay,' in Brij V Lal (ed.), *Pacific Places, Pacific Histories: Essays in Honor of Robert C Kiste* (Honolulu: University of Hawaii Press, 2004), 237-258

2. 'The Muses' written in 1956 and published in 1963. Quoted in CK Stead, *Book Self* (Auckland, 2008), 8.

3. *Pacific Island Portraits* (Wellington: AH & AW Reed, 1970). Those 'portrayed' were Peter Dillon, the Henrys of Tahiti, King George Tupou 1 of Tonga, Cakobau and Ma'afu, Xavier Montrouzier, John Coleridge Patterson, Kwaisulia of the Solomon Islands, Lauaki Namulau'ulu Mamoe, Baiteke and Binoka of Abemama, Pacific beach communities, the Pacific labour trade and the planter community in Fiji.

4. Sione Tupouniua was the editor, and Editorial Committee members included Isoa Gavidi, Lionel Brown, John Samy, Finau Tabakaucoro and Gary Finlay besides academics Peter Stone and Brian Lockwood.

5. I published a set of senior prize-winning graduate essays at the University of Hawaii titled *Wansalawara: Soundings in Melanesian History* (University of Hawaii Center for Pacific Islands Studies, Occasional Paper 31, 1987), and Honours essays done under my supervision at the ANU in my *Chalo Jahaji: On a journey through indenture in Fiji* (ANU: Division of Pacific and Asian History and Suva: Fiji Museum, 2000).

6. *Peasants in the Pacific: A Study of Fiji Indian Rural Society* (Berkeley and Los Angeles: University of California Press, 2nd ed. 1973).

7. *Fiji's Indian Migrants: A history to the end of indenture in 1920* (Melbourne: Oxford University Press, 1962)

8. *Fiji and the Franchise, 1900-1937* (Australian National University thesis, unpublished, 1973).

9. Sione Tupouniua, Ron Crocombe, Claire Slatter (eds), *The Pacific Way: Social Issues in National Development* (Suva: Institute of Pacific Studies, 1975).

10. Sister Mary Stella, Raymond Pillay and Asesela Ravuvu, 'Pacific History and National Integrity,' in *Pacific Perspectives* 1:2 (1973), 1-7

11. 'Pacific History: Past, Present, Future,' *Journal of Pacific History* 6 (1971), 24. Maude retired to an academic career after a lifetime as a colonial civil servant. His academic colleague, JW Davidson, was active in advising island people during their transition to independence.

12. For more on this, see Nicholas Thomas, 'Partial Texts: Representation, colonialism and agency in Pacific history,' *Journal of Pacific History* 25 (2), 1990, 139-58.

13. His two published collections of short stories include *The Celebration* (Suva: Mana Publications and South Pacific Creative Arts Society, 1980) and, posthumously, *The End of the Line* (Suva: Fiji Institute of Applied Studies, 2008).

14. 'Marama,' in the *Mana Annual of Creative Writing 1973*, 91.

15. See his 'Novelists and Historians and the Art of Remembering,' in Anthony Hooper et al (eds), *Class and Culture in the South Pacific* (Suva: Institute of Pacific Studies, 1987), 78-92.

16. See, for instance, Peter Novick, *That Noble Dream: The 'Objectivity Question' and the American Historical Profession* (New York: Cambridge University Press, 1988).

17. KS Inglis, *This is the ABC: The Australian Broadcasting Commission, 1932-1983* (Melbourne: Melbourne University Press, 1983), 1

18. See my *Mr Tulsi's Store: A Fijian Journey* (Canberra: Pandanus Books, 2001), and *Turnings: Fiji Factions* (Lautoka: Fiji Institute of Applied Studies, 2008).

19. *Mr Tulsi's Store* was selected as one of the 'Ten Notable Books of Asia Pacific' by the San Francisco-based Kiriyama Prize in 2002 and chosen as 'Highly Commended 2002 ACT Book of the Year.'

20. See, for example, in addition to Nicholas Thomas (above), David Routledge, 'Pacific History as Seen from the Pacific Islands,' *Pacific Studies* 8:2 (1985), 81-100, and FX Hezel, 'New Directions in Pacific History: A Practitioner's Critical View,' *Pacific Studies* 11 (3), 1988), 107 ff

21. Roger M Keesing, 'Creating the Past: Custom and Identity in the Contemporary Pacific,' *The Contemporary Pacific: A Journal of Island Affairs* 1&2 (1989), 19-42, 'Reply to Trask,' in *The Contemporary Pacific,* 3:4 (1990), 168-71, and Haunani-Kay Trask, 'Natives and Anthropologists: The Colonial Struggle, *ibid*, 159-167.

22. Vilsoni Hereniko is Director of Center for Pacific Islands Studies at the University of Hawaii, Peggy Dunlop-Fairbairn is Professor of Pacific Studies at the Auckland University of Technology, Teresia Teaiwa is Convenor of Pacific Studies at Victoria University of Wellington and Katerina Teaiwa is Convenor of Pacific Studies at The Australian National University.

23. See, for instance, essays by Epeli Hau'ofa and others in Eric Waddell and Vijay Naidu (eds), *A New Oceania: Rediscovering Our Sea of Islands* (Suva, USP: School of Social and Economic Development, 1993).

24. The names are legion: JW Davidson, HE Maude, Dorothy Shineberg, OHK Spate, Deryck Scarr, Hank Nelson: these are all people associated with the Australian National University.

25. 'History's wily liberal endures,' *Weekend Australian Review*, July 3-4 (2010), 23.

26. See Doug Munro, 'Pacific Islands History in the Vernacular: Practical and Ethical Considerations,' in *New Zealand Journal of History*, 29:1 (1995), 83-96

27. Matthew Arnold, 'A Summer Night,' 1.68.

28. CK Stead, *Book Self* (Auckland) 2008), 8

29. *Hyperion*, Bk 1, chapter 8.

30. 'Editors' Introduction,' *Humanities Australia,* no 1 (2010), 4

## Chapter Nine

1. For reflections on the Coombs Building itself, see essays in Brij V Lal and Allison Ley (eds), *The Coombs: A House of Memories* (Canberra, 2006).

2. My thesis was on the origins of Fiji's North Indian indentured migrants titled 'Leaves of the Banyan Tree: Origins and Background of Fiji's North Indian Migrants, 1879-1916,' 2 vols, ANU, 1980. A considerably shortened version was published as *Girmitiyas: The origins of the Fiji Indians* (Canberra, 1983).

3. Mostly about my views on Hugh Tinker's *A New System of Slavery: The Export of Indian Labour Overseas, 1830-1920* (London, 1974) about which I had made some critical comments in my thesis.

4. *The Spanish Lake, Monopolists and Freebooters* and *Paradise Found and Lost*, all published by ANU Press between 1979 and 1988.
5. *Fiji's Indian Migrants: A history to the end of indenture in 1920* (Melbourne, 1962).
6. *The Fiji Indians: Challenge to European dominance, 1920-1946* (Canberra, 1977).
7. *The Fijian People: Economic Problems and Prospects* (Fiji Legislative Council Paper 13/1959).
8. *Broken Waves: A history of the Fiji islands in the 20th century* (Honolulu, 1992).
9. Wm Roger Louis, 'Sir Keith Hancock and the British Empire: the Pax Britannica and the Pax Americana,' *English Historical Review*, 120, no. 488 (2005), 942.
10. And the subject of Jim Davidson's splendid biography, *The Historian WK Hancock: A Three-Cornered Life* (Kensington, NSW, 2010). Doug Munro is writing JW (Jim) Davidson's life.
11. Her collection of poems *Peeling Apples* was published by Pandanus Books in 2005. Some of Tessa's and Mark's fiction and poetry appeared in *Conversations*, a literary journal I founded in 2000 but which closed in 2005.
12. See more generally his "Making History Now (An Inaugural Lecture) delivered as the Director of the Institute of Historical Research in the University of London in 1996 at http://www.history.ac.uk/ihr/Focus/Whatishistory/cannadine.html.
13. Dorothy Shineberg, 'The Early Years of Pacific History,' *The Journal of Pacific Studies 20 (1996), 9*.
14. For a damning indictment of the British system, see Stefan Collini, *Common Reading: critics, historians, publics* (Oxford, 2008), 317-38.
15. *A Vision for Change: AD Patel and the politics of Fiji* (Canberra, 1997), to be re-issued by ANU E Press in 2011 along with a volume of his speeches and writings.
16. *In the eye of the Storm: Jai Ram Reddy and the politics of postcolonial Fiji* (Canberra, 2010).
17. David Reynolds, *In Command of History: Churchill Fighting and Writing the Second World War* (Penguin, 2005), 525.
18. Arthur M Schlesinger Jr. *Journals, 1951-2000* edited by Andrew Schlesinger and Stephen Schlesinger (New York, 2007), 535.

## Chapter Ten

1. Kishore Nangrani, 'We Indians,' *Desh Videsh*, August 1997, 55.
2. 5 August 1980.
3. Colin Clarke, Ceri Peach and Steven Vertovec (eds), *South Asians Overseas Migration and Ethnicity* (Cambridge, 1990). Now the size of the Indian diaspora is estimated at over 20 million.
4. Aisha Khan, 'Homeland, Motherland, Authenticity, Legitimacy, and Ideologies of Place among Muslims in Trinidad,' in Peter van der Veer (ed), *Nation and Migration: The Politics of Space in the South Asian Diaspora* (Pennsylvania, 1995), 93.
5. See, among others, Hugh Tinker, *A New system of Slavery: The export of Indian labour overseas, 1830-1920 (London, 1974)*.
6. See my *Girmitiyas: The origins of the Fiji Indians* (Canberra, 1983), 37-39.

7. Among those who wrote about the problems of indenture in Fiji included CF Andrews, Mahatma Gandhi's emissary, and JW Burton, *Fiji of Today* (London, 1910). Totaram Sanadhya wrote of his indenture experience in *Fiji Dwip Men Mere Ikkis Varsh*. My Twenty One Years in the Fiji Islands (Kanpur, 1913).
8. See generally my *Chalo Jahaji: On a journey through indenture in Fiji* (Canberra, 2000).
9. The literature on Chinese migration is vast. I have leaned on Wally Look Lai's succinct summary, 'Origins of the Caribbean Chinese Community,' in the *Journal of Caribbean Studies*, 14 (1&2), (2005), 25-38. Brinsley Samaroo in the same issue looks at 'Chinese and Indian Coolie Voyages to the Caribbean,' 3-24.
10. Lai, 'Origins of the Caribbean Chinese Community,' 34. An extended treatment is in his *Indentured Labor, Caribbean Sugar* (Baltimore, 1993). My debt to Lai's work is enormous.
11. Lai, *Indentured Labor*, 95-96.
12. See Lai for more discussion.
13. Lai, *Indentured Labor*, 204.
14. Leo Despres, *Cultural Pluralism and Nationalist Politics in British Guyana* (Chicago, 1967), 58.
15. 'East Indian women in the Caribbean: Experience and Voice,' in Brinsley Samaroo and David Dabydeen (eds.), *India in the Caribbean* (Warwick, 1987), 232.
16. Roy Glasgow, *Guyana: Race and Politics among Africans and East Indians* (The Hague, 1970), 79.
17. See generally Hugh Tinker, *Separate and Unequal: India and the Indians in the British Commonwealth, 1920-1950* (St Lucia, Qld, 1976).
18. For a survey, see KS Sandhu, *Indians in Malaya: Some Aspects of their Immigration and Settlement* (Cambridge, 1969).
19. See his *The Indian Minority in Burma: the rise and decline of an immigrant minority* (London, 1971)
20. See Chandra Jayawardena's important article, 'Migration and Social Change: A survey of Indian communities overseas,' *Geographical Journal*, LVIII:3 (1968), 426-429.
21. In books such as *An Area of Darkness, India: A Wounded Civilization* and *India: A Million Mutinies Now*.
22. Samaroo, 'The India Connection: The Influence of Indian Thought and Ideas on East Indians in the Caribbean,' in Samaroo and Dabydeen (eds), *India in the Caribbean*, 56. He quotes Naipaul: 'India is for me a difficult country. It isn't my home; and yet I cannot reject it or be indifferent to it; I cannot travel only for the sights. I am at once too close and too far …Any enquiry about India—even an enquiry about the Emergency—has quickly to go beyond the political. It has to be an enquiry about the Indian attitudes; it has to be an enquiry about the civilization itself.'

## Chapter Twelve

1. See my *Girmitiyas: The origins of the Fiji Indians* (Canberra, 1983) and other works cited elsewhere in this volume.
2. See 'Hinduism Under Indenture' in my *Chalo Jahaji: on a journey through indenture in Fiji* (Canberra and Suva, 2000).

*Notes*

3. For the Caribbean experience generally, see Brinsley Samaroo and David Dabydeen (eds), *India in the Caribbean (Warwick, 1987),* and *Across the Dark Waters: Ethnicity and Indian Identity in the Caribbean* (London, 1996).

4. Adrian Mayer, *Peasants in the Pacific: A Study of Fiji Indian Rural Society* (Berkeley and Los Angeles, 2nd ed. 1973), 6

5. See Chandra Jayawardena, 'The Disintegration of Caste in Fiji Indian Rural Society,' in LR Hiatt and Chandra Jayawardena (eds.), *Anthropology in Oceania* (Sydney, 1971), *88-119.*

6. For more on this see my *Mr Tulsi's Store (Canberra, 2001).*

7. See, among many others, Peter France, *Charter of the Land: Custom and colonisation in Fiji* (Melbourne, 1969).

8. See Michael Moynagh, *Brown or White? A history of the Fiji sugar industry, 1873-1973* (Canberra, 1981).

9. JW Coulter, *Fiji: Little India of the Pacific* (Chicago, 1942), *93*

10. WEH Stanner, *South Seas in Transition: A Study of Post-War Rehabilitation and Reconstruction in Three British Pacific Dependencies* (Sydney, 1953), *179-180..*

11. See generally John D Kelly, *A Politics of Virtue: Hinduism, Sexuality and Countercolonial Discourse in Fiji* (Chicago, 1991).

12. See Vijay Mishra, *Bollywood Cinema: Temples of Desire* (New York, 2002).

## Chapter Thirteen

1. I use Hindi for the sake of brevity, but my usage incorporates Urdu. In that sense, Hindustani is probably a more accurate term for the language I have in mind.

2. But see Rodney Moag, *Fiji Hindi: A Basic Course and Reference Grammar* (Canberra: Australian National University Press, 1977), and Subramani's *Dauka Puran* (Delhi: Star Publications, 2001)

3. For the regional background of Fiji's Indian migrants, see Brij V. Lal, *Girmitiyas: The Origins of the Fiji Indians* (Canberra: Journal of Pacific History Monograph, 1983, rep. Lautoka: Fiji Institute of Applied Studies, 2004). See also Jeff Siegel, *Language Contact in a plantation environment: A sociolinguistic history of Fiji* (Cambridge: Cambridge University Press, 1987).

4. I am concerned here with those descended from the indenture experience. In urban areas in post-indenture times, Gujarati words and expressions entered the language as well. To make a *Khichri* (mixed dhall-rice dish, a staple of the Gujarati community) of something was to make a mess of things.

5. See generally Adrian C Mayer, *Peasants in the Pacific: A study of Fiji Indian rural society* (Berkeley: University of California Press, 2nd rep. 1973).

7. J R Pearson, Preface to AW MacMillan, *Hindustani Handbook*: *Specially Prepared for Colonial Use* (Suva: Government Printer, 1931).

8. *Fiji Samachar,* 27 June 1931 comments on MacMillan's book: 'This Handbook has been prepared for Europeans. The compiler himself admits this; but Indian teachers can derive benefit from this work.' For the language controversy in the 1940s, see my *A Vision for Change: AD Patel and the politics of Fiji* (Canberra: ANU National Centre for Development Studies, 1997), pp.109-110.

9. This is treated in my *Chalo Jahaji: On a journey through indenture in Fiji* (Suva: Fiji Museum, 2000).

10. For more discussion, see KL Gillion, *The Fiji Indians: Challenge to European Dominance, 1920-1947* (Canberra: Australian National University Press, 1977).

11. I concentrate here on the majority Hindu community. For the experience of Muslims, see Ahmed Ali, 'Remembering,' in Brij V. Lal (ed.) *BitterSweet: The Indo-Fijian Experience* (Canberra: Pandanus books, 2004), 71-88. See also Zarina Ahmad, 'Muslim Caste in Uttar Pradesh,' *The Economic Weekly*, 325-336, 17 February 1962.

12. See my *Mr Tulsi's Store: A Fijian Journey* (Canberra: Pandanus Books, 2001) for fuller discussion.

13. MacMillan, a LMS missionary and long-time Inspector of Indian Schools, had served in India before coming to Fiji and joining the government in 1929. The first (quarterly) issue of the *School Journal* was published in 1931, replacing *Raj Dut* which published government gazette notices and some children's reading material.

14. The *Pothis* were used in Fiji until independence in 1970 when a new curriculum emphasising nation building came into effect.

15. A copy of this text is in my possession.

16. I have discussed this in my 'Primary Texts,' in this volume.

17. But things have changed considerably in the last two decades or so as migration and urbanisation have brought the two communities into great contact. Now nearly half of Fiji, both Fijians and Indo-Fijians, live in urban or peri-urban areas.

18. If truth be told, as editor of several journals over the years—*The Contemporary Pacific: A Journal of Island Affairs*, *The Journal of Pacific History*, and *Conversations* (a Canberra-based literary journal), I myself make little concession to the linguistic handicaps of the contributors.

19. This is particularly evident in the work of 'Niu Wave' writers at the University of the South Pacific in Fiji.

20. I am unsure of the usage in India, though in some parts *dada*, for instance, can mean grandfather.

21. I should use the past tense here because things are much more mixed in contemporary life. I still don't call my *bhabhis* by their name. I don't know their names! But I now address my younger brothers' spouses by their first names.

## Chapter Seventeen

1. Published as *Fiji: British Documents on the End of Empire* (London: The Stationery Office, 2006), lxxxix+547

# About the Author

Photo by Belinda Pratten

Brij Vilash Lal, Fiji-born but long-time resident of Canberra, among other places, describes his life as a series of haphazard intersections between the primitive and the modern, colonial and postcolonial, past and present, and scholarship and political activism. Of eclectic disposition, he inhabits several worlds at once, but finds the greatest pleasure in reading and writing imaginatively, including about Fiji, from which he has been exiled by that country's military regime for his unceasing opposition to military coups there. Non, je ne regrette rien, he says, after Edith Piaf, 'No, I regret nothing.' He is at present a Professor of Pacific and Asian History and Deputy Director of the School of Culture, History and Language in the College of Asia and the Pacific at The Australian National University where he is now researching Australia's engagement with the South Pacific in the second half of the 20th century, and writing 'faction' on the side.

www.ingramcontent.com/pod-product-compliance
Lightning Source LLC
Chambersburg PA
CBHW040243240426
43663CB00047B/2972